Steps Toward a Tibetan Understanding of Purity

Evangelical Missiological Society Monograph Series

Anthony Casey, Rochelle Scheuermann, and Edward L. Smither
SERIES EDITORS

A Project of the Evangelical Missiological Society
www.emsweb.org

The EMS Monograph Series publishes the best book-length works of EMS members. The monographs may be reworked dissertations or original works based on missiological research focused on aspects of history, theology, culture, strategy, or spiritual formation all relating to the academic and practical nature of the missionary enterprise. EMS monographs are peer-reviewed and authors work with an editing team from Pickwick Publications (Wipf and Stock). Typically, 3–5 monographs are published each year.

Steps Toward a Tibetan Understanding of Purity

A Semantic and Textual Analysis

James E. Morrison

Foreword by R. Daniel Shaw

◦PICKWICK *Publications* • Eugene, Oregon

STEPS TOWARD A TIBETAN UNDERSTANDING OF PURITY
A Semantic and Textual Analysis

Evangelical Missiological Society Monograph Series

Copyright © 2025 James E. Morrison. All rights reserved. Except for brief quotations in critical publications or reviews, no part of this book may be reproduced in any manner without prior written permission from the publisher. Write: Permissions, Wipf and Stock Publishers, 199 W. 8th Ave., Suite 3, Eugene, OR 97401.

Pickwick Publications
An Imprint of Wipf and Stock Publishers
199 W. 8th Ave., Suite 3
Eugene, OR 97401

www.wipfandstock.com

PAPERBACK ISBN: 979-8-3852-0875-3
HARDCOVER ISBN: 979-8-3852-0876-0
EBOOK ISBN: 979-8-3852-0877-7

Cataloguing-in-Publication data:

Names: Morrison, James E., author. | Shaw, R. Daniel, foreword.
Title: Steps toward a Tibetan understanding of purity / James E. Morrison ; foreword by R. Daniel Shaw.
Description: Eugene, OR: Pickwick Publications, 2025. | Evangelical Missiological Society Monograph Series. | Includes bibliographical references and index.
Identifiers: ISBN 979-8-3852-0875-3 (paperback). | ISBN 979-8-3852-0876-0 (hardcover). | ISBN 979-8-3852-0877-7 (ebook).
Subjects: LCSH: Buddhism—Tibet Region. | Atonement (Prayer)—Buddhism. | Spiritual life—Buddhism. | Buddhism—Rituals.
Classification: DS785.A1 M67 2025 (print). | DS785.A1 (ebook).

VERSION NUMBER 03/25/25

Unless otherwise indicated, Scripture quotations are from The ESV® Bible (The Holy Bible, English Standard Version®), © 2001 by Crossway, a publishing ministry of Good News Publishers. Used by permission. All rights reserved.

The cover photograph shows Tibetan pilgrims circumambulating around the sacred mountain of Mount Kailash in far western Tibet. Pilgrimage is believed to be a foundational way of removing sin and defilements, and purifying one's heart and mind. Snow mountains are also symbolic of purity. The photograph was taken by the author.

Contents

Illustrations and Tables | vii
Foreword by R. Daniel Shaw | ix
Preface | xv
Acknowledgments | xvii
Abbreviations | xix

Introduction | 1
1. Setting the Scene | 34
2. Monastic Texts of Praxis | 86
3. Texts of Lay Aspiration and Folk Traditions | 150
4. Ritual Texts and Symbols | 198
5. Missiological Reflections and Considerations | 222

Bibliography | 255

Illustrations and Tables

Figure 1.1 Diagrammatic Representation of the Findings | 228
Figure 1.2 Word Diagram of Three Key Elements
 with Associated Praxis | 231
Table 1.1 Three Key Elements with Associated Praxis | 230

Foreword

THE VERY MENTION OF Tibet conjures a host of thoughts about the "roof of the world," the "lost kingdom," ethereal visions of temples and palaces high on hilltops. Mention Tibet and thoughts turn to Lhasa with its innumerable monasteries where monks engage in spiritual practices that remain secretive and ensnared in privacy, where Lhasa Apso dogs are bred to be foot warmers so monks can survive the intense cold during the long Himalayan winters. Similarly, there are accounts of the exiled Dalai Lama and his entourage living in India and jet setting around the globe with his message of world peace. Stereotypes all, but all with tantalizing elements of truth—as all stereotypes are.

James Morrison has moved beyond these stereotypes to research a semantic schema that has enabled him, as a Bible translator, to appreciate how Tibetans, particularly the laity, capture the concept of purity through highly formulated and ancient texts, mantras, and proverbs along with a host of rituals. And not just purity as understood by the people, but how those concepts weave together to create a constellation of meaning encased in the reality of tradition, contemporary life on the Tibetan plateau and as they anticipate a future that progressively removes those who adhere to these ideas from being bound in the filth of samsara toward an unimagined nirvana. Furthermore, Morrison contrasts purity with impurity or pollution and demonstrates the value of a progression that moves people from one state to the other, a process of purification that ensures escape from samsara. The progression represents a continuum that lifts human spirituality from worldly filth to heavenly bliss. If that has a biblical ring to it, Morrison assures us we are right as he captures the depth of monastic texts (ch. 2) mantras and proverbs (ch. 3) and rituals and symbols (ch. 4) that holistically reinforce each other into a cognitive schema to reflect on objective meaning in an esoteric Buddhist world. More specifically, Morrison focuses on how this mega-schema brings out a Tibetan focus on the role of purity. He demonstrates how it becomes a national symbol of identity. He highlights the contributions of all the elements to the importance of purity as a high and lifted up domain in contrast to demeaned and earthly pollution. He goes on to make clear that in the Tibetan schema of spiritual engagement, the pollution-purity progression is central to their worldview and all other schema bow down to purity to create a holistic, meaningful means of dealing with reality.

He illustrates this with the proverb: "Words and thoughts must be truthful, just as bodies and hands must be clean" (Morrison, p. 233–34 this ms.). Clean bodies and clean hands symbolize a person who does not steal, is trustworthy, refrains from sexual misconduct or anything that defiles the body. "The idiom of 'clean hands'" represents "an extension of the body and thus both the body and the hands must be morally clean" (p. 186 this ms.). Morrison uses such deep analysis of texts, mantras, proverbs and rituals to bring out three realms that blend into a spiritual totality: ontology, cosmology and soteriology. Interestingly, Paul Hiebert blended these concepts into his analytical model for understanding belief systems. The ontological corresponds to what Hiebert called "transcendent," the soteriological corresponds to the "immanent," and the cosmological blends these poles into a middle layer energized by all manner of spiritual beings, the gods and deities that populate folk Buddhism throughout Tibet, and indeed all of South East Asia. This model serves as the dominant heuristic device in our book *Understanding Folk Religion: A Christian Response to Popular Beliefs and Practices,* recently published in a 25th Anniversary Edition (Hiebert, Shaw, and Tienou 2024, 45–72). The model affirms Morrison's detailed analysis of extensive texts, mantras, proverbs and rituals that manifest the purity schema in Tibet. Morrison elaborates:

> The need for spiritual power to influence the unseen spiritual realm is clearly evident through the use of spells, incantations, and mantras. Indeed, all the rituals and practices presented here are dependent upon mantras for their efficacy. No spiritual pursuit is attempted without them . . . Likewise, the pursuit of merit accumulation . . . specifically, the merit derived from circumambulations, prostrations, the spinning of prayer wheels, water rituals, incense burning, and the recitation of mantras.

Such conceptual accounting of these culturally loaded elements reflect on the totality that is the purity schema: what must Tibetan Buddhists, both formal and informal, the specialists and the laity, know in order to behave in a manner acceptable to people who hold to the purity schema? This adheres to Ward Goodenough's well known dictum (Goodenough 1956) and encourages outsiders to take a deep dive into such cognitive domains that, by virtue of the rich collection of sub-domains and componential interlocution communicate a rich segment of cultural expectation, i.e. religious beliefs and practices epitomized by the concept of purity. This is what Morrison, as one who seeks to communicate the biblical concepts that parallel the Tibetan understanding, needs to know in order to present the one true God's desire to make sin burdened human beings righteous before him by accepting what Jesus did on Calvary, that hilltop place of slaughter that residents of Lhasa can identify with.

In the final chapter, Morrison confirms my approach as an anthropologist; "dig deep" into cultural expressions, "study closely" what people say and do and then "carefully construct some possible conclusions" (p. 290 this ms.). Avoid placing a conceptual overview from another culture on the time and place of your particular study. You need what truly resonates with the people of that context and then blend it both with Scripture and other cultures to get a fuller perspective of the concept (purity in this material). Then, compare and contrast; determine what is new and what more generally documents what it means to be human. Having created human beings in his image, God understands us, knows our innermost thoughts and is able to speak to people's particular needs in ways that truly make sense to them. To that end Morrison provides some insightful diagrams and enhances the specifics of his narrative to anticipate how Tibetans will bring God's Word in line with their cultural proclivities.

This information gives us an appreciation for views we could not process ourselves because we are not Tibetan, but from which Tibetans will benefit because Morrison penetrated deeply into the key elements of Tibetan purity. Morrison provides a new perspective on what purity is, how it is manifest in texts, mantras, parables and rituals that all interrelate to create what Samuel Law calls a "mazeway". Such complex systems move research from a traditional linear approach to a complex systems science focus with four main characteristic adjustments: "1) reductionism to holism; 2) linear to nonlinear analysis; 3) static to dynamic; and 4) empirical to metaphor" (Law 2016, 79).

FOREWORD

This book is a clear example of such an approach to data collection, analysis and presentation. Understanding how Tibetans express their spirituality and move from impure to pure by making others (including gods and deities) pure, is the essence of Morrison's extensive presentation. The purification process enlightens all and moves the world to a better place. We now have a view of the Bible through Tibetan eyes, which in turn, teaches us new things about God we would not see without Morrison's guidance. Humanity is by definition impure and unclean, i.e. polluted. Those who reach the heavenly realm, are in Tibetan terms, considered pure. Therefore any texts, mantras, proverbs and all the associated rituals that exude purity can raise impure human beings to a heavenly realm (Morrison p. 260 this ms.). But we cannot leave it there, we must bring the Biblical view alongside the Tibetan view and recognize that the way forward, is not only to understand the purity system of Tibetan Buddhism, "but to see it as a reference point, as a bridge or a link to frame the gospel in a way that may make sense to a Tibetan" (p. 298 this ms.). Like the Apostle Paul, we must "communicate clearly within the framework and thought patterns of the receptor culture so that the gospel both comes to authentic expression in the local context and at the same time prophetically transforms the context." (Flemming 2005, 19) And I would add, those who process this perspective and gain new understanding.

To that end I commend this book to you. I pray that you may appreciate the depth of Morrison's research for the purpose of not only using the right constellation of words that communicate purity, but that those words will speak to the hearts and minds of Tibetans. In this way they can see a way to move from their earthly reality to the undefiled presence of God because of Jesus Christ through the power of the Holy Spirit.

R. Daniel Shaw
Sr. Prof. of Anthropology and Translation
Fuller Seminary School of Mission and Theology
Pasadena, California
June 2024

References

Flemming, Dean E. *Contextualization in the New Testament: Patterns for Theology and Mission*. Downers Grove, IL: InterVarsity, 2005.

Goodenough, Ward H. "Componential Analysis and the Study of Meaning." *Language* 32 (1956) 195–216.

Hiebert, Paul.G., R. Daniel Shaw, and Tite Tienou. 2024. *Understanding Folk Religion: A Christian Response to Popular Beliefs and Practices*. 25th Anniversary Edition. American Society of Missiology Series. Eugene, OR: Wipf & Stock. Original ed., 1999.

Law, Samuel K. *Revitalizing Missions on the Cusp of Change: Complex Systems Science Mazeways for Mission Theory amid Twenty-first Century Realities*. Lexington: Emeth, 2016.

Preface

STUDIES OF PURITY AND pollution have typically been conducted through a social anthropological framework, demarcating the ritually impure and unclean from the clean and pure, and examining the impact of this on social interactions. This study has sought to answer the question of how Tibetan Buddhists conceptualize notions of purity and purification, not delineated as a social phenomenon, but through the religious framework of Tibetan Buddhism. To that end, this research has explored notions of purity from within the religious domain and soteriological discourse of Tibetan Buddhism. While some studies have examined Tibetan purity demarcations from an anthropological and sociological perspective, there has been a paucity of studies examining purity as it appears in the religious realm of Tibetan Buddhism. Furthermore, no studies exist that have sought a Tibetan understanding of purity with the express purpose of exploring potential missiological considerations and applications.

In this research, the primary method for answering the question of Tibetan notions of purity has been to seek an emic voice through examining a comprehensive range of indigenous Tibetan texts, which explicitly deal with notions of purity, across a broad spectrum of genres, incorporating both the monastics and laity. This approach was considered efficacious in gaining an objective and in-depth understanding from an emic, "insider" perspective. This study, then, has undertaken a semantic and textual analysis of Tibetan Buddhist notions of purity, drawing from the large Tibetan corpus of salient texts.

Though other factors which emerged from the data set were the pursuit of spiritual power and merit accumulation as essential elements to

Tibetan Buddhist praxis, the predominant finding of this study suggests that purity and purification are of significant concern to Tibetans, both monks and laity, and foundational to their worldview. Notions of purity and purification have considerable bearing on how Tibetans view themselves, the world around them, how they respond to those perceptions, and how they conduct their daily lives. The ontological and soteriological findings of this study suggest that presenting a contextualized gospel within a purification framework may find more resonance with a Tibetan Buddhist audience. These findings also suggest that an awareness of purity and purification concerns may be beneficial to those who are ministering to Tibetan Buddhists. An understanding of the purity schema of Tibetans, coupled with a Biblical perspective of purification, may also be informative in the fostering of indigenous ecclesial praxis.

The manuscript for this book is a modified version of my PhD dissertation. For the full version, including extensive footnotes and appendices, please see: https://independent.academia.edu/JamesMorrison284.

Acknowledgments

GRATEFUL THANKS ARE DUE to Dr. Ken Nehrbass, formerly of Biola University, for kindly welcoming me to Biola's Master's Degree program, and helping to reacquaint me with formal studies in the new era of hybrid and online courses. Thanks, Dr. Ken, for treating me to fried rice at the café with the red benches as you carefully outlined the curriculum and the path forward. Your friendship and encouragement are appreciated. Thanks, too, to Dr. Tom Steffen, also formerly of Biola University, for your lively classes and for persistently nudging me to publish some of my research papers. Thank you for introducing me to the doctoral program at Columbia International University. Thank you to Dr. Aminta Arrington, of John Brown University, for encouraging me to continue studying beyond an M.A. and pursue a doctoral degree.

Dr. Edward Smither of CIU deserves particular thanks for warmly welcoming me into the doctoral degree program. Thank you for being so supportive of my research. A special thank you to my research mentor, Dr. David Cashin. Your cheerful and encouraging support has been greatly appreciated. I enjoyed our Zoom calls. To the staff at CIU of the doctoral program, you have been very friendly and efficient. Thank you to everyone at CIU for your prompt replies to my emails!

Thanks to Sarah Hill for carefully reading over each of the chapter drafts, for your comments, encouragement and for keeping the writing consistent with punctuation and formatting. A special thanks to my wife, who also patiently and carefully read over each chapter as it emerged. You have been incredibly supportive of my involvement in this program, and I thank you for the many sacrifices you have made over the years. Thanks

ACKNOWLEDGMENTS

also to my wonderful children who allowed me to spend too many hours locked away in my office. Hopefully, I will have more time to play Settlers with you now!

Above all, thanks and gratitude are due to God for making all things possible. There were numerous moments in the midst of the heady congestion of pulling together so many pieces of data from a variety of source materials, mulling over conversations, and attempting to harness wandering and disparate thoughts, when I had a strong sense of God directing my way and highlighting certain things to me. I am forever grateful for the opportunity God opened up for me and my family to spend so many years living with Tibetans, and to be deeply immersed in their language and culture. Finally, I am grateful to all the Tibetans, who I cannot name here, who have very generously shared their lives, their language, their secrets, their butter tea, and their culture and religion with me over many years. One of the great joys of my life is spending time with Tibetans and being welcomed into their world. My hope and prayer is that many more Tibetans will personally come to faith in Savior Jesus, who can indeed cleanse them from all impurity.

Abbreviations

BDRC	Buddhist Digital Resource Center: https://www.tbrc.org/
DGCM	Dung dkar blo bzang 'phrin las. *Dung Dkar Tshig Mdzod Chen Mo [Dung Dkar's Great Dictionary]*. Beijing: krung go'i bod rig pa dpe skrun khang [China's Tibetology Press], 2002.
ITED	Lotsawa Tony Duff and Peter Schaffranek. *The Illuminator Tibetan-English Dictionary*. 4.20. Padma Karpo Translation Committee, 2003.
NTED	Melvyn C. Goldstein, T. N. Shelling, and J. T. Surkhang. *The New Tibetan–English Dictionary of Modern Tibetan*. Berkeley: University of California Press, 2001.
MTD	Tshe ring rdo rje, rdo sbis, ed. *Deng Rabs Bod Skad Tshig Mdzod [Modern Tibetan Dictionary]*. Chengdu: bod ljongs mi dmangs dpe skrun khang [Tibet People's Press], 2016.
TDCM	Yisun Zhang and Bian Zhu, ed. *Bod Rgya Tshig Mdzod Chen Mo [The Great Tibetan–Chinese Dictionary]*. Beijing: Nationalities Press, 1984.
RJYS	Rangjung Yeshe. *Rangjung Yeshe Tibetan-English Dharma Dictionary 3.0*. Rangjung Yeshe Publications, 2005.
SCD	Das, Sarat Chandra. *Tibetan-English Dictionary*. 1902. Reprint, Delhi: Book FaithIndia, 2000.
TWE	Tibetan Works: https://tibetan.works/etext/
Sk.	Sanskrit (Note that apart from certain proper nouns diacritics have not been used in the transliteration of Sanskrit terms).

Introduction

TIBETAN BUDDHISTS, AND INDEED Buddhists at large, have long proved resistant to the gospel.[1] Despite various efforts, relatively few Tibetans are followers of Jesus. There are multiple reasons for this. For example, geographical isolation, limited missionary access, demonic opposition, cultural pride, Christianity being perceived as a "foreign" religion or "just the same as Buddhism," are to mention just a few.[2] An additional factor may be that gospel presentations have been speaking to a misinformed set of needs, speaking superficially or just not speaking at all. Contextualizing the gospel for a Tibetan context remains a needed area of development. Fresh approaches are still required and hence the need to probe further into Tibetan culture and worldview. One area that needs to be explored is how Tibetans understand purity.

I have had the privilege of living and working with Tibetans for more than three decades. My interest in the purity concerns of Tibetans was first sparked back in 2002 when I was grappling with various key terms and looking for a suitable term for baptism for our New Testament translation project. In the process of researching this term, I discovered a water purification ritual (*byabs khrus*) which seemed to indicate the issue of purity and impurity was of significant concern for Tibetans. In exploring the lexical range of purity terms, I learned that there were many terms for purity and defilement and their lexical weighting within the vernacular register was more than initially imagined. I further discovered that the *byabs khrus* water cleansing ritual, performed daily in the *byams khang* temple, in the

---

1. A. Smith, *Buddhism through Christian Eyes*, 27–28.
2. See Morrison, "Christianity's Journey."

heart of Lhasa, was a popular one that attracted hundreds of people, often with long waiting lines.

Though anthropologists have documented the purity and pollution systems of an array of people groups over many years, little has been written about these systems from a missiological perspective. Currently, much of the discussion regarding contextualizing the gospel has been formed around the cultural paradigms of honor/shame, guilt/innocence, and fear/power. While these cultural lenses have been used as tools for analyzing culture and formulating approaches to contextualization, the paradigm of purity/pollution may have been overlooked.

According to anthropologist and Bible translator Eugene Nida, there are three basic human responses to religious transgressions—"guilt, fear, and shame."[3] In recent years, this tripartite division has been a foundation for cultural analysis and formulations of contextualized gospel presentations.[4] There may be something missing from Nida's statement. Is there not also a fourth possible basic response to transgression; a sense of defilement, pollution, uncleanness or simply "being dirty"?

While much has been written about the purity system as revealed in the Biblical record, little has been written from a missional viewpoint.[5] To be sure, the purity code of Hinduism has been well documented, and a small band of reflective practitioners in Islamic contexts have studied purity from a missiological perspective.[6] In contrast, little, if anything, has been written about purity from a missiological perspective in a Buddhist setting. In order to address this apparent gap in the literature, and to provide another window into Tibetan culture and worldview, and to perhaps move forward the discussion of contextualizing the gospel in a Tibetan context, an in-depth study of a Tibetan understanding of purity may reveal certain insights.

---

3. Nida, *Customs and Cultures*, 150.

4. See Müller, *Honor and Shame*; Georges, *The 3D Gospel*; Mischke et al., *Global Gospel*. To be clear, I am not suggesting that this tripartite paradigm is necessarily a robust framework, or an accurate reflection of the complexities of human communities, or a nuanced emic approach; rather, I am noting the existence of the framework as a predicating factor in current contextualization discussions.

5. See Neyrey, "Idea of Purity," 91–128; Neyrey, "Clean/Unclean."; deSilva, *Honor*; Neusner, "Idea of Purity."

6. See Hibbert, "Defilement and Cleansing"; B. Thomas, "Gospel for Shame Cultures,"; Davis, "Philoxenus"; Dale, "Ritual Purity."

INTRODUCTION

Rationale and Need

Given the fact there are gaps in our understanding of the Tibetan purity system, and how an understanding of it might be illuminating from a missiological perspective, there is value in making an initial attempt to fill this void. A study of this kind may help to provide further insights into Tibetan culture and worldview, which could then be beneficial to cross-cultural practitioners ministering to Tibetans. Indeed, in the first instance, those who may directly benefit from this research are people working with Tibetans in whatever context they may find them—in either Tibetan native homelands or scattered throughout the diaspora in Nepal, India, or the West. Those living and working in a Tibetan context, however, may find this study especially pertinent. Practitioners working in the broader Buddhist World may also find this research relevant.

To the larger community of missiologists and reflective practitioners this study may contribute to the ongoing conversation about contextualization. Any who are interested in the cultural frameworks of honor/shame, fear/power, and guilt/innocence may find this research beneficial. This same group is typically in dialogue about the various atonement theories and motifs which are considered more appropriate to particular people groups in initial presentations of the gospel. This study could hold some further interest in that regard. Bible translators in Buddhist contexts may also find this study relevant as they consider how to approach the purity passages in Scripture and in the development of contextually relevant scripture engagement resources.

Analyzing the purity system of Tibetans could perhaps be propaedeutic in stimulating further research and prompt others to consider how doing such a study may be relevant in their contexts. In that vein, this research could be used as a foundation to build upon or as a source of reference.

In 2016, I wrote a brief overview of some of the ways Tibetans understand pollution and purity.[7] In that paper, I was making the case that pollution and purity were of significant concern to Tibetans and worthy of further exploration. While an introduction to Tibetan purity and pollution has previously been attempted, there are questions that remain for a fuller and deeper understanding. For example, how do Tibetans understand purity according to their sacred texts, according to their folk literature, their rituals, symbols, and everyday practices? How might this understanding

---

7. Morrison, "Sharing the Gospel."

be formational in gaining a deeper understanding of a Tibetan worldview? What are some missiological implications and how might this be relevant for contextualizing the gospel? If part of the process of contextualization is to discover what questions a given people group might be asking about reality, then researching the purity concerns of Tibetans would seem to be a valid and important topic of investigation.

The purity system of Tibetans has not been extensively studied, neither as an anthropological study or as a bibliographic and text-based study. Broadly speaking there are two gaps in our understanding: firstly, of a thorough understanding of Tibetan purity and secondly, of analyzing purity concerns in a Tibetan context through a missiological lens. It is the intention of this study to begin to address this lacuna.

In short, Tibetans have remained resistant to the gospel and attempts at culturally relevant gospel presentations are still needed. The purpose of this study, then, is to help in gaining a deeper insight into Tibetan culture by exploring their understanding of purity with the missional intention of reflecting upon how this may be informative in reaching Tibetans for Christ.

Research Problem

In this dissertation, my aim is to research how Tibetans understand purity, and to reflect on some possible missiological implications. In order to facilitate a structured approach to this research, further sub-questions are needed. These are as follows:

- What do the terms "purity" and "impurity" mean in a Tibetan context?
- What do indigenous texts in the Tibetan language reveal about purity?
- What purity rituals do Tibetans observe and what symbols represent purity?
- What does this understanding of purity teach us about the Tibetan worldview?
- What are some missiological implications that arise from an understanding of Tibetan purity?

INTRODUCTION

Limitations

While the concept of impurity will be included in this study, the primary focus is on exploring a Tibetan understanding of purity. To be more specific, this research is not intended as a detailed anatomy of how Tibetans regard filth, disgust, defilement, pollution, or impurity.[8] Rather, this is a study of how Tibetans understand and conceptualize purity. The question of what Tibetans consider impure, or defiling will be addressed, but that question will be researched in order to bring further illumination to an understanding of Tibetan purity.

The primary data source for this research will be Tibetan texts and related secondary sources. As such, this study will be textual and bibliographic. The research will not be pursuing a diachronic, historical approach tracing the development of impurity and purity concerns among Tibetans over a given time period. Rather, the approach will be more synchronic—to explore indigenous Tibetan texts, across a variety of genres, and assess what this data may reveal about a Tibetan understanding of purity. The purview of this study, then, will not involve standard anthropological methods such as interviews, participant observation, or focus groups. Even if such an approach were possible, not only would this be a significant security risk, as interviewing people, particularly those in the religious establishment, can be a delicate activity, there is the question as to whether this would represent a meaningful and valid way of collecting data. Written texts, revered by Tibetans, on the other hand, provide an objective and valid data source.

The focus of this research is with primary source texts that have influenced Tibetans living in Tibet and Tibetan areas. Though the teachings of the current Dalai Lama, and other contemporary lamas, some of whom now reside in the West, will be studied and analyzed where relevant, the primary data sources will not be drawn from Western Tibetan Buddhism, a form of Buddhism which can be at variance to that practiced in Tibet itself.[9] Though purification rituals do form part of the "self-realization"

---

8. Robert Priest, for example, has detailed the filth system of a certain people group. His goal was "to provide a comprehensive and systematic exposition of defilement and dirt symbolism in a single culture." Priest, "Defilement," 22. In contrast, the focus of this study is on Tibetan notions of purity rather than a detailed analysis of Tibetan notions of filth, disgust, and impurity.

9. Peter Bishop, among others, has traced the development of Western Tibetan Buddhism and the Western fascination of Tibet. See Bishop, *Dreams of Power*; Lopez, *Prisoners of Shangri-La*; Dodin and Rather, *Imagining Tibet*; and Schell, *Virtual Tibet*.

meditation retreats offered by Tibetan dharma centers scattered throughout the major cities of the Western world, this research will not be focusing attention there. Further, while Pure Land Buddhism will be addressed in this study, and related texts discussed, tracing the development of Pure Land Buddhism in Tibet will not be attempted.[10]

Were one to study every instance of purification rites within the panoply of Tibetan ritual, that would also exceed the scope of this study. While acknowledging purification rites typically form part of all rituals, not all rituals can or will be studied in depth. Therefore, it will be necessary to selectively focus on those rituals perspicacious to purity and which provide a clear data set for analysis. In terms of other limitations, it will not be possible to research all the written texts that deal with purity or purification. The ocean of Tibetan literature is simply too vast.[11] Therefore, it will be necessary to selectively look at the salient texts which deal with purity.

A limitation that may seem apparent then, is that a key text dealing with purity could be overlooked. This is certainly possible, but to help mitigate against this, Tibetan friends and colleagues will assist in providing guidance to those texts which speak of purity most prominently.[12] Though texts will be placed in their historical, religious, and literary context, discussions about textual variants or issues of authenticity will not be entered into. Texts that have been widely accepted will be the primary data source.

Defining of Terms

Various technical terms will be used throughout this dissertation but only some of the major ones will be outlined below. The terms for purity and impurity will be discussed in detail in a subsequent chapter and therefore have not been included here. Except for certain Buddhist terms which appear to have an established form of lexicalization in English, for example, "nirvana", "samsara", "karma", "Mahayana" and so forth (though these terms

---

10. Such an endeavor would entail a separate dissertation.

11. The Tibetan canon, the Kangyur, is 108 volumes, and the Tengyur, the commentaries, is more than 200 volumes. These figures do not include all the thousands of indigenous writings that have been preserved over the centuries. To provide another example: a detailed study of all the texts from the genre known as "mind purification" (*blo sbyong*) would require a separate dissertation.

12. This approach does not in itself invalidate the study. The study will be based upon the data collected from available salient texts and the argument and conclusions will be informed by and generated from those texts and relevant secondary sources.

INTRODUCTION

have been derived from Sanskrit and not Tibetan), I will use an established system of transliteration for Tibetan terms rather than Tibetan orthography. This transliteration system, first developed by Turrell Wylie,[13] is not phonetic but instead corresponds to Tibetan spelling and readily transfers into Tibetan orthography. The Wylie schema is the most accurate way to transliterate Tibetan and those who wish to can then easily search for the Tibetan terms used in this dissertation in standard Tibetan lexicons and Tibetan texts.[14] Note that while many sacred texts and Buddhist terms have been translated from Sanskrit into Tibetan, the focus here will be on Tibetan terminology. Where appropriate, Tibetan transliterations will be provided in italics within parenthesis.

Key terms surrounding the study of Tibetans and Tibetan Buddhism are not without controversy. Tibetologists, both Tibetan and otherwise, have, for example, engaged in rigorous debates about what constitutes Tibet,[15] what does it mean to be Tibetan,[16] and what is Tibetan Buddhism.[17] However, below are modest attempts at "standard" definitions.

Tibet (*bod*): contemporary Tibet suggests the Tibetan Autonomous Regions (TAR) which became a province of China in 1959 after the annexation of Tibet during the reign of Mao Zedong and today remains under Chinese jurisdiction.[18] Greater Tibet (*bod chen po*) is the traditional area that incorporates all Tibetan areas in other provinces of China, predominantly Qinghai and Sichuan.[19]

Tibetans (*bod rigs*) may be categorized as those who self-identify as Tibetan, who follow Tibetan Buddhism and speak Tibetan or a Tibetic

---

13. Wylie, "Standard System of Tibetan."

14. Following this transliteration scheme, rather than my own phonetic rendering of Tibetan terms, is the most transparent approach, and one could perhaps argue that this is also part of a data validation strategy. That is, anyone can readily locate these lexical items in the Tibetan contexts from which they are derived and can study them further should they so desire.

15. See, for example, Van Schaik, *Tibet*, xv–xviii.

16. See Kapstein, *The Tibetans*; Bell, *The People of Tibet*; Richardson, *Tibet and Its History*; Shneiderman, "Barbarians at the Border"; and Van Spengen, "Ways of Knowing."

17. See Samuel, *Introducing Tibetan Buddhism*; Powers, *Introduction to Tibetan Buddhism*; Kapstein, *Tibetan Buddhism*.

18. The TAR is known in Tibetan as *bod rang skyong ljongs*.

19. The authoritative lexicon, *The Great Tibetan-Chinese Dictionary*, compiled by Tibetan scholars, has an entry for both *bod* and *bod chen po* which incorporates the tradition Tibetan areas of Ngari, U-Tsang, Kham and Amdo. See Zhang and Zhu, *Bod Rgya Tshig Mdzod Chen Mo [The Great Tibetan-Chinese Dictionary]*, 1846–48.

language. Many scholars have claimed that the link between being a Tibetan and a Tibetan Buddhist is an inseparable part of ethnic identity.[20] Robert Ekvall, who lived among Tibetans for many years, found that the highest value Tibetans placed on their identity was their religion.[21] The focus of this study is Tibetans in the region of Greater Tibet and others in the Himalayas who may self-identify as Tibetan.[22]

Tibetan Buddhism (*nang pa'i chos lugs*) is understood as belonging to the wider branch of Mahayana (*theg chen*) Buddhism but more narrowly restricted to Tantric or Vajrayana (*rdo rje theg pa*) Buddhism. Tibetan Buddhism is further predicated upon an eclectic mix of shamanism and animistic Bön practices derived from the ancient Bön religion.[23] Tibetan Buddhism has various schools or sects that are carefully preserved through the lineages of incarnate lamas.

Bön (*bon*) is the indigenous religion of Tibet widely established before Tibetans embraced Buddhism in the seventh century. Bön resembles a shamanistic and animistic religion of the worship and appeasement of mountain, sky, river, and lake deities. In recent years, Bön has absorbed Tibetan Buddhist practices and there exist a number of Bön monasteries throughout the Tibetan Buddhist World.[24]

Bodhisattva (*byang chub sems dpa'*) is one who has vowed to become a Buddha in order to liberate all beings from the suffering of samsara or who has delayed enlightenment for the sake of others.[25] The system of Bodhisattvas is unique to Mahayana Buddhism.

Vajrayana (*rdo rje theg pa*) is a form of Buddhism that focus on esoteric teachings or tantras (*rgyud*), the recitation of mantras (*sngags*), secret yogic practices (*rnal 'byor*) and the use of mandalas *(dkyil 'khor)* for meditation and guidance through the spirit world. Though Vajrayana is believed to be efficacious in leading to enlightenment, it is typically regarded as potentially dangerous (because of the focus on the occult) and requires specialized training.

20. See Goldstein and Kapstein, *Buddhism in Contemporary Tibet*, 4–6, 142–45; B. Miller, "Tibetan Culture(s) without Buddhism?"; M. Tsering, *Sharing Christ*, 97–98; Tsomo, "Review of Buddhism," 124–26.

21. Ekvall, "Tibetan Self-Image," 629–30.

22. Tibetans are also known as (*bod pa*), though this distinction is more typically reserved for Central Tibetans living in the U-Tsang central plateau.

23. See Samuel, *Civilized Shamans*.

24. Practitioners of Bön are known as Bönpo (*bon po*) and Bön is also spelled Bon.

25. Van Schaik, *Spirit of Tibetan Buddhism*, 35

Mahayana (*theg chen*) in contrast to Hinayana (*theg chung*) or Theravada Buddhism, maintains a system of Bodhisattvas and posits that enlightenment is possible in one lifetime.

Kangyur (*bka' 'gyur*) is the Buddhist canon containing both the sutras (*mdo*) and the tantras (*rgyud*) which are considered to be the words of Buddha. The Tibetan canon is typically either 104 or 108 volumes.[26]

Tengyur (*bstang 'gyur*) are commentaries on the words of Buddha recorded in the Tibetan canon (*bka' 'gyur*). These commentaries are translations from the Indian Buddhist masters who explained and elaborated upon the words of Buddha. This set of more than 220 volumes is also referred to as the "canonical treatises."

Mantra (*sngags*) are formulaic spell-like phrases pervasive in the tantras and believed to contain special powers. With such an emphasis on mantras, Tantric Vajrayana Buddhism is often called Mantrayana—the mantra vehicle.

Samsara (*'khor ba*) is the perpetual cyclic existence of birth, death, and rebirth predicated upon the unrelenting law of karma. The end goal of Buddhist practice is to be released from the affliction of samsara.

Literature Review

Edgar Elliston suggests that a critical aspect to the integrity of one's research is in conducting an honest, fair, and thorough review of the precedent literature.[27] What follows is an attempt to do justice to the studies that have gone before—studies which have been undertaken in the fields of social anthropology and Tibetan Buddhist religious studies. While the intended focus of this literature review is research conducted among Tibetans in Tibet, of necessity, this has been expanded to Tibetan Buddhist people groups outside of Tibet. Though there are obviously differences between these groups, there is also enough commonality to warrant doing so. The literature review is divided into two sections. The first section deals with studies undertaken in the broader Tibetan Buddhist world and the second with studies undertaken in Tibet. Keeping to a tight focus, I have not drawn on the immense corpus of literature from the wider area of anthropological and religious purity/pollution studies.

---

26. The variation in the number of volumes is dependent upon which edition of the Kangyur one is referencing.

27. Elliston, *Missiological Research Design*, 88–89, 168–69.

Studies from the Tibetan Buddhist World

Moving on from a structuralist-functionalist approach, which posits purity as being framed primarily upon caste lines, anthropologist Sherry Ortner, in her study of Sherpa purity, provides an alternative approach. She contends that purity is symbolic of a larger embedded system that needs to be viewed within that context. In her article, "Sherpa Purity," Ortner outlines the various causes of pollution among the Tibetan Buddhist Sherpa of the Solu-Khumbu in northeastern Nepal and the solutions they have developed to deal with it.[28]

Ortner suggests the Sherpa have a three-pronged approach to dealing with pollution. A monk deals with pollution by striving for "perfect purity/spirituality, and to excise and eliminate the forces which pollute him and hinder his quest for salvation."[29] For the lay person, strategies are embodied in two rituals. The first is a water ritual (*tu*) which deals with the physical aspect of ritual pollution "most prominently performed during the rituals surrounding birth and death."[30] The second ritual is burning incense (*sang*) to appease the multiplicity of demons, perceived to be the source of much pollution: "The struggle against antireligious demons in fact covers every aspect of purity/pollution action."[31]

In her subsequent book, *Sherpas Through Their Rituals*,[32] Ortner adds a fourth way of dealing with the pollution caused by demonic activity: that of ritual exorcism. Though she provides little detail about demon possession or exorcism itself, she maintains that, "Culturally, exorcisms are considered to be rites of purification, 'to clean all the dirty things out of the village,' 'to clean all the bad smells out of the village.'"[33] The results of purification for the Sherpa, according to Ortner, are "better pragmatic functioning in the world, and to the pursuit of salvation."[34] Her most comprehensive work, *High Religion: A Cultural and Political History of Sherpa Buddhism*,[35] provides further insightful reflections about pollution concerns.

---

28. Ortner, "Sherpa Purity."
29. Ortner, "Sherpa Purity," 58.
30. Ortner, "Sherpa Purity," 59.
31. Ortner, "Sherpa Purity," 60.
32. Ortner, *Sherpas Through Their Rituals*.
33. Ortner, *Sherpas Through Their Rituals*, 103.
34. Ortner, *Sherpas Through Their Rituals*, 104.
35. Ortner, *High Religion*.

INTRODUCTION

Ortner's research relates to this dissertation in that she has documented and provided commentary on the pollution system of a Tibetan Buddhist people group. Her approach of moving on from the structuralist tendency to explain pollution as merely a social construct is affirming as I plan to explore purity within the larger context of Tibetan Buddhism. Ortner's research focused on the Sherpa of Nepal. While there is some commonality, there are also differences from Tibetans living in Tibet. Ortner's anthropological work dealt with pollution and defilement, but less on purity and purification, and she did not access any written texts.[36] In contrast, this study aims to examine Tibetan purity texts that have influenced Tibetans in Tibet.

In her detailed ethnography of the Khumbo (neighbors to the Sherpa) in northeastern Nepal,[37] anthropologist Hildegard Diemberger outlines how the main opposition to prosperity in the highland village of Sepa was considered to be defilement caused by "dip"—pollution.[38] For the Khumbo, they can be inflicted with pollution by any association with birth, death, inter-personal conflicts, ethical transgressions, and contact with anyone who is polluted.[39] Diemberger observes that pollution derived from childbirth is eliminated by a name giving ceremony in which the child is both purified from the stain of birth and is socially born into society. In this process, a lama purifies the birth with water and bestows a name on the child as a rite of passage.[40] Diemberger further relates that the process of birth means that women are more prone to defilement and have less access

---

36. It is curious that though there are monasteries in her fieldwork area, and highly literate monks, Ortner did not access any written sources. This concern was also raised by Alexander Macdonald in his review of her book, *High Religion*. See Macdonald, review of *High Religion*, 341–44. Distinguished anthropologist and Tibetologist, Melvin Goldstein, in his review of Ortner's work, though appreciating her contribution, questioned her lack of supporting evidence and the data that was used he described as often "forced and unconvincing," and in some cases presented no data at all. Goldstein, Review of *Sherpas Through Their Rituals*, 216–19.

37. Diemberger, "Blood, Sperm, Soul."

38. Diemberger, "Blood, Sperm, Soul," 105. Note that "dip" is the Sherpa, Khumbo, and Ladakhi pronunciation of the more standard Tibetan term "drip" and the spelling is how Ortner, Diemberger, Schicklgruber, and Mills phoneticize the term in their writings.

39. Diemberger, "Blood, Sperm, Soul," 106.

40. Diemberger, "Blood, Sperm, Soul," 116. In an earlier article, Diemberger analyzes the role of the lama and lay priest of the Khumbo and the purification rituals they perform. See Diemberger, "Lovanga (Lo 'bangs Pa?)", 421–33.

to the sacred forces of religious life than men.[41] The Khumbo have various myths related to pollution where it is perceived as casting a dark shadow upon individuals and the community as a whole. Though not necessarily permanent, "dip" for the Khumbo can be profoundly disruptive of human relations and needs to be avoided at all costs.[42]

Though she does not detail all pollution concerns, nor delve deeply into purification, or access written texts, Diemberger's study relates to this current research in providing an understanding the Tibetan Buddhist Khumbo have of the profound sense of societal damage pollution can wreak. The moral element to pollution, though obviously to be interpreted through a Buddhist lens, provides a certain foundation for further exploration with reference to missiological application, something which Diemberger had no cause to investigate.

Anthropologist Christian Schicklgruber, a contemporary of Diemberger, provides another layer of understanding to the concept of "dip" pollution among the Khumbo of northeastern Nepal.[43] By examining an oral myth that tells of the pollution that arises from incest, Schicklgruber traces the strict marriage rules of the clan system, which ensure there is no communal defilement through marriage. He also outlines how birth and death are defiling events and how the breaching of socially prescribed norms can lead any individual into pollution. This defilement can then infect a whole family, clan, or wider community with potentially disastrous effects such as sickness, epidemics among livestock, or hail, which can destroy crops.[44]

Schicklgruber's main discussion is concerned with shamanist rituals for neutralizing the impurity that arises from childbirth and death. He concludes that pollution is unavoidable in the life of the Khumbo as are the rituals dealing with the elimination of it.[45] His analysis of pollution adds to our understanding of the social ramifications of communal defilement. Schicklgruber does not, however, deal directly with purity or purification. While he does engage with oral narratives, which are certainly valid data points, he provides no examination of written texts. This contrasts with the study at hand.

41. Diemberger, "Blood, Sperm, Soul," 117.
42. Diemberger, "Blood, Sperm, Soul," 117.
43. Schicklgruber, "Grib."
44. Christian Schicklgruber, "Grib," 728.
45. Christian Schicklgruber, "Grib," 734. These elaborate rituals, which call on the spirit world, require ritual specialists who may be a trained lay person or a lama.

INTRODUCTION

In her dissertation, "Embodying Spirits: Village Oracles and Possession Ritual in Ladakh, North India," Sophie Day examines how village oracles in an area of Tibetan Buddhist Ladakh provide certain ritualized services when they are in a trance or possessed by a spirit.[46] While primarily concerned with the role of the oracle, she does document a purification rite intended for the conquest of demons and demonic forces. Day details the *sang* incense burning ritual and its significance for ritual cleansing and purification. She relates that in Ladakhi Tibetan Buddhist cosmology, there exist certain household gods (*phas lha*) who require daily purification in order for their anger towards humans to be placated. These gods can be polluted by the activities of humans, such as cultivating the land, building a house, burning fuel, or cooking.[47] The burning of incense (*sang*) is believed to remove the pollution from the gods and clean an entire area.[48] Failure to do so would cause problems such as illness, crop failure, and dead livestock. Day concludes that, "rites of such as *sang* have to be performed regularly."[49]

Day has focused on one area of pollution and ritual purification and provided insights into the cosmology of Tibetan Buddhists in Ladakh. Her identification of the relationship between pollution and wrathful numina is reflective of beliefs held in many Tibetan Buddhist areas. In contrast to this current research, her study focused on certain villages in Ladakh and not in Tibet itself, nor did she interact with textual sources.

Three of the universal polluting activities in cultures for whom purity/pollution concerns are prevalent appear to be birth, death, and bodily discharges—typically menstruation.[50] In their article, "Tibetan and Indian Ideas of Birth Pollution: Similarities and Contrasts," Santi Rozario and Geoffrey Samuel provide insights into Tibetan conceptions of birth pollution (*skye drip*).[51] In 1997, Rozario and Samuel conducted fieldwork in a Tibetan refuge community in Himal Pradesh, north India, studying Tibetan attitudes towards childbirth and comparing these with the wider Indian context.[52] In researching why childbirth was considered to be polluting, one

---

46. Day, "Embodying Spirits."
47. Day, "Embodying Spirits," 140.
48. Day, "Embodying Spirits," 138.
49. Day, "Embodying Spirits," 140.
50. There are others, of course, but these are the main three that appear to be consistent in the literature.
51. Rozario and Samuel, "Tibetan and Indian Ideas."
52. Rozario and Samuel, "Tibetan and Indian Ideas," 182.

of their Tibetan informants stated that "birth and its associated substances were 'dirty' (Tibetan *tsokpa*) and that they cause sickness, including conjunctivitis and *drip*."[53] Other Tibetans reported that those who help during the birth process are "routinely subjected to *drip*," experience "burning or irritation of eyes, tiredness and general body ache," and sometimes it was believed to lead to blindness.[54] Rozario and Samuel outline the perceived solution: to observe the purification rituals of incense burning and washing with consecrated water.[55]

Rozario and Samuel have highlighted the seriousness with which Tibetan refugees living in exile in north India take childbirth pollution.[56] Their research is helpful in providing another window into the pervasiveness of pollution in the daily lives of Tibetans. A consideration, however, is that their research took place outside of Tibet and was not focused on textual concerns.

Lawrence Epstein conducted a sociological study of Tibetan refuges in Mysore, southern India, which included seventeen months of fieldwork during 1969–1970. His dissertation "Causation in Tibetan Religion: Duality and Its Transformations,"[57] though primarily dealing with the outworking of the Buddhist notion of cause and effect in secular and religious life, does delve into the concept of pollution. Epstein identifies six distinct types of pollution and details its contaminating nature.[58] He further suggests that pollution may "initiate or invite demonic attack" which can lead to illness,

---

53. Rozario and Samuel, "Tibetan and Indian Ideas," 191. Note that the term "drip" (a standard Tibetan word for pollution) is the same term as "dip"—which reflects the Sherpa, Khumbo and Ladakhi pronunciation.

54. Rozario and Samuel, "Tibetan and Indian Ideas," 194.

55. Rozario and Samuel, "Tibetan and Indian Ideas," 192–93. On the third or fourth day after birth (three if a boy, four if a girl), the purification rituals can begin. The first of these rituals is the burning of incense for the baby, mother, and the maternity ward. Then, upon arriving at home, to rid themselves of any impurities, the family sprinkle consecrated water on themselves and conduct a ritual cleaning of the house and all their clothes.

56. A pertinent observation that Rozario and Samuel make is that there is a tendency to highlight only the polluting aspect of birth, and the danger of contaminating others, and to discount that giving birth can also be seen as meritorious. Rozario and Samuel, "Tibetan and Indian Ideas," 186. The meritoriousness of birth is notable if one gives birth to a son and if the timing is auspicious, that is, giving birth on a lucky day, month, or year.

57. L. Epstein, "Causation in Tibetan Religion."

58. L. Epstein, "Causation in Tibetan Religion," 90–91.

outbursts of anger or even insanity.⁵⁹ The theory behind this, according to Epstein, is that various protective deities have been impacted by human pollution and thus have their protective powers reduced resulting in sickness and trouble. The solution to pollution is incense offerings and water purification rituals.⁶⁰

Epstein's work has provided helpful insights into the larger schematic of the Tibetan worldview and how the various tensions of mitigating demonic attacks, accumulating merit, and being subject to spiritual opposition relate to the all-encompassing doctrine of karma. His delineation between *bar chad* (demonic opposition) and *drip* (pollution) is insightful as are his observations about Tibetan worldview. His research, however, was conducted in southern India among Tibetan refugees and needs to be viewed within that context. This current research, on the other hand, has its focus on Tibetans within Tibet.

Martin Mills, in his comprehensive book, *Identity, Ritual and State in Tibetan Buddhism: The Foundations of Authority in Gelukpa Monasticism*,⁶¹ presents the results of his fieldwork conducted in a village area in southern Ladakh during 1993–1995. Mills' primary area of study was a Gelukpa (*dge lugs pa*) monastery situated in a village area in southern Ladakh.⁶² Though Mills was researching "the nature of religious authority in Tibetan Buddhist monasticism,"⁶³ he also provides insights into purity/pollution and associated ritual practices. Consistent with previous studies, Mills highlights the ubiquitous nature of pollution (*dip*), which is attributed to be the direct result of the perceived chthonic order. He also documents the process of removing pollution through rituals conducted by monks, villagers, or local oracles.⁶⁴ Mills does add another level of understanding in the area of commensality. Mills relates that pollution concerns had a profound impact on the social structure of hospitality where polluted classes could only mix if particular protocols were observed. He outlines the necessary hierarchical arrangement of guests at a communal meal and found that "what was

---

59. L. Epstein, "Causation in Tibetan Religion," 92.

60. L. Epstein, "Causation in Tibetan Religion," 94–95.

61. Mills, *Identity, Ritual and State*.

62. The Gelukpa sect is the largest school of Tibetan Buddhism and the lineage through which the Dalai Lamas are preserved.

63. Mills, *Identity, Ritual and State*, xviii.

64. Mills, *Identity, Ritual and State*, 206. Note that the term "dip" (which is the same term for the standard Tibetan word for pollution "drip") reflects Ladakhi pronunciation.

important was the maintenance of the correct order, lest it generated dangerous pollution."[65] He also outlined how food could be purified and how the leftovers of high lamas were considered pure and a source of blessing to others.[66]

In a subsequent article on pollution in Buddhist Ladakh,[67] Mills analyzes pollution practices through the time portal of the Tibetan Buddhist astrological calendar. He found that those who had become ritually polluted, through, for example, involvement with birth or death, were unable to participate in the auspicious activities within the Tibetan calendar, dislocating them from "the ordinary astrological tempos that organize social life within village communities."[68] He further examines the times within the astrological calendar when it is more efficacious to perform purification rituals.[69]

Both of Mills' studies relate to this dissertation in that he has brought another layer of understanding to the various elements of pollution and its out-working in monastic and village life. Further, his work was undertaken in areas under the influence of the Gelukpa sect of Tibetan Buddhism, which is the largest and most influential sect within Tibet. Of note, however, is that these studies were undertaken in Ladakh and there was no specific engagement with purity textual sources.

Christine Daniels' study, "Defilement and Purification: Tibetan Buddhist Pilgrims at Bodhnath, Nepal," traces Tibetan refugees who travelled as pilgrims from Tibet to the sacred site of Bodhnath in Kathmandu, Nepal.[70] Daniels reveals a certain ontological perception of pilgrims regarding themselves as defiled and pilgrimage as the path to purification. In exploring why these pilgrims considered themselves defiled, Daniels notes there were six main reasons: "wrongdoing, pollution, supernaturally caused harm, inauspiciousness, ignorance and the condition of being a woman."[71] It was not, Daniels observes, only the end result of visiting the sacred site of Bodhnath that was seen as purifying, but the whole pilgrimage from Tibet

---

65. Mills, *Identity, Ritual and State*, 208–9.
66. Mills, *Identity, Ritual and State*, 211.
67. Mills, "Living in Time's Shadow," 349–66.
68. Mills, "Living in Time's Shadow," 357.
69. Mills, "Living in Time's Shadow," 359.
70. Daniels, "Defilement and Purification," 299–306. Note that, try as I might, I have not been able to access Daniels' full dissertation but only excerpts.
71. Daniels, "Defilement and Purification," 301.

INTRODUCTION

and the interaction with sacred sites along the way that had a combined purificatory effect.⁷²

Daniels' research provides an understanding of purity/pollution concerns among Tibetan pilgrims who journeyed to Nepal.⁷³ Her dissertation is helpful in highlighting the perception that the process of pilgrimage is believed to remove the stain of defilement and the belief that the harder the pilgrimage, the more effective it is. Daniels' primary data points were interviews and interactions with Tibetan pilgrims residing in Nepal over a number of years and was not focused on textual analysis. Daniels also had no need of a missiological analysis, which stands in contrast to this present study.

In her dissertation "Purity, Embodiment and the Immaterial Body,"⁷⁴ Gemma Clay explores the notion of purity in a Tibetan Buddhist monastery in southern India, among a Tibetan refugee community. One of her main concerns is to understand how "attitudes towards purity and the embodiment of purity perpetuates the social hierarchy of the monastery."⁷⁵ Clay explores the doctrinal teaching of the Dzogchen (*rdzogs chen*) monastic order which maintains that all human beings are innately pure.⁷⁶ She further traces how the lama at this monastery, Dzogchen Rinpoche, was considered to be the embodiment of purity and how his purity could be transferred to others. The transferal, Clay observes, was performed through a consecration ritual (*rab gnas*) which culminated in the lama's purity being bestowed upon others through contact with a ritually pure white scarf.⁷⁷ Prostrations and circumambulating the monastery and other sacred sites were also believed to be efficacious in the process of moving towards embodied purity.⁷⁸

---

72. These overland pilgrimages can be long and arduous, sometimes thousands of kilometers in distance. Pilgrims may even prostrate themselves for most of the journey, which may extend the pilgrimage into a year or more.

73. Though Nepal is a Hindu country, there are many Tibetan refugees living there and a variety of Tibetan Buddhist people groups who have lived for centuries in the highlands. There are also many Tibetan Buddhist temples, monasteries, and sacred sites.

74. Clay, "Purity."

75. Clay, "Purity," 11.

76. The Dzogchen school of Tibetan Buddhism is one of six schools that belong to the larger sect of the Nyingmapa (*rnying ma pa*), which is the oldest school of Buddhism in Tibet. The incarnate lamas from this school, the Dzogchen Rinpoche, are believed to be the living embodiment of purity. See Clay, "Purity," 65.

77. Clay, "Purity," 33, 143, 152–57, 168–73, 195–96, 198.

78. Clay, "Purity," 201–2, 214, 215–20.

Clay's research relates to this dissertation in that she has focused on purity rather than pollution, and rightly identified the Dzogchen school as one of the major proponents of purity teachings. She has identified purification rituals which are not necessarily for the elimination of pollution but rather for the pursuit of a purified state. Her study though, does need to be balanced against certain considerations. Her research was conducted in southern India at a monastery where many foreigners were in residence, the monastic teachings were all in English, her interviews were conducted in English and the official language of the monastery is English.[79] She also did not consult any texts in the Tibetan language. In contrast, this current study is focused on indigenous Tibetan texts which have exerted influence among Tibetans in Tibet. In addition, the delineation between the doctrine of purity, with its multiple layering, and ritualized purity praxis will be further explored in this dissertation.

Studies undertaken within Tibet

In her book, *Commoners and Nobles in Tibet*,[80] social anthropologist Heidi Fjeld's ethnographic study documents the traditional stratification of Tibetan society and the extent to which these traditional categories are still evident in contemporary Lhasa, the capital of Tibet. In her research, she found that the lower classes, such as blacksmiths and butchers, were classified in terms of "impurity," while the upper stratum "were not defined in terms of purity."[81] Building on these initial findings, Fjeld later carried out a more detailed study, the findings of which she published in a paper entitled, *Pollution and Social Networks in Contemporary Rural Tibet.*[82]

In her study of ritual pollution in rural Tibet, Fjeld traces the lives of Tibetans in a certain village who had been deemed to be of an unclean type or kind (*rigs gtsog pa*)—literally "dirty kinds."[83] Her aim was to document

---

79. Clay, "Purity," 57, 59. Clay is also a practicing Buddhist, and is on the board of trustees which financially supports the monastery where she undertook her research. She readily admits, however, that these personal associations made it more difficult to be objective.

80. Fjeld, *Commoners and Nobles*.

81. Fjeld, *Commoners and Nobles*, 5.

82. Fjeld, "Pollution and Social Networks." Fjeld's fieldwork involved various stints in the mid 1990s and early 2000s in Lhasa, the capital of Tibet, and the rural area of Pannam.

83. Fjeld, "Pollution and Social Networks," 113.

INTRODUCTION

those who were considered "unclean," in what ways they were considered unclean, how their social networks functioned within the larger societal framework and the extent to which this prejudicial demarcation was still evident. Fjeld identified the most unclean peoples as being corpse cutters and corpse handlers,[84] blacksmiths,[85] butchers,[86] and beggars.[87] These four groups were collectively known as *smad rigs*—"inferior kinds."[88] Those born into these families were marked as being unclean with no room for social advancement. They were further considered to be polluting agents who could ritually pollute others in three ways. Firstly, through the sharing of bowls, secondly, through contact with clothes and, thirdly, through sexual intercourse.[89] Fjeld found that in observing some basic taboo practices, such as never sharing bowls or making physical contact, unclean individuals could interact with those who were considered clean. However, this only allowed for interactions between clean and unclean individuals and did not include interactions on a collective basis between clean and unclean households.

Fjeld's research relates to this current study in that she has identified certain aspects of social pollution in highly prescribed social networks in a rural area of Tibet. She rightly distinguishes between ritual and moral pollution and exposes the ongoing prejudice towards those who are born into certain unclean family lines.[90] Though making a valuable contribution

---

84. "Corpse-cutters" (*stob ldan*) are used to cut up corpses and feed them to vultures as part of the funerary sky burial process. Corpse handlers are known as (*rags rgyab pa*).

85. Blacksmiths (*mkhar ba* or *mkhar ra*) are considered unclean because of the dirty nature of their work, because they make knives that kill, and because they take minerals from out of the ground which may upset local deities. Blacksmiths are also known as *lcags ra*. There is a saying about them: *rus khog nag po*, which means "black to the bone." Conversely, people of a "clean" birth are said to be *rus khog gkar po*—"white to the bone." There is also a proverb about blacksmiths: *mgar ba rang gi ral gris bsad*, which means "blacksmiths are killed by their own swords." See *Bod kyi dtam pe* [*Tibetan Proverbs*], 80, and Pemba, *Tibetan Proverbs Bod-kyi-gtam-dpe*, 42.

86. Butchers *shan pa* (also *shen pa*) are unclean and polluting as killing animals is a grave sin and a morally polluting activity in Tibetan Buddhism.

87. Beggars (*slong mkhan*, also *sprang po* and *spang go*) are polluting since they engage in all manner of activities.

88. While Fjeld has identified four inferior classes, fishermen (*nya pa*, also *nya gdol pa*), horse and dog sellers (*rta tsong mkhan* and *khyi tsong mkhan*), and lepers (*mdze can*) are seen as defiled and low class and are thus social outcasts. Morrison, "Sharing the Gospel," 122–23.

89. Fjeld, "Pollution and Social Networks," 113.

90. This stigma appears impossible to dispense with and is still a major factor in determining marriage.

to our understanding, Fjeld does not discuss purity or purification rites in her research, nor does she explore any written texts that deal with purity/pollution. Her primary data sources were the informants she used during her fieldwork. This dissertation, however, seeks to discover what Tibetan textual sources reveal about purity.

In his book, *The Cult of Pure Crystal Mountain: Popular Pilgrimage and Visionary Landscape in Southeast Tibet*,[91] anthropologist Toni Huber provides a comprehensive study of Tibetan pilgrim practices. His work reveals a high level of preoccupation with purity/pollution concerns among pilgrims who visit sacred sites, particularly holy mountains.[92] Huber, in his study of the pilgrimage to the holy mountain Tsari (*tsa ri*) in southeast Tibet, found that pilgrims considered themselves to be polluted both with ritual pollution (*drip*) and sin (*sdig pa*) and were seeking purification through pilgrimage to, and circumambulation of, a sacred, holy mountain. He maintains that pilgrims saw pilgrimage as the fundamental method of removing and purifying the stain of pollution and sin.[93] Huber further suggests that Tibetans believe pollution and sin are removed through the physical act of pilgrimage and coming into direct contact with a holy and sacred site.[94] His study with Tsepak Rigzin, of the pilgrim sites of Mount Kailas and Lake Manasarovar, revealed similar findings.[95] Likewise, Katia Buffetrille, in her study of the pilgrim guide of sacred sites in northern Tibet, found that circumambulating them multiple times was believed to result in an individual being purified from defilements.[96]

In a similar way to Daniels, Huber, Rigzin and Buffetrille provide another layer of understanding of purity/pollution, both ontologically, how Tibetans perceive themselves as polluted, and soteriologically—pilgrimage as part of the perceived salvific solution. Huber is careful to note that pilgrimage has other functions in the Tibetan mindset, such as the accumulation of merit. Huber has provided insights into one aspect of the purity/

---

91. Huber, *Cult of Crystal Mountain*.

92. Huber's book represents research undertaken between 1987–1995, where he interviewed many Tibetans from a variety of locations.

93. Huber, *Cult of Crystal Mountain*, 16. Huber makes a similar observation in his article, Huber, "Putting the Gnas Back," 23–60.

94. Huber, *Cult of Crystal Mountain*, 17. One of the most efficacious ways of removing *drip* and *sdig pa* is to prostrate around the entire sacred mountain, or prostrate all the way to a holy site, even if this takes many months.

95. Huber and Rigzin, "Tibetan Guide," 125–53.

96. Buffetrille, "Blue Lake," 12, 14–15.

pollution landscape among Tibetans and his definition of "sin" needs to be understood through a Tibetan Buddhist filter. This present study seeks to provide a broader understanding of purity through an examination of texts from a variety of Tibetan literary genres. Huber, Rigzin and Buffetrille, like previous authors, have no concern for missiological reflections, which marks a contrast to the study at hand.

Indigenous Tibetan scholar Sa mtsho Skyid and anthropologist Gerald Roche conducted a study of the purity concerns of a small village in a Tibetan area on the northwestern edge of Greater Tibet.[97] By studying the daily, monthly, and annual life cycle rituals of Tibetans in Phug Sde village, they found the pursuit of purity was linked to the avoidance of bad fortune and a necessary prerequisite for good fortune. Purity, for these villagers, was considered to be not just the absence of ritual pollution but also the presence of morally pure behaviors such as pure speech and a pure mind devoid of pride and jealousy.[98] The motivation for the villages to observe ritual purity was primarily to avoid harm from malevolent spirits and to acquire meritorious good fortune. Skyid and Roche concluded that for Phug Sde villagers, "purity is the primary condition for creating fortune."[99]

Skyid and Roche's research relates to this current dissertation by adding another element to our understanding of Tibetan purity by introducing what they have called "social purity," or purity based on ethical behavior. They have also linked the pursuit of purity to another overarching aspect of the cultural worldview—that of accumulating merit and creating good fortune. There is, however, a question about the linking of purity to "fortune" which may not be as neatly connected as they suggest.[100] Also of consideration is that Skyid and Roche studied one small village on the fringes of Tibet and were not attempting to engage written sources.

---

97. Skyid and Roche, "Purity and Fortune."

98. Skyid and Roche, "Purity and Fortune," 248.

99. Skyid and Roche, "Purity and Fortune," 249. Skyid and Roche reached their conclusions through careful linguistic analysis, observing many rituals and asking the people directly what they understood by the term "clean" (*gtsang ma*).

100. As Skyid and Roche are aware, there are many factors which contribute to accumulating good fortune or good luck. By their own admission, the term Skyid and Roche use for "fortune" (*rten 'brel*) has a wide semantic domain and may not necessarily be immediately associated with "good fortune." There are other terms such as *g.yang*, *rlung rta*, and *bsod nams* which are more suggestive of "good fortune."

STEPS TOWARD A TIBETAN UNDERSTANDING OF PURITY

In a careful and detailed exposé of the role and function of Tibetan Buddhist and Bön ritual dance in Tibet,[101] Mona Schrempf shows how dance is used as a medium for purification and blessing for both the participants and the audience. In examining a variety of ritual dances, and analyzing associated ritual texts, Schrempf suggests that the complex array of ritualized dance serves to create purified and sacred space on both the microcosmic and macrocosmic level.[102] In other words, these dances need to be seen as interacting with a perceived Tibetan cosmology of deities—gods and demons, which impact the earthly and the supernatural realm. In studying the monastic *cham* dance,[103] very popular in Tibet, she notes that the main purpose is "the expulsion of 'evil forces' by which all participants and the local environment is purified."[104] Even Tibetan folk opera (*lha mo*), Schrempf suggests, begins with consecration and purification rites to rid the ground of evil forces.[105] Schrempf concludes that though the powerful symbolic ritual dances do provide the chance for increasing merit and bringing prosperity to the community, the primary function is so that "purification and blessing can take place on microcosmic and macrocosmic levels correspondingly."[106]

Though this dissertation will not be examining ritual monastic dances, nor the genre of *cham yig* (monastic dance texts), the point of connection here is that the notion of purification is spread widely across a range of religious activities and deeply connected to Tibetan cosmology. What Schrempf's study does is provide further grounds for framing the argument for Tibetan purification on cosmological and religious grounds rather than, as anthropologists have tended to do, as primarily a social construct for determining who is temporarily (or even permanently) deemed "in" or "out." In other words, the concept of purity and associated purification rituals needs to be examined through the cosmological world of Tibetans and not as a separate system that functions only to demarcate the clean from the unclean. A wider system is in play. And this is the approach of this current

---

101. Schrempf, "Taming the Earth."

102. Schrempf, "Taming the Earth," 199.

103. Monastic *cham* dances are typically performed over a period of two to three days and are observed by most monasteries in Tibet. They also involve many tantric practices with the dancers using highly elaborate masks and costumes.

104. Schrempf, "Taming the Earth," 200.

105. Schrempf, "Taming the Earth," 211–12.

106. Schrempf, "Taming the Earth," 214.

study; to examine purity within the larger Tibetan cultural milieu through the examination of relevant Tibetan texts.

In a slightly unusual anthropological study, Gillian Tan examines the differences between types of smoke evident in the lives of Tibetan pastoralists in the eastern Kham area of the Tibetan Plateau. In her study, "Differentiating Smoke: Smoke as *duwa* and Smoke from *bsang* on the Tibetan Plateau,"[107] Tan suggests there is a marked difference between smoke used for secular purposes such as cooking, smoke generated from cigarettes, and the smoke generated for religious purposes such as burning incense. Though smoke is ubiquitous on the Tibetan plateau being a necessary part of everyday life, it is not, Tan notes, all considered in the same way. She suggests that smoke from cooking is benign and harmless, cigarette smoke is harmful and polluting, and smoke from the *sang* incense burning ritual is a purifying fumigation used to "please and purify numerous deities."[108] Tan elaborates on the polluting effects of tobacco smoke on individuals, communities and even as being capable of defiling deities themselves.[109] In contrast, the smoke of incense, Tan concludes, is "viewed positively because its fragrance pleases the gods and it is able to purify these deities."[110]

In a subsequent study on smoke, "Smoky Relations: Beyond Dichotomies of Substance on the Tibetan Plateau,"[111] where Tan explores the transformative effect of incense smoke, she further concludes that "fragrant smoke does not only please the gods: it purifies the deities themselves, securing not only their goodwill and fortune but also their continued presence in a particular place."[112] Consistent with other studies, Tan has shown how the ritual of *bsang* incense offerings are believed to be efficacious in purifying various anthropogenic polluting agencies. Her studies further highlight the pervasiveness of incense burning as perceived as purifying deities, people, places, and communities. Though her juxtaposition of smoke from cooking and smoke from incense, is a slightly curious framework, even by her own admission,[113] she nonetheless has given further insights into Tibetan

107. Tan, "Differentiating Smoke."
108. Tan, "Differentiating Smoke," 127.
109. Tan, "Differentiating Smoke," 129.
110. Tan, "Differentiating Smoke," 134.
111. Tan, "Smoky Relations."
112. Tan, "Smoky Relations," 152.

113. Tan states that "Tibetans themselves regard *duwa* and *bsang* as indexing different actions, contexts, and motivations and would likely note a comparison of these as an awkward logical manouevre." Tan, "Differentiating Smoke," 134.

cosmology and ritual praxis. She has provided a basis for exploring related literary genres of *bsang yig* and *bsang mchod* texts which will help to gain a more comprehensive understanding of Tibetan purity.

Tibetan scholar Chabpel Tseten Phuntsok provides further insight into incense burning in Tibet in his article, "The Deity Invocation Ritual and the Purification Rite of Incense Burning in Tibet."[114] He begins by tracing the history of incense burning in Tibet, which he suggests has been an integral part of Tibetan society, having existed for centuries and predating the introduction of Buddhism to Tibet.[115] Phunstok suggests that though the origins of the ritual clearly come from the indigenous Bön religion, it has been widely adopted by all schools of Buddhism and also impacted by Buddhist doctrines in that it was later reinterpreted as a means for attaining a better rebirth.[116] However, Phuntsok makes it clear that the purification rite of incense burning was an essential part of the deity invocation ritual and was performed to "purify the ground from innate defilements" and "make a place pure enough to invite deities."[117] Phuntsok also outlines the major ways the invocation ritual is performed in modern daily life in Central Tibet.[118]

By tracing the history of this ritual, Phuntsok has further shown the ubiquitous nature of incense burning as an invocation ritual to purify both humans and spaces from defilements in order to attempt to win the favor of deities. His research is instructive here as it continues to build the case that purity concerns among Tibetans are best framed through an understanding of their cosmological worldview. As with other authors, Phuntsok has focused on one aspect of Tibetan purity/pollution concerns, albeit one universal to the Tibetan Buddhist world. However, for a comprehensive understanding of purity, one needs to look at other rituals, festivals, symbols, and written sources—which is the express goal of this research.

In a recent study, Daniel Berounský traces the history of purification rituals in a remote area of eastern Tibet.[119] His research confirms Phuntsok's work of placing purification rituals within the ancient Bön tradition. Berounský's focus was on a particular ritual for purification from incest. In studying one of the associated texts tracing the mythical origins of the

114. Phuntsok, "Deity Invocation Ritual."
115. Phuntsok, "Deity Invocation Ritual," 4.
116. Phuntsok, "Deity Invocation Ritual," 12–13.
117. Phuntsok, "Deity Invocation Ritual," 9.
118. Phuntsok, "Deity Invocation Ritual," 20–24.
119. Berounský, "Tibetan Purificatory Sel Rituals."

ritual, he suggests that the sacrifice of animals, in particular the flying squirrel, formed a necessary part of this purification ritual.[120] There is little evidence to suggest such a practice continues today,[121] but it does perhaps further reveal a long and unbroken Tibetan consciousness of defilement, in this case from incest, and the need to be purified from it.

In a deeply philosophical study, Eva Rolf explores various themes in the writings of the celebrated Gelukpa monk Tsong Khapa.[122] The focus of Rolf's study is an exploration of Tsong Khapa's understanding of the tantra texts and his commentaries on them. Of particular interest to Rolf is the philosophical elements of Tsong Khapa's teachings and how his understanding of tantra related to his Middle Way doctrine (*lam rim chen mo*), for which he became renowned.[123] She attempts to answer questions about "themes of illusion, purity, and creation within Tsongkhapa's thought."[124] In her dissertation she provides lengthy discussions regarding the interplay between the Buddhist concepts of karma, emptiness, and illusion. In terms of purity, Rolf suggests Tsong Khapa saw a distinction between purity, which is free from defilement, and purity, which is free from any inherent existence and from grasping at self. According to her understanding, Tsong Khapa also saw purity as "a final attainment to be realized."[125] Though not her express intention, Rolf further revealed the profound influence of the Great Perfection teachings on Tsong Khapa's doctrinal development as he frequently espoused the primordially pure nature of the mind.[126] She rightly identifies the sutras as providing a philosophical or doctrinal basis for purity and the tantras as the practical orthopraxis.[127]

---

120. Berounský, "Tibetan Purificatory Sel Rituals," 4. In a previous work, Berounský traces an ancient purification rite of burning foxes. He maintains that the burning of fox hair, in a northern area of Tibet, is still in practice today. See Berounský, "Burning the Incestuous Fox."

121. This is not to suggest that animal sacrifices are nonexistent today, rather that it is not the flying squirrel which is sacrificed. There is also a question in Berounský's paper if the animal referred to in the myth does exactly correspond to the flying squirrel or if it refers to a bat. There is a strong body of evidence (including my own observations) to suggest that in a limited and selected way, animal sacrifice is still practiced in certain areas of Tibet today.

122. Rolf, "Sacred Illusion."
123. Rolf, "Sacred Illusion," 6.
124. Rolf, "Sacred Illusion," 4.
125. Rolf, "Sacred Illusion," 259.
126. Rolf, "Sacred Illusion," 351.
127. Rolf, "Sacred Illusion," 263.

STEPS TOWARD A TIBETAN UNDERSTANDING OF PURITY

Rolf's research relates to this present study in that she has, among other themes, explored purity within a specific corpus of texts. She also provides a brief discussion of purity terms, though with a focus on technical Buddhist meanings.[128] The points of difference from this current study are that her scope was narrowly defined to one Tibetan author, from one school of Tibetan Buddhism (albeit the largest), and a specific set of tantric texts. The study of purity was not her sole focus, nor did she seek to develop a folk understanding of purity. Her dissertation is highly philosophical and theoretical, being aimed at those well-versed in Tsong Khapa's writings and experienced in Tibetan Buddhist praxis.[129] Though she expresses a personal interest in inter-religious dialogue,[130] this was not the focus of her research, and naturally she had no need to provide any missiological application.

For a more complete understanding of Tibetan purity, it is necessary to examine the Mahayana branch of Buddhism known as Pure Land Buddhism. Though more popular in China and Japan, Georgios Halkias' comprehensive survey of Pure Land Buddhism in Tibet suggests a high degree of consciousness of Buddha Amitābha and his pure land abode of Sukhāvatī.[131] In essence, Amitābha's teachings claim that through certain practices and recitation of particular prayers, one can arrive at a pure land "free of sickness, suffering, and all impurities, where the dharma is perpetually taught."[132] Halkias is careful to note that the Pure Land school did not establish itself as a major school of Buddhism in Tibet.[133] However, his comprehensive study of Pure Land literature in Tibet clearly shows how this eschatological teaching impacted all the schools of Tibetan Buddhism and continues to impact monastic institutions and the laity today.[134]

Halkias' work relates to the current study in that he has provided an excellent base from which to examine some key Pure Land texts that have impacted a Tibetan understanding of purity. For thorough missiological

---

128. Rolf, "Sacred Illusion," 8–10.

129. Rolf, "Sacred Illusion," 539.

130. Rolf, "Sacred Illusion," 537–38.

131. Halkias, *Luminous Bliss*. Note that within the literature, Amitābha is also spelled Amitabha and Amitåabha, and Sukhāvatī as Sukhavati.

132. Halkias, *Luminous Bliss*, Kindle location 427.

133. Halkias, *Luminous Bliss*, Kindle location 333–34.

134. Halkias also notes that Pure Land Buddhism in Tibet has been under-represented in academic literature, which is at variance to the multitude of Pure Land texts available in the Tibetan language.

reflections, further examination of Pure Land eschatology is consonant with the goal of this present study.

In a similar vein, noted scholar Matthew Kapstein, in his chapter, "Pure Land Buddhism in Tibet?"[135] suggests that the Pure Land teachings were an integral part of the Mahayana tradition in Tibetan Buddhism and that it held, and continues to hold, a privileged position within the Tibetan religious imagination.[136] Kapstein traces some of the major Pure Land Amitābha texts which were embraced by all the schools of Tibetan Buddhism. In particular, he mentions that the aspirational Tibetan prayers for a rebirth into the Pure Land of Sukhāvatī are so numerous that they form their own genre of liturgical works.[137] Kapstein also briefly traces the development of the *'pho ba* "consciousness transfer" ritual, which became widely popular in Tibet, and its connection to Amitābha's Pure Land teaching. This tantric yogic technique, performed at the point of death, was believed to be able to immediately transfer the consciousness of the dying individual, through an opening in the crown of the skull, to a pure land resulting in enlightenment.[138] Kapstein concludes that there is "evidence for a broad, popular promulgation of the teaching of salvation in Amitābha's realm."[139]

Like Halkias, Kapstein's work provides a strong base for examining Pure Land texts which will help to give a fuller picture of a Tibetan understanding of purity. It would appear that in Pure Land doctrine, there is both an eschatological and soteriological perspective that needs to be further explored for a nuanced understanding of purity.

Summary

This review has shown that the precedent literature on Tibetan Buddhist purity/pollution has been orientated more towards pollution and less towards purity per se. Though studies from the broader Tibetan Buddhist world do show a level of commonality with studies undertaken in Tibet, differences between the groups do exist and cannot be taken as directly

---

135. Kapstein, "Pure Land Buddhism," 16–51.
136. Kapstein, "Pure Land Buddhism," 41.
137. Kapstein, "Pure Land Buddhism," 25.
138. Kapstein, "Pure Land Buddhism," 26. This ritual is still popular today. Kapstein has also documented the revival of the *powa* transfer ritual in Kapstein, "Pilgrimage of Rebirth," 95–119.
139. Kapstein, "Pure Land Buddhism," 32.

universal. However, that said, all these studies relate to this current dissertation in that they highlight common elements in a Tibetan Buddhist understanding of pollution—that it is harmful both to individuals and communities, that it can be spread to others, that there is both a ritual and moral component, and that there is an unseen cosmological connection that must be dealt with through purification rituals of some kind.

This literature review has also demonstrated that the major purification ritual that has been researched, albeit with good reason, is that of incense burning. These studies have reinforced the cosmological worldview which places this ritual as apotropaic—the perceived solution to individual and corporate defilement, and the primary way to placate fickle and cantankerous deities. These findings are confirming of the approach of this study to examine purity within a religious and cosmological framework and not merely as a social construct. The precedent literature also demonstrates that purity/pollution concerns are prevalent across a range of Tibetan religious endeavors. However, while each study has provided a certain window into Tibetan purity and pollution, we have only snippets and not a fuller picture. There are still gaps in our understanding. What exactly do some of the key Tibetan texts reveal about purity? And what of the folk literature, symbols, and other rituals?

Moreover, there has been no specific study which focuses solely on purity among Tibetans in Tibet.[140] Perhaps it goes without saying that none of the precedent research has applied a missiological hermeneutic to the data. The researchers have had no cause to do so. This current study is a modest attempt to begin filling this void.[141]

Research Methodology

The methodology for this research will be textual and bibliographic. In terms of the academic discipline, this research would be placed in missiology or inter-cultural studies. Skreslet and Elliston have noted the hybrid nature of missiological research in that it draws from a range of disciplines.[142] Skreslet

---

140. That is, at least, no studies that I have been able to find.

141. As mentioned earlier, to date, I have not been able to find missiological studies concerning purity in Buddhism, much less in Tibetan Buddhism. To be sure, missiological studies of Buddhism do exist, as does a body of literature on contextualization with Buddhist people groups, but none that explore the issue of purity.

142. Elliston, *Missiological Research Design*.

suggests missiology is the "intersection point among the many disciplines that take an interest in mission-related phenomena."[143] With the multi-discipline nature of missiology in mind, this study will involve elements of anthropology, linguistics, and theology. Secondary sources typically come from the fields of anthropology, ethnography, and Tibetan religious studies. The textual analysis will involve a linguistic and hermeneutic component, and the missiological reflections a theological one. In framing the context of the study in more detail, a historical component will be needed. Thus, the integrative nature of missiology will also be apparent in this study.

The main bibliographic method of this research will be an examination of Tibetan primary sources. Pablo Deiros has described bibliographic research as the "analytical survey of previous scholarship and the location of secondary literature or precedent research in the chosen field. It also has to do with the finding and identification of primary sources."[144] In order to delineate between personal experience and reliable data, Elliston further relates that, "Primary sources are generally reserved for the central focus of the study."[145] As both authors have suggested, the first task then is in identifying relevant primary source texts.

In this study, identifying primary sources will be based on the degree to which a text is considered germane to the topic of purity. In order to facilitate this process, I will be guided by relevant secondary sources, Tibetan friends and colleagues, and previous study I have undertaken. Texts will be placed in their historical, literary, and religious context. "Religious context" refers to the school of Tibetan Buddhism that a text is primarily or typically associated with. Many texts have influence across all the schools of Tibetan Buddhism but often are connected to one particular lineage.

While the express goal is to examine texts, wherever possible, in the Tibetan language, there may be occasions where the original Tibetan version cannot be accessed, but an established English translation is in existence. In such cases, the English text will provide the data set. There will be numerous occasions when I will need to provide my own English translations, particularly for translating the names and publishers of Tibetan texts. These translations will be placed in brackets after the Tibetan title. There

---

143. Skreslet, *Comprehending Mission*, 12.

144. Deiros, "Historical Research," 207.

145. Edgar J. Elliston, *Introduction to Missiological Research Design* (William Carey Library, 2011), 59.

will also be occasions where I will access secondary sources written by Tibetan scholars in Tibetan.

The first necessary methodological step is a detailed exploration of the semantic domains of the Tibetan terms for purity and pollution. Lexicons, both in Tibetan and English, precedent literature and Tibetan informants will guide this process. This semantic framework will provide the essential base from which to explore native texts. This foundation will also provide an axiological framework in helping to inform which aspect of purity is in focus. For example, is the focus of the text the doctrine of purity, the pursuit of purity, social or moral purity, ritual purity, or the elimination of defilement? In most cases there will be a mix and blending of these aspects. However, a frame of reference is necessary in order to navigate the complexities and nuances. Another necessary frame of reference is that of literary genre. With more than a thousand-year literary tradition, Tibetan literature is vast and diverse. Codification of some basic genre categories, as well as using existing Tibetan ones, will help to move the study along in a guided fashion. While "genre" on the surface may seem an etic designation, Tibetans themselves have for centuries classified texts into certain categories and genres.[146] Wherever possible, I will be looking at texts through their emic categories.

Part of the validity of the study rests on my ability to adequately read and interpret the texts. As an advanced reader of Tibetan, and one who has been privileged to have had a long and intimate association with the language, I feel that I am in a position to accurately reflect the source text. When issues of clarification arise, I will be able to call upon trusted Tibetans with whom I have had long and close relationships. Since all of the texts are available for careful scrutiny, my understanding, interpretation, and analysis of the texts can be judged against the texts themselves, for any who may wish to do so.

As previously mentioned, this study will not engage in interviews, participant observation or focus groups. It is not possible to pursue this study as a standard anthropological or ethnographic research project. But, even if it were, one wonders whether this would be the preferred method for an accurate understanding of Tibetan purity.[147] There is a certain ob-

---

146. See Rheingans, *Tibetan Literary Genres;* Cabezón and Jackson, *Tibetan Literature;* E. Smith, *Among Tibetan Texts.*

147. Joy Hendry, among others, has mentioned some of the pitfalls of anthropological research, especially anthropologists who rely solely on interpreters to collect their data. Not to diminish the work of anthropologists, but such reliance has resulted in mixed

jectivity that a textual study can bring. Georges Dreyfus has noted a trend in ethnographic and anthropological studies which suggests the "real" understanding of culture is found in the folklore, oral narratives, and oral literature.[148] He aptly notes, however, that in the case of Tibetan culture, to focus only on that aspect, valid though it is, would be to overlook a central component. He comments that, "the sophisticated intellectual culture that developed in the large monastic institutions has been at the center of traditional Tibetan life for centuries."[149]

Naturally, the solution then, is to look at both the established texts within the monastic tradition, and the texts in the genre of folklore and folk literature. What, for example, do Tibetan proverbs have to say about purity? To fill this out in more detail, I will, for example, examine the literature of the texts of practice (*sgrub thabs*, Sk. sadhana), which will focus on the preliminary texts (*sgon 'gro*), and confessional and purification (*gso sbyong*) texts of the monastic tradition. These texts incorporate the larger genres of the sutras (*mdo*), tantras (*rgyud*), and incantations (*gzungs*). The texts of Pure Land aspirational prayers (*bde smon*) will also be examined. To gain a wider perspective, the folk genres of Tibetan proverbs (*gtam dpe*), ritual manuals (*man ngag, gdams ngag*), liturgies (*kha 'don*), prayers (*smon lam, gsol ba*), symbols (*rtags mtshan*), festivals (*dus chen*) and incense offering texts (*bsang yig, bsangs mchod*) will also be examined.

The traveler to Tibet would be struck by the preponderance of Tibetan Buddhist temples, monasteries and sacred sites, and the profound level of devotion by Tibetans who flock to them. It may be stating the obvious that it would be worthwhile exploring what the monastic clerics, through the tradition of their texts, have to say about purity. The observant traveler would also be struck by the ubiquity of the Tibetan script. Prayer flags covered with Tibetan text, prayer cairns engraved with Tibetan mantras, *mani* walls with invocations chiseled on stone tablets, prayer wheels embossed with mantras and encased with scriptures, auspicious words spelled-out on mountainsides with white rocks, monasteries filled with Buddhist texts, protective mantras hung on doorframes and household bookshelves

---

fortunes. See Hendry, *Introduction to Social Anthropology*, 324–27. In my experience, Tibetans have been reluctant to share their "cultural secrets" with outsiders and, understandably, it takes considerable time to gain their intimate trust. Sjaak van der Geest provides an interesting discussion about the relationship between anthropologists and missionaries. See Van der Geest, "Anthropologists and Missionaries."

148. Dreyfus, *Sound of Two Hands*, 8–9.
149. Dreyfus, *Sound of Two Hands*, 3.

replete with sacred texts all speak of a preoccupation with the written word. Though not all Tibetans are literate, all Tibetans venerate their written language. And words can be seen everywhere. Words are powerful and authoritative. Indeed, the written word is a power in itself.[150] Kurtis Schaeffer observes that,

> The book in Tibet is variously the embodiment of the Buddha's voice, a principal tool in education, a source of tradition and authority, an economic product, a finely crafted aesthetic object, a medium of Buddhist written culture, and a symbol of the religion itself. From the earliest examples of Tibetan writing upon imperial stele to the mass production of printed canons a thousand years later, Tibetan scribes, scholars, and kings have explicitly made reference to the importance of books and the written word in areas of life from social authority to soteriology.[151]

Given this historical precedent, and the present-day reality of the power Tibetans ascribe to words, it would seem only fitting to dig into some of their preserved writings to see how they may inform the topic at hand.

Chapter Breakdown

The introduction has outlined the rationale, need, research problem and methodology of the study as well as provided a review of the precedent literature.

Chapter one will set the scene for the study and provide the contextual background. For this study, a description of the context will involve a brief history of missionary engagement to Tibet, an overview of Tibetan Buddhism, including an introduction to the major schools that have developed, and a brief overview of Tibetan cosmology. This will be followed by an introduction to the Tibetan language and literary genres. In order to establish a theoretical framework, there will be a discussion about purity studies and the argument this study will take. The last section of the chapter will be devoted to exploring the semantic domains of purity and pollution

---

150. A very common Tibetan practice is to touch one's head with a sacred book or scripture to receive a blessing from it and pay homage to it. A regular part of a monastic visit involves walking crouched down underneath shelves of scriptures (*dpe cha*) so that one's head can come into close proximity with them in order to receive a blessing or empowerment. Some pilgrims circumambulate libraries or other buildings known to contain sacred Buddhist manuscripts.

151. Schaeffer, *Culture of the Book*, vii.

terms in Tibetan. This will lay the foundation for the textual analysis of the ensuing chapters.

Chapter two will explore purity as it appears within Tibetan Buddhist scriptures and sacred texts. The focus will be the texts of praxis of the monastic tradition that have been taught and practiced for centuries. More specifically, this chapter will focus on the confessional, preliminary, and purification texts of practice which are located within the sutra, tantra, and mantra and incantation literature of the monastic tradition. The emphasis will be on examining the prescribed orthopraxis, meditation practices, and incantations associated with purity.

Chapter three will examine texts which have influenced a lay understanding of purity and purification praxis. Texts from the genres of Pure Land prayers of aspiration, proverbs and texts of moral instructions will be the subject of this chapter. The most well-known Tibetan mantra will also be examined. The emphasis will be on exploring texts which inform a lay understanding of notions purity and purification.

Chapter four will explore the rituals and symbols associated with purity. Texts associated with the rituals of prostration, incense burning, and water purification will be analyzed. The annual incense burning festival "World Purification Day" (*'dzam gling spyi bzang*) will be discussed. The Tibetan prayer wheel and symbols which represent purity will also be examined.

Chapter five will be engaged in reflecting on the data through a missiological lens. Questions such as, "What is the data suggesting about the Tibetan worldview?" and "What are some possible missiological applications?" will be addressed. This chapter will also include a discussion regarding the purity language found in the Bible and explore possibilities for contextualizing the gospel in a Tibetan context. Any potential applications will be discussed in light of on field practitioners, translators, and missiologists at large. Potential areas of further research will be addressed, and some concluding remarks will be made.

I

Setting the Scene

Introduction

IN FRAMING ONE'S RESEARCH, Elliston suggests that "a description of the context of the study provides a justification for the study and a perspective for understanding the research."[1] This chapter will attempt to provide the necessary contextual background for this study. Exploring the context will involve a brief outline of the history of missionary endeavors to Tibet, an overview of Tibetan Buddhism and Tibetan cosmology, and an introduction to the Tibetan language and literary genres. A discussion of purity and pollution within the broader discipline of anthropology will follow, including a discussion regarding Mary Douglas and her approach to purity studies.[2] A critique of her approach will be given while offering an alternative theoretical lens by which this study will be guided. The argument that will be developed is that purity is not just a social categorization of temporary or permanent "in groups" or "out groups." Rather, purity concerns for Tibetans are more than a social construct and manifest a deeper religious and soteriological concern. The remainder of the chapter will be taken up with working through Tibetan purity and pollution terms and their various semantic domains. A discussion of these terms will provide the requisite linguistic framework through which this study will then analyze a variety of Tibetan texts.

---

1. Elliston, *Missiological Research Design*, 58.

2. Mary Douglas' work, *Purity and Danger* is regarded as one of the definitive texts in purity studies.

A Brief History of Missions to Tibet

Though the mystique of Tibet has perhaps reached new heights since the coming of the Dalai Lama to the West in the latter part of the twentieth century, and the opening up of Tibet for tourism during the late 1980s and early 1990s, the land of Tibet has for centuries captured the Western imagination as an exotic "Shangri-La" for the spiritual seeker, and the "last frontier" for the intrepid explorer and pioneer missionary.[3] Part of the aura associated with this may have been that for many centuries Tibet had been closed to foreigners as it isolated itself from the rest of the world in a self-imposed exile. However, missionary engagement with Tibet, though somewhat sparse and intermittent, and largely unsuccessful, does have a long history.[4]

The Influence of the Church of the East

There is strong evidence to suggest that the influence of the Church of the East (also known as the Nestorian Church) reached Tibet as early as the sixth or seventh century AD. Geza Uray, in exploring the connections between Nestorians and Tibet, cites a letter attributed to Timothy 1, the celebrated patriarch of the Church of the East between 780–823, to his confidential friend Sergius. In that letter, Timothy 1 writes that he "recently consecrated a metropolitan bishop for the Turks and that he is preparing to anoint one for the land of the Tibetans."[5] On a list of places where the *Trisagion*, one of the oldest Christian prayers, is recited, Timothy 1 records

---

3. Popular works that fueled the mystique of Tibet were books like Rudyard Kipling's *Kim*, James Hilton's *Lost Horizon* from where the term "Shangri-La" became popularized, Lobsang Rampa's fanciful *The Third Eye*, and Henrich Harrier's remarkable account, *Seven Years in Tibet*. These books (three of which became feature films), among a bevy of others, reflect the Western fascination and romanticization of Tibet. While they are several works which address the subject of the Western obsession and idolization of Tibet, Donald S. Lopez' *Prisoners of Shangri-La*, and Orville Schell's *Virtual Tibet* are two of the more comprehensive ones.

4. This section on missions to Tibet has been shaped in part by a paper I wrote in 2019. Some of the material in that paper has been adapted and abbreviated for this brief introduction. For a more detailed overview see Morrison, "Christianity's Journey." See also Hattaway, *Tibet*; and Covell, "Buddhism and the Gospel," 130–34.

5. Uray, "Tibet's Connections with Nestorianism," 402. See also Jenkins, *Lost History of Christianity*, 63, and Jenkins, Campbell Lecture.

Tibet (known as Tangut in Syriac) on that list.[6] Further textual evidence suggests engagement with Tibetans by the Church of the East. A divination text found in Dunhuang, and dating to the ninth or tenth century, contains a surprising reference to "the god called 'Jesus Messiah.'"[7] After careful analysis of this manuscript, Uray concludes the text to be "rightly categorized in the literature as a Nestorian work."[8] Matthew Kapstein has found numerous Biblical references in ancient manuscripts, including the famous story of Solomon's dealing with a disputed maternity case.[9] The time of Timothy 1 roughly coincided with Tibet's assimilation of Buddhism and perhaps there was a season of open curiosity towards Christianity before Tibetan Buddhism became widely entrenched.

Further evidence of the influence of the Church of the East can be seen by the distinctive symbol of a cross joined to a lotus (a Buddhist symbol of purity and enlightenment), which has been found inscribed on Tibetan manuscripts dating back to the ninth or tenth century.[10] A cave painting dating to the ninth-century Tang dynasty shows a Nestorian cross on the crown of the head of a Buddhist saint and crosses adorning the necklace. Historian Phillip Jenkins states that "some historians believe that Nestorian missionaries influenced the religious practices of the Buddhist religion then developing in Tibet."[11] Paul Carus has gone so far as to suggest that the Nestorians were so active and successful that "for a time it seemed that Nestorian Christianity would be the state religion of Tibet."[12]

---

6. Uray, "Tibet's Connections with Nestorianism," 401. It is unclear whether Tangut refers to Tibet proper or a Tibetan area in the province of Gansu. Marku Tsering suggests Tangut may have been in modern day Gansu province of China and not Tibet itself. See M. Tsering, *Sharing Christ*, 322, footnote 390.

7. Uray, "Tibet's Connections with Nestorianism," 412–13. Note that this text is also referred to as the "Jesus Sutra." See Jenkins, *Lost History of Christianity*, 92, and Schaeffer et al., *Sources of Tibetan Tradition*, 95–96.

8. Uray, "Tibet's Connections with Nestorianism," 416.

9. Kapstein, *Tibetan Assimilation of Buddhism*, 30. This story of Solomon can also be found in Tibetan textbooks such as *Lha Sa'i Dmangs Khrod Sgrung Gtam*, 112–13. I have also found other borrowings from the book of Revelation in Tibetan Buddhist writings. Perhaps such borrowings were the result of Nestorian influences.

10. See Hattaway, *Tibet*, 22–24, and Smither, *Christian Mission*, 38–39, 45.

11. Jenkins, *Lost History of Christianity*, 92. See also Thom Wolf who makes a compelling case that the institution of Bodhisattvas in Mahayana Buddhism was the result of contact with Christianity. Wolf, "The Mahayana Moment."

12. Carus, "Nestorius and Nestorians," 173. Carus' assertion may be somewhat exaggerated as he provides little evidence to support this claim.

The Jesuits

Portuguese Father Antonio de Andrade was the first Jesuit to make it into Tibet proper. Disguised as a Hindu pilgrim, Andrade set out from India in 1624. After ploughing his way up through the Himalayas, enduring altitude sickness and snow blindness, he finally arrived in Tsaparang, the capital of the Guge kingdom in western Tibet in 1625.[13] The king of Guge welcomed the strange visitor, considering him to be a high lama. Andrade was allowed by the king to teach his religion and on April 12, 1626, the foundation stone of "the first church was laid in Tibet with the name of Our Lady of Hope."[14] In subsequent years, twelve Tibetans were baptized including the queen.[15] The mission, however, was short-lived. In 1630, due to political turmoil, and an uprising led by monks who felt jealous and threatened by the mission, Andrade and others stationed there had to flee. The church was completely destroyed and a few years later the door to Tibet had closed.[16]

On August 17, 1715, the Italian Jesuit Ippolito Desideri, who had long-held ambitions of starting a mission in Tibet, began the long and hazardous journey from Ladakh to Lhasa. During his journey, while fighting frost bite, lice, and bandits, Desideri fortuitously met the caravan of a Mongol princess who took pity on him and allowed him to travel with her to Lhasa. Her band of soldiers protected him from thieves and her yaks kept him supplied with yak-butter tea. He finally arrived in Lhasa, after a six-month journey, on March 18, 1716.[17] Desideri was welcomed by the Mongol governor (who had recently deposed the sixth Dalai Lama) and given freedom to preach and a room to stay in the prestigious Sera monastery.[18]

Desideri was a scholar trained in medieval philosophical debate and gave himself wholeheartedly to language study. He attained a high degree of fluency in both written and spoken Tibetan. Desideri's studies paid off as he wrote five major works on Christian theology in Tibetan, attempting to prove the truth of Christianity and expose the flaws of Lamaism.[19] He

---

13. M. Tsering, *Sharing Christ*, 112; Houston, "Jesus and His Missionaries," 18–20.

14. Aguilar, "Jesuits in Tibet," 62.

15. Aguilar, "Jesuits in Tibet," 62.

16. Aguilar, "Jesuits in Tibet," 62.

17. Trent Pomplun, *Jesuit on the Roof of the World: Ippolito Desideri's Mission to Tibet* (Oxford University Press, 2010), 67–68.

18. M. Tsering, *Sharing Christ*, 113–14.

19. Gispert-Sauch, "Desideri and Tibet," 32–33, and Pomplun, *Jesuit on the Roof*, 14. For an English translation of two of Desideri's major works see Lopez and Jinpa,

primarily spent his energies debating with monks and used philosophical methods to justify the Christian faith with a focus on the Trinity.[20] Unfortunately, Desideri's superiors in Rome decided that the Capuchins were to take charge of the mission in Tibet, and he very reluctantly left Lhasa in April 1721. As Tsering notes, "His withdrawal from the field for administrative reasons seems one of the less fortunate episodes in church history."[21]

The Capuchins

Once the Capuchins were settled in Lhasa, they opened a small dispensary and worked on translating catechisms and prayers. They did not have the facility of language of Desideri, and rather than engage directly with monks, they distributed tracts among them. This did not prove to be a wise move. Much of the literature was trampled into the ground and two monks who were caught reading them were publicly flogged. Despite the tension this caused, the Capuchins persisted and in 1726 they opened a small chapel. By 1742, there were twenty-seven baptized converts. However, when the new believers refused to bow down to the Dalai Lama, a revolt led by monks insisted that all missionaries and Christians be expelled from Lhasa. The Capuchins were lucky to escape with their lives. No sooner were they out of the city when their chapel was destroyed.[22] The only thing that remains to this day is their church bell, which they had lugged with them all the way from Rome.[23]

The French Catholics

In 1846, the Vatican assigned the *Missions Etrangeres de Paris* (MEP) to be responsible for mission work in Tibet.[24] The MEP primarily worked on

---

Dispelling the Darkness.

20. M. Tsering, *Sharing Christ*, 114; and Pomplun, *Jesuit on the Roof*, 74–75, 87–89.

21. M. Tsering, *Sharing Christ*, 114.

22. M. Tsering, *Sharing Christ*, 115–16.

23. The bell is still housed in the famous Jokhang temple in Lhasa. I have seen it and photographed it on a several occasions, though it is now no longer available for public viewing. The monks call it the "Jesus bell." The inscription in Latin reads TE DEUM LAUDAMUS TE DOMINUM which can be translated as "We praise you, O God, we acknowledge you as Lord." See also Hattaway, *Tibet*, 42.

24. Bray, "French Catholic Missions," 83. The MEP is also known as Societe des Missions Etrangeres (SME).

the fringes. They did make attempts to establish a mission in Lhasa, but the Lhasa government suspected they were politically motivated and refused them entry.[25] The MEP did, however, have some success on the eastern border. In 1863, the MEP were able to claim seven hundred converts,[26] and in 1896 they published in Tibetan *A Summary of the Deeds of Jesus Christ and the Books of the Bible*.[27] The Lhasa government reacted strongly to this substantial number of converts and issued an edict that all Tibetan converts were to recant and return to Buddhism or be killed. Some fled, others were killed, including some of the missionaries.[28] The mission relocated further to the fringes, yet remarkably, a Catholic church still exits today in Markham and the 1896 publication is still in use.

The Moravians

At about the same time the MEP were working on the fringes, the Moravians, in 1853, had commenced work in Ladakh. Though they never made it to Lhasa, their story is still noteworthy. The first Moravians who set out to reach Tibetans focused on Bible translation. The brilliant linguist, Henrich Jäschke, made a significant contribution to the study of the Tibetan language and translation work. In 1881, Jäschke published a Tibetan-English dictionary which is still in print today.[29] Jäschke also translated the New Testament. Translation work continued after his death, most notably by August Francke and Joseb Gergan, who, through an epic struggle, translated and published the Tibetan Bible in 1945.[30] Today, there remains a Moravian church in Leh, Ladakh, and it has been accepted as a small minority in that culture. One of the great grandsons of Joseph Gergan is preparing a New Testament in colloquial Ladakhi.[31]

25. Bray, "French Catholic Missions," 96.
26. Bray, "French Catholic Missions," 88.
27. In Tibetan, the book is: *ye shu kri sto'i spyod pa dang gsung rab rnams kyi mdo bsdud zhes bya ba bzhugs so*. The parents of one of my neighbors attended the Catholic church there. Many years ago, he gave me a copy of this book, originally published in 1896, which is still used by the congregation today.
28. Bray, "French Catholic Missions," 88.
29. Jäschke, *A Tibetan-English Dictionary*.
30. Bray, "Heinrich August Jäschke," 50, 52. Allan Maberly has told this remarkable story in his book, *God Spoke Tibetan*.
31. Bray, "Sacred Words," 114.

Mission Stations on the Fringes

From the 1800s onwards, the door to Tibet was firmly closed. Protestant missionaries set up mission stations on the fringes, hoping to make it to Lhasa. None of them did. Their efforts on the borders were zealous, though not entirely successful. In 1888, the China Inland Mission (CIM) established a mission base on the north-east border of Tibet. In 1895, the Christian Missionary Alliance (CMA) also set up a base there.[32] In 1897, CIM set up another base in the east of Tibet, in Kanding. Petrus and Susie Rijnhart, Jessie and William Christie, French Ridley, Albert Shelton, George Kraft, Victor Plymire, Frank and Annie Learner, Geoffrey Bull, George Patterson, Robert Ekvall, and Annie Tyler are some of the notable missionaries of this era.[33] Their biographies record accounts of lawlessness, death of spouses, resistance to the gospel, and "persistent political instability."[34] The story of angry Tibetans revolting against the missionaries is a common theme.[35] Ultimately, political instability in these areas, combined with the rise of Communism in China, forced missionaries to leave with little to show for their efforts. From the 1950s until mid-1980, no missionaries were allowed in these border areas.[36]

In the 1920s, Indian evangelist, Sadhu Sundar Singh, made a number of forays into Tibet from India over a period of ten years. Though battling ill health, and against the advice of friends, in April 1929, Sundar Singh made one last trip into Tibet and was never seen or heard of again. His disappearance and death were never solved, and the impact of his preaching is unknown.[37] In the mid-1990s, Tibet started to open up to foreign influences, and a trickle of language students, English teachers, and businesspeople have been able to reside there somewhat tenuously.

---

32. M. Tsering, *Sharing Christ*, 121.

33. For a more comprehensive account of missionary activity see Hattaway, *Tibet*. See also Hopkirk, *Trespassers*; and Covell, "Buddhism and the Gospel."

34. Bray, "Sacred Words," 111.

35. M. Tsering, *Sharing Christ*, 122.

36. Bray, "Sacred Words," 113.

37. Thompson, *Sadhu Sundar Singh*.

Missions Summary

Despite a long and costly history of missionary engagement, the indigenous Tibetan church in Tibet remains in its infancy with only small pockets of believers in a handful of locations.[38] There are various reasons as to why Christianity has yet to take root in Tibet. The high altitude, the tyranny of distance, and the harsh topography are perhaps contributing factors. Other factors are the political machinations that have inflicted Tibet over the centuries, the various empires that have come and gone in China, and, in more recent history, the rise of Communism, which both closed and more recently opened up Tibet. Another factor is the political workings of ecclesiastical orders and various mission societies where the best outcome for the gospel did not always result. Presentations of the gospel, with perhaps the exception of the Church of the East, were largely done from a Western perspective. Contextualizing the gospel so that it resonated with the Tibetan mindset may have seen greater fruit.[39] One does not want to overlook the spiritual dimension. In 1892, Hudson Taylor stated: "To make converts in Tibet is similar to going into a cave and trying to rob a lioness of her cubs."[40] Even if Taylor made a slight overstatement, an element of spiritual warfare is clearly at play.[41]

Introduction to Tibetan Buddhism

There are various features which distinguish Tibetan Buddhism from other forms of Buddhism. One of those features is its eclectic nature. While falling within the broad school of Indian Mahayana Buddhism, with its developed system of Bodhisattvas, Tibetan Buddhism has been deeply influenced by the indigenous Tibetan religion of Bön, with its system of shaman priests

---

38. For more specific locational details, see Hattaway, *Tibet*.

39. Bray notes that pioneer missionary Victor Plymire's evangelistic tracts were "simple expositions of Christian teaching written in Tibetan, but in a style that would have been recognizable at an American revivalist meeting." Bray, "Sacred Words," 111.

40. Hattaway, *Peoples*, 316.

41. Geoffrey Bull, pioneer missionary on the fringes of Tibet, who had a lengthy incarceration for his faith, wrote in one of his accounts, "If one examines the history of those who have sought to enter Tibet it is significant to notice that many, if not all of those who have presumed to go up against these gates of evil, have been mauled in one way or another by the very talons of the devil. In my own case I had no inkling at that time how severe that mauling was ultimately to be." Bull, *Tibetan Tales*, 70.

(*bon po*). The influence of shamanism on Tibetan Buddhism is profound and may be a factor as to why the tantric practices of Vajrayana have been so widely adopted by all schools of Tibetan Buddhism. As others have observed, the shamanism already prevalent in Tibet was fertile soil for tantric Buddhism to take root.[42] Geoffrey Samuel, in his book *Civilized Shamans*, traces the relationship between shamanism and monastic or clerical Buddhism in Tibet. He states that, "The contrast between shamanic and clerical aspects of Buddhism is a complex one, in part because the two are closely interwoven in practice. Virtually all Tibetan Buddhism, whether that of the Gelugpa scholar with his *geshe* diploma or that of the Nyingmapa yogin in his or her mountain hermitage, contains elements of both shamanic and clerical orientations."[43]

Another feature of Tibetan Buddhism, which Samuel has alluded to, is that the line between what one might consider "folk practices" and "monastic" ones is blurred. While there is a dichotomy between the clerical training provided by the monasteries and the praxis of Buddhism at the folk level of the laity, who are not privy to such a training, in reality, this gap may not be as large as one might imagine. In fact, there is a certain co-dependency between monks and the laity. Village life typically revolves around the activities of the local monastery, where the laity focus their efforts on merit collection through acts of devotion and worship, offerings, and alms. In return, the laity expects to be serviced by the monks to keep capricious and malignant evil forces at bay. As Kapstein observes, "The bread-and-butter concerns of the Tibetan Buddhist clergy required that they devote considerable efforts to realizing the broad range of ritual demands for the protection, peace, and prosperity of their patrons, and to furnishing them with divinations and astrological consultations."[44]

A further distinguishing feature is that by the time Buddhism entered Tibet in the seventh century, Buddhism had been in existence in India and other places for over a thousand years and had gone through a considerable transformation. One such transformation was the acceptance of the tantric texts and practices which had developed from the sixth century BC onwards.[45] Tibetan Buddhism does of course hold to the basic tenets of Buddhism such as the four noble truths, the eight-fold path, the law of karma,

---

42. M. Tsering, *Sharing Christ*, 55–57, 84, and M. Tsering "Islands in the Sky," 252.
43. Samuel, *Civilized Shamans*, 10.
44. Kapstein, *Tibetan Buddhism*, 3.
45. Van Schaik, *Spirit of Tibetan Buddhism*, 5–6.

cyclical samsaric existence, the pursuit of enlightenment and so forth. However, as Samuel has rightly observed, "any real attempt to understand the religion of Tibet has to recognize that the Vajrayana is at the center of Tibetan spiritual life."[46] The Vajrayana practices served two main purposes. One is the belief that tantra is efficacious in leading to enlightenment, even in one lifetime.[47] The other is that they augmented shamanism and thus became another means by which Tibetans came to deal with dangerous and ubiquitous demonic forces.[48]

Padmasambhava

One prime example illustrating the dual functionality of Vajrayana, that is, as a means to enlightenment for the tantric practitioner and as an intersection point between the clergy and the laity, is in the legendary figure of Padmasambhava.[49] According to legend, this tantric shaman visited Tibet during the eighth century, where he subdued, tamed, and, in some cases, slew powerful Tibetan gods and spirits, thereby subjugating them to future Buddhist tantric practitioners.[50] Padmasambhava's many conquests are celebrated all over Tibet and his image can be found throughout monasteries and households. Sam Van Schaik observes that "Padmasambhava became a kind of cult hero, seen as a second Buddha."[51] He is credited with being the founder of the Nyingma order of Tibetan Buddhism, the first and hence the oldest school. His tantric practices were preserved by successive practitioners, many of whom went to India to study tantra further.[52] Padmasambhava's system of burying certain texts and prophecies,

---

46. Samuel, *Civilized Shamans*, 12. David White suggests that "Tibetan Buddhism is by definition a Tantric tradition: this applies to the four major orders (the Nyingmapas, Kagyupas, Sakyabas, and the Gelugpas), as well as to the Dzogchen and other syncretistic traditions." White, *Tantra in Practice*, 7.

47. John Powers concurs with the thoughts of others in saying that the tantric path is "considered by Tibetans to be the most effective means for attaining Buddhahood." Powers, *Introduction to Tibetan Buddhism*, 24. See also 259.

48. Samuel, *Introducing Tibetan Buddhism*, 10.

49. Padmasambhava is known in Tibetan as Guru Rinpoche (*gu ru rin po che*)—"Precious Lama"—and also Pema Junge (*pad ma 'byung gnas*)—the "Lotus-Born One."

50. Powers, *Introduction to Tibetan Buddhism*, 148; Thurman, *Essential Tibetan Buddhism*, 3.

51. Van Schaik, *Spirit of Tibetan Buddhism*, 6.

52. Van Schaik, *Spirit of Tibetan Buddhism*, 7.

to be revealed as "treasures" (*gter ma*) by future generations, further added to his following. Through the example of Padmasambhava, one can see the origins of the adoption of Vajrayana as the primary vehicle for both the monastics and the laity. For the monastic world, the tantras represented the "fast", though potentially highly dangerous, route to enlightenment. For the laity, monks or lay shamans who were skilled in Vajrayana, and had the power to control the spirit world, were highly sought after. Vajrayana built on existing shamanistic rituals and further provided the occult technology to combat the nefarious spirit world that plagued the lives of Tibetans.[53]

Lamaism

Another distinguishing feature of Tibetan Buddhism, which is closely related to the practice of Vajrayana, is the relationship between the guru and disciple, or lama and monk. Tantric teachings are considered esoteric and require complete faith in one's lama in order to be transmitted. The transmission of these secret teachings is performed orally and only when a student is considered ready to receive them. Tantra is dangerous and an error in transmission can have disastrous results.[54] Therefore, the relationship between lama and monk is paramount. This close association was not lost on Augustine Weddell, who in the nineteenth century famously called Tibetan Buddhism "Lamaism."[55] While his label was construed pejoratively, as he desired for Tibetans to rid themselves of such a system and return to a "pure" form of Buddhism, his observation of Tibetan Buddhism being inextricably located in the bond between lama and novice is an accurate one and still essential to this day.[56]

---

53. M. Tsering, *Sharing Christ*, 87–88. Samuel, *Introducing Tibetan Buddhism*, 10.

54. Powers, *Introduction to Tibetan Buddhism*, 61, 258; Kapstein, *Tibetan Buddhism*, 26; Samuel, *Introducing Tibetan Buddhism*, 61. The many Tibetans that I have asked all speak of the superiority of Vajrayana as the path to enlightenment, but caution about the potential dangers of being harmed by evil forces, which can often lead to insanity.

55. Waddell, *Buddhism of Tibet*.

56. As Van Schaik observes, "The relationship between teacher and student is taken very seriously and is often compared to that between a patient and a doctor." Van Schaik, *Spirit of Tibetan Buddhism*, 2.

The Schools of Tibetan Buddhism

While Tibetan Buddhism can be described as an eclectic mix of shamanism, tantra, and Buddhist philosophy, various schools of Tibetan Buddhism developed into an elaborate and complex monastic system that has been in existence for well over a millennium. After Buddhism was embraced during the seventh century, various schools or sects slowly emerged. Songtsen Gampo (*srong btsang sgam po*, c. 614–50), Tibet's most celebrated king, is credited with introducing Buddhism to Tibet. Not only did he manage to unite Tibet, but he forged it into a dominant military force within Inner Asia.[57] Such was the reach of his empire that he received two princess wives as tribute—one from the court of the Chinese Tang Dynasty and the other from the royal family in Nepal.[58] According to legend, both of his new wives were Buddhist and managed to convert him to the ways of the dharma.[59] Songtsen Gampo later dispatched an envoy to India to learn Sanskrit and develop a standard written Tibetan language.[60] His motivation appears to have been more that just attempting to further unify Tibet with a written language, but also to promote Buddhism through the translation of Buddhist texts.

When referring to the "schools," "sects," "orders," or "denominations" (terms that are used interchangeably in the literature in English) of Tibetan Buddhism, the Tibetan term used to delineate the various schools is *chos lugs*, which technically means "religious system." It is a term that can also be used to refer to the major religions of the world. However, as Lopez has pointed out, a more correct delineation of the schools would be to use the term "lineage" because all schools support a system of lineages (*rgyud pa*) believed to be preserved through carefully selected reincarnations (*sprul sku*).[61] This system of adherence to a lineage over and above a strict doctrinal position also supports the view that Tibetan Buddhism can indeed be categorized as "Lamaism."

In Tibetan Buddhism, it is traditionally held that there are four main orders (*chos lugs bzhi*), though some of the literature stresses that there are

---

57. Sam Van Schaik, *Tibet: A History*, 6, 8.
58. Thurman, *Essential Tibetan Buddhism*, 7.
59. Lopez, *Religions of Tibet*, 6.
60. Dreyfus, *Sound of Two Hands*, 18.
61. Lopez, *Religions of Tibet*, 24; Van Schaik, *Spirit of Tibetan Buddhism*, 5.

five main systems, placing the indigenous religion of Bön as the fifth.[62] There are many other smaller schools within these orders and the system is complex. It is not the intention of this outline to elaborate on those intricacies but rather to focus on the four main schools.

Nyingma (rnying ma)

As previously mentioned, the celebrated sorcerer Padmasambhava is credited with being the founder of this school. The establishment of the Nyingma ("old") school occurred during what is known as the first diffusion (*snga dar*) of Buddhism in Tibet. The teachings of this order are based on tantras that Padmasambhava introduced to Tibet. His teachings can be divided into the exoteric "general" teachings and esoteric tantras. One distinctive of this school is the reliance on *gter ma* "treasure" teaching texts that were allegedly buried by Padmasambhava to be revealed by select disciples in the future.[63] This practice was perpetuated throughout the centuries (and continues today) and gave an authorial basis to Nyingma beliefs.[64] It also ensured the longevity of Padmasambhava's teachings. Padmasambhava brought with him tantric weapons and implements, the most notable being the vajra (*rdo rje*)—a cross-shaped implement symbolizing clarity and indestructibility,[65] essential to all tantric practice (hence the name Vajrayana).

The apex of the Nyingma teachings is the Great Perfection (*rdzogs chen*) or Supreme Yoga (Sk. Atiyoga). These teachings stress that the nature of the mind is primordially pure (*ye dag* and *ka dag*) and that through an

---

62. Tonba Shenrap (*ston pa gshen rab*) is credited with being the founder of the Bön religion and he is regarded by Bönpo as an enlightened Buddha. Bön has retained many of its original shamanistic beliefs and practices but has also absorbed teachings and practices from Buddhism. Some of the teachings are similar to the Nyingma school of Tibetan Buddhism. There are several Bön monasteries in Tibet and an increasing number of Bön monasteries in Nepal. See Karmay and Nagano, *Survey of Bonpo Monasteries*; Karmay and Nagano, *New Horizons*; Bellezza, *Spirit-mediums*.

63. For an overview of treasure texts see Thondup, *Hidden Teachings*, and Doctor, *Tibetan Treasure Literature*.

64. For a comprehensive analysis of treasure revealers and their place in contemporary Tibetan society, see Terrone, "Bya Rog Prog Zhu"; Terrone, "Householders and Monks."

65. Beer, *Encyclopedia of Tibetan Symbols*, 233–34. The vajra has other symbolic meanings, one being representative of a phalanx and the accompanying tantric bell, the pudenda.

elaborate process of secret yoga, one can return the mind to that originally pure state.[66] Though this teaching of primordial purity is found in other schools, it is most prominent in the Nyingma order.[67] The Great Perfection lineage has been well preserved by Tibetan exiles in India and is popular among Western Tibetan Buddhists.[68] The Nyingma have produced a number of famous scholars, namely Rongzom Chokyi Zangpo (*rong zom chos kyi bzang po*, 1012–1088), Longchenpa (*klong chen rab 'byams*, 1308–1363), Jigme Lingpa (*'jigs med gling pa*, 1730–798) and Mipham Namgyal (*'ju mi pham rnam rgyal*, 1846–1912).[69] One of the famous treasure texts, which is attributed to Padmasambhava, is the so-called *Tibetan Book of the Dead* (*bar do'i thos grol*), which is read aloud by monks while the deceased passes through an intermediary stage into the next life in the hope of safe passage.[70] It is a text still widely used in Tibet today. Another treasure text (revealed during the twelfth and thirteenth centuries) which has had a profound impact on Tibetan culture, is the *Mani Kabum* (*ma Ni bka' 'bum*). This work is a large collection of texts attributed to King Songtsen Gampo and is primarily concerned with the cult of Avalokiteshvara (*spyan ras gzigs*) and the six-syllable mantra *om mani padme hum*.[71]

Kagyu (bka' brgyud)

The Kagyu ("word lineage") order traces its origins to the famous translator Marpa Lotsawa (*mar pa lo tsa wa*, 1012–1099) from the beginning of the eleventh century.[72] During his visits to India to study under the Indian

66. Lopez, *Religions of Tibet*, 24; Wangchuk, "Relativity Theory," 225.

67. The Great Perfection teaching is also prominent in the indigenous Bön religion. Tibetan scholar Samten Karmay suggests that the *rdzogs chen* "is the heart of the Bön religious tradition." Karmay, *Great Perfection (RDzogs Chen)*, ix, 201–5. See also Namdak, *Bonpo Dzogchen Teachings*. The doctrine of the original purity of the mind is a foundational tenet of yoga praxis (*rnal 'byor spyod pa*, Sk. yogachara). Keenan, "Original Purity."

68. See Clay, "Purity," 70. There are six main lineages of Nyingma with the Dzogchen being most prominent.

69. Lopez, *Religions of Tibet*, 25; Van Schaik, *Spirit of Tibetan Buddhism*, 8.

70. See Trungpa and Fremantle, *Tibetan Book*; and S. Rinpoche, *Tibetan Book*. A small point of nomenclature; the title *Tibetan Book of the Dead* is somewhat of a misnomer. A more literal rendering is "Hearing Liberation of Bar do," which means being liberated from the intermediatory stage through the hearing of the "bar do" text. *See also* Kapstein, *Tibetans*, 109.

71. Kapstein, "Remarks on the Mani"; Kapstein, "Royal Way."

72. Lopez, *Religions of Tibet*, 26; Van Schaik, *Spirit of Tibetan Buddhism*, 9.

masters of the day, Marpa received a direct transmission of tantric teachings from the tantric master Naropa (*nA ro pa*, 956–1041) who was a disciple of the tantric sage Tilopa (*ti lo pa*, 988–1069).[73] Marpa Lotsawa's most famous student was Milarepa (*mi la ras pa*, 1052–1135), who is alleged to have achieved enlightenment in one lifetime, an incredibly rare feat. Milarepa was once a sorcerer who practiced black magic. After destroying his wicked relatives through his sorcery, he repented of his ways and became Marpa's loyal disciple. Milarepa composed many songs and poems and his autobiography, known as the *One Hundred Thousand Songs of Milarepa*, became one of the most celebrated works in Tibetan literature.[74] He remains to this day a Tibetan folk hero.

It was Milarepa's disciple, Gampopa (*sgam po pa*, 1079–1153), who formally established the Kagyu order from which later sub-schools were formed. The two most notable of these sub-schools were the lineages of the Karmapa and the Drukpa. The Drukpa Kagyu became widespread in Ladakh and also became the primary order of Bhutan, remaining so to this day.[75] The defining doctrine of the Kagyu was the Mahamudra or Great Seal (*phyag rgya chen po*), which, like the Great Perfection teachings, emphasized liberation from the worldly, deluded mind, which has a distorted view of reality, by resting in or relying upon the natural or primordial pure state of the mind.[76] The qualified guru, who, having deemed his students to be worthy recipients, leads them through elaborate tantric practices to bring them to the realization that "natural purity pervades all existence."[77] Both the Nyingma, through the Great Perfection teachings, and the Kagyu schools propound a similar doctrine of the ultimate reality of all phenomena being inherently pure, though the means they use to arrive at this state of awareness varies.[78]

---

73. Powers, *Introduction to Tibetan Buddhism*, 399.

74. Lopez, *Religions of Tibet*, 26. See also Lhalungpa, *Life of Milarepa*.

75. Van Schaik, *Spirit of Tibetan Buddhism*, 10; M. Tsering, *Sharing Christ*, 60; Phuntsho, *History of Bhutan*, 141–50.

76. Powers, *Introduction to Tibetan Buddhism*, 401.

77. Lopez, *Religions of Tibet*, 27.

78. Kapstein, *Tibetan Buddhism*, 34; Wangchuk, "Relativity Theory," 225–26, 231–34.

Sakya (sa skya)

Like the Kagyu school, the Sakya ("grey earth") school became established during what is known as the second or later (*phyi dar*) dispersion of Buddhism during the eleventh century.[79] The founder of this school was Khon Konchog Gyalpo (*'khon dkon mchog rgyal po*, 1034–1120) who established a monastery in the area of Sakya in south-central Tibet in 1073. Khon Konchog Gyalpo was a disciple of the translator Drogmi Shakya Yeshe (*'brog mi sha kya ye shes*, 993–1050), a tantric adept who translated the famous Hevajra Tantra into Tibetan.[80] This text became a foundational text for the Sakya school and was the basis for the specialized meditational practices of the "Path and Result" (*lam 'bras*) tradition.[81]

The most well-known of the Sakya masters is Gunga Gyaltsen (*kun dga' rgyal mtshan*, 1181–1251) who later became known as Sakya Pandita. One of his works, the *Treasury of Reasonings* (*rigs gter*), became so influential that it was translated from Tibetan into Sanskrit.[82] Sakya Pandita's most famous work is his *Treasury of Wise Sayings* (*sa kya legs bshad*) which contains over four hundred pithy sayings and proverbial moral lessons.[83] This text is still venerated and read today. Many of the sayings appear in Tibetan textbooks and are studied and memorized by school students.[84] Sakya Pandita was influential in the spread of Tibetan Buddhism to Mongolia, where he was invited to the Mongol court in 1244 and remained there until his death.[85]

Another famous scholar from the Sakya order is Budon (*bu ston*, 1290–364) who systematized the huge body of translated Tibetan texts into the Tibetan canon of the Kangyur (the alleged words of Buddha) and the Tengyur (the commentaries). This was no small feat since the wave of translation that occurred during the second diffusion of Buddhism in Tibet

---

79. The name of the Sakya school is based on the unusual grey color of the soil around the area where the first Sakya monastery was established. The monastery is distinctive from other monasteries in Tibet with its grey, rather than white, walls. The grey soil was considered auspicious.

80. M. Tsering, *Sharing Christ*, 60. See Snellgrove, *Hevajra Tantra*.

81. Van Schaik, *Spirit of Tibetan Buddhism*, 8.

82. Lopez, *Religions of Tibet*, 27.

83. See Sakya Pandita, *Ordinary Wisdom*; Sakya Pandita, *Legs Par Bshad Pa*.

84. One popular text is Sakya Pandita, *Sa Skya Legs Bshad*.

85. Van Schaik, *Spirit of Tibetan Buddhism*, 9; Snellgrove and Richardson, *Cultural History of Tibet*, 148.

resulted in perhaps one of the largest collections of sacred literature in all of Asia.[86] Indeed, sifting through the thousands of texts and codifying them accordingly was a task of epic proportions.

Geluk (dge lugs)

The origin of the Gelukpa ("virtuous ones") order, which is now the largest and most prominent school of Tibetan Buddhism, differs from the other schools in that it does not hold an Indian master as the source of their tradition. Rather, the founder of the Gelukpa (who is accredited retrospectively as "founder") is the highly acclaimed Tibetan adept Tsong Khapa Lobsang Trakba (*tshong kha pa blo bzang grags pa*, 1357–1419).[87] Tsong Khapa is remembered as a "reformer" of Tibetan Buddhism as he sought to recapture the teachings of Buddha as he understood them. He was also a reformer in the sense that he held to a strict form of monasticism and attempted to keep monks accountable to their vows, to increase their skills as debaters, and engage in higher level tantric practices.[88] Tsong Khapa was a highly regarded debater, with an outstanding capacity for memorization. He became a prolific writer. Tsong Khapa studied at various monasteries in Tibet and was heavily influenced by the tantric practices of the Sakya school.[89]

Tsong Khapa was also influenced by the earlier teachings of the Kadam (*bka' gdams*) school, a sect which claimed to hold firmly to the words of Buddha alone. The Kadam were founded by Atisha (*a ti sha*, 982–1054), a renowned Bengali Buddhist master who spent many years in Tibet teaching and translating.[90] The Kadampa were known for their strict monasticism and for their "mind purification" (*blo sbyong*) texts and practices.[91] These texts strongly influenced Tsong Khapa's writings and practices. The

---

86. Tsepag, "Traditional Cataloguing & Classification," 49.

87. Lopez, *Religions of Tibet*, 28.

88. Powers, *Introduction to Tibetan Buddhism*, 467. The Gelukpa order is known for its monastic debating while the other orders are not.

89. Van Schaik, *Spirit of Tibetan Buddhism*, 10.

90. Samuel, *Introducing Tibetan Buddhism*, 32, 38, 137. A more literal meaning of the term *bka' gdams* is "choose words" but the connotative meaning is "choosing to live only by the words of Buddha." The Kadampa order basically died out during the thirteenth to fourteenth centuries and the Gelukpa order was seen as the new and reformed Kadampa. See Roesler, "Kadampa."

91. Sweet, "Mental Purification (Blo Sbyong)," 249; Powers, *Introduction to Tibetan Buddhism*, 482. See also Jinpa et al., *Mind Training*.

Kadampa also developed a teaching known as the Gradual Path (*lam rim*) to enlightenment. This, too, influenced Tsong Khapa and is reflected in his epic work, *The Great Stages of the Path to Enlightenment* (*byang chub lam rim chen mo*).[92] Tsong Khapa wrote many other works, including *The Great Exposition of Secret Mantra* (*sngags rim chen mo*).[93] Though credited as a reformer, Tsong Khapa was a devoted tantric practitioner and occult practices remain integral components of Gelukpa teaching and practice.[94]

Tsong Khapa established Ganden monastery in 1409 and his disciples would later establish Drepung (*'bras spungs*) and Sera (*se ra*) monastery. These three monasteries would become foundational centers for the Gelukpa order and for centuries attracted vast numbers of monks. In 1950, the Drepung monastery was home to more than 10,000 monks and at one time was the largest monastery in the world.[95] A major factor of the supremacy of the Gelukpa order was the establishment of the system of the Dalai Lama, the first of whom was one of Tsong Khapa's disciples.[96] The Dalai Lamas were proclaimed to be emanations of Avalokiteshvara (*spyan ras gzigs*), the embodiment of Buddha's compassion.[97] As well as being the head of the dominant Gelukpa order, the institutionalization of the Dalai

92. This tome is more than 800 A4 pages in Tibetan and has been translated into English in three volumes. See Tsong Khapa Blo bzang grags pa, *Great Treatise*.

93. This text has been translated into English in three volumes with a commentary from the present Dalai Lama. See Tsong Khapa Blo bzang grags pa and Bstan 'dzin rgya mtsho, *Great Exposition Volume One*.

94. There are multiple examples of this, even in the preliminary practices of tantric initiation, but one of the more popular practices is the Kalachakra initiation. See The Dalai Lama, *Kalachakra Tantra*.

95. Goldstein, "Revival of Monastic Life," 15, 20. Goldstein further suggests that in 1951 there were 2500 monasteries in Tibet, with approximately 115,000 monks, comprising 10–15% of the male population.

96. The word Dalai (*tA la'i*) is a transliteration of a Mongolian term which means "ocean." TDCM, 1023.

97. Avalokiteshvara (also spelled Avalokitesvara) is also referred to as the Buddha of Compassion and the Bodhisattva of Compassion. The cult of Avalokiteshvara can be traced back to the seventh century as the *Mani Kabum* text indicates. Tara (*sgrol ma*), Avalokiteshvara's consort, is also widely revered throughout Tibet. She is seen in multiple ways as a savioress (as her name implies), as a protector, as the mother of the Tibetan people, and as the mother of Buddha. See Thurman, *Essential Tibetan Buddhism*, 5. Her image, like that of Avalokiteshvara, is seen all throughout monasteries, temples, and households. See Beyer, *Magic and Ritual*. Together with Padmasambhava and Avalokiteshvara, a case could be made that these three deities may well be the most invoked deities in the Tibetan pantheon. Their popularity remains strong to this day. See Lopez, *Religions of Tibet*, 21.

Lama lineage would see the Dalai Lamas become both the religious and political leaders of Tibet. This system of theocracy remained in place until the middle of the twentieth century.

Pure Land Buddhism

Although never an official school of Tibetan Buddhism, the cult of Pure Land Buddhism is profound in Tibet. As Kapstein and Halkias have shown, consciousness of a "pure land," and the possibility of arriving there in one lifetime, is a doctrine which gained wide appeal.[98] There appears to be no sectarian association with Pure Land teachings as it has pervaded all Tibetan orders and proved to resonate strongly with laity sensibilities. The adoption of many prayers and related practices (for example, funeral rites and the '*pho ba* transferal), which focus on rebirth in Buddha Amitābha's (*'od dpag med*) pure land abode of Sukhāvatī (*bde ba can*), is evidence of that.[99] Kapstein further states that, "all of the Tibetan Buddhist orders affirmed rebirth in the Land of Bliss as a preeminent, though not exclusive, spiritual goal. Innumerable tantric as well as exoteric devotions, meditations, and rituals were composed to ensure this happy outcome."[100]

Tibetan Buddhist Cosmology

Noted Tibetologist Giuseppe Tucci, in summarizing the folk religion of Tibet, states that, "The entire spiritual life of the Tibetan is defined by a permanent attitude of defense, by a constant effort to appease and propitiate the powers whom he fears. These powers have their residence everywhere."[101] Tsering further notes that, "The world of the folk Tibetan Buddhist is filled with aggressive spirits, capricious gods, malignant demons."[102] It could be argued that all layers of society—the folk and the clergy—have a preoccupation with the spirit world and navigation of it is a necessary part of daily existence. Given the plethora of terms to describe a complex array of demons, it is no surprise that words such as *klu* (nagas), *gdon dre* (demons), *lha*

---

98. Halkias, *Luminous Bliss*; Kapstein, "Pure Land Buddhism," 16–51.
99. Kapstein, *Tibetan Buddhism*, 97.
100. Kapstein, *Tibetan Buddhism*, 98.
101. Giuseppe Tucci, *Religions of Tibet*, 187.
102. M. Tsering, *Sharing Christ*, 86.

(gods) are used frequently in the spoken vernacular. In fact, as Lopez notes, there are too many beings in the underworld that English lacks sufficient terms to render them adequately.[103] Kapstein provides a helpful summation: "without the cooperation of the local spirits, the community cannot hope to achieve prosperity; without the prosperity of the community, the material basis for religious achievement is lost; and without achievement in religious practice and learning, the cooperation of the local spirits cannot be won. This cycle of interdependence undergirds the religious life of Tibet in all its aspects, whether in settings denoted as Buddhist or Bön."[104]

Wheel of Life

The diagram which best represents the cosmology of the Tibetan Buddhist,[105] and further illustrates the preoccupation with the unseen world, is the so-called "Wheel of Life" (*srid pa'i 'khor lo*).[106] This ubiquitous diagram, typically found at the entrance to all temples and monasteries, is a picture containing three concentric circles. In the smaller, central, inner circle are illustrations of three animals—a pigeon, snake, and pig which symbolize, respectively, desire, hatred, and ignorance (*'dod chags, zhe sdang,* and *gti mug*). These three are known as the "three poisons" (*dug gsum*). They are the root cause of all suffering and drive the turning of the wheel of samsara thus subjecting all beings to it. The second, larger circle, is divided into six

---

103. Lopez, *Religions of Tibet*, 8. For a more comprehensive list of demons and spirits see Kohn, "Offering of Torma," 255–58. In my early years in Tibet, I also attempted to document the names and classes of the various demons, spirits, and gods, which resulted in pages of copious notes.

104. Kapstein, *Tibetan Buddhism*, 7.

105. In defining cosmology, I will follow Eliran Arazi's definition: "a term used here to denote a given society's complex of assumptions about the organization of the world and the distribution of agency, authority, and responsibility among the human and non-human entities of which it is constituted." Arazi, "Corpse Impurity," 355.

106. The term "Wheel of Life" in Tibetan is more literally "Wheel of Possibilities." The word *srid pa* means "possibility" or "that which is possible." The wheel gives six possibilities for rebirth or transmigration. It is also of note that the wheel of samsara is a wheel of endless suffering. In translating this term into English many years ago, my Tibetan colleague insisted that I add the word "suffering" as he repeatedly made the case that this samsaric system is a curse of suffering, not a cause for celebration, and that Tibetans want to be rid of it. The Western fascination of the "Wheel of Life" was puzzling to him and it remained further perplexing why a westerner would want to choose to become a Buddhist and wish to voluntarily be trapped in this endless cycle of misery and suffering.

sections which depict the six realms of existence and the six classes of beings (*'gro ba rigs drug*) caught in samsaric existence. The three upper realms are known as the "pleasant migrations" (*bde 'gro*) of gods (*lha*), demigods (*lha ma yin*) and humans (*mi*). The three lower realms (*ngan 'gro*) are known as the "evil migrations" of the realm of hungry ghosts (*yi dwags*), beasts (*dud 'gro*), and hell-beings (*dmyal ba*) in hell itself.[107] (There are eighteen hells, nine hot and nine cold.) The greater likelihood is of being reborn into one of the three lower realms.[108]

The third, outer circle, contains twelve illustrations depicting the cause and effect or interconnection and interdependence of samsara. For example, the first illustration is of a blind man who symbolizes walking through life in ignorance of the dharma, and the final three illustrations are of a pregnant woman, a child, and an elderly person, which represent the endless cycles of birth, aging and death. The Lord of Death (*gshin rje chos rgyal*, Sk. Yama), the one who weighs up the deceased's accumulated karma and presides over their next rebirth, holds this wheel in his jaws.[109] Outside of the wheel, and the clutches of Yama, are depictions of Buddhas who have escaped the endless cycle of suffering and who offer teachings to those beings still trapped.

There are many other realms and categories of demons, gods and spirits which are too numerous to outline here, but the Wheel of Life synthesizes the core beliefs of all layers of Tibetan society.[110]

---

107. TDCM, 2976–77. The TDCM labels the upper realms as representing "the white path" and the lower realms "the black path" (*bde 'gro dang /ngan 'gro'i lam mtshon byed lam dkar nag gnyis*).

108. Lopez, *Religions of Tibet*, 23. It is commonly believed, and somewhat fatalistically accepted, that one's next reincarnation will likely be worse than one's current state. This is because being born as a human is rare, and is considered highly auspicious and meritorious, as one has maximum opportunities, especially if male, to listen to and heed the dharma.

109. The Lord of Death is frequently spoken of in daily life, with parents often threatening their children that *aku gshin rje chos rgyal* will deal with them if they do not behave properly.

110. There are three main realms (*khams gsum*) within samsara; the desire realm (*'dod khams*), the form realm (*gzugs khams*), and the formless realm (*gzugs med khams*).

The Tibetan Language and Written Texts

According to legend, Thonmi Sambhota (*thon mi sam bhoT*) is credited with having developed the Tibetan written script. Sent by King Songtsen Gampo in the seventh century, Thonmi studied Sanskrit and the orthographies of various Indian languages, basing Tibetan orthography on the Lensa and Wadu scripts.[111] Upon returning to Tibet, he developed the Tibetan alphabet and codified the grammar.[112] Thonmi wrote eight grammatical treatises on the Tibetan language, two of which have survived today—*The Thirty Verses* (*sum ju ba*) and *The Guide to the Signs* (*rtags mjug pa*).[113] Both of these works are still studied and memorized by school students today, being considered sacred grammar texts.[114] The introduction of a writing system produced a literate elite, who later would be dominated by the monastic community.

The translation and dissemination of Tibetan texts proliferated under King Trisong Detsen (*khri srong sde btsan*, 742–98). After he founded Samye, the first monastery in Tibet, in 779, Trisong Detsen invited the Indian master Santaraskita (*zhi ba mtsho*) to ordain the first monks.[115] The Tibetan written language was carefully preserved in the translation of thousands of texts and the autochthonous writings of many Tibetan masters. Perhaps it goes without saying that the indigenous literature produced by Tibetans was overwhelmingly religious in nature. The famous three "dharma kings" (Songtsen Gampo, Trisong Detsen and Tritsug Detsen Ralpachen) presided over one of the most extensive translation efforts of sacred texts in all of Asia, resulting in a corpus of Tibetan literary works perhaps unparalleled by any major religion.[116] Mention should also be made of the staggering

---

111. For an account in Tibetan of the Thonmi legend see U lhan, *Rna Ba'i Bdud Rtsi [Collection of Beloved Folk Stories]*, 23–25.

112. Van Schaik, *Tibet*, 12.

113. Dung dkar blo bzang 'phrin las, *Dung Dkar Tshig Mdzod [Dung Dkar's Great Dictionary]*, 1417. Dung dkar's entry for "Tibetan letters" (*bod kyi yi ge*), which traces the history of the Tibetan written language, is an essay that extends for five pages, 1416–20. See also R. Miller, *Studies*.

114. Tournadre, "Classical Tibetan Cases." There are many commentaries on the grammars of Thonmi Sambhota and other treatises on aspects of Tibetan language and literature.

115. Dreyfus, *Sound of Two Hands*, 18.

116. Ngawang Tsepag estimates the combined total of the Tibetan canon and commentaries is "4,502 texts in 73 million words." Tsepag, "Traditional Cataloguing & Classification," 52.

achievements of producing scriptures, firstly copying them by hand and later through carved wood block printing.[117]

Tibetan Language

In broad terms, Tibetic languages share some features of Sanskrit in that they are both inflected languages and employ case endings as grammatical markers. Written Tibetan uses a syllabary based on an alphabet of thirty consonants, four vowels and various diacritics. Words are comprised of combinations of independent syllables. Syllables are comprised of letters which can be as simple as a single letter or made up of a combination of six letters not including vowel markers. Complex syllables can have a prefix, root letter, superscribed and subscribed diacritics, a suffix, a post suffix, and a vowel marker. Tibetic languages vary in their tonal aspect; Central Tibetan is distinctly tonal whereas other major Tibetic languages are not or vary in degrees of tonality.[118] The Tibetan language has traditionally been classified as Tibeto-Burman, a subset under the larger umbrella of the Sino-Tibetan language family.[119] More recently, Nicolas Tournadre, among others, has proposed a classification of a "Tibetic" language grouping, and this has been increasingly accepted in the literature.[120]

The general misconception is that there is one Tibetan language with various Tibetan dialects. Tournadre and others have suggested there may be closer to fifty Tibetic languages across Tibet and the Himalayas, and up to two hundred related dialects.[121] Tibetans themselves have traditionally regarded their language as belonging to one of three main linguistic groupings—Central (*dbu gtsang*), Kham (*khams*), and Amdo (*a mdo*).[122] For a general overview of the Tibetan language, these three broad categories can suffice. Though there exist many regional varieties of Tibetan at the

---

117. See Schaeffer, *Culture of the Book*, 4–11.

118. Denwood, *Tibetan*, xi.

119. Denwood, *Tibetan*, xii; Cabezón and Jackson, *Tibetan Literature*, 13; Tournadre, "Tibetic Languages," 105.

120. Tournadre, "Tibetic Languages." See also Matisoff et al., *Languages and Dialects*.

121. Tournadre, "Tibetic Languages," 118. See also Roche, "Introduction"; Chamberlain, "Linguistic Watersheds"; Roche and Suzuki, "Tibet's Minority Languages."

122. Sum bha don grub tshe ring, *Bod Kyi Yul Skad Rnam Bshad [General Introduction]*, 51.

vernacular level, the written language, preserved through the sacred texts, has remained remarkably uniform.

Given such a focus on translation, and the preservation of written texts, it is no surprise that the literary form of Tibetan gained prominence over the spoken, vernacular or "common" (*kha skad* and *phal skad*) forms of the language, forms which were never committed to writing.[123] As such, over the centuries, the divergence between the spoken and written forms of the language became profound.[124] The high-register literary language of the sacred texts became known as *chos skad* ("religious language") and was generally accessible only to educated monks. This literary level of language served to unite Tibetans both linguistically and religiously, even when their spoken vernaculars were often mutually unintelligible. Thus, anyone within these three broad linguistic areas, who was educated in literary Tibetan, could read the written texts regardless of their regional dialect. The literate lamas could also teach the written texts using their vernacular regional dialects.

This preservation of the literary language ensured that the dharma could be disseminated far and wide, regardless of location or dialectical variations. It also cultivated the sanctity of the written word, where the language itself, and by extension any grammatical treatise on the language, were, along with the vast corpus of writings, considered sacred.[125] Hence, the written language was not to be altered, modernized, or tampered with in any way. This "sanctity of language" still prevails today and any attempts to standardize or modernize the literary form have been strongly resisted. Here one can indeed see a close alignment to the axiom "language is culture."

---

123. It is worth mentioning that while the oral language was not committed to writing, the oral language did influence the sacred writings in that many teachings were transmitted orally and these oral teachings, which included commentaries and elaborations on the texts, were later committed to writing. Indeed, a strong oral tradition has been in existence for centuries, in part due to literacy rates having been so low. Cabezón and Jackson are right to point out the important role oral traditions played in the transmission of Tibetan culture. Cabezón and Jackson, *Tibetan Literature*, 13–14.

124. This divergence between the written language and the spoken variety is known as diglossia. Arabic, for example, is another language which is considered diglossic. This divide between the written and spoken language can be a cause of confusion for the Tibetan language student. However, if one learns literary Tibetan, one can then read texts over one thousand years old, texts which have been preserved and remain largely untouched from when they were first translated or composed.

125. Tournadre, "Classical Tibetan Cases," 87–88.

STEPS TOWARD A TIBETAN UNDERSTANDING OF PURITY

Literary Genres

Given the significant Indian influence upon Tibet's religious and scholastic development, with many Indian teachers disseminating Buddhism, and the translation of Buddhist texts from Sanskrit to Tibetan, it is no surprise that the traditional Tibetan categorization of texts follows an Indian system of codification. This classification is based on the five major areas of knowledge (*rig gnas che ba lnga*) and the five minor areas of knowledge (*rig gnas chung ba lnga*). The five major learnings are, in order of priority, Buddhism (*nang rig pa*), logic (*gtan tshigs rig pa*), linguistics (*sgra rig pa*), medicine/healing (*gso ba'i rig pa*), and arts and crafts (*bzo rig pa*). The minor areas of knowledge are poetics (*snyan ngag*), synonymics (*mngon brjod*), literary composition (*sdeb sbyor*), theatrical performance (*zlos gar*), and astrology (*skar rtsis*).[126] While these categories are still extant today, and offer a broad, content-based approach to literary texts, other systems of classifying texts based on their style and authorship also emerged. Indeed, an elaborate autochthonous system of cataloguing (*dkar chag*) Tibetan texts produced encyclopedic lists (*gsan yig*) and copious collections (*gsung 'bum*).[127]

For the purposes of this study, more specific genre-based categories will prove helpful. Putting to one side the potentially contentious term "genre,"[128] what is intended here is some general points of demarcation of broadly accepted categories in navigating the complex and vast body of Tibetan literature. Broad classifications such as the Buddhist canon (*bka' 'gyur*) and the commentaries (*bstan 'gyur*) have previously been mentioned. Drilling down further, the Buddhist canon can be divided into two: the sutras (*mdo*), or discourses of Buddha, which are general, exoteric teachings open to everyone, and the tantras (*rgyud* or *sngags*), secret or esoteric teachings suitable only for the specially qualified.[129] An important division within the Kangyur is the class of texts known as *gzungs* (Sk. dharani),

---

126. Dung dkar blo bzang 'phrin las, *Dung Dkar Tshig Mdzod [Dung Dkar's Great Dictionary]*, 1900–1.

127. Roesler, "Classifying Literature," 40. *Dkar chag* also refers to a table of contents, and there exist copious tomes dedicated to documenting the tables of contents of various bodies of sacred works.

128. Rheingans, *Tibetan Literary Genres*, ii–iv, and Roesler, "Classifying Literature," 31, discuss how problematic the term genre can be when applied to non-Western contexts.

129. Ngawang Tsepag identifies six broad categories of tantra texts. See Tsepag, "Traditional Cataloguing," 56. Snellgrove suggests ten categories of tantra. See Snellgrove, "Categories of Buddhist Tantras."

which can be glossed as "incantations" or "magical spells." These are similar to mantras though they tend to be longer strings of syllables and the texts themselves typically do not contain tantric rituals.[130] Some collections of the Kangyur subsume these texts within the tantra section, while others, such as the authoritative Dege Kangyur, list them as a separate section.[131] These incantations form a significant part of the Kangyur.

The sutras can be further divided into three, known as the "three baskets of teachings" (*sde snod gsum*, Sk. Tripitaka).[132] The first "basket" is the basket of discipline (*'dul ba'i sde snod*, Sk. Vinaya), containing the rules and expectations for Buddhist practitioners, but particularly for monks. The second is the basket of discourses (*mdo sde'i sde snod*, Sk. Pitaka), containing the discourses of Buddha on spiritual training. The third is the basket of metaphysics (*chos mngon pa'i sde snod*, Sk. Abhidharma), containing teachings of a higher knowledge or understanding of all phenomena.[133] A further division of the sutras is the popular teachings known as the *Perfection of Wisdom* literature (*phar phyin* or *pha rol tu phyin pa* also *shes phyin*, Sk. Prajnaparamita), which teaches the path to a transcendent level of wisdom necessary for enlightenment.[134] Another popular sutra text is the recounting of the Buddha's previous lives (*syes rabs kyi sde*, Sk. Jataka).[135]

A helpful way to navigate the commentaries, and indeed the entire literary corpus, is to look at the titles of the texts themselves. Though Eugene Smith and Orna Almogi have highlighted that this approach can be problematic,[136] as some Tibetan terms do not always have clear equivalence

---

130. See ITED entry under *gzungs*. These incantations are related to mantras and are delineated not only by their length but the fact that they are considered to be "retention mantras" that need to be committed to memory and recited repeatedly in order for their magical powers to take effect. See also RJYS entry under *gzungs*. There are many *gzungs* included in tantra rituals. The study of *gzungs* will form a considerable part of chapter two.

131. The Dege Kangyur lists 265 incantation or *gzungs* texts, which is approximately one quarter of the texts contained within the collection. See Dege Kangyur.

132. Roesler, "Classifying Literature," 35–36.

133. TDCM, 834.

134. There are twenty-three sutras, varying in length, concerned with the topic of the Perfection of Wisdom.

135. Almogi, "Analysing Tibetan Titles," 40.

136. Eugene Smith's approach was to categorize Tibetan literature based on the four major sects of Tibetan Buddhism, the literary arts and encyclopedias, and the nonsectarian (*ris med*) literary. See E. Smith, *Among Tibetan Texts*. While true that not all works necessarily have titles, or titles that clearly indicate genre, and some texts have

in English, Roesler's suggestion of looking at text titles is one of the more accurate ways of codifying texts, and helpful in providing insights into autochthonous classifications.[137] It is true that many of the titles are long and ornamental, and, as Almogi suggests, perhaps somewhat "flowery" in language for Western sensibilities, however, to the trained eye, these terms can readily identify established literary genres.[138]

Though not exhaustive, the following are some further literary categories which also have bearing upon this study. A large class of writings are known as the biographies (*rnam thar*) of exalted saints who may or may not have achieved enlightenment. Related to these are narrative accounts (*rtogs pa brjod pa*), often in the form of a parable or moral lesson. Other types of works include mind purification texts (*blo sbyong*), Great Perfection texts (*dzogs chen*), preliminary practices (*sngon 'gro*), royal lineages (*rgyal rabs*), historical accounts (*lo rgyus*), annals or chronicles (*deb ther*), prophecy (*lung bstang*), "treasure" texts (*gter ma*), monastic textbooks (*yig cha*), instruction manuals (*khrid yig*), hymns or spiritual songs (*mgur glu*), supplication prayers (*gsol 'debs*), prostration prayers (*na mo*), liturgies and chants (*kha don*), ritual manuals (*cho ga*), essential instructions (*man ngag*), consecration manuals (*rab gnas*), and pilgrim guidebooks (*gnas yig*). In the realm of folk literature (*dmangs khrod*), there are books of proverbs (*gtam dpe*), wise sayings (*legs bshad*), moral instructions (*zhal gdams, bslab bya*) oral traditions (*gtam rgyud*), opera (*lha mo*), and folk stories (*sgrung gtam*), to mention some of the main ones.

As stated at the outset of this chapter, the purpose of giving an overview of Tibetan Buddhism, the development of written Tibetan, and a brief overview of literary categories, is to help place texts within their historical, religious, and literary contexts. This contextual mapping highlights the breadth and complexity of Tibetan texts and provides an axiological framework for the study of texts relating to purity. Attention will now be turned to defining purity and pollution, outlining an anthropological frame of reference, and exploring the relevant Tibetan terms.

---

abbreviated titles, even with those limitations, genre identification using titles can still provide meaningful data.

137. Roesler, "Classifying Literature"; See also Almogi, *Contributions*, 87–127.
138. Almogi, "Analysing Tibetan Titles," 29.

Defining Purity and Pollution

Thomas Kazen has suggested that "Ideas of purity/impurity are found globally,"[139] and James Preston notes that "concepts of purity are found in virtually all the religions of the world."[140] Petra Bahr adds that "the distinction between purity and impurity belong to the basic conditions of every religion."[141] Against this perceived ubiquity, Nikolas Jaspert suggests that "notions of purity, impurity, and pollution seem to have lost their relevance to societies of the twenty-first century."[142] At least, one might add, among the younger generations in the secularized Western world, conceptions of purity and impurity may have indeed been lost in recent times. Once, where "purity" may have denoted sexual purity, chastity, virginity or heterosexual monogamy, such notions now appear to have dropped out of mainstream consciousness. Given such a backdrop, there may be merit in beginning by first looking at what the term purity means in English, or perhaps what it once may have meant.

Among the meanings listed in the Merriam-Webster dictionary under the adjective "pure" are: unmixed with any other matter; free from dust, dirt or taint; spotless, stainless; free from what vitiates, weakens or pollutes; free from moral fault or guilt; marked by chastity; of pure blood and unmixed ancestry; ritually clean.[143] The noun "purity" is then defined as "the quality or state of being pure."[144] As an introductory baseline, these definitions can be informative. As will be explored in the next section, though cross-linguistic correspondence can clearly be problematic, these terms in English do have some semantic correlation with Tibetan notions of purity and thus are a valid starting point.

---

139. Kazen, "Purity/Impurity," 1.

140. Preston, "Purification," 91.

141. Bahr, "Purity," in *The Brill Dictionary of Religion*, ed. Kocku von Stuckrad, vol. 1–4 (Leiden: Brill, 2006), 1562.

142. Jaspert, "Introduction to Discourses," 1. Jaspert does, however, further elaborate that ethnic cleansing and issues related to Islamic and Hindu ideals of cleansing does make the notion of purity "alive and effective" in the modern day.

143. Merrriam-Webster online dictionary, "pure."

144. Merrriam-Webster online dictionary, "purity."

Pollution

The term "pollution," to the modern reader, may be imagined as referring to air pollution with images of factory chimneys spewing thick clouds of smoke into the atmosphere. In anthropological terms, the pairing of "purity/pollution" (p/p) is used to describe notions about dirt and cleanliness in a given society, and particularly where there is an added connotation of associated spiritual powers.[145] Sjaak Van Der Geest has suggested that pollution and purity are in fact about "very mundane matters: being dirty and being clean."[146] While not untrue, there is clearly more to it. Put simply, pollution is that which defiles someone, makes them unclean, dirty, or filthy, and causes them to be categorized as being in a state, often temporary, outside of what is typically deemed normality.[147] The impure person's condition is adjudged unclean, outside of normally accepted and safe boundaries for human interaction, leading the defiled to be forced into a state of alterity. Some external condition—birth, sickness, menstruation, or association with the dead, has made the person unfit for socialization. For this type of pollution, the standard classification is "ritual" or "ceremonial" impurity, or "ritually defiled." This is largely no fault of the person, rather it is part of the cycle of life. Though typically temporary, it still necessitates isolation before returning to one's daily life.[148] Moral or ethical impurity, however, is largely controllable and is often preserved for heinous crimes such as incest or patricide.

As noted earlier, classes of people can also be considered unclean, vulgar, dirty, or unsavory. The caste system of Hinduism is well known as being demarcated on clean and unclean lines. These are typically permanent designations. In the Tibetan schema, for example, those who are corpse handlers, metal workers, or lepers are permanently anomic.

Kazen provides a helpful definition of impurity, which includes both the ritual and moral components: "Impurity is used to designate a diversity of conditions and behaviors, including besmirched items, repelling substances, bodily fluids, certain physical states and diseases, corpses and carcasses,

---

145. Hendry, *Introduction to Social Anthropology*, 38.
146. van der Geest, "Pollution and Purity," 1844.
147. Bendlin, "Purity and Pollution," 178.
148. Bendlin, "Purity and Pollution," 178.

Purity

Though notions of purity are culturally determined,[150] in general terms purity is not seen just as the absence of defilement but rather as a transcendent state free from all filth, contamination, disease, and sickness. In many cases purity is often related to radiant light, white radiance, or shining clear light.[151] In other cases, purity is related to cleanliness, but often with religious connotations of being considered clean in order to appease a spiritual being or communicate with the supernatural.[152] Unlike defilement, which is contagious, one cannot contract purity; it is something that one aspires to attain. Purity can have a certain illusive quality. As Bahr observes, "The condition of purity is either very fragile, or else denotes a future ideal condition worth the striving."[153] Places and spaces can also be considered pure, and one must be careful not to contaminate pure places or unfavorable outcomes will result. Moshe Blidstein provides a balanced summation of the various layers of purity concerns: "Purity served all ancient religions to negotiate the difference between the divine and human realm, to construct borders between social groups, and to signify and embody changes people underwent in their lives."[154]

A Note on Nomenclature

The terms "pollution", "defilement," and "impurity" are typically seen as being synonymous and are used interchangeably in the literature, as are the pairings of "purity/pollution" and "purity/impurity"—they will also be for this study. As already mentioned, these terms, depending on the context,

---

149. Kazen, "Purity/Impurity," 2.

150. Frevel and Nihan, in their introduction to *Purity* state that "Conceptions of 'purity' and its counter-concept 'impurity' are strongly related to a certain worldview and hence they may vary between cultures." 12–13. See also Kazen's entry "Purity/Impurity," for other examples of cultural notions of purity.

151. Feder, "Semantics of Purity."

152. Hendry, *Introduction to Social Anthropology*, 43.

153. Bahr, "Purity," in *Brill Dictionary of Religion*, 1562.

154. Blidstein, *Purity, Community, and Ritual*, 4.

can have either a ritual or moral association. The terms "unclean," "dirty," and "disgusting" can also have ritual or moral connotations. "Ritual" pollution can also be referred to as "ceremonial" pollution and "moral" pollution as "ethical" pollution. The distinction between ritual and moral pollution is culturally defined and this dichotomy may not always be clearly demarcated.[155] Other categories of collective purity are "genealogical" or "ethnic," derived from a sense of the existence of a pure or undefiled ethnicity.[156]

Purity/Pollution as a Binary Category?

While the "clean/unclean" categorization may be more clearly binary, for example, either food is clean or it is not, or either one's body is clean or it is not, the purity/pollution binary classification cannot be seen as strict opposites. The non-existence of pollution does not equal purity, nor does the non-existence of purity equal pollution or a polluted state. Thus, this binary category of "purity/pollution" can be misleading. Unlike impurity, purity is not contagious. Purity typically cannot be spread or shared but remains an individualized state. However, the impure can be purified and have their impurity cleansed through specific agents (typically water) and performative rituals often conducted by a specialist. This does not, however, mean that the person has become "pure" as such, rather that the impurity has been removed and an equilibrium state of normality has been restored. The state of impurity is often constrained by time, that is, one can be temporarily impure. In contrast, one is typically not temporarily "pure." One can be temporarily defiled, cleansed, or purified by a ritual resulting in being restored to the community. However, this does not of necessity lead to a state of purity. While there are degrees of defilement, that is, some states of defilement are considered worse than others, and these can be accumulative,

---

155. Kazen states that "no clear distinction between ritual and morality—not to speak of convention—holds cross-culturally, since these categories are culture-specific and at least in part arbitrary." Kazen, "Purity/Impurity," 3.

156. A related category is that of "language purism" where speakers of particular languages ascribe a value of purity or "cleanness" to either a prestige dialect or to reference speakers who speak in a pure, unadulterated manner, being the epitome of how a language should be spoken. Language purism also reveals a pejorative posture towards related dialects which are considered to be impure derivations of the "pure" language form. In Tibetan areas, particularly Central Tibet, notions of language purism among speakers of the prestigious Lhasa dialect are pronounced. An examination of this aspect of purity is beyond the scope of this study.

purity is not typically amplified by accrual or accumulation.[157] Purity is thus an ultimate state which is free from any possible defilements, free from the stain of either ritual or moral impurity. Though a convenient dyad in English, the binary pairing of "purity/pollution" does not do justice to the nuances and complexities involved.

Anthropological Frameworks

Anthropological studies in purity and pollution first began with the study of the notion of "taboo," a Polynesian term which came to prominence through the work of James Frazer in the late nineteenth century.[158] Concepts of what was considered taboo, prohibited, or off-limits were studied with a view to how these demarcations related to a wider system of classification. Notions of what was considered sacred and profane were further investigated through the taboo lens.[159]

The scholar who has made the most significant contribution to purity studies, and the development of a theoretical framework, is Mary Douglas through her seminal work *Purity and Danger*.[160] Central to Douglas' structuralist theory is that purity concerns are symbolically representative of an ordered social system. Purity rules are explained through their social function, which, she suggests, is for the purpose of maintaining and preserving the basic structures of a given society. The key metaphor in her thesis is that of "dirt." She claims that "dirt is essentially disorder" and that "dirt offends against order."[161] According to Douglas, dirt, in its proper place, is not "dirty" or "defiled" per se, but it is defiling when in an improper or inappropriate setting. When something is out of place, an order or system has been violated, contamination has occurred resulting in certain alienating consequences. To consider the nature of dirt, is to consider an underlying system. Douglas further elaborates, "dirt is matter out of place ... [it is] a set of ordered relations and a contravention of that order. Dirt, then, is never a unique isolated event. Where there is dirt there is a system. Dirt is the

---

157. Frevel and Nihan, *Purity*, 14.
158. Radcliffe-Brown, *Structure and Function*, 133–52.
159. Hendry, *Introduction to Social Anthropology*, 38–29.
160. Douglas, *Purity and Danger*.
161. Douglas, *Purity and Danger*, 2. Developing her theory further, Douglas concluded that, "Dirt was created by the differentiating activity of mind, it was a by-product of the creation of order," 162.

by-product of a systematic ordering and classification of matter, in so far as ordering involves rejecting inappropriate elements."[162]

In the practice of everyday life, as Douglas shows through many examples, "the pollution rule draws very precise lines of incorporation and exclusion."[163] A polluting person, then, is one who has stepped outside the normal boundaries set down by society, is in some way seen as contaminated, and as a result suffers from marginalization and exclusion. Douglas notes that defilement can occur intentionally or unintentionally (such as a skin disease), however, the result is the same; the polluter has violated a code, is in the wrong, and must face the consequences.[164]

The impact of Douglas' schema has been profound, and her theory has been followed by many. Bruce Malina, in echoing Douglas, states that, "Garden dirt in the back yard is in its proper place. When the same dirt gets into the house, the house is considered "dirty, defiled, unclean, impure." Dirt is a way of speaking of something out of place."[165] David deSilva, also following Douglas, defines purity as the state where things are as they should be: the right thing, is in its right place, at the right time. DeSilva suggests purity is, "fundamentally concerned with the ordering of the world and making sense of one's everyday experiences in light of that order."[166]

In recent years, however, Douglas' theory has received increasing criticism, primarily because of the over-emphasis she placed on the social aspect and her seeming disregard for the spiritual dimension.[167] Yohan Yoo observes that one of the main shortcomings of Douglas' theory is "by over-emphasizing societies, social systems, and social order for understanding purity, Douglas overlooks the religious dimensions of purity ideas that cannot always be explained by social systems."[168]

---

162. Douglas, *Purity and Danger*, 35.
163. Douglas, *Purity and Danger*, 107.
164. Douglas, *Purity and Danger*, 133.
165. Malina, *New Testament World*, 153.
166. deSilva, *Honor*, 246.
167. Blidstein, "All is Pure," 6.
168. Yoo, "Theory of Purity," 11. Christian Frevel and Christophe Nihan in criticizing Douglas state that "purification rituals. . .need to be described and explained first and foremost for themselves, and not merely as the concrete 'translation' of a preexisting symbolic order." Frevel and Nihan, *Purity*, 10.

A Critique of Mary Douglas

One of the premises upon which Douglas began to develop her theory was in the rejection of analyzing culture through the lens of fear, something she felt was an unproductive exercise. She maintained that anthropologists found little evidence of fear in their studies of "primitive cultures" and concluded that the fear paradigm "seems to be a false trail . . . hygiene, by contrast, turns out to be an excellent route."[169] Robert Priest, who has provided a robust critique of Douglas, suggests that this is where Douglas makes her first mistake. He argues that "Many scholars have noted the universality of funeral rites and have concluded, contra Douglas, that a central religious impulse is the anxiety generated by death."[170] He goes on to construct a powerful counterargument.

Priest raises a valid point. An analysis of the outworking of fear within a culture may indeed prove to have considerable heuristic merit. While this study is not about Tibetan notions of fear, Douglas may have been too quick to dismiss fear as an avenue of exploration and, in something so universal as funeral rites, which clearly generate purity/pollution tensions, may have missed the centrality of this important "religious impulse." Furthermore, in any cultural analysis, one needs to weigh up various cultural dynamics. Notions of fear of the demonic world and interaction with spirits, in the case of Tibetans, for example, as previously observed by many (see Tucci, M. Tsering, Kapstein, Samuels, Powers, and Lopez), are indeed profound and need to be borne in mind.

Central to Douglas' argument is that pollution and defilement are symbolically seen as dirt being matter out of place. If, however, one was to change the image of "dirt" to feces, saliva, or any other type of excrement, then the metaphor of dirt simply being the wrong stuff in the wrong place is less likely to carry. Some things, including many defiling substances, are dirty, filthy, and reviling regardless of where they are located. Indeed, their location does

---

169. Douglas, *Purity and Danger*, 2.

170. Priest, "Defilement, Moral Purity," 42. Thomas Kazen further elaborates, "Dirt is to humans more than matter out of place. Danger stems from more than surprise. Fear of death, decay, and animality are important factors, too." Kazen, "Dirt and Disgust," 63. Kazen further posits that it is the basic notion of disgust, universal in all cultures, that actually defines purity/pollution boundaries both morally and ritually. Blidstein has also suggested that Kazen's approach can be useful in explaining how "morality is emotionally embodied through practices of purity and defilement." Blidstein, "All is Pure," 7. Yitzhaq Feder continues this line of argument in his article, "Defilement, Disgust, and Disease."

not define the degree of their defilement. As Priest and others have pointed out, defiling substances are defiling wherever they may be found.[171]

When one considers the array of purification rites (for example, apotropaic, cleansing, consecrative and protective), rather than view them only from a social-functionalist perspective of preserving social hierarchy,[172] one could equally view them from the religious perspective of the cultural milieu in question. In light of the literature review, this perspective would be more closely connected to the perception of the practitioners themselves, and particularly for Tibetan Buddhists, who have an elaborate system. Tracey Lemos provides valuable insight in suggesting that the etic posture can often over analyze while disregarding the emic posture, which may well offer a sound explanation. As she notes, "the type of analysis that seeks ever to schematize almost always sees ritual as secondary to belief and the body as secondary to the mind."[173]

In contrast to Douglas, Jacob Neusner, who spent much of his life studying and writing about Mishnaic purity laws, could not find any rational or ordered system. He claimed it was full of "irrational compulsions" and "chaotic phobias."[174] However, in attempting to compare purity laws of Ancient Near East cultures, Neusner concluded that it was a hopeless endeavor because one ended up comparing the cosmological systems.[175] But here, he may have incidentally provided a key to exploring purity—that it is undergirded by a particular cosmological worldview and is not just creating social order out of chaos, as Douglas had proposed. Stanley Tambiah has observed that a significant ritual within a culture will "enact and incarnate cosmological conceptions."[176]

The point to be made here is that Douglas, in only seeing purity and pollution as reflected of a system of order out of chaos, has perhaps fallen short of a potentially deeper understanding. "Primitive" cultures often see their attempts at removing defilement, attaining cleansing, and moving towards a state of purity as a religious, cosmological, and soteriological endeavor. Tibetans have a profound sense of the unseen world and even,

---

171. Priest, "Defilement, Moral Purity," 586–87.
172. Douglas, *Purity and Danger*, 101, 104, 125–26.
173. Lemos, "Where There Is Dirt," 294.
174. Neusner, *History of the Mishnaic*," 19.
175. Neusner, *History of the Mishnaic*," 19.
176. Tambiah, "Performative Approach to Ritual," 121. As quoted in Dennis, "Purity and Transformation," 51.

for example, in the daily task of burning incense may not necessarily be attempting to create order from their chaotic world, as Douglas would have it, but rather are attempting to satisfy the spirit world who they believe they have defiled through their actions here on earth.

Summary Argument

This study will view purity as governed primarily by religious sensibilities and not social ones. In other words, the primary concern is not how purity is construed to measure social demarcations or create order out of disorder and preserve a social hierarchy, but rather how purity is connected to the religious domain. Ortner is right to suggest that the world of Tibetan Buddhists, both monastic and laity, cannot be separated from their religion or cosmology and therefore neither can their concerns for purity/pollution.[177] Douglas' theory does not appear to adequately take this into account.

The main problem with Douglas' schema is not so much that she has led us down the wrong path, but rather that her schema does not lead us far enough down the path. While there is a socially defining aspect to purity and pollution, a holistic approach, which is not attempting to imagine a social order from every action, but which examines purity in consideration of a larger religious and cosmological schema, is needed. Elian Azari has provided a balanced approach by suggesting that, "trying to grasp impurity per se is futile and mistaken, because in actuality, no *single* concept of impurity has ever existed. We should rather account for specific impurities, for how each one was experienced and understood, based on an empirical investigation of how these individual impurities interconnected with other cultural categories and social practices."[178]

I further concur with Yoo that, "purity ideas and purification rituals should be studied not just in relation to society but also in terms of a religion's central doctrines."[179] It is on this basis, then, of analyzing purity from a religious, cosmological, and soteriological perspective, a perspective that would seem to be more indicative of an emic reality, that will undergird this study.

---

177. Ortner, "Sherpa Purity," 49, 56.
178. Arazi, "Corpse Impurity," 355; italics original.
179. Yoo, "Theory of Purity," 25.

Tibetan Terms for Purity and Pollution

As a basic theoretical framework for analyzing Tibetan purity terms and their semantic domains, what I will follow here is the broad approach of cognitive linguistics, which posits that meaning is directly related to human experience. Feder elaborates that, "Taking consideration of the communicative context of language, one might state that the exchange of linguistic meanings by communicating parties is dependent on their shared world knowledge."[180] In practical terms, this means that language indexes human experience and assumes a common shared experience between communicating parties. Kazen adds that, "As all linguistic expressions relate to human experience, lexical meaning is bound to contain an affective element . . . as becomes particularly obvious in the field of purity/impurity."[181] In short, in semantic studies, to gain a fuller understanding of the range of meaning, the cultural context also needs to be considered and not just the lexemes themselves.

However, it also needs to be borne in mind that while meaning is derived from shared human experience, semantic meaning is also derived from the larger lexical corpus into which lexemes are embedded and interconnected. Susan Bean, in her study of purity and pollution terms among the Kannada in India, suggests that, "It is a basic tenet of structural semantic analysis that the meanings of words are a product of the relations among them in a corpus, and not simply of their relations to the cultural world each describes."[182] For this study, this will mean exploring the purity terms in themselves, their various cognates, their relations to other terms, and the reach of their semantic domain in the wider cultural context. This approach to semantic analysis allows for the multivalent and polysemous nature of many of the terms within the domains of purity and impurity and thus provides a broad theoretical approach.[183]

The following analysis is based on discussions with Tibetan colleagues, authoritative Tibetan lexicons—both Tibetan to Tibetan and Tibetan to

---

180. Feder, "Semantics of Purity," 89.

181. Kazen, "Purity/Impurity," 2.

182. Bean, "Toward a Semiotics," 577.

183. This broad approach of cognitive linguistics could be summed up in William Croft's statement that "everything you know about the concept is part of its meaning." For example, the generic word for defilement in Tibetan *grib* means "shadow", but as will be seen, it has multiple meanings and associations beyond that single English gloss. Croft, "Role of Domains," 163, as quoted in Feder, "Semantics of Purity," 89.

English, Tibetan literary sources, and observations from relevant secondary sources. Purity terms have been broken down into sections based on their meanings and lexical weighting.

Pollution Terms

Defilement and Impurity

The most common term for "defilement" or "impurity" is the word *grib*. The term in its literal sense means "shade" or "shadow," though this meaning can also be expressed in the cognate terms *grib ma* or *grib nag*. This term is used as a noun to describe a state of impurity or defilement, which is considered to be a type of *nad*—a disease, sickness, or illness. *grib* (also *btsog grib*) can describe a sickness that one is afflicted with (*grib phog pa*) or a disease one can catch from someone else (*grib gos pa*). For example, the pollution from a woman who has just given birth, or the pollution from handling a corpse, is transferable to others who come into close contact with those who are polluted. The term *grib* can be divided into both ritual and moral defilement. The primary meaning is of a particular type of physical illness that arises from being in a state of impurity. The TDCM gives the following definition: "A type of disease that comes from impurity" and "the filth of uncleanness."[184]

There are various types of ritual pollution, caused by unclean food (*zas grib*), leprosy (*mze grib*), contaminated clothes (*gos grib*), a bride through marriage (*bag grib*)—this term is applied if, after marriage, there is sickness in the household; the sickness is ascribed to the new bride and thus considered a polluting illness—childbirth (*skye grib*),[185] being a widow

---

184. TDCM, 399. The Tibetan is: *mde btshog la brten nas 'byung ba'i nad cig/mi gtsang ba'i dme btsog.*

185. There is a related term *pang grib* which also refers to pollution from childbirth, but more specifically to uterine blood that may spill onto the lap or the apron of a woman during childbirth. The term *pang khrag* refers to uterine blood (MTD, 1027). The term *pang grib* is more common in remoter regions. Charles Ramble and Lawrence Epstein have both noted the term in their respective research. Tibetan women traditionally wear colorful aprons (*pang gdan*), which in some areas is a sign of marriage. If blood spills on an apron, this is of course considered defiling. The lower half of the body, for both men and women, is considered impure, but especially so for women. If a woman waves her apron at anyone (for example out of anger or spite) this is considered a highly defiling act for those she is waving it at. Though Tibetans are less fastidious about menstruating women than Hindus, there is still a concern about the inherent impurity of women. This

(*yugs grib*), being a butcher (*bshan grib*), and corpse pollution (*ro grib*). Pollution can lead to permanent physical damage such as cataracts (*grib ling*) and blindness (*grib long*).

Pollution considered "moral" or "ethical" includes pollution arising from; breaking a promise (*dam grib*), breaking a monastic vow (*nyams grib*),[186] making a wrong or corrupt vow (*mna' grib*), fights, arguments or holding a grudge (*'khon grib*), incest (*nal grib*), parricide (*dme grib*),[187] and blood (*dmar grib*).[188] The term *rme grib* refers to a particular type of contamination or mental disturbance that arises from meeting a person who is a murderer, or even walking past them, or by being at a murder site. Rangjung Yeshe glosses this type of defilement as "the killer's defilement," whereby the moral defilement of the murderer can inflict an innocent bystander.[189] There is a certain type of pollution that arises from the birth of an illegitimate child (*mug phrug*) which requires a particular type of purification.[190]

Other terms cognate with *grib* include *btsog grib*, (also *grib btsog* and *dme grib*) which can be glossed as "filth and defilement pollution." This term is typically used when one has become defiled through contact with

---

is reflected in the prohibition of women entering certain areas in temples and monasteries (typically the *mgon khang*—the room/chapel of the protector deities) and certain areas of sacred sites. Toni Huber has documented this restriction of females in certain pilgrim areas and the sacred mountain Tsari in particular. See also Ramble, *Navel of the Demoness*, 224; L. Epstein, "Causation in Tibetan Religion," 90–91; Huber, *Cult of Pure Crystal*.

186. The term *nyams grib* refers to breaking monastic vows in general but also more specifically relates to the breaking of a promise or vow between a monk and a lama, which is also known as *dam tshig nyams chags*. The violation of a monastic vow requires a purification ritual called *gso sbyong*.

187. The term *nal grib* can also refer to parricide and *dme grib* can also refer to incest.

188. The generic term *dmar drib* is associated with menstruation (*zla mtshan* and *skyed pa rgyag pa*), coming into contact with the blood of an animal, blood from killing an animal or simply having blood on one's hands. Women's underwear is also considered polluting, and men are not to touch women's apparel that is drying out on a clothesline or walk underneath it.

189. RJYS entry under *rme grib*.

190. Note that the term *nal* (for incest) can also refer to an illegitimate child, as in the term *nal phrug* (also *byi phrug*). In an ancient text dating to the fourteenth century (though the text itself is referencing events much earlier) in a story about Shenrap Mibo, (*gshen rap mi bo*) the founder of the Bön religion, a demon inflicts him with nine impurities (*mi gtsang rdzas cha sna dgu*). These are listed as impurities stemming from: "*dme* (murder), *mug* (illegitimate children), *nal* (incest), *grib* (pollution), *byur* (misfortunes), *yug* (widowhood), *rme* (impurities), *mnol* (defiling actions), and *than* (bad omens)." Clemente, "SGra-Bla, Gods," 133.

an impure person.[191] Another generic term for defilement is *mnol*, which refers to filth, uncleanness, and defilement. The term *mnol rigs* refers to dirty, unclean classes of people. When combined with *grib*, the term *mnol grib* references a particular kind of pollution that arises from being in a state of physical weakness, listlessness, mental torpor, or dullness. This particular affliction can occur through association with a defiled person. There is a particular cleansing ritual (*mnol bsang*) of burning incense associated with this type of pollution. According to textual sources, the Tibetan king Trisong Detsen (eighth century) suffered from this type of pollution and his guru, Padmasambhava, was able to perform rituals which cured him.[192] The tradition of *mnol bsang* has been passed down through the Nyingmapa tradition.

Another related term is *grib mdos* which refers to a woven cross-shaped image that serves as a trap for evil spirits which have caused some kind of polluting sickness, often believed to have been caused by *klu*—nagas.[193] In order to rid the afflicted person of pollution, *grib mdos* are placed on street corners or intersections.[194] Nagas are considered one of the prime causes of *grib*.[195] (Nagas are serpents undetected by the human eye who inhabit streams and lakes and the underground, and who cause intentional harm to humans who have disturbed their habitat). The term *grib khrus* is a generic term which refers to ritual purification rites which are believed to eliminate *grib*.[196] The term *grib sel* is a generic term referring to the method of removal or clearing away of *grib*. The term *grib skyon* (pollution + faults) refers to epilepsy or seizures. Epilepsy is believed to be caused by the wrathful tantric deity Rahula where burst blood vessels in the brain result in seizures and fainting.[197]

---

191. ITED, entry under *gstog grib*.

192. ITED, entry under *mnol bsang*.

193. Morrison, "Sharing the Gospel," 126.

194. There are other kinds of offerings for dealing with *grib*, one common one being the *glud*—a ransom offering, where a small effigy of the sick or polluted person is also placed on a street corner, representing the exorcism of the demons causing the polluting sickness. Both the effigy (*lgud*) and the cross (*mdos*) are often placed together in a box. For more on *lgud* and *mdos* see Barnett, "Notes on Contemporary Ransom."

195. All Tibetan informants confirmed such a statement.

196. MTD, 299.

197. TDCM, 399 and MTD, 298. The archaic terms *gza' grib* and *steng grib* also refer to strokes or seizures. In ancient Tibet, it was believed that an eclipse of the sun or moon could cause seizures. See ITED, entry under *gza' grib*.

Though the term *grib* does occur frequently in Tibetan literature, it is a term commonly associated with the laity who live in direct contact with the defiled world more so than monks in their cloistered monasteries. The problem of *grib*, however, does become a monastic affair as monks are frequently called upon to perform purification rituals of various kinds. Here one can see the pervasive nature of *grib* and the ongoing struggle to deal with it at both the monastic and lay level.

Dirt and Filth

Another term for defilement is *sbags* which means to "contaminate," "defile," or "pollute." One can be defiled by bad habits (*ngan gsom kyis sbags pa*) or by making mistakes (*skyon gyis sbags pa*).[198] The noun *gtsog pa* means "dirt," "filth," "feces," "excrement" and also has the sense of being contaminated and defiled. The term can be applied to someone who has been afflicted with *grib* and is also used to described unclean and dirty classes of people (*rigs gtsog pa*), occupations or families.[199] Certain households can be considered filthy (*mi tshang gtsog pa*) and need to be avoided in marriage.[200] A related term is *gtsog lhag* which refers to the filthy leftovers or remainders of food or offerings, particularly in relation to tantric feasts and offerings.[201]

Clean and Unclean

The term *mi gtsang ba* means "filthy," "dirty," "impure," and "unclean." The term is a negation of its opposite *gtsang ba/ma* which denotes purity, cleanness, or to be free of stain or blemish. As well as referencing general cleanliness, the term *gtsang* also has a strong connotative moral meaning. When someone has done wrong, committed a crime, or violated a social code, they are considered *mi gtsang ba*. Ritual and confessional practices help in clearing away the violations. There is a commonly used idiomatic collocation *lag pa gtsang ma* (literally "clean hands"), which refers to someone who is honest, trustworthy and does not steal. It is an expression often used when recommending a person to someone else. An untrustworthy

---

198. TDCM, 2013.

199. For classes of unclean people see Heidi Fjeld in the literature review section and associated footnotes for more details.

200. Morrison, "Sharing the Gospel," 122.

201. ITED, entry under *gtsog lhag*.

person has dirty hands (*lag pa btsog pa*).²⁰² The compound *gtsang spyod* (also *tshangs spyod*) refers to clean and pure behavior.²⁰³ Places and spaces can also be considered clean or unclean. A pure, untouched place, free of litter, (such as a grassland meadow) is considered to be completely clean (*gtsang kyang*). Pure realms, free from the afflictions of samsara, are known as *gnas gtsang*. (See the *Pure Realms* section below for further discussion.)

Stains and Taints

A commonly used word to denote impurity or defilements is the term *dri ma*. This term literally means "smell" or "odor"—as in pleasant or bad odors, but also refers "stains," "taints," or "defilements." As a Buddhist term, *dri ma* refers to the sufferings, misery, and afflictions (*nyon rmongs*) that arise from samsara.²⁰⁴ The three primary stains (*dri ma gsum*) are desire, enmity, and ignorance—also known as the three poisons (*dug gsum*). The quest for the Tibetan Buddhist is to be free from all stains (*dri ma med pa*). This state of being free from all stains (*dri ma med pa'i sa*) is the second of ten stages of a Bodhisattva (*byang chub sems dpa'i sa bcu*) on the path to enlightenment. This same expression *dri ma med pa* (also *dri med*) is an epithet of the Buddha "Stainless One"—denoting purity and perfection—and is frequently used in sacred texts.²⁰⁵ The description of being stainless is also given as one of the qualities of the Supreme Being (*dkon mchog*), a being who exists independently from samsara.²⁰⁶ There is a particular tantra called the *dri ma med pa'i bshags rgyud* ("The Stainless Confessional Tantra") a confessional text for monks who have broken their vows (*nyams grib*).²⁰⁷

Obscurations and Hindrances

A related word to *grib* is the term *sgrib*. These two terms are sometimes mistakenly used interchangeably. The pronunciation between the two

---

202. Tibetans maintain a pejorative view about left-handedness being dirty and impure. The left hand is the "bad hand" (*sdug lag*), and the right hand is the "good hand" (*yag lag*).
203. TDCM, 2190.
204. ITED, entry under *dri ma*.
205. TDCM, 1327.
206. TDCM, 61.
207. RJYS, entry under *dri ma med pa'i bshags rgyud*.

differs slightly only in tone and voicing, (though they are often pronounced the same in vernacular speech) and the spelling is distinguished only by the suprafixed letter *sa*. As an active transitive verb, *sgrib* means to "cover over", "conceal," or "obscure." As a noun, *sgrib* has a technical Buddhist meaning of "that which obscures", "obscuration" or "mental hindrance." Though the term does not refer to pollution in the same sense as *grib*, the etymology suggests a clear semantic link. The term could be regarded as "mind pollution," which is in need of cleansing through "mind purification" (*slo sbyong*). The term *sgrib* occurs frequently in Buddhist texts to mean that a true understanding is obscured, hidden, or covered over because of wrong perceptions about reality or impure moral conduct. A large part of Tibetan Buddhist study and meditation is devoted to cleansing or clearing away these obscurations. The five primary obscurations (*sgrib pa lnga*) are craving and desire (*'dod pa la 'dun pa*), restlessness and regret (*rgod 'gyod*), harmful thoughts (*gnod sems*), dullness and drowsiness (*rmugs pa dang gnyid*), and doubt (*the tshom*).[208] These obscurations need to be cleansed (*sgrib sbyong*) and this is an essential part of the preliminary practices (*ngon 'dro*) of the Tibetan Buddhist monk.[209] Such purification practices are particularly associated with meditation upon the tantric deity Vajrasattva (*rdo rje sems ba*) of which more will be discussed in the following chapter.

A common collocation with *sgrib* is the term *sdig* which means "negativity," "non-virtue," or "sin." The compound *sdig sgrib* means "obscuration and non-virtue"—something from which all sentient beings need to be purified. Prostrations and circumambulations are one way of working towards purification. There is a prostration term *phyag skor sgrib sbyong* "prostration circumambulation for purifying obscurations/hindrances," which expressly refers to prostration circuits as efficacious in purifying *sgrib*.[210] (More will be discussed about prostration in chapter four.) The compound *sgrib sel* refers to the clearing away or purification of *sgrib*. The verb *sel* is used in respect to clearing away or cleansing both *sgrib* and *grib*.

---

208. TDCM, 612. There are other kinds of obscuration which are codified as the "two," "three," and "four" obscurations, and they vary according to the school of Tibetan Buddhism. Though *grib* and *sgrib* are clearly distinct yet overlapping terms, because the pronunciation of the terms is very similar, *sgrib* is often understood as referencing *grib*, particularly at the vernacular register. In other words, *grib* is the generic term for pollution more widely understood by the laity.

209. RJYS, entry under *sgrib sbyong*. Texts of the preliminary practices will be examined in chapter two.

210. Huber, *Cult of Pure Crystal*, 17.

The verb *sel* requires active agency, that is, someone or something has to mediate the clearing away. The term *sgrib sel* is also an abbreviation of one the Buddha's closest eight disciples *sgrib pa rnam sel*, whose name could be glossed as "Completely Purified from Obscurations."[211]

A related term to *sgrib* is *zag pa*. As a verb, in its literal sense, *zag pa* means "to drop" or "to fall down." As a noun it can refer to excreta. In a technical Buddhist sense, the term means "harmful outflows"—things which defile the pristine primordial mind. Thus, the term is often glossed as "contamination" or "defilement." A related Buddhist term is *zag bcas* which also references defilement. There are four "outflows"—desire, belief in existence, ignorance, and wrong doctrines.[212] One of the terms for purification, or more precisely of having arrived at a purified state, is the negation *zag med*—the absence of outflows. The term *zad med* appears frequently in Buddhist texts to mean uncontaminated and unpolluted from the afflictions of samsaric existence.[213]

Purity Terms

Purity

The term *dag pa* means "clean," "pure," "pristine," or "free from any blemishes or stains." This term can be used to describe clean clothes after they have been washed and when a person has been cleansed from *grib*. There are four purified states (*dag pa bzhi*), which all Buddhas have attained—a pure body (*lus dag pa*), pure awareness (*dmigs pa dag pa*), a pure mind (*sems dag pa*) and pure wisdom (*ye shes dag pa*).[214] A related term *yang dag pa* has the sense of being "perfect," "completely clean," and "flawless," and can also mean "right," "correct," or "faultless." The term *yang dag pa* is used to qualify each of the characteristics of the eight-fold Buddhist path. Each aspect of the path—the right view, thought, speech, action, living, effort, mindfulness, and focus—is modified with *yang dag pa*. One could, based on the etymology, make a case that this path might also be understood as the "eight-fold path of purity." The closely related term *rnam par dag*

---

211. TDCM, 612 and ITED entry under *nye ba'i sras brgyad*.

212. TDCM, 2445.

213. Eva Natanya Rolf glosses this term as "immaculate," which is also an appropriate translation. Rolf, "Sacred Illusion," 10.

214. TDCM, 1237 and RJYS entry under *dag pa bzhi*.

pa means to be "completely clean or pure" and is the goal of the Buddhist practitioner, and naturally, the final state of an enlightened Buddha.[215] A commonly used term related to *rnam par dag pa* and *yang dag pa* is the term *dam pa* which means "sublime," "supreme," "holy," or "sacred." *dam pa* can be used to describe a lama or a teacher, a "sacred teaching" (*dam pa'i chos*), or the "highest truth" (*don dam*), and all enlightened beings are described as *dam pa*.[216]

The compound *dag ther* means to correct, rectify, or "clean up" a wrong way of thinking or behaving. A related compound *dag 'khrol* means to wipe away or wipe clean a grievance or difference or "wipe the slate clean."[217] Other cognates of *dag* include *dag yig* "pure letters" which refers to the correct spelling of literary Tibetan. The term *zhu dag* refers to proofreading and correcting a text, making it clean and pure. The related term *dag bcos* also means to correct the mistakes in a written text. The compound *dag 'bud* means to testify to the truth or to give true or "pure" testimony. The term *dag snang* "pure vision" is a technical Buddhist term which describes the tantric practice of changing one's perception to seeing everything as being innately pure.[218]

Purification

The verbs *dag* and *sel* are both used to describe the process of being cleansed from pollution and defilement. The distinction in meaning is that *sel* means to "clear away" or "remove" and *dag* means to "make clean." Both verbs are used in ceremonial, ritual, moral and ethical contexts. The compound *dag sel* means to have all impurities removed and to be made clean from all faults and defilements.[219] Both verbs are used to describe being purified from *grib*, *sgrib* and *sdig pa* (negativity or "sin"). A closely related term *byang ba* also means to be cleansed or made clean from filth, stains, and defilements but with the added element of being made whole, pure, or holy.[220]

---

215. The term *rnam par dag pa* is one of the main terms for "righteousness" in the Tibetan New Testament. *The New Testament– A Radiant Light to the Ends of the Earth*. See, for example, Romans 4:2.

216. TDCM, 1246, MTD, 898–99.

217. NTED, 524.

218. ITED, entry under *dag snang*.

219. TDCM, 1238.

220. MTB, 1313, ITED entry under *byang ba*, and RJYS entry under *byang ba*.

These terms are used in common expressions associated with performing religious deeds which help to cleanse or purify one's sins. For example, "If you do circumambulations, it will cleanse your sins" (*sdig pa dag*).[221] The everyday expression "I'm sorry" *dgongs dag* (mind + clean) is more literally a request by the speaker to the offended party to please clean their minds from the misdemeanor or harm that has just occurred. The expression *dgongs dag* also represents one way to ask for forgiveness.

Another term which denotes purification is *sbyong ba*. This active transitive verb typically means "to study" or "to train." In a religious context, it means "to purify," with the emphasis on the individual themselves working towards being purified, to make effort through correctly training the mind, meditation, and correct moral conduct. It is a term used frequently in Buddhist literature; for example, in the expression *sdig sgrib sbyong ba*—"purify [your] sins and obscurations." The term *sbyong ba* then contrasts to *dag*, *sel* and *byang* where there is typically an outside agency (for example water, incense or a qualified lama or shaman) responsible for facilitating cleansing. A related term is *sbyong gzhi* which means the "basis of purification", referencing both what needs to be purified and how to purify it.[222] A related term is *gso sbyong* ("restoring purification"), which refers to a ceremony that monks and nuns must perform in order to purify any violations of their monastic vows. It is a ceremony that is typically performed twice a month.[223] A related term is *sbyang chog* which is a tantric purification ritual for purifying evil deeds and obscurations particularly associated with purifying one's mind.

Another key term denoting cleansing and purification is the term *bsang*. As a verb *bsang* means "to cleanse," remove," "clean out," or "purify." It can be used in contexts of cleansing impurities such as *btsog grib* and for clearing away evil deeds and moral failings.[224] As such, it is similar in usage to the verb *sel*. As a noun, *bsang* refers to a smoke offering for the purposes of purification. This offering is the most common one Tibetans make. The term frequently occurs in religious texts to denote purification and cleansing through an offering of incense; it can also be referred to as purification through fumigation. The verbalized compound *bsang gtong*

221. NTED, 524. Also, "(He) is cleansing his sins by doing prostrations and circumambulations" (*phyag 'tshal skor sbyongs byas nas sdig pa 'byang gi yod pa red*), NTED, 766, and, "Sins and defilements will be cleansed" (*sdig sgrib 'byang bar 'gyur*), SCD, 923.

222. For further discussion of this term see Rolf, "Sacred Illusion," 74.

223. RJYS entry under *gso sbyong*, and ITED entry under *gso sbyong*.

224. TDCM, 3036.

refers to the action of burning incense, something most Tibetans do every day. The compound *bsang mchod* (also *bsang gsol*) refers to a fragrant smoke offering, typically from burning juniper. The related terms *bsangs chog* and *bsangs yig* refer to rituals and liturgies associated with offering *bsang*.[225] Most Tibetan houses have a *bsang khung*—incense burner. There is a particular *bsang* ceremony called *lha bsang* ("purifying gods") which is believed to be efficacious in purifying wrathful gods (*dra lha*) and local deities (*yul lha*).[226] There is an annual festival of making *bsang* offerings at sacred sites known as World Purification Day—*'dzam gling spyi bsang*. As the literature review has shown, Tibetans have a certain preoccupation with the practice of *bsang*.

The Purified State

The primary meaning of the very closely related term *sangs* (which is a homophone of *bsang*) means to have been cleansed or purified; it is the result of having gone through the process of cleansing or purification. This becomes more significant as this word forms the base for the Tibetan term for an enlightened Buddha *sangs rgyas*—which could be literally glossed as "purified-expanded" (*rgyas* means "extensive," "wide," or "expansive"). Among the many definitions provided for this term, such as "Enlightened One", "Fully Realized," and "Fully Awakened" (all of which are valid translations since *sangs* can also mean "to be awakened"), one of the underlying meanings is to have become completely purified. All major dictionaries list the first quality of an enlightened Buddha as having been cleansed or purified from all obscurations.[227] A closely related term is *byang chub* (purified

---

225. Note that the difference in spelling between *bsang* and *bsangs* (*bsangs* has a postsuffix *sa*) is one of aspect marking; *bsangs* is past tense, but can also be used, as here, in nominalized compounds. There is no difference in pronunciation.

226. TDCM, 3091.

227. RJYS under *sangs rgyas* lists, among the meanings, "purified from obscurations" and "eradicated all obscurations." See also ITED under *sang rgyas*, DGCM, 2028, TDCM, 2913 & TMD, 2086–87. The glossary of terms in the authoritative website *Translating the Words of Buddha* defines *sangs rgyas* as "purified and perfected." See entry g.86. Rolf discusses the primary meaning of *sangs rgyas* as referencing purity. See Rolf, "Sacred Illusion," 155–56, 268, 277–78. Kapstein, among others, also suggests the etymology allows for the term enlightenment to be viewed primary as a state of ultimate purity. See Kapstein, *Tibetan Buddhism*, 8. In my discussions with Tibetans about this term, they all agree that one of the main elements of enlightenment is to have become *rnam par dag pa*—completely purified.

+ understanding), which is typically glossed in English as "enlightenment." However, a more nuanced sense of the term means to have pure and complete understanding free from all flaws, defilements, stains and imperfections.[228] The term *byan chub* is the base root for the term *byang chub sems dpa'*—a Bodhisattva.[229]

Though the study of purity in Theravada Buddhism is not within the purview of this study, it is pertinent that in describing nirvana, the famous commentary, *The Path of Purification*, provides this definition: "Herein, *purification* should be understood as Nibbana, which being devoid of all stains, is utterly pure. *The path of purification* is the path to that purification; it is the means of approach that is called the path"[230] (italics in original). The term *sangs rgyas* then denotes an ultimate state free from all pollutions, stains, and afflictions of samsara. As previously mentioned, included in this ultimate state of *sangs rgyas* are the notions of being "stainless" *dri med* and "uncontaminated" *zag med*. As Bahr has suggested, purity concerns often animate "a future ideal condition worth the striving."[231]

Primordial Purity

The terms *ye dag* and *ka dag* express the concept of the primordial or innate purity of the mind, which exists in all humans but has been lost because of the afflictions of samsara.[232] The term *ka dag* could be glossed "alpha purity" because *ka* is the first letter of the Tibetan alphabet and communicates the idea of "first" or "original" purity. A related term is *dag pa rab 'byams* which means "universal" or "all-encompassing" purity. This is also considered to be the innate condition of the mind. This lost, innate purity

---

228. DGCM, 1471, MTD, 1269. One of the first definitions listed in RJYS is "purified and perfected," see RJYS entry under *byang chub*. SCD, also lists the first meaning as "purified and perfected", 883.

229. Note that the term *sems dpa'* (literally "heroic mind") refers to the resolution of pursuing enlightenment for the sake of others.

230. Buddhaghosa, *Path of Purification*, 6. Note that Nibbana is a transliteration from Pali. Though Dreyfus has suggested that the commentaries in Theravada do not carry as much weight as they do in Tibetan Buddhism (since they prioritize the Buddhist canon), this text is still significant and does provide further insights into a wider understanding of purity in Buddhism. Dreyfus, *Sound of Two Hands*, 109.

231. Bahr, "Purity," in *Brill Dictionary of Religion*, 1562.

232. *ka dag* is an abbreviation of *ka nas dag pa* and *ye dag* is also written as *gdod ma'i dag pa*—"purity from the very beginning."

needs to be restored through elaborate practices which will be explored in the following chapter.²³³

Pure Realms

There is a certain perception among Tibetans that Tibet itself was once a pure, pristine land, a *sa gtsang* (literally "pure land") free from polluting outside influences. Snellgrove and Richardson have traced this perception by documenting the expression *ri mtho sa gtsang* "high peaks pure land" in ancient documents.²³⁴ Michael Aris has further traced this expression to documents dating to the ninth century and notes that the expression is still found in Tibetans works published in the late twentieth century.²³⁵ There is also an idiomatic expression "pure earth pure stones" (*sa gtsang rdo gtsang*) which is used to describe that which is completely pure, unmixed (*bsres med*) or unadulterated (*lhad med*). This idiom is also used as an epithet for the land of Tibet.²³⁶

There are numerous realms that are considered pure places free from all defilements and the terms *dag* and *gtsang* are the primary cognates. A generic term for a pure realm is *gnas gtsang*. The heavenly pure realm of the gods is known as *gtsang ris lha gnas* and there are five pure level realms of the heavens (*gnas gtsang ma'i sa lnga*).²³⁷ The pure realm of a Buddha is known as *rnam dag pa'i zhing khams* (also *dag pa'i zhing khams, dag pa'i khams* and *dag zhing*), a realm which manifests the complete purity of a Buddha.²³⁸ The final three levels of a Bodhisattva's journey to enlightenment are known as the *dag pa sa gsum*—"the three pure places," so named because Bodhisattvas who dwell there have had all their pride completely purified.²³⁹ The pure Sukhāvatī realm of Pure Land Buddhism is known as *bde ba can*—the Land of Bliss, being the place Tibetans hope to arrive at

---

233. The notion of primordial purity was evident in cultures of the Ancient Near East, particularly among the Sumerians. See Frevel and Nihan, *Purity*, 22–23.

234. Snellgrove and Richardson, *Cultural History of Tibet*, 23–25.

235. In Michael Aris' Introduction to Richardson, *High Peaks, Pure Earth*, iii.

236. TMD, 2077, entry under *sa gtsang rdo gtsang*. Also, TDCM, 2904.

237. ITED, entry under *gnas gtsang ma*.

238. ITED, entry under *rnam dag pa'i zhing khams*.

239. TDCM, 1237, RJYS and ITED entries under *dag pa sa gsum*.

after escaping from samsara. This land is also known as the Lotus Mound (*pad ma btsheg*), with the lotus flower symbolic of purity.[240]

Symbolic Terms for Purity

For Tibetans, the color white is symbolic of purity and the color black of impurity. White scarfs (*kha rtags*), white lotus flowers (*pad ma dkar po*) and white conch shells (*dung dkar*) all symbolize purity. Lhamo Pemba states, "Black and white: Symbolizes impurity and purity, respectively. Expressions like a black dog, a crow, and coal personify impurity. On the other hand, a white dzo, a white felicity scarf, a conch shell represent purity."[241] The term for vegetarian food is *dkar zas* "white food" with the associated meaning of being "pure" and "clean." "White food" typically refers to milk, yogurt, and cheese. The negative term *dkar min* "not white" refers to things that are evil, sinful, and impure. In an annual festival (*dkar rtsi dus chen*), whitewash is splashed on houses and buildings as a cleansing, purifying, and protective agent and for merit accrual. There is the tradition of putting white handprints (*dkar rtags rgyag pa*) on the walls of houses just prior to the new year in order to usher in good luck for the coming year. The compound *dkar gtsang* (white + clean) denotes the color "pure white" and is used to describe things that are pure and without blemish.[242] Traditionally, when a shaman conducted a divination, he wore white clothes symbolic of being cleansed and pure and thus more efficacious. Shamans were given the name "white-clothed-one"—*gos dkar lcang lo can* (also *gos bkar can*).[243] One of the four goddesses, Pandura, is known as the "White Clad One" (*gso dkar mo*), symbolizing purity.

Water Ritual Purification Terms

The term *khrus* means "to wash" or "bathe," but also refers to a cleansing ritual involving water. The honorific term *khrus gsol* refers specifically to this ritual, a ritual which involves the sprinkling of water over polluted spaces and the recitation of particular liturgies and mantras. The term *khrus chog*

---

240. RJYS, entry under *bde ba can*.
241. Pemba, *Tibetan Proverbs*, xiii.
242. TDCM, 57.
243. TDCM, 376.

(wash + ritual) refers to a purification bath.²⁴⁴ A popular water purification ritual, mediated by a qualified lama, is known as *byabs khrus*. The verb *byabs* means to wipe clean or to wipe off dust or stains. The compound *byabs khrus* (wiping + wash) involves water being poured upon the heads of those polluted by *grib* while various mantras are chanted. Water which is drawn from a well early on the first day of the new year (*tse chu*) is considered auspicious because of its pure qualities and is considered a sign of good luck. More will be discussed about water rituals in chapter four.

Purity/Pollution Terms Summary

This discussion has shown that purity and pollution terms form a significant part of the Tibetan lexicon and are highly nuanced in meaning and application.²⁴⁵ These terms have both a ritual and moral aspect. Many of the terms are widely used in everyday life and across the strata of both monastics and laity. Other terms have technical Tibetan Buddhist meanings more relevant to the tantric practitioner. The language of purity rituals and symbols has been outlined, but the rituals and symbols themselves will be explored in more detail in chapters three and four. Some of the key terms for pollution are *grib, btsog, dri ma, sgrib* and *zag pa*, while some of the key terms for purity are *dag, sel, sbyong, dri med, zag med, bsang* and *sangs*. From this initial data, and as the literature review would seem to indicate, one could make the preliminary suggestion that purity forms a significant part of Tibetan consciousness; it informs their ontological self-perception, how they see the world and act within it. Purity would further appear to be an aspirational and desired state, as is rebirth in a pure realm.

Chapter One Summary

This chapter has provided an historical, religious, and literary context for the study at hand, as well as provided a semantic analysis of relevant Tibetan purity and pollution terms. Missionary efforts to Tibet faced numerous challenges and despite their best efforts, the early pioneers saw little

---

244. RJYS, entry under *khrus chog*.
245. By way of contrast, terms for shame and honor are more restricted with only a small number of lexical items. This does not mean that honor/shame (h/s) is not part of the cultural mix, nor that it is unimportant to Tibetan society (as indeed it is important) but rather is an observation about lexical richness and lexical weighting.

fruit. Tibetan Buddhism is a complex and eclectic system with a wide variety of texts, accumulated over many centuries, which form its religious corpus. The Tibetan written language has been uniformly preserved and the written word in Tibetan is considered sacred. Notions of purity and impurity draw upon a large lexicon of multivalent terms. A broad linguistic approach of studying words both as they relate to the larger corpus and to extra-linguistic cultural understandings will frame the semantic analysis of the Tibetan texts. Understandings of purity will be studied from a religious, cosmological, and soteriological perspective, based on the discussion in this chapter. The study will now proceed to explore selected monastic texts dealing with purity and orthopraxis in Tibetan Buddhism, and which exhibit lexical content germane to purity.

2
Monastic Texts of Praxis

Introduction

THIS CHAPTER WILL EXPLORE purity as revealed in selected Tibetan scriptures and sacred texts. The focus will be monastic texts of praxis (*sgrub thabs*, Sk. sadhana) associated with purity which have been taught and practiced over the centuries. Though the term *sgrub thabs* can refer to specific tantric and yogic practices, the term will be applied more broadly to refer to texts of monastic practice. To be more specific, this chapter will examine confessional (*gso sbyong*), preliminary (*sngon 'gro*), and purification (*rnam par dag pa*) tantra texts of praxis. The purification tantra texts will focus on the deity Vajrasattva (*rdo rje sems ba*) and the associated *sgrub thabs* or orthopraxis. These texts are embedded in the larger genres of sutra (*mdo*), tantra (*rgyud*), and incantation (*gzungs*) texts. These texts of praxis have been selected for analysis because it would appear that they most clearly reveal Tibetan notions of purity, as opposed to, for example, the texts of philosophical treatises *(bstan bcos)*. As these texts of praxis are still followed today, they are of contemporary relevance.

The texts analyzed here represent a small sample of extant texts available. As this synchronic study seeks to gain a broad overview of notions of purity, the approach employed has been to investigate a range of texts rather than a deep dive into only one or two. The texts examined are reflective of purity praxis widely held across all schools of Tibetan Buddhism. There appears to be no sectarian view of purity and these conceptualizations of purity and purification orthopraxis are generic to all lineages.[1] The texts also represent those in current use in monastic communities.

Though the focus of this chapter is monastic texts, this does not mean these texts are the exclusive domain of monks and removed from the domain of laity consciousness. Over the centuries, certain monastic texts, with the exception of esoteric tantras which require privileged access, have been exposed to the laity in public readings, teachings, festivals, and rituals. This preservation and exposure have thus impacted lay beliefs and orthopraxis. As mentioned in the introduction to Tibetan Buddhism, the dichotomy between the monastics and the laity is not a fixed one, rather it is blurred. Many Tibetans have copies of sacred texts in their homes, even if they cannot read them. It is common for householders, given certain circumstances, for example, illness or death, to invite monks to their house in order to read a particular scripture. The laity are also familiar with the major lamas and deities within the Tibetan pantheon. The vast majority of households have a shrine or altar room with images and statues of saints and deities. While this chapter carries the title "monastic texts," it should not be assumed that their influence and notoriety are only among monastic communities.[2] Furthermore, many of the sacred texts, in either a traditional Tibetan scripture *dpe cha* form or a modern book, can be purchased from monasteries and bookstores throughout Tibetan areas, and in recent years many are now accessible through digital online sources.[3] However, the main difference could be summed up this way: the laity have a general level of devotion and awareness of the deities mentioned in the texts that

---

1. In the foreword to the translation of Patrul's *Kunzan Lama'i Shelung*, a text which contains some definitive teachings on purity, Dilgo Khyenste Rinpoche maintains that the text "sets out the paths of the four main schools of Tibetan Buddhism without any conflict between them." xxviii. In Yeshe, *Becoming Vajrasattva*, which examines the definitive Vajrasattva text on purity, Lama Thubten Yeshe claims that the teaching and practice is "common to all four traditions of Tibetan Buddhism—Nyingma, Kagyu, Sakya, and Geluk—where it is used to purify obstacles, obscurations, negative karma, and illness." x.

2. To be clear, this dissertation is not attempting to measure the influence of monastic texts upon the laity, but rather notes, as an observation in passing, (and one which was discussed in the introduction to Tibetan Buddhism in chapter one) the historical and continuing interplay between monks and the laity. The observation here is that monastic texts dealing with purity and orthopraxis have had a greater influence beyond monastic communities.

3. There are currently more than two hundred indigenous Tibetan websites which house copious amounts of texts.

will be explored in this section, but the specialized tantric practices largely remain the domain of monastic communities and initiated practitioners.

As a generalization, Western culture has a bias towards that which is new or "the latest." This also holds true for Western scholarship—we are typically attracted to the date something was published and the more recent, the better. This value is not necessarily shared by Tibetans. For them, and other cultures with long, well-preserved histories, the older something is, the more it is valued and esteemed. Likewise, the elderly have a higher esteem than they enjoy in Western societies. This veneration of that which is old can be seen in the following proverbs: "Better are the ways of the elderly than the vigor of the young"[4] and, "As steps descend from a stupa, so instruction is from old to young."[5] The image of a stupa is insightful because contained inside a stupa, as well as the ashes of esteemed lamas and ancient relics, there are copies of ancient sacred texts. The image portrayed in this proverb is that of the ancient traditions, and the ageless wisdom of the texts, as being the teachers and guides for the young. Just as steps come down from a stupa, so this wealth of knowledge and tradition descends from time immemorial to the current generation. In the monastic tradition, one can see a very deliberate and careful preservation and transmission of ancient texts and teachings. Thus, many of the texts discussed in this chapter are ancient texts (certainly by contemporary Western standards), that have stood the test of time, and are still in circulation and mainstream consciousness among both the monastics and laity today.[6]

The majority of primary sources that will be analyzed in this chapter have been taken from these websites: Buddhist Digital Resource Center, The Buddhist Canons Research Database, Translating the Words of Buddha, Adarsha and Lotsawa House. Texts on these websites have been well preserved. Tibetan texts and commentaries that appear in published books have also been consulted. In terms of the Kangyur, a certain priority has

---

4. Pemba, *Tibetan Proverbs*, 181, and Hor Khang, *Bod kyi dtam dpe*, 361. Another proverb concerning the veneration of the aged is "One must obey the words of the elderly, just as one must observe the flavor of delicious tea." Hor Khang, *Bod kyi dtam dpe*, 296.

5. Hor Khang, *Bod kyi dtam dpe*, 453.

6. For example, the works of Tsong Khapa (among many others), written in the fourteenth century are still studied and recited today, being the core of the Gelukpa tradition. Likewise, the Nyingmapa and other schools still adhere to texts of yore. Sonam Tsering claims this of Tsong Khapa's influence: "The works of Tsongkhapa remain central to Gelukpa spirituality" and "his writings have been studied and transmitted in unbroken continuity to this day." S. Tsering, "Role of Texts," 333.

been given to the Dege Kangyur because of the completeness of the corpus and the authoritative weight it seems to carry, and to the Lhasa Kangyur, which is likewise another authoritative corpus of the Buddhist canon in Tibetan. For this study, a primary source is considered to be the Tibetan text itself, Tibetan commentaries about a text, and the writings of contemporary Tibetan lamas and Rinpoches, including the Dalai Lama, who may have given teachings on these texts.

Confessional Texts

The first selection of texts to be analyzed are those from the broad genre of confessional texts. One genre of confessional texts is known as *gso sbyong* (Sk. poshadha) which means "to restore and purify." These texts form an essential part of the practice of a monk or nun, being used frequently as part of their restoration and purification practice. In a general sense, this practice is not unique to Tibetan Buddhism since monks and nuns of all persuasions throughout Asia engage in such confessional ceremonies. In the Gelukpa system, fully ordained monks take a set of two hundred and fifty-three vows and nuns three hundred and sixty-four. The five most important vows are not to kill, steal, engage in sexual misconduct, lie, or use intoxicants.[7] The confessional texts are the basis of monthly or biweekly confessional sessions where monks and nuns confess their short comings and any breakages of their vows, and seek purification and restoration. The practice of confession is thus a regular part of monastic life.

These confessional texts fit within the broad category in the Kangyur of the *bdul ba* (Sk. Vinaya) or monastic "moral discipline" texts. The broader categorization is that the confessionals are considered texts of praxis in that they follow a prescribed set of practices. The lengthy outline for the prescribed practices of confessions is found in the discipline text *gso sbyong gi gzhi—The Basis for Restoration and Purification*.[8] However, the primary confessional text in Tibetan Buddhism is *The Confession of Downfalls of the Bodhisattva* (*chang chub sems dpa'i ltung ba bshags pa*).[9] Attention will now be turned to this text.

---

7. Lopez, "Rite for Restoring," 387.

8. See *Adarsha*: Vinaya under section *gso sbyong gi gzhi 'chad pa*. There are thirteen volumes of Vinaya in the Lhasa Kangyur and twenty-four texts in the Dege Kangyur.

9. The term "confession" (*bshags pa*) means "laying aside," "to put something down," or "to put to one side," and in some cases "to abandon something." Though glossed as

The Confession of Downfalls of the Bodhisattva

Though this text is considered to be a confessional text, its place within the Kangyur canon is in the sutra section (*mdo sde*) and is also known by the name, *The Sutra of the Three Heaps* (*phung po gsum pa'i mdo*).[10] Nagarjuna (*klu sgrub*), a great Indian master of Buddhism, who lived during the second to third centuries AD, in his commentary on the *Three Heaps*, suggested that the classification of this text, though it has been placed in the sutra "basket," technically is a text of moral discipline (*'dul ba*, Sk. Vinaya) and should be categorized as such.[11] Though the text, being a sutra, is an exoteric text available to all, it has also become widely used in the more esoteric tantric practices, particularly the preliminary practices which are necessary in order to progress to tantric yoga. The confession itself forms part of the *Three Heaps* sutra and was later popularized as the *Confession of Downfalls of the Bodhisattva*, which then became in itself one of the premier confessional and purification texts.[12] The background to the sutra is that during a certain time some 2,500 years ago, when thirty-five of Buddha's disciples, who had each taken the vow of a Bodhisattva, were collecting alms, they accidentally caused the death of a child. One of the disciples then asked the Buddha how to confess and purify what they had done. In reply, the Buddha spoke out this sutra and, as he did so, thirty-four other

---

"confession," the term does not correspond with the notion of confession in the Christian sense of acknowledging one's sin before a holy God. There is another, separate genre of confessional texts known as *bshags pa*, but these do not appear to be as widely known or used as the general confessional texts of *gso sbyong*. The classification of Tibetan texts and their placement in the Kangyur or Tengyur is a matter of ongoing discussion and tension. As mentioned in the introduction, this research does not seek to get bogged down in such matters. For more on the complexities of textual classifications and doxography see Eimer and Germano, *Many Canons*; Dalton, "Crisis of Doxography." Though the systematic codification of texts is an important issue, the focus of this study is the analysis of extant texts still in current use which have been foundational in Tibetan consciousness in the formation of notions of purity, rather than how the texts are classified and where they are placed within the corpus.

10. In the Lhasa Kangyur, the text is placed in the sutra section (*mdo sde*), volume zha. See Tibetan Works. The full title is *'phags pa phung po gsum pa zhes bya ba theg pa chen po'i mdo*—*The Exalted Mahayana Sutra of the Three Heaps*. In the Dege Kangyur it is also placed in the sutra section, Toh 284.

11. Nagarjuna, "Explanation of the Confessions," 8.

12. Such is the popularity of this text that is also well-known in Tibetan by the abbreviated form *ltung ba*—"Downfalls."

Buddhas appeared around him and light emanated from his body.[13] The disciples then paid homage to all thirty-five Buddhas through prostrations and offerings, confessed their sin, reaffirmed their vows, and took refuge in the Buddhas surrounding them.

An Exposition of The Confession of Downfalls of the Bodhisattva

Turning to the text itself, after beginning with taking refuge in one's lama, the Buddha, the dharma and the sangha, each of the thirty-five Buddhas are then individually named and paid homage to with prostration—*phyag 'tshal lo*, the words which conclude each of the thirty-five lines of homage.[14] Of relevance here is that homage is paid to, among others, the Buddhas "Stainless One" (*dri ma med pa*, Sk. Vimala), "Pure One" (*tshangs pa*, Sk. Brahma), and "Bestowed with Purity" (*tshangs pas byin*, Sk. Brahmadatta). In his commentary of this text, Nagarjuna suggests the name Stainless "indicates his pristine awareness without obscurations" and that he has "the ability to make others stainless." The role of the Pure One, he suggests, is "to purify since he cleanses all sentient beings from cyclic existence" and to cleanse because "he cleanses both himself and others."[15] In his commentary on the *Confession of Downfalls*, Sanggye Yeshe (*sangs rgyas ye shes*, 1525–1591), the celebrated Gelukpa monk, lists the benefits associated with prostrating to each one of the thirty-five Buddhas individually. For example, prostrating to the Pure One "purifies the negativities motivated by attachment" and prostrating to Bestowed with Purity "purifies the

---

13. Though the legend surrounding the origins of the context to the *Sutra of the Three Heaps* suggests that the thirty-five disciples of Buddha had taken the vows of a Bodhisattva, this may be anachronistic because the system of Bodhisattva's did not develop until much later, well after the time of Buddha Shakyamuni. (See Wolf, "Mahayana Moment," 1–35). This has likely occurred during the process of the *Sutra of the Three Heaps* becoming popularized as *The Confessions of the Downfalls of a Bodhisattva* and thus the origin story of the text was reinterpreted through a Bodhisattva framework.

14. This text is the version used predominantly by the Nyingma school and is an excerpt from the sutra *Ascertaining the Discipline: The Sutra of Upali's Questions* (*'dul ba rnam par gtan la dbab pa nye bar 'khor gyis zhus pa*). I also consulted *The Exalted Mahayana Sutra of the Three Heaps* (*'phags Pa Phung Po Gsum Pa*). There were no major differences between the other Tibetan texts I examined. Other Tibetan versions consulted were the text in the Appendices of G. J. Gyatso, *Purification in Tibetan Buddhism*, Kindle location 1853–56, as well as the version in the Lhasa Kangyur cited earlier.

15. Nagarjuna, "Explanation of the Confessions," 16.

negativities of ten thousand eons."[16] Sanggye Yeshe goes on to add that "reciting or remembering the names of these tathagatas one time purifies the negativities of countless eons."[17] The commentaries of Nagarjuna, Sanggye Yeshe, Geshe Kelsang Gyatso and Lama Zopa Rinpoche, each list the names of the thirty five Buddhas along with their specific purification ability.[18] In short, they suggest that collectively the Buddhas can purify all negativities and moral defilement accumulated over many eons. But what is it that one is exactly being purified from? The text itself makes that explicit.

After the homages are complete, the text then introduces the first-person pronoun, inviting reciters to personally self-identify (by saying their name out aloud) with the list of short-comings, sins, negativities, and misappropriations that follow.[19] This list includes all of the negativities one has done and rejoiced in doing in this samsaric cyclical existence and previous existences. More specifically, the list includes committing the five inexpiable sins (*mtshams med pa lnga*),[20] the ten non-virtues (*mi dge ba bcu*),[21] and being veiled by the polluting obscurations of karma (*las kyi*

---

16. Sanggye Yeshe, *A Significant Sight: An Explanation of the Bodhisattva's Confession of Downfalls* (*byang chub sems dpa'i ltung ba shags pa'i don ldan ces bya ba bzhugs so*) in G. J. Gyatso, *Purification in Tibetan Buddhism*, Kindle location 734.

17. Sanggye Yeshe, *A Significant Sight* in G. J. Gyatso, *Purification in Tibetan Buddhism*, Kindle location 759. Note that the Sanskrit term *tathagatas* is an epithet of a Buddha. The term has been translated into Tibetan as *de bzhin bshegs pa* which can be glossed as "One Thus Gone," meaning one who has left samsara and been liberated into nirvana.

18. Nagarjuna, "Explanation of the Confessions," 13–22; Sanggye Yeshe, *A Significant Sight*, in G. J. Gyatso, *Purification in Tibetan Buddhism*, Kindle location 734–59, G. K. Gyatso, *Bodhisattva Vow*, 57–59; L. Z. Rinpoche, *Preliminary Practice of Prostrations*, Kindle location 828–920.

19. That is, "I (insert name) confess to the following." This formula is common in other texts of praxis which will be explored in following sections.

20. Of relevance is that these five sins, which, without being purified, if indeed they actually can be, lead straight to hell, include the serious polluting sins (mentioned in the Purity Terms section of chapter one) of patricide (*pha bsad pa*) and matricide (*ma bsad pa*), as well as the killing of a Bodhisattva (*dgra bcom pa bsad pa*), causing a schism in the sangha (*dge 'dun gyi dbyen byas pa*), and drawing blood from a Tathagata with evil intent (*de bzhin gshegs pa la ngan sems kyis khrag phyung ba*). The term *mtshams med* more literally means "without a boundary, interval or pause" meaning there is no interval in the intermediate state after death in *bar do*, where one's next reincarnation is determined. Rather, if one has committed any of these five sins, one goes immediately to hell. (Note that the term *dgra bcom pa*, in the third vice listed above, more literally means "Overcomer of Enemies" and is an epithet of Bodhisattvas and Buddhas.)

21. The ten non-virtues, which are essentially the negation of the ten virtues, are: 1.

sgrib).²² The section concludes with an open confession in the presence of all the Buddhas, and a pledge not to commit any of these misdeeds henceforth. The final section of the text is a resolution and vow that any future virtuous actions, no matter how great or small, will be dedicated to the sublime and perfectly complete attainment of purified enlightenment. The text concludes with a final confession, praise to the Buddhas, and the taking of refuge in the thirty-five Buddhas.

The Practice of the Confession of Downfalls

The reference to the "three heaps" (*phung po gsum*), in the alternative title, *The Three Heaps Sutra*, is perhaps suggestive of the structure of the text itself. Geshe Kelsang Gyatso (1932–2007) claims the three heaps refer to "three 'heaps' or collections of virtue: prostration, purification, and dedication."²³ Geshe Ngawang Dhargyey and Thupten Zopa Rinpoche suggest, "The first of the 'Three Heaps' is the heap of confession, the second, dedication, and third, rejoicing."²⁴ Sanggye Yeshe claims the three are indicative of "the heap of confessing negativities, the heap of dedicating virtues, and the heap of rejoicing."²⁵ In any case, as outlined above, there is a natural structure to the text of homage, confession, and dedication. It is this structure which represents how the practice of the *Confession of Downfalls* is to be undertaken.

It is not sufficient to merely recite this confession; one must prostrate before the thirty-five Buddhas, clearly visualize and meditate upon them, sincerely confess and regret one's past actions, and promise to dedicate any future virtuous actions to the pursuit of enlightenment.²⁶ This fourfold approach is known as the "four powers of the antidotes" (*gnyen po'i stobs*

---

taking a life (*srog gcod pa*), 2. theft (*ma byin len pa*), 3. sexual misconduct (*'dod log spyod pa*), 4. lying (*rdzun du smra ba*), 5. divisive speech (*phra ma*), 6. harsh words (*tshig rtsub*), 7. gossip (*ngag kyal*), 8. covetousness (*brnab sems*), 9. harmful intentions (*gnod sems*), 10. wrong views (*log lta*).

22. Geshe Kelsang Gyatso in his commentary on this text elaborates further on the downfalls (though they do not appear in the text itself) listing forty-six secondary downfalls and eighteen primary or "root" downfalls. G. K. Gyatso, *Bodhisattva Vow*, 14–26, 27–33.

23. G. K. Gyatso, *Bodhisattva Vow*, 45.

24. Geshe Ngawang Dhargyey and Thupten Zopa Rinpoche, *An Explanation of the Practice of the Sutra of Three Heaps*, in Beresford, *Confession of Downfalls*, 16.

25. G. J. Gyatso, *Purification in Tibetan Buddhism*, Kindle location 1553.

26. A *thangkha* of the thirty-five Buddhas is often used in the visualization process.

bzhi),²⁷ and is elaborated upon in many of the commentaries. These powers, which are typically used in confessional practices for the laying aside of moral transgressions, are:

1. The power of reliance (*rten gyi stobs*) by visualizing the appropriate deities.
2. The power of total repudiation of one's misdeeds (*rnam par sun 'byin pa'i stobs*) by confession and profound regret.
3. The power of turning away from one's wrongs (*nyes pa las slar ldog pa'i stobs*) through renewing vows and rededication.
4. The power of all the antidotes (*gnyen po'i kun tu spyod pa'i stobs*) through prostrations and reciting mantras.²⁸

This fourfold practice requires the guidance and direction of a trusted lama or guru, one whom the practitioner has given his or her complete allegiance.²⁹ This approach is also used in preliminary tantric practices, particularly those associated with the deities Vajrasattva and Heruka. The current Dalai Lama is likewise an exponent of the four antidotes, vouching for their efficacy in this way: "When an individual goes through a process of purifying the mind by applying the antidotes to the mental afflictions,

---

27. See TDCM, 984 and ITED entry under *gnyen po'i stobs bzhi*. This technical Buddhist term is also glossed as the "four opponent powers" meaning the four powers one should use to oppose and deal with one's negativities. However, the term "antidote" in English seems to better capture the meaning and follows the recurrent metaphor in the Kangyur of sentient beings afflicted with endless cyclical existence who require the antidote of the Buddha's teachings.

28. Geshe Kelsang Gyatso and Geshe Jampa Gyatso, among others, have varying forms of how to practice the power of the four antidotes, but the essence is similar. See G. J. Gyatso, *Purification in Tibetan Buddhism*, Kindle location 317–57, and G. K. Gyatso, *Bodhisattva Vow*, 61–73.

29. The first line of the text begins with paying homage to one's lama. This is standard practice in deity yoga (*bla ma'i rnal 'byor*) where one imagines one's lama to be the actual deity of the particular meditational practice. In some practices of this confession, prostrations to the seven medicine Buddhas (*sman bla bdun*) is performed after prostrating to the thirty-five Buddhas. This is typically at the discretion of one's lama, is not part of the main practice, and is less common. The Seven Medicine Buddha sadhana is also used as a purification practice. There is a further Medicine Buddha sadhana (*sangs rgyas sman bla*). To complicate things, there are a total of eight Medicine Buddhas (*sman bla bde gshegs brgyad*), ITED, entry under *sman bla bde gshegs brgyad*, TDCM, entry under *bde gshegs mched brgyad*, 1369.

over time, the mind becomes totally free of all these obscurations. The emptiness of this undefiled mind is the *true nirvana* or liberation."[30]

It is not sufficient to recite this confession only once or practice the four powers of the antidotes only once. These four must be performed repeatedly and earnestly to be effective, but particularly the aspect of regret needs to be emphasized. Lama Zopa Rinpoche, among others, has suggested that "the stronger the regret, the greater the purification."[31] The great yoga master of the eleventh century, Milarepa, is alleged to have said, "When I examined whether or not confessions could purify the negativities, I found that it is regret that cleanses them."[32] Celebrated monk and scholar, Shantideva (*zhi ba lha*), in his highly regarded eight-century classic, a text still studied and revered today, *A Guide to the Bodhisattva's Way of Life*, proposed that,

> Three times during the day and the night
> I should recite The Sutra of the Three Heaps;
> For by relying upon the Buddhas and the Awakening Mind
> My remaining downfalls will be purified.[33]

Nagarjuna suggested that for heinous actions "you should, without any break, apply the four forces of confession with extremely strong regret for months or years" and for lesser evil actions six sessions a day for six months, or at a bare minimum three times a day for a week.[34]

The question may be rightly asked as to how does one know if one has been purified? What are the signs of purification? The text itself does not answer that question, but the commentaries offer numerous suggestions. Sanggye Yeshe, along with others, claims the purification signs will occur in dreams. For example, dreams of vomiting bad food, of drinking the pure food of yogurt and milk, or of visualizing the sun or moon or a blazing fire.[35] Geshe Jampa Gyatso adds that dreaming of wearing white clothes is

---

30. The Dalai Lama, *Essence of the Heart Sutra*, Kindle location 1561; italics original.

31. L. Z. Rinpoche, *Preliminary Practice of Prostrations*, Kindle location 167. He also claims that the purification process is more powerful if, along with visualizing the thirty-five Buddhas, the color white is also visualized. Kindle location 511. The color white, of course, being symbolic of purity.

32. The Dalai Lama, *Complete Foundation*, Kindle location 881. The term "regret" (*'gyod pa*) should not be equated with the Christian concept of guilt. There is no direct equivalent for the term "guilt," as in guilty before a holy God for one's transgressions, and the concept of a "guilty conscience" is not attested to.

33. Shantideva, *Guide to the Bodhisattva*, 48, stanza 98.

34. Nagarjuna, "Explanation of the Confessions," 9.

35. G. J. Gyatso, *Purification in Tibetan Buddhism*, Kindle location 1572.

a clear sign of purification.³⁶ Geshe Ngawang Dhargyey and Thupten Zopa Rinpoche further add to the list of dreams with, among others, dreams of flying through the sky, overcoming figures dressed in black, and riding a horse or elephant as sure signs of having been purified. They further suggest that "a clearer indication of successful purification is your intelligence becoming sharper, enabling you to penetrate into deeper subjects with increased comprehension."³⁷ The second Dalai Lama (*rgyal ba dge 'dun rgya mtsho*, 1475–1542), in his *Treatise on the Six Yogas of Niguma* (*ni gu chos drug rgyas pa khrid yid*), a text which also contains a significant purification practice, suggests that "as a sign of purification of negativity and obscurations, one dreams of flying through the sky" and "the sign of purification on hindrances and evil spirits is that one dreams of many insects being driven out of one's body."³⁸

Commentaries on *The Confession of Downfalls*

Though some of the commentaries on this text have been mentioned already, it is worth further noting that Tibetan masters who have written on this text are effusive in their praise and in the perceived efficacy of this confessional practice. Indeed, the great Tsong Khapa himself strongly endorsed this confessional practice and is alleged to have performed 100,000 prostrations to each of the thirty-five Buddhas, which equates to 3.5 million prostrations.³⁹ Geshe Kelsang Gyatso, in his commentary on this text, exhorts the reader: "We should make use of this precious opportunity to purify our negative karma . . . Since purification is the root of future happiness and spiritual realizations, we should strive to cleanse our minds of

---

36. G. J. Gyatso, *Purification in Tibetan Buddhism*, Kindle location 1572.

37. Beresford, *Confession of Downfalls*, 50.

38. Mullin, *Dalai Lamas on Tantra*, 109. In my experience over the years, Tibetans are highly sensitive to dreams. They have often told me what they have dreamt about on a previous evening. Periodically, they have dreams about myself and my family. If they felt uneasy about the dream, they would contact us to make sure that nothing untoward had happened. On many occasions when visiting friends, they would often say that they had recently dreamt about us. One of my closest colleagues, who frequently shared his dreams with me, considers the most auspicious dream possible is to dream that one is flying through the sky.

39. Beresford, *Confession of Downfalls*, 50; G. J. Gyatso, *Purification in Tibetan Buddhism*, Kindle location 96.

delusions and negative karma by engaging in the practice of the *Sutra of the Three Superior Heaps*."[40]

Geshe Jampa Gyatso's book, *Purification in Tibetan Buddhism*, which provides some additional commentary to Sanggye Yeshe's sixteenth-century commentary, is solely devoted to the *Confessions of Downfalls* and examines no other purification text. Likewise, Kelsang Gyatso in his book, *The Bodhisattva Vow: The Essential Practices of Mahayana Buddhism*, also only includes the *Confessions of Downfalls* and no other text. One could perhaps conclude that this indicates the importance of this text in the purification schema of the monastic system. Convinced of the efficacy of this confessional text and practice, Geshe Jampa Gyatso states,

> Therefore, just as we clean our dirty clothes with soap and water, we need to purify our mental continuum of non-virtuous actions of body, speech, and mind. To avoid experiencing their unpleasant results, it is vital that we develop the habit of regularly purifying our inner dirt, the impure mind. For this purpose, we engage in a practice of purification such as The Bodhisattva's Confession of Downfalls. When this practice is done in conjunction with the application of the four opponent forces, not only will we purify the non-virtuous actions committed in this life, we will also purify those committed during all our beginningless lives in cyclic existence.[41]

Though originally conceived as a text for the purification and restoration of those who had taken the vows of a Bodhisattva, the text grew in popularity and became used as a general confessional text for all who had committed evil conduct in this life and for the bad karma accumulated in previous lives. The semantic sense of the purification term (*dag*) used in this text, is that of being cleansed and made clean from the stains of samsara and human misdemeanors. The clear focus is on the moral conduct of the practitioner and the necessary foundational step of purification in the process of leading to the ultimate purified state of enlightenment. This confessional continues to be an essential daily practice and, along with Vajrasattva, is used in preliminary practices prior to progressing to the tantric practices of guru and deity yoga. More will be discussed about Vajrasattva in a following section.

---

40. G. K. Gyatso, *Bodhisattva Vow*, 45.
41. G. J. Gyatso, *Purification in Tibetan Buddhism*, Kindle location 242–47.

The Essence of the Practice for Restoring and Purifying the Three Vows

The next confessional text, *The Essence of the Practice for Restoring and Purifying the Three Vows* (*sdom pa gsum gyi gso sbyong gi cho ga mdor bsdus snying por dril ba bzhugs so*)[42] is attributed to the Tibetan master Dudjom Rinpoche (*bdud 'joms 'jigs bral ye shes rdo rje*, 1904–1987). Dudjom Rinpoche was a revered figure throughout Tibet and later in life became highly respected among the diaspora. He was considered to be the incarnate lama of the great Guru Rinpoche (Sk. Padmasambhava). Like Padmasambhava, Dudjom Rinpoche was also a treasure revealer (*gter ston*) and became a prolific writer composing over forty volumes.[43] Though he was an incarnation of the Nyingma lineage, his teachings were widely accepted across all four schools of Tibetan Buddhism. The text being analyzed here is no exception in that regard. As the title suggests, his confessional text is considered an essential practice in restoring the three general vows of a Buddhist monk. These three vows, which are sets of vows or a particular class of vows, are:

1. The vows of individual liberation (*so sor thar pa'i sdom pa*), these being the vows of the Hinayana.

2. The vows of pursuing the mind of a Bodhisattva (*byang chub sems kyi sdom pa*), these being the vows of the Mahayana.

3. The vows of secret mantra (*gsang sngags kyi sdom pa*), these being the vows of the Vajrayana.[44]

These vows reflect a progression from the general vow of individual liberation of Hinayana, to the more specific vow of pursuing enlightenment for the sake of others of Mahayana, and the final specialized secret mantra "fast track" vow of enlightenment of Vajrayana.

---

42. bDud 'joms, *sDom pa gsum*.

43. D. Rinpoche, *Nyingma School*, xxv–xxvi.

44. TDCM, 1481, ITED entry under *sdom pa gsum*, and RJYS entry under *sdom pa gsum*.

An Exposition of *The Essence of the Practice for Restoring and Purifying the Three Vows*

The text opens with a paragraph of exhortation addressed to the practitioner prior to undertaking the practice. Here Dudjom Rinpoche outlines that the most important practice for those who have set out on the path and broken their vows is to purify or clean out (*sbyong*) any shortcomings through the practice that follows. Before doing this practice, however, Dudjom Rinpoche strongly recommends reciting the previous text, the *Confession of Downfalls of the Bodhisattva*. After that is completed, he then suggests to arrange as many offerings as one can afford and to take refuge in one's lama and the victorious Buddha.[45]

Dudjom Rinpoche does not include any specific homage or refuge but moves directly into a renewal of the vows not to commit any unwholesome actions and to pursue virtue. He then reminds the practitioner of the interconnection between the vows of the body, mind, and speech (*lus yid ngag gi sdom pa*). This is followed by a thirty-nine-syllable mantra incantation which is in Sanskrit (as are all mantras and incantations), the recitation of which acts as invocation for, or a summoning of, the attainment of pure moral discipline (*tshul khrim rnam dag*). Dudjom Rinpoche recommends reciting this mantra at least twenty-one times or as many times as one can. This is then followed by a prayer of aspiration that one's moral discipline may be free from any flaws, devoid of pride, and become completely pure (*rnam par dag dang ldan*). After another resolution to follow in the ways of all the Buddhas, and pursue pure and flawless conduct and discipline, the text then invites the practitioner to restore and cleanse their vows of Bodhicitta (*byang chub kyi sems*), that is, of having the mind of a Bodhisattva to pursue enlightenment for the sake of all beings, as much as one is able, through the seven-branch offering (*yan lag bdun*) of confession and dedication. The text then works through each of the seven branches.

This seven-branch offering of dedication, which is also performed in many other practices, and is considered to represent a complete session of devotion and worship, is as follows:

1. The branch of prostration (*phyag thsal ba'i yan lag*)
2. The branch of offering (*mchod pa'i yan lag*)

---

45. No indication in the text is given as to the type of offering but grain, rice, and fruit are typical offerings.

3. The branch of confession/laying aside (*bshags pa'i yan lag*)
4. The branch of rejoicing (*rjes su yi rang ba'i yan lag*)
5. The branch of urging the turning of the wheel of dharma (*chos kyi 'khor lo bskor bar bskul ba'i yan lag*)[46]
6. The branch of supplicating Bodhisattvas not to enter nirvana (*mya ngan las mi 'da' bar gsol ba gdab pa'i yan lag*)[47]
7. The branch of dedicating virtue to complete enlightenment (*dge ba rdzogs byang du bsngo ba'i yan lag*)[48]

These seven branches are also known as the "seven limbs" and are used in other preliminary or meditational practices. The current Dalai Lama, among others, has further elaborated on the practices of the seven branches. He notes that, "The seven parts of the practice are encompassed by two practices—the purification of negativities and the enhancing of the store of merit."[49]

Working through each of these seven branches, the text elaborates on the expressions of worship to be recited in each of the branches. Space does not permit a full explanation, but in essence each branch is to be performed with sincere devotion with the object in each case being the sublime Buddhas. The text then concludes with an invocation to Vajrasattva and the recitation of his one hundred syllable mantra. The practitioner is again encouraged to recite the mantra as many times as possible and to visualize the Buddha Vajrasattva. The final line of the text is a supplication to all lamas and tutelary deities (*bla ma yi dam lha tshogs dgons su gsol*).[50] As

---

46. That is, so that the teachings of the dharma will be ongoing.

47. That is, so that Buddhas and Bodhisattvas can keep teaching the dharma.

48. TDCM, 2554–55, MTD, 1780, ITED entry under *yan lag bdun*, and RJYS entry under *yan lag bdun*. The dedication of virtue for enlightenment is parallel to the final section of the *Confessions of Downfalls*. Other parallel elements are prostration and confession.

49. The Dalai Lama, *Complete Foundation*, Kindle location 703, and for further instructions see 705–892. See also The Dalai Lama, *Introduction to Buddhism*, Kindle location 745–46, and 1825–27.

50. The term *yi dam* refers to one's personal deity or spirit guide, generally regarded to be a manifestation of one's lama or guru, who enables the practitioner to seek enlightenment. A *yi dam* is necessary for tantric practices and essential for progressing beyond the preliminary stages. This explanation may be a polite or veiled way of saying that in tantric practice one must in essence give oneself over to demonic direction and possible demonic possession.

Vajrasattva will be dealt with in a separate section, an analysis will not be given here other than the comment that the inclusion of Vajrasattva in this text, and in the commentaries to the *Confessions of Downfalls*, illustrates the importance of Vajrasattva in the purity schema.

This confessional text deals with the cleansing and clearing away of any infractions of the vows of a monk and provides the model for a complete worship session of restoration and dedication. The aspect of purity that appears to be in focus is again one's moral conduct. This confession and renewal practice, then, is the means to clean (*sbyong ba*) any stains and defilements in order to become clean and pure (*dag*). Prostrations, visualization, and multiple mantra recitations form the bulk of the practice. Dudjom Rinpoche extolled this practice as an essential and regular requirement for any practitioner on the path to enlightenment. It remains a practice of wide appeal.

A Concise Confession to the Lords of the Earth

The third confessional text, *A Concise Confession to the Lords of the Earth* (*sa bdag bshags 'bum bsdus pa bzhugs so*)[51] is perhaps a little unusual, yet is representative of another type of confessional text. Here, the composer is offering a confession not to the sublime Buddhas, but rather to the earthly gods who inhabit the realm of samsara. Though a short confession, it does reveal, and perhaps further confirm, another level of understanding about notions of purity. While the text itself may be less well known, the author is certainly well known, being famous throughout all Tibet. This confession is attributed to Karma Chagme (*karma chags med*, 1613–1678), who at one time had thousands of disciples. Legend has it that during his first public examination at the age of twenty-one, after having only been a monk for two years, twelve thousand monks attended.[52] He was a remarkably gifted child and learned the dharma quickly once he entered monastic life. Karma Chagme, who was a monk of the Karmapa Kagyu lineage, was believed to be an authentic emanation of the Avalokiteshvara, the Bodhisattva of Compassion. He predicted his death to the thousands of his disciples, and when he finally died it is said that "he dissolved his mind into the heart of Buddha Amitābha."[53] In one sense, that such a feat should be ascribed to

---

51. Karma Chagme, *Sa bdag bshags 'bum*.
52. Karma Chagme and G. Rinpoche, *Spacious Path to Freedom*, 8.
53. Karma Chagme and G. Rinpoche, *Spacious Path to Freedom*, 9. It was also

him is not surprising since of the sixty or so works he composed, his most famous and enduring text was the *Aspiration to be Reborn in the Pure Realm of Sukhāvatī* (*rnam dag bde chen zhing gi smon lam*).[54]

Translation and Exposition of *A Concise Confession to the Lords of the Earth*

It is not known exactly when Karma Chagme wrote this text, but it is alleged that he did most of his writing during a thirteen-year retreat. Being a short confession, I have provided a translation of the full text as follows:

> Pay heed! Whatever I, and my generous patrons,
> Have committed against you, the gods, nagas and spirits,
> Including the deeds of our ancestors and,
> Children of future generations,
> Whatever digging up of earth spirits and raising of stone spirits,
> Of agitating water spirits and harming tree spirits,
> Of disturbing charnel grounds,
> And whatever has been done in ignorance,
> I confess and admit; may you be purified![55]

Karma Chagme's tone is apologetic and humble. He identifies himself with the transgressions of past, present and future generations and makes clear against whom the offenses have taken place—these being the gods (*lha*), who inhabit the higher realms of samsara such as the skies and heavens, nagas (*klu*), who inhabit the underground places such as lakes, rivers and fields, and (*gnyan*), the ubiquitous malevolent spirits who inhabit the intermediate space between the earth and sky.[56] Though he does not make the reference explicit in the text itself, in the title of the text, Karma Chagme is also addressing the Lords of the Earth (*sa bdag*), who are cantankerous local deities easily offended by human activity. His confession corresponds

---

claimed that after he died, images of Avalokiteshvara were found embossed all over his bones. See Karma Chagme and G. Rinpoche, *Naked Awareness*, 8.

54. This text will be analyzed in detail in chapter three.

55. This text is in poetic form, and I have attempted to render it in English as such. Tibetan poetry has strict metrical demands, typically requiring a syllable count of an odd number per line. In this text, each of the nine lines has seven syllables in a standard 2-2-3 metrical structure. Tibetan verse form is usually formulated in lines of seven, nine or eleven syllables. The length of stanzas can vary greatly. For the Tibetan text see Karma Chagme, *Sa bdag bshags 'bum*.

56. The term *gnyan* can also refer to pestilence, infectious diseases, and a cognate term *nyan kha* means "infection."

directly to the Tibetan perception that humans have disrupted the spirit world, particularly nagas (*klu*), by their presence on earth and are thus subject to their wrath. These spirits in turn need to be placated or purified through prayers, supplications, and offerings to quell their proclivities for bringing harm upon humans. As the review of the precedent literature showed, such offerings typically take the form of incense, where the offended spirits are themselves purified through the apotropaic fumigating powers of incense smoke. Karma Chagme appears to have been well aware of this practice and wrote a lengthy invocation of incense offering to purify nagas called *A Great Sang Offering to Nagas* (*klu bsangs bla sel chen po bzhugs so*).[57] Through the composition of these texts, Karma Chagme appears to have been well attuned to laity sensibilities, since it is the laity who typically perform *sang* incense offerings. This identification with the laity, which may have been perceived to be an act of benevolent service to them, could have been another reason for his wide following.

In this confession, Karma Chagme appears not to be asking for himself to be purified, as is the case in the previous two confessional texts, where the confessor is the object of the desired purification, but rather that through his admission and confession of human wrongs, may the gods and so on, be purified, and the stain of disturbing human activity be removed from them.[58] Though it is not made explicit here, it is quite likely that this confession accompanied the burning of incense. Yet, it remains a confessional text in its own right. The text reveals that human activities, such as tilling the soil, lifting rocks out of the ground to construct houses, for example, or chopping down trees or branches, or performing funeral rites, while not necessarily morally repugnant actions in themselves, nevertheless require confession. In contrast to the previous two confessional texts, there appears to be a projected sense of purification upon the offended rather than the offender. Perhaps then one could conclude that moral transgressions, which have clearly broached an established moral boundary, and mundane

---

57. This text, and the one analyzed here, again demonstrates the interplay between monks and the laity.

58. The referent in the final line is not made explicit but it seems unlikely to refer to the transgressions themselves or the transgressors, rather the sense is for the objects of the petition to be purified. Not only is this more likely grammatically, (since the gods are in the accusative) but the title of the text makes the focus clear and the opening vocative address of "Pay heed!" places the object of purification as the gods themselves. Further, the optative *gyur cig*—the term used for expressing a wish, is typically used for second and third persons.

infractions of humans going about their earthly business on the earth, both require, though the orthopraxis is at variance, purification. The former orthopraxis of the confessionals is working explicitly to an ultimate salvific end, while the later is perhaps, notwithstanding the accumulation of merit derived from reciting a confession, more concerned with the here and now, the temporal world of making life more bearable from oppressive spirits. The former confessions are concerned with the supramundane, while the later the mundane. The moral cleansing of the two previous confessions required focused attention upon a higher moral source than that of the offender. Here in this text the offended themselves, the local deities, in order to be placated, are the ones who require purification from the offenders.

Preliminary Practices

Essential to Vajrayana Buddhism are the "preliminary practices" (*sngon 'gro*), being the foundation for all tantric practices. These preliminary practices are generic to all schools of Tibetan Buddhism.[59] Whereas the confessional practices are an exoteric and general practice, the preliminaries prepare the practitioner for the esoteric practices of tantra (*rgyud*). Though there may be minor differences in the practice, the formulation of the preliminary or foundational practices follows a standard pattern.[60] There is a progression from exoteric or "outer" (*phyi*) preliminaries, to the esoteric or "inner" (*nang*) preliminary practices.[61] It is within the inner preliminary practices where the focus is centered on purity and purification. The importance of the preliminaries in being able to achieve purification and transformation is highlighted in the various commentaries about them. For example, Dilgo Khyentse Rinpoche states that, "To accomplish the good of others, we must first perfect ourselves by purifying and transforming our minds. This is the aim of what we call the preliminary practices, which establish the foundations of all spiritual progress. You may feel like dispensing with these foundations in order to practice other teachings that you

---

59. P. Rinpoche, *Kunzan Lama'i Shelung*, xxviii; Namkhai Norbu and Shane, *Crystal*, 116–17.

60. Rabten, *Preliminary Practices*, 28.

61. The inner preliminary practices are also known as the "extraordinary preliminaries" or "special practices."

think are more profound, but if you do so, you are building a palace on the surface of a frozen lake."[62]

The progression from the outer to the inner preliminary practice leads to the essential tantric practice of guru yoga (*bla ma'i rnal 'byor*). When one is ready to progress from the inner preliminary practices, one can, assuming the necessary initiations have been attained, begin the highest tantric yoga practices (*bla na med pa'i rgyud*). This progression will also be followed here. In fact, there has already been a natural progression from the foundational confessional texts to the foundational preliminary practices. Here, a brief outline of the preliminary practices will be given, followed by a closer look at the purification ritual of the inner preliminary practice. This will be followed by a separate section examining one of the highest yoga purification practices. Essential to all these practices are mantras and incantations, and a separate section following the highest yoga section will be devoted to exploring some of those incantations in detail.

The Outer Preliminary

The outer section of the preliminary practice is typically centered around the "four thoughts," "contemplations," or "reminders" (*blo ldog rnam bzhi*), which turn one's mind away from the worldly existence of samsara to being centered upon the dharma. These four contemplations are:

1. Contemplating the rarity of human existence (*dal 'byor rnyed dka'*)
2. Contemplating death and impermanence (*'chi ba mi rtag*)
3. Contemplating karmic cause and effect (*las rgyu 'bras*)
4. Contemplating the evils and defects of samsara (*'khor ba'i nyes dmigs*)[63]

Often added to this core are two other contemplations: "the possibility of liberation" and "the need for a spiritual guide."[64] In outlining the five main stages of the inner preliminaries, the process prescribed by Shabkar

---

62. D. K. Rinpoche, *Excellent Path to Enlightenment*, 10.

63. RJYS, entry under *blo ldog rnam bzhi*; Rabten, *Preliminary Practices*, 3.

64. D. K. Rinpoche, *Excellent Path to Enlightenment*, 12–13, and P. Rinpoche, *Kunzan Lama'i Shelung*, xxxv.

STEPS TOWARD A TIBETAN UNDERSTANDING OF PURITY

Tsodruk Rangdrol (*zhabs dkar tshog drug rang grol*, 1781–1851), in his *Concise Preliminary* (*sngon 'gro nyung 'dus bzhugs*), will be followed.[65]

The Inner Preliminary

Shabkar Tsodruk Rangdrol was considered to be an emanation of the renowned yogin and poet Milarepa, and Shabkar Tsodruk was thus likewise considered a great poet.[66] His *Concise Preliminary* neatly works through the five core elements of the inner preliminary. After visualizing the field of merit, the text begins in typical fashion by taking refuge (*skyabs 'gro*) in one's guru, the Three Jewels of the Buddha, the dharma, and the Sangha, this being stage one. The text then moves directly to the second stage of arousing or generating the mind of a Bodhisattva (*byang chub sems bskyed*). The practitioner is invited to recite these lines as many times as possible. The text then moves to the third stage of visualizing and reciting the Vajrasattva mantra. The practitioner is to imagine the deity Vajrasattva appearing at the crown of one's head, with nectar flowing from his body which purifies one's illnesses, harmful actions, negativities and defiling mental obscurations. In the fourth stage, one performs the mandala offering, which is both a physical offering of precious objects and a mental one of handing over important treasures in one's life.[67]

In the fifth and final stage, the practitioner performs guru yoga, where the intention is for the mind of the guru and the mind of the practitioner

---

65. Shabkar Tsodruk Rangdrol, "sNgon 'gro Nyung 'dus," 75–76.

66. His most famous work is the *Flight of the Garuda* (*mkha' lding gshog rlabs*). This text became a famous Dzogchen text which expounded the view of *khregs chod*—the practice of "cutting through" or "breaking through" the mental barriers of delusion and linking directly back to one's primordially pure mind. See Dowman, *Flight of the Garuda*; D. Khyentse, *Primordial Purity*.

67. The mandala offering (*maN+Dal 'bul ba*) can take various forms but in short it is an offering where one symbolically gives over all things for the purpose of accumulating merit. A mandala offering can involve the handing over of a special kind of circular plate, often with two or three stacked layers, which symbolically represent the universe. Offerings such as rice, grain, and fruit can also be made. These offerings are typically made to one's lama. The term mandala (*dkyil 'khor*–literally "center and surroundings") is a multivalent one, but usually refers to a certain representation of the universe in which one is guided through by a spirit guide/demon (*yi dam*) in order to progress to further stages of tantric practice. Suffice to say, much more could be said about the central role of the mandala, but in short, they require detailed and intricated preparations and practices. The use of the mandala is crucial to tantric practice and a thorough examination is beyond the scope of this study.

to meld, without distinction, into one. Here, the guru is perceived as being equal to the meditational deity Vajrasattva. The text closes with a dedication and aspiration, which, like the opening homage and refuge, is not considered one of the five stages.[68] As with the confessions, the inner practice is not intended to be performed just once as a prelude to other advanced practices. It is to be repeated many times, and for the duration of one's life. A tradition has emerged to perform each element of the practice at least 100,000 times, and in particular Vajrasattva and guru yoga.[69] Others suggest a higher number for a total over 500,000 repetitions.[70] Attention will now be turned to stage three of this preliminary practice: the meditation upon, and practice of becoming Vajrasattva.

Vajrasattva

Vajrasattva is always practiced within the inner preliminaries but can also be performed separately as a special method or practice (*sgrub thabs* Sk. sadhana) in its own right. As the preeminent deity for purification, Vajrasattva practice can also be incorporated into confessional practices, as in the case of Dudjom Rinpoche's confessional which was examined earlier, the preliminary practices and various tantric yogic practices.[71] The centrality of Vajrasattva in the purity schema cannot perhaps be overstated. The nineteenth-century master, Patrul Rinpoche, stated that,

> The main obstacles that prevent all the extraordinary experiences and realizations of the profound path from arising are negative actions, obscurations and habitual tendencies. Just as it is important to clean the surface of a mirror if forms are to be reflected in it, so too it is important to eliminate our obscurations so that realization can appear like a reflection in the mirror of the Ground of All. The Conqueror taught countless methods of purification for

---

68. Though not made explicit in this text, the inner preliminaries also include prostrations, usually in the second stage. See Rabten, *Preliminary Practices*, 51. Prostrations are also an essential part of the third stage of Vajrasattva practice, as are practicing the four antidotes within that stage.

69. D. J. Khyentse, *Not for Happiness*, 749–67.

70. Kongtrul, *Torch of Certainty*, 9–10.

71. For example, see Shabkar Tsodruk Rangdrol's *Concise Song of Praise* (*nyams len bsdus don gyi glu*) This texts contains the purification rite through visualizing Vajrasattva and reciting his mantra (*rdo sems bsgom bzlas*).

this purpose, but the best of them all is meditation and recitation related to the teacher as Vajrasattva.⁷²

In his *Commentary on the Practice of Vajrasattva*, Gyatrul Rinpoche (b.1925–) further extols Vajrasattva by claiming,

> The Buddhas and Bodhisattvas taught many different methods to purify these obscurations. Amongst all of these methods that were taught, the most profound, excellent and supreme method is the visualization and meditation upon Lama Vajrasattva (Dorje Sempa) which is the method used in the secret Vajrayana. With this, one can, in a very profound way, purify every inkling of delusion and obscuration.⁷³

The question then may well be asked as to why Vajrasattva is the deity most associated with purity and purification within the Tibetan Buddhist pantheon of deities. The name Vajrasattva (*rdo rje sems dpa'*, often shortened to *rdor sems*) means "heroic-minded vajra," "indestructible adamantine," or "diamond-like enlightened one." Vajrasattva is considered to be the "Buddha of Purification" and he is believed to be bathed in pure radiant light. According to legend, the Bodhisattva Vajrasattva was greatly troubled by all the misdeeds and negativities generated by sentient beings, but he was particularly distressed by disciples of the dharma who broke their vows and fell away from their sacred commitments. This led him to take a vow that if he attained Buddhahood, he would do so for the sake of purifying all those who had violated their vows, even those who had committed the five inexpiable sins. He formulated his mantra for the express purpose that all beings may have their negativities and obscurations completely purified.⁷⁴

In the iconography, Vajrasattva is typically pictured on a throne of lotuses, with the shape of a moon-like disc behind him. His body is white in color, and he radiates brilliant, pure light.⁷⁵ He is also believed to be one of the Buddhas of the "five families of Buddhas" (*sangs rgyas rigs lnga*), being a member of the second family, the Vajra family of Buddhas (*rdo rje rigs*).⁷⁶ Patrul Rinpoche goes further by claiming that Vajrasattva embodies all the manifestations of enlightenment in a single form, embodying "the hundred

---

72. P. Rinpoche, *Kunzan Lama'i Shelung*, 263–64.
73. G. Rinpoche and T. N. Rinpoche, *Commentaries*, 6.
74. Khenpo Yeshe Phuntsok, *Vajrasattva Meditation*, Kindle location 68, 259–79.
75. Landaw and Weber, *Images of Enlightenment*, plate 17 and 18.
76. ITED, entry under *sangs rgyas rigs lnga*.

deities in one." He continues that, "Of the whole inconceivable infinity of peaceful and wrathful yidam deities, there is not one whom he does not embody."[77] Vajrasattva's one hundred syllable mantra is believed to be highly efficacious in purifying all breakages of vows, the stains of karma, and defiling obscurations and negativities.[78]

Becoming Vajrasattva as a Foundational Tantric Practice

The Vajrasattva tantra belongs to the class of tantra known as "mother tantras" (*ma rgyud*, Sk. yoginatrantras). Within this esoteric class of tantra, the male deity is typically cojoined with his female consort (*rig ma*). This practice of Buddhas with their consorts is also commonly referred to in tantric texts as *yab yum*—literally "father and mother."[79] The female deity is perceived to be the embodiment of wisdom (*shes rab*), and the male the embodiment of method (*thabs*). Thus, in this class of tantra, the iconography portrays the male deity cojoined with his consort in sexual embrace, symbolizing wisdom and method in blissful union. This union, combined with various tantric practices, is believed to move the practitioner more rapidly along the stages towards enlightenment. In the case of Vajrasattva, he is often depicted with his consort Vajratopa (*rdo rje snyems ma*—literally "Vajra consort"), and they are typically adorned with white silk and precious jewels, being symbolic of purity. Both Vajrasattva and Vajratopa are the objects of worship, devotion, and visualization in the Vajrasattva practice. There is ongoing conjecture about whether such sexual imagery is to be understood literally or figuratively, but sexual fluids as the preferred offerings to tantric deities has been well documented,[80] and semen in particular has long been considered highly efficacious in the pursuit of enlightenment.[81]

---

77. P. Rinpoche, *Kunzan Lama'i Shelung*, 279.

78. Khenpo Yeshe Phuntsok, *Vajrasattva Meditation*, Kindle location 279; Dragpa, *Overview of Buddhist Tantra*, 78–79, 83; Yeshe, *Becoming Vajrasattva*, x–xi.

79. RJYS entry under *yab yum*.

80. White, *Tantra in Practice*, 16; Gray and Overbey, *Tantric Traditions*, 235; Dragpa, *Overview of Buddhist Tantra*, 79.

81. White observes the iconography of Vajrasattva as being "depicted as engaging in endless sexual marathons." White, *Tantra in Practice*, 15. It is not the place of this study to enter into the debate about how literally practitioners do or do not understand sexual union, other than to say, as an observation in passing, that in more contemporary times, literal sexual union, while still clearly a part of tantric practice, has been de-emphasized

STEPS TOWARD A TIBETAN UNDERSTANDING OF PURITY

It is worth noting that the goal of tantric practice is to actually become the essence of the deity that one is worshipping, to meld into them and thus become enlightened by dissolving into their essence. Tantra is designed to move beyond the visualization of a deity within a particular practice, and to actually become one with the deity of one's meditation. Lama Yeshe has made that explicit in the title of his book, *Becoming Vajrasattva: The Tantric Path of Purification*.[82] In guru yoga, one visualizes one's teacher as the living embodiment of the deity to which one is giving allegiance. This visualization and meditation process, repeated many times, is central to the attainment of enlightenment in the Vajrayana system. Indeed, when one has fully dissolved oneself into the deity, one is then in fact enlightened. Though there are many stages, levels, and secret practices, in short, this melding of oneself into a Buddha or Bodhisattva is the "fast track" of Vajrayana. For the Tibetan Buddhist practitioner, the Vajrasattva practices are essential on this path to enlightenment. It could be stated this way: the final goal is the purified state of enlightenment, and the means to that end is the purification of the practitioner. Gray observes that the meditator, in visualizing a deity, is attempting to join the "impure world with the deity who is of the pure supramundane world." The goal then, he states, "is for this dichotomy to dissolve with the impure meditator being absorbed into the purity of the deity."[83]

---

and become a highly secretive practice among monks who have taken vows of celibacy. A widely held view is that sexual union is permissible provided that it is devoid of desire or attachment. Should desire or attachment arise, sexual union is then considered a defiling act of passion. See, for example, Namdak, *Bonpo Dzogchen Teachings*, 96. It would seem that some of the more debased elements of the early heterodox tantric practices, such as sacrificial violence and the consumption of impure bodily substances, have largely been eliminated from current day practice. That is not to say the practice of a male practitioner taking a consort no longer exists, rather, that the rhetoric seems to be that in "standard" yogic practices, one is, at least initially, to view sexual union as symbolic rather than literal, and to be imagined rather than practiced. These debased practices were why tantra was initially banned in Tibet, but after these practices were consecrated and purified, through various means, tantra became widely accepted as the dominant mode of practice in Tibet. See White, *Tantra in Practice* 15–17, and Gray and Overbey, *Tantric Traditions*, 235, 238–39. For a more recent study on the practice of taking a consort see Gayley, "Revisiting the 'Secret Consort.'"

82. Yeshe, *Becoming Vajrasattva*.

83. Gray, "Purification of Heruka," 240–41. Hopkins, in his introduction to *The Kalachakra Tantra*, suggests that visualization can take the practitioner even further, to ultimately become a divine self: "With success in visualizing the deity, both mind and body appear to be pure; hence, the sense of self that the meditator has in dependence upon purely appearing mind and body is of a *pure* self, a *divine* self." (italics in the original).

With these considerations in mind, attention will now be turned to exploring various Vajrasattva texts. There are many texts one could draw from, but these texts are representative of those in current usage. The first text, *A Concise Vajrasattva Visualization and Mantra Recitation* (*rdo sems sgom bzlas mdor bsdus*), is believed to have been composed by Jamyang Khyentse Chokyi Lodro (*'jam dbyangs mkhyen brtse chos kyi blo gros*, 1893–1959).[84]

A Concise Vajrasattva Visualization and Mantra Recitation

Well versed in the four main schools of Tibetan Buddhism, Jamyang Khyentse became a champion of the non-sectarian movement (*ris med*—"nonpartisan") which maintained a certain posture that the differences between the Tibetan Buddhist orders were immaterial so as not to be reason for aversion or acrimony towards each other.[85] This movement actively promoted a dialogue of ecumenical cooperation. Jamyang Khyentse appeared to live by this creed and received teachings and transmissions from all the four major schools. His text is indicative of that position, being intentionally aimed for a wider audience among all four schools.

The opening lines of the text begin in the typical fashion of homage and supplication to the Buddha, the dharma, and the supreme assembly of the sangha—*tshogs kyi mchog*. This is followed by an affirmation of the Bodhisattva's pledge of attaining Buddhahood for the benefit of all sentient beings. The practitioner is then invited to repeat the same opening lines three times.

The text then moves into a visualization, which consists of imagining Vajrasattva seated on a white lotus and moon-shaped disc, appearing upon the crown of one's own head. Vajrasattva is described as being radiant white, holding a dorje (*vajra*) in one hand and a bell in the other. Enveloped in his

---

The Dalai Lama, *Kalachakra Tantra*, 70.

84. I examined two texts: *rdo sems sgom bzlas mdor bsdus* and *rdo sems kyi sgom bzlas mdor bsdus bya tshul bzhugs so*. The second text is a slightly longer version. Though there are some minor differences between the texts, the essence of the two texts is the same. The extended version of this text provides more detail regarding Vajrasattva and his consort, detailing what they are holding in their hands and their positionings. In that text there is more focus centered on them as a cojoined couple as the *yab yum* pairing– a tantric term which occurs repeatedly throughout the text. *yab yum* (honorific for father and mother) is a term which in general refers to a Buddha with his consorts.

85. RJYS, entry under *ris med*.

own radiance, and with his white consort Vajratopa, who holds a hooked knife and skull-bowl,[86] the two are imagined as enmeshed together in the vajra and lotus positions, adorned with silk and precious jewels.[87] Vajrasattva's one hundred syllable mantra encircles them both and at Vajrasattva's heart appears the letter HUM.[88] Practitioners then request to be purified by Vajrasattva, along with all sentient beings, without exception, from all negativities, defiling obscurations, downfalls, broken vows and promises.

Nectar is then imagined flowing like a stream from Vajrasattva's body.[89] This nectar, which is perceived to remove ailments, evil spirits, negativities, and the pollution of broken vows and promises, and expel them in the form of smoke, soot, steam, pus, blood, and insects, then fills the inside of one's body. Following this, the practitioner is to recite the

---

86. The hooked knife (*gri gug*) and skull-bowl (*thod pa*) are very common images in tantric literature and iconography. They have multiple meanings and associations but are typically perceived as symbolic of wisdom and method respectively. The hooked knife represents the wisdom that cuts through ignorance and symbolizes cutting through the pollution of emotional defilements (*nyon mongs sgrib ba*). See Landaw and Weber, *Images of Enlightenment*, 141; Beer, *Encyclopedia of Tibetan Symbols and Motifs*, 261, 263–66; Beer, *Handbook of Tibetan Symbols*, 110–13. See also Gega, *Principles of Tibetan Art*, 158–59. The skull is associated with death. There is a long history in tantric Buddhism of death being associated with awakening. The terrifying imagery of a skull, often pictured as filled with blood, is believed to aid the practitioner in visualizing death and thus leading to an enlightened awakening. See Gray, "Skull Imagery," 25, 32. Patrul Rinpoche suggests that some yogis used the top of a skull as a bowl as it "symbolizes egolessness." P. Rinpoche, *Kunzan Lama'i Shelung*, 158 in footnote.

87. Silk and precious jewels are symbolic of purity. The vajra and lotus positions (*rdo rje pad ma'i skyil krung*) are common postures in tantric meditation.

88. HUM is an important "seed" (*sa bon*, Sk. bija) syllable in tantric mantras. HUM is a multivalent, and much debated term but typically refers to the indestructible mind of enlightened beings (*rdo rje thugs*).

89. Nectar (*bdud rtsi*) is a frequent motif in tantric texts. The allusion to sexual fluids is a common interpretation and though not made explicit in the text, the connection seems apparent, and some commentators have certainly viewed it that way. Gyatrul Rinpoche explains: "This nectar drips down and begins to fill up the lower part of their bodies. This nectar is the nectar of the union of intrinsic awareness and great bliss. As it fills the bodies of Vajrasattva and his consort, it begins to drip out of the place where they are in union. It comes from this opening down to the crown of your head, entering your head at the opening of the crown chakra." G. Rinpoche and T. N. Rinpoche, *Commentaries*, 18. Gyatrul Rinpoche goes on to add that "As the nectar enters your crown, you should have a sensation similar to milk being poured into a very clear glass." 20. The Sanskrit term chakra (*'khor lo*) refers to particular focal or energy points in the body. There are five chakras (*lus kyi gnas lnga*); crown of the head (*spyi bo*); throat (*mgrin pa*); heart (*snying kha*); navel (*lte ba*); "secret place" (*gsang gnas*) which is a euphemism for genitalia. TDCM, 1544.

one hundred syllable mantra. The mantra is to be repeated as many times as possible. Then, the essence of the mantra, the short and quintessential form of the Vajrasattva mantra—"OM Vajrasattva AH" is to be recited. The practitioner is again invited to recite the mantra as many times as possible. It is suggested in the text that this visualization and mantra recitation be repeated from start to finish many times before continuing further.

The text concludes with a final seeking of refuge in, and paying homage to, Vajrasattva. A final confession follows, and then a supplication requesting to be completely cleansed and purified (*byang zhing dag par*) of all negative actions, obscurations, short-comings, defilements, and contaminations—*dri ma'i tshogs*. This is followed by a reassurance that the lama has been pleased and thus has bestowed purification upon the practitioner. Vajrasattva is then imagined to melt into light and dissolve into the practitioner. In the final dedication, the practitioner, through the merit attained from this practice, and the realization of becoming Vajrasattva, without delay, wishes for all sentient beings, without exception, to likewise be established in Vajrasattva.

An Exposition of A Concise Vajrasattva Visualization and Mantra Recitation

Central elements here appear to be the visualization of Vajrasattva, the request for purification before the transferal of nectar, the one hundred mantra, the bestowal of purification, the fusion of the mind of the practitioner with the deity—the impure being cojoined with the pure, and the dissolution of the practitioner into the deity.[90] Though the practice of the four antidotes is not outlined here, the underlying assumption is that Vajrasattva practice is to be undertaken only by performing each of the four aspects of the antidotes (or "opponent powers"). The commentaries consulted expand on the necessity of doing so. Yeshe Phuntsok states, "The effectiveness of purification depends entirely on the fulfillment and strength of the four opponent powers."[91] Karma Chagme has made it clear that without sincere regret one cannot be purified.[92] Patrul Rinpoche notes that "purification

---

90. These same elements appear in the Vajrasattva section of D. Rinpoche's *Essence of the Practice*, the text studied in a previous section.

91. Khenpo Yeshe Phuntsok, *Vajrasattva Meditation*, Kindle location 257. The "opponent powers" are the same as the "four antidotes."

92. P. Rinpoche, *Kunzan Lama'i Shelung*, 266.

only takes place when you confess sincerely in the right way, using the four powers as antidotes."[93] He has further stressed the need for urgency, as there is a perceived time limit on purification: "If faults are confessed immediately, purification is easy. The longer you wait, however, the more powerful the fault grows, and the more difficult confession becomes. If you wait more then three years. . .no purification will take place."[94]

While the earnestness and sincerity of the practitioner is of course paramount in the process of purification, what engenders this practice to be seen as powerful is the alleged power of Vajrasattva's mantra. Khyentse Rinpoche claims Vajrasattva's mantra is "the quintessence of all mantras."[95] The text *The Stainless Confession Tantra* (*dri med bshags pa'i rgyud*)[96] states that, "the hundred-syllable mantra is the essence of all the buddha's wisdom, and it can purify all the obscurations of broken precepts and conceptual thoughts. It is the king of purification."[97] Another text claims, "If you recite it [Vajrasattva's mantra] a hundred thousand times, you will become the very embodiment of utter purity."[98] Patrul Rinpoche exhorts his disciples: "the hundred syllable mantra is superior to all other mantras, you must know that there is no more profound practice than this."[99] In a lengthy poem extolling the virtues of the mantra, praise is given for its efficacy in gaining merit equal to that of all the Buddhas and in overcoming sickness, pain, or premature death.[100]

Why is the mantra believed to be so powerful? Attempts have been made to render the mantra into English, but this is a fruitless exercise, as the Sanskrit letters are phonetic transliterations of sounds and have no inherent meaning—nor are they intended to.[101] The power of a mantra is in

---

93. P. Rinpoche, *Kunzan Lama'i Shelung*, 264.

94. P. Rinpoche, *Kunzan Lama'i Shelung*, 279.

95. D. K. Rinpoche, *Excellent Path to Enlightenment*, 51.

96. This text is also known as *dri ma med pa'i rgyal po*—*The Stainless King*.

97. As quoted in Khenpo Yeshe Phuntsok, *Vajrasattva Meditation*, Kindle location 385.

98. *The Essential Ornament Tantra* (*dpal rdo rje snying po rgyan gyi rgyud*) as quoted in P. Rinpoche, *Kunzan Lama'i Shelung*, 276.

99. P. Rinpoche, *Kunzan Lama'i Shelung*, 280.

100. Kongtrul, *Torch of Certainty*, 86–87. Kongtrul does not provide a source for the poem but claims the sentiment encapsulates both the old and new tantras.

101. Various attempts have been made to render the mantra in English. For example, L. Z. Rinpoche, *Daily Purification*, 15. This translation may have been generated into English more for a fawning Western audience rather than representing the Sanskrit. In

the combination of the sounds, the sounds themselves, and the symbolic representation of the sounds. Within this mantra, which is typical of many, are the three main "seed" syllables (*sa bon*, Sk. bija) OM, AH, and HUM. In the secret mantra Vajrayana vehicle, these syllables are extremely important and ubiquitous throughout the texts. The OM is indicative of the indestructible body (*rdo rje sku*), the AH representative of indestructible speech (*rdo rje gsung*), and the HUM representative of the indestructible mind of enlightened beings (*rdo jre thugs*). In the shorter, quintessential mantra—"OM Vajrasattva AH", Vajrasattva's name is bracketed with OM and AH respectively, thus the three elements of these seed syllables have been woven throughout the text. In this text, HUM is imagined at the center of Vajrasattva's mind, with the one hundred syllable mantra encircling him. It is from this center where the purifying nectar is believed to emanate before transferring from his body to the practitioner. Though not made explicit in this text, the implication is that these three main constituent elements—body, speech, and mind, need to be purified in order for one to be considered completely purified. In other texts, to be examined in a following section, the purification of these three elements is made explicit.

Khyentse Rinpoche provides a further layer of explanation of Vajrasattva's mantra: "the mantra of Vajrasattva, the hundred-syllable mantra, is the hundred peaceful and wrathful deities in the form of sound; it embodies all the wisdom and power of Vajrasattva himself."[102] Yeshe Phuntsok concurs: "Each syllable is a representation of each of the heart syllables of all the hundred peaceful and wrathful deities" and concludes that "Vajrasattva pervades all the enlightened spheres."[103] In short, the sounds represented by the syllables are efficacious in themselves to produce the desired state of purification. This is, of course, predicated upon the sincerity and endeavor of the practitioner, following the necessary praxis, and the sheer number of repetitions. As has been mentioned, 100,000 recitations with 100,000 prostrations are the standard measure for an initial initiation, but it is a life-time endeavor.[104]

---

any case, a mantra is powerless if the sounds themselves are not intoned. In other words, a mantra has no efficacy when translated into another language.

102. D. K. Rinpoche, *Excellent Path to Enlightenment*, 61.

103. Khenpo Yeshe Phuntsok, *Vajrasattva Meditation*, Kindle location 385.

104. Gyatrul Rinpoche recommends 100,000 repetitions of the *sngon 'gro* practice, 100,000 recitations of the one-hundred syllable mantra in the Vajrasattva practice, and 600,000 recitations of the short Vajrasattva mantra. He concludes that "The real meaning of the practice is a life-time endeavor; one never ceases to practice one's deity." G.

STEPS TOWARD A TIBETAN UNDERSTANDING OF PURITY

The sign of having been purified in the Vajrasattva practice, apart from the visualization of the bestowal of purity from the pleased lama, are auspicious dreams, in a similar manner to the dreams accompanying success in the confessional practices.[105] In addition, one may "experience a feeling of physical buoyancy, little need for sleep, good health, clear thinking and glimpses of realization."[106]

King of Purification, The Heart Essence of Confession

This next text is a short excerpt that appears to have been taken from another text, *The Stainless Secret Vajrasattva* (*rdo rje sems dpa' gsang ba dri med*), and given the title *King of Purification, The Heart Essence of Confession* (*bshags pa'i snying po sbyong ba'i rgyal po bstan*). The arrangement of the text is credited to Do Khyentse Yeshe Dorje (*mdo mkhyen brtse ye shes rdo rje*, 1800–1866), who was believed to be an emanation of Jikme Lingpa (*'jigs med gling pa*, 1730–798), a significant figure within the Nyingma school. What adds to the interest of this text, beyond the actual content, is that it is structured around Vajrasattva's short, six-syllable mantra OM VAJRASATTVA AH, in a type of acrostic format.

The first stanza of the text begins with OM, which is followed with four lines, each nine syllables in length, paying homage to Vajrasattva, for being, among other things, the primordial All Perfect Buddha (*kun tu bzang po*, Sk. Samantabhadra).[107] The second stanza begins with the seed syllable AH,

---

Rinpoche and T. Norbu Rinpoche, *Commentaries*, 63.

105. Rabten, *Preliminary Practices*, 56.

106. Kongtrul, *Torch of Certainty*, 82.

107. The All Perfect or All Good Buddha *kun tu bzang po* refers to the primordial Buddha, or "original" Buddha, the Buddha who is in all things excellent and good and who is ever-present. Samantabhadra is also the name of one of Shakyamuni Buddha's eight closest disciples (*nye ba'i sras brgyad*). See RJYS, entry under *kun tu bzang po* and ITED, entry under *kun tu bzang po*. The ascription of Vajrasattva as the primordial Buddha seems to have been first recorded in the yoga tantra text *The Purification of Evil Destinies* (*ngan song sbyong rgyud*), a tantra devoted to avoiding the three lower realms of reincarnation. Vajrasattva is attributed as being efficacious in this process. This text, which has two slightly variant forms, is found in the Kangyur. Vajrasattva is also referred to frequently as Samantabhadra in the two texts, *The Great Tantra of Vajrasattva: Equal to the End of the Sky* (*rdo rje sems dpa' nam mkha'i mtha dang mnyam pa'i rgyud chen po*) and *The Tantra on the Mirror of the Heart of Vajrasattva* (*rdo rje sems dpa' snying gi me longs gi rgyud ces bya ba*). Both texts are significant in the Dzogchen tradition, which propounds the view of the innate or primordial pure nature of the mind and the pure

and expresses remorse that though everything in existence is primordially pure, ignorance and delusion have caused the breaking and impairments of one's vows. This unfortunate reality is confessed before the Great Pure One, mother of the vast expanse of all the dharma.

The third stanza begins with VAJRA. In the presence of the Lord of Secrets, Vajrapani, Proclaimer of Vajrayana,[108] all the 100,000 secrets of broken vows and promises of body, speech, and mind, with great remorse and regret, are thereby confessed. The fourth stanza commences with SATTVA.[109] Further confession is made to the sky goddesses, the custodians of karma, who will punish sentient beings harshly for the defilement caused in this life and the next, and for contributing to the accumulation of torment in the great hells.[110] The fifth stanza begins with HUM (and concludes with AH), thus employing all three of the primary mantra seed syllables by bracketing Vajrasattva's name with OH AH at the beginning and concluding with HUM AH. Further homage is paid to the great primordial Vajra, King of Desire, one who is free from deficiencies and the need for confession, the unassailable, All Perfect Buddha, dwelling in the vast expanse of the dharma.

Though the text does not explicitly reference the practitioner becoming purified, the title, *King of Purification* (*sbyongs ba'i rgyal po*) clearly implies that purification is being sought through this short practice. As Vajrasattva's mantra is woven throughout this short poem, the mantra is not explicitly recited. Do Khyentse Yeshe Dorje provides a brief explanation at the end of the text which would indicate that the text is in fact a *gter ma*—a buried text from a previous generation. The colophon reads that the text has been formulated for future generations and is still in use today.[111]

---

essence of all things.

108. Vajrapani (*phyag na rdo rje*) was one of Buddha's closest disciples and was considered to be worthy of teaching the tantras and thus became known as "Lord of Tantra."

109. "Sattva" is a Sanskrit term translated into Tibetan as *sems dpa'*—"heroic mind," which refers to one who has resolved to pursue enlightenment for the sake of others.

110. This stanza affirms the Tibetan perception of humans defiling the unseen spirit world through their actions.

111. Such *gter ma* "hidden treasure texts" are particularly sacred to the Nyingma school.

Vajrasattva as a Daily Practice

The text *A Concise Daily Practice of Vajrasattva* (*rdor sems rgyun khyer mdor bsdus bzhugs*), is a short liturgy which is encouraged to be practiced every day.[112] The term for "daily practice" in the title—*rgyun khyer* more literally means to "continually take" as in, to perform something continuously. The text is broken up into four parts and follows a similar pattern to the previous texts—taking refuge, the main yoga of visualization and confession, the recitation of the short quintessential form of the mantra, and the dedication that all sentient beings, including oneself, will become Vajrasattva. Another even shorter liturgy, but with a long title, *Purifying the Pollution of Broken Vows by Adherence to Glorious Vajrasattva* (*dpal ldan bla ma rdo rje sems dpa' la brten nas nyams grib sbyang ba'i thabs bzhugs*), is also encouraged to be a daily practice.[113] This short liturgy condenses the elements of the previous ones into eight lines of terse poetic verse and concludes with Vajrasattva's short mantra. Both of these shorter texts appear to have been composed with memorization and frequent use in mind.

The Wide Appeal of Vajrasattva

Vajrasattva is foundational to confessional and preliminary texts and praxis. The confessional and preliminary texts share common elements of homage, devotion, confession, prostration, mantra recitation, visualization, and dedication. Vajrasattva visualization and mantra recitation are key elements in the process of purification—that is, of being cleansed from moral failings, breakages of vows and defiling obscurations. The visualization practice is based on one's lama as being identified as Vajrasattva, and ultimately the practitioners themselves as becoming Vajrasattva. Vajrasattva practices have wide appeal. The deity Vajrasattva is of particular importance to the Dzogchen tradition which, as mentioned earlier, propounds the view of the innately pure or primordially pure nature of the mind, and the pure essence of all things. Vajrasattva practice is essential in restoring the innate pristine

---

112. This text is credited to Dilgo Khyentse Rinpoche (*dil mgo mhkyen brste rin po che*, 1910–991), who has considered to be a Vajrayana master and was one of the teachers of the current Dalai Lama. Though of the Nyingma lineage, he was a proponent of the non-sectarian movement.

113. This text is attributed to Mipham Rinpoche (*'ju mi pham*, 1846–1912), who was considered a great Nyingma master and author.

mind of understanding.[114] In Tsong Khapa's *The Great Exposition of Secret Mantra* (*sngags rim chen mo*), Vajrasattva is referenced frequently throughout the text. He outlines a similar pattern to the preliminary practices in imagining oneself as Vajrasattva: "Reciting Vajrasattva's essence-mantra and constructing his great seal, contemplate yourself as Vajrasattva."[115] The influence of Vajrasattva is not limited to Tibet nor Tibetan Buddhism. Images of Vajrasattva, either as statues, frescoes, paintings or *thangkha*, have been found throughout all areas where tantric Vajrayana Buddhism spread—India, Nepal, Java, Khmer, Tibet, China, Mongolia, and Japan.[116]

Perhaps one of the reasons for the widespread appeal of Vajrasattva is the influence of the tantra text, found in the Kangyur, *The Purification of Evil Destinies* (*ngan song sbyong rgyud*)[117] which purports to have the ability to purify both the living and the dead.[118] Though the text expounds a way to be purified from rebirth in one of the lower realms of existence, (that is, from the realms of hungry ghosts *yi dwags*, beasts *dud 'gro* or hell beings *dmyal ba*) it also outlines the way to enlightenment through initiation, consecration, devotion and visualization. Central to this process appears

---

114. An examination of the main texts of Dzogchen is beyond the scope of this study. Suffice to say that Vajrasattva is one of their most important meditation deities. Three of their main tantra texts, which all reference Vajrasattva, are, *The Essence of the Mind of all Buddhas* (*sangs rgyas thams cad kyi dgongs pa 'dus pa'i mdo*), *The Great Tantra of Vajrasattva: Equal to the End of the Sky* (*rdo rje sems dpa' nam mkha'i mtha dang mnyam pa'i rgyud chen po*), and *The Tantra on the Mirror of the Heart of Vajrasattva* (*rdo rje sems dpa' snying gi me longs gi rgyud ces bya ba*).

115. Tsong Khapa Blo bzang grags pa and Bstan 'dzin rgya mtsho, *Great Exposition Volume One*, Kindle location 3725. The "great seal" refers to a particular hand gesture or mudra (*phyag rgya*) that has symbolic significance. There are many mudras in tantric practice.

116. Linrothe, "Mirror Image," 11. Linrothe traces images of Vajrasattva dating back to the tenth and eleventh centuries. Tibetan *thangkha* are religious paintings and representations of Buddhist deities and cosmological conceptions.

117. The longer name of this text is (*de bzhin gshegs pa dgra bcom pa yang dag par rdzogs pa'i sangs rgyas ngan song thams cad yongs su sbyong ba gzi brjid rgyal po'i brtag pa zhes bya ba*).

118. Tsong Khapa also wrote a famous commentary on this text *An Explanation of the King of Purification of the Evil Realms* (*ngan song sbyong ba'i rgyal po'i rgyud rje'i gsung gi mchan 'gral bcas pa*) and that may have added to the text's appeal. Tsong Khapa, as previously noted, regularly practiced Vajrasattva meditation. Tsong Khapa Blo bzang grags pa and Bstan 'dzin rgya mtsho, *Great Exposition Volume Three*, Kindle location 432. This tantra may have also become popular because it fostered a belief that through practicing it one could attempt to purify those who had already died, being an obvious attraction for the close kin of the deceased.

to be devotion to Vajrasattva who is, "Purifier of all Sins, Pure most pure in respect of the obscurations of all acts" and to whom the initiate pledges: "OM I offer myself for the service of worshipping all the Tathagatas. Vajrasattva of all the Tathagatas empower me."[119] Throughout the text are repeated references to Vajrasattva, his mantra and the seed syllables. The practitioner is also invited to imagine that "OM Vajrasattva today himself opens your eyes" and "to let Vajrasattva descend upon him."[120] The initiate is reassured that "Today Vajrasattva himself has entered your heart."[121] Vajrasattva is described in various places along similar lines as these: "Purifier of Imperfections of Desires and Hatred, of desire, hatred and deep ignorance, of existence and non-existence he is the Purifier. Peaceful and docile and totally pure, his is Buddha bestowing Buddhahood. He is Buddha-Essence, Buddha-Form, Vajrasattva, Vajra-Born, Samantabhadra All-Good, Adorned with all Buddha-marks. He pervades the whole universe. He is the Pure One, the Whole Essence of the Vajra."[122]

As the collection of texts in this section indicate, Vajrasattva is perceived to be the Buddha of Purification and one of the central deities within the purity schema. Jacob Dalton suggests that Vajrasattva "represents the highest buddha of the Buddhist Yoga-tantra pantheon" and "incorporates all other buddhas."[123] Visualizing him, and reciting his mantra are paramount in the cleansing and purification process. The tantra-yoga practices of Vajrasattva, which have been analyzed here, remain foundational texts of praxis within all schools of the monastic communities in Greater Tibet and further abroad. Attention will now be turned to tantra texts of the highest yoga practices.

---

119. Skorupski, *Sarvadurgatipariśodhana Tantra*, line 19b, 20, line 13a, 14.

120. Skorupski, *Sarvadurgatipariśodhana Tantra*, line 20a, 20, line 103a, 104.

121. Skorupski, *Sarvadurgatipariśodhana Tantra*, line 102b, 103. Sonam Dragpa Panchen, in detailing the praxis of a certain empowerment ritual, also suggests that the outcome is that Vajrasattva dwells within one's heart. Dragpa, *Overview of Buddhist Tantra*, 83.

122. Skorupski, *Sarvadurgatipariśodhana Tantra*, line 108b, 108.

123. Dalton, "Questions and Answers," 190.

Highest Tantric Yoga

The land which embraced the bulk of the Indian tantric Buddhist texts was Tibet.[124] The Dege Kangyur contains over five hundred tantra texts. Of these, one hundred and twenty are classified as belonging to the "highest" or "unparalleled" *bla med rgyud*—literally "nothing above" tantra.[125] In general, the highest tantras are considered to be most effective in leading to enlightenment. Tadeusz Skorupski observes that the highest tantra class was considered by all schools of Tibetan Buddhism to be "the most adventurous and efficacious path towards spiritual perfection."[126] Practicing the highest tantras requires special initiation and is predicated upon adequate completion of the confessional and preliminary practices.[127] Specific to highest tantra are the pantheon of fearsome and wrathful meditational deities. In the Tibetan Buddhist pantheon, many deities are believed to have both a peaceful and wrathful form *zhi khro*—literally "peace and anger." There are forty-two peaceful deities and fifty-eight wrathful ones.[128] In the lower tantras, the peaceful form of a deity is typically the object of devotion, and in the higher forms the angry or gruesome form. This focus on the wrathful deities is one reason Tibetans consider tantra to be dangerous, yet the attraction is that these deities are believed to be more powerful for advancing the stages of enlightenment.[129] Concentrating on the terrifying aspect of a deity is also believed to facilitate awakening.[130]

---

124. Herrmann-Pfandt, "Lhan Kar Ma," 132; Skorupski, "Canonical Tantras," 98–99, 106. The spread of the tantras predominantly occurred during the second dissemination of Buddhism to Tibet during the tenth to twelfth centuries.

125. The Dege Kangyur lists 508 tantric texts in the *rgyud 'bum* Tantra Collection. The collection is broken down into these categories: 15 yoga tantra (*rnal 'byor gyi rgyud*), 8 conduct tantra (*spyod pa'i rgyud*), 19 dedication and aspiration tantra (*bsngo sngon shis brjod*), 316 action tantra (*bya ba'i rgyud*) and 120 highest tantra (*bla med rgyud*) texts. The Lhasa Kangyur does not divide the tantra texts so neatly, instead it has twenty-one large volumes.

126. Skorupski, "Canonical Tantras," 101.

127. Some traditions also considered Vajrasattva, being a "mother" (*ma rgyud*) tantra, particularly when practiced as a separate sadhana outside of the confessional or preliminaries, to be a highest tantra. But, as already mentioned, these textual groupings can be problematic and are not the focus of this study. See also Skorupski, "Canonical Tantras," 99.

128. ITED, entry under *zhi khro*, and RJYS entry under *zhi khro*.

129. G. K. Gyatso, *Essence of Vajrayana*.

130. Gray, "Skull Imagery."

Some of the main elements of highest tantra are sexual yoga, literal or symbolically imagined, and the meditation upon and visualization of wrathful deities. Sexual passions are used as a means for facilitating enlightenment, either through tantric sexual practices or by channeling desire to pursue higher virtuous actions to expedite the process of enlightenment.[131] The current Dalai Lama has said this about the highest tantras: "For us Tibetans, Highest Yoga Tantra is like our daily diet, and thus we are more familiar with this class of tantra."[132]

The practices of the highest tantras, and the wrathful deities worshipped, have long been associated with heretical practices such as ritual violence, sorcery, blood sacrifice, eating meat, consuming alcohol and impure bodily substances, sexual marathons, the use of skulls, swords and daggers, a preoccupation with charnel grounds, human bones and corpses, and even anthropophagy.[133] Indeed, during the tenth and eleventh centuries, various Tibetan kings sought to outlaw tantric deities and practices, considering them to be impure and unfit for inclusion among the sacred gods of Tibet.[134] Though this prohibition of the tantras may have only added to their esoteric appeal, there was also a process of sanitizing or purifying that took place in the transmission of these tantric deities into Tibet. This then paved the way for these tantric texts to become part of mainstream Vajrayana. Some of the more antinomian and heterodoxic elements of the early tantra seem to have died out over the passage of time, but the objects of the practice, that is, the central deities, have not changed. One significant deity in the purity schema of the higher tantras is Heruka.

---

131. White, *Tantra in Practice*, 15. Geshe Kelsang Gyatso defines highest yoga tantra as an "instruction that includes the method of transforming sexual bliss into the spiritual path." G. K. Gyatso, *Essence of Vajrayana*, 490.

132. The Dalai Lama, *The World of Tibetan Buddhism: An Overview of Its Philosophy and Practice*, trans. Geshe Thupten Jinpa, Kindle location 1567. In recent years one of the more popular highest tantras, and one the current Dalai Lama has performed in numerous Western locations, is the Kalachakra Tantra. See The Dalai Lama, *Kalachakra Tantra*.

133. See Gray, "On Supreme Bliss," 477; Gray, "Purification of Heruka," 235; White, *Tantra in Practice*, 12, 15. See also Dalton, *Taming of the Demons*; Gray, "Compassionate Violence"; Barstow, *Food of Sinful Demons*, 92–96.

134. Herrmann-Pfandt, "Lhan Kar Ma," 146; Gray, "Purification of Heruka," 238–39.

Heruka

The term *heruka*, as a class noun, refers to a general class of wrathful deities known as *khrag 'thung*—"blood drinkers."[135] The term used to describe the fifty-eight wrathful deities is "blood drinker" or *heruka*. Aside from having Indian origins, the myth of the deity Heruka is not clearly attested to, and he remains a somewhat enigmatic figure. David Gray, however, makes a convincing case that Heruka is a projection of the Hindu deity Shiva, particularly of his destructive forms.[136] Curiously, the term *heruka* may have been a loanword which was absorbed into Sanskrit, all of which adds further speculation about his origins.[137]

In some traditions, Heruka is equated with being a wrathful manifestation of Vajrasattva, while others consider him to be the wrathful form of Buddha Aksobhya (*mi bskyod pa*).[138] Heruka is also known by other names such as Sriheruka, Samvara, Cakrasamvara, Korlo Demchog (*'khor lo bde mchog*), Korlo Dompa (*'khor lo sdom pa*), Che Chog (*che mchog*) and Demchog (*bde mchog*).[139] Being an emanation of Aksobhya, who is depicted as dark blue and wrathful, Heruka is likewise depicted as dark blue or black. Heruka has a gruesome appearance, often iconized with twelve arms, four legs and four heads, adorned with a crown of skulls and wielding a knife, axe or sword in his hands.[140] His consort, Vajravahari (*rdo rje phag mo* "Adamantine Sow"), is depicted as bright red and typically holds skull bowls in her hands filled with blood. Red in color, she is said to be representative of passion. The explanation given is that she is able to help those with

---

135. ITED, entry under *he ru ka*, and TDCM, 3069.

136. Gray, "On Supreme Bliss," 474; Gray, "Purification of Heruka," 237–38.

137. Lokesh Chandra has noted there is a similarity between *heruka* and the Greek word heruko which means "to restrain or control." This meaning corresponds to the Sanskrit term *samvara*, which is an alternative name for Heruka. Gray, "On Supreme Bliss," 475.

138. G. K. Gyatso, *Essence of Vajrayana*, 32; Herrmann-Pfandt, "Lhan Kar Ma," 146; White, *Tantra in Practice*, 621; Snellgrove, *Hevajra Tantra*, 30. The epithet *mi skyod pa* means "unshakeable" or "immovable."

139. TDCM, entry under *bde mchog*, 1366. Gelukpa teacher Lama Thubten Yeshe's personal *yi dam* or spirit guide is Heruka, or, as he prefers to call him, Korlo Demchog—"The Wheel of Supreme Happiness." Yeshe, *Becoming Vajrasattva*, 280.

140. Heruka is not to be confused with Tsangnyon Heruka (*gtsang smyon he ru ka*, 1452–1504), the Mad Heruka of Tsang, who wrote a famous biography of Milarepa and carefully collected and collocated all his songs. See Schaeffer, Kapstein, Tuttle, *Sources of Tibetan Tradition*, 437; Tsangnyon, *Life of Milarepa*.

strong desire to overcome their passions and focus these lustful desires towards the virtuous pursuit of enlightenment.[141] Gray has described Heruka as a "fierce deity" who has "nonetheless become a quintessential deity of the "higher" Buddhist Tantra," and who also features prominently in the "mother" tantras (*ma rgyud*).[142] The question then may well be asked, how is it that such a terrifying and grotesque figure could become so directly associated with purity and purification? The answer to that may lie partly in a small, yet significant text composed perhaps in the later part of the tenth century.

The Purification of Heruka

The tantric text, *The Purification of Heruka* (*he ru ka'i rnam par dag pa*) is attributed to Sraddhakaravarma, a Kashmiri scholar who travelled to Tibet in the late tenth century, and the great translator Rinchen Sangpo (*lo tswa ba rin chen bzang po*, 958–1055). The text is found in the tantra section of the Tengyur.[143] A full exposition of the text is not warranted here, but certain salient points are worth highlighting. The text provides no Sanskrit title which suggests an original Tibetan composition. The title of the text is also curious. That is, the object of purification, indeed complete purification (as the term *rnam par dag pa*, discussed in the purity key terms section earlier, denotes) is not for the practitioner, but for Heruka himself.[144] There seems to be an effort in this text to sanitize this wild deity in order for him to become accepted into the Tibetan pantheon of deities. The text itself seems to bear out this postulation.

Unlike other tantras, *The Purification of Heruka* has no detailed meditational instructions, no visualization, and no mantras to recite. The term *rnam par dag pa* occurs seventeen times and most frequently in relation to purifying the objects that Heruka holds in his twelve hands. In the opening line of the text, Heruka himself is first declared as having the innate nature

141. Heruka's other main consort is Vajrayogini (*rdo rje rnal 'byor ma*, Sk. Vajrayogini) who is similar in form to Vajravahari.

142. Gray, "On Supreme Bliss," 473. For example, according to my calculations, the name Heruka appears twenty-five times in the highest tantra text *The Foundation of All Tantras, the Great Compendium* (*yang dag par sbyor ba zhes bya ba'i rgyud chen po*), also known as *The Emergence from Samputa* tantra. Vajrasattva is also referenced some twenty times.

143. Sraddhakaravarma and Zangpo. "He Ru Ka'i [Purification of Heruka]."

144. "Heruka," in the title of the text, is in the genitive case—"Heruka's Purification."

of the purity of meditative concentration. The text then works through the various tantric tools of Heruka declaring them to be purified. These same objects are then reinterpreted through a Mahayana framework by equating each of these objects to one of the ten perfections of a Bodhisattva, and one of the ten stages of a Bodhisattva's journey towards enlightenment.[145]

The first object declared as purified is Heruka's drum. Rather than simply state that the drum has become cleansed, the authors pronounce the drum as being the perfection of pure generosity. The virtue of generosity is the first of the ten perfections of a Bodhisattva. The drum is reinterpreted this way because, according to the text, "it continually sounds forth the dharma, is the antidote for jealousy that steals the happiness of others and has become the stage of Great Enjoyment."[146] Other implements Heruka is holding are likewise purified, sanitized, and reinterpreted through the Bodhisattva framework of Mahayana Buddhism. His battle axe (*dgra sta*) is declared to be purified as the purity of moral discipline (*tshul khrims*) which cuts off the non-virtuous actions of killing and eating and thus, because it turns one away from all negativities and sins, is beneficial in assisting one to arrive at the Stainless stage.[147] Heruka's hooked knife (*gri gug*) is declared to be the purification of forbearance because it completely cuts away all impatience and disturbances caused by weapons and so forth. The hooked knife becomes the stage of Radiance, where an untroubled mind, devoid of fear, becomes unsullied, pure understanding.[148] His trident becomes purified as the symbol of pure perseverance, dispelling listlessness, and laziness,

---

145. The ten perfections of the Bodhisattva (*pha rol tu phyin pa bcu*, Sk. dasha paramitas) are 1. generosity (*sbyin pa*), 2. moral discipline (*tshul khrims*), 3. forbearance (*bzod pa*), 4. perseverance (*brtson 'grus*), 5. meditative concentration (*bsam gtan*), 6. wisdom (*shes rab*), 7. skillful means (*thabs*), 8. prayer (*smon lam*), 9. strength (*stobs*), 10. primordial wisdom (*ye shes*). These ten are more typically condensed to the Six Perfections of the Bodhisattvas (*phar phyin drug*), with the first six being considered the primary perfections. The practice of these perfections is the central focus of the sutras known as the *Perfection of Wisdom* (*phar phyin, pha rol tu phyin pa* or *shes phyin*, Sk. Prajnaparamita). There are approximately twenty-three such sutras in the Kangyur, being foundational texts of the Mahayana Bodhisattva path. The ten perfections in this text are linked to the ten stages of the Bodhisattva (*byang chub sems dpa'i sa bcu*, Sk. dasabhumi), which are 1. Great Joy (*rab tu dga' ba*), 2. Stainless (*dri ma med pa*), 3. Light Making (*'od byed pa*), 4. Radiance (*'od phro ba*), 5. Difficult to Cleanse (*shin tu sbyang dka' ba*), 6. Made Manifest (*mngon du gyur pa*), 7. Gone Far (*ring du song ba*), 8. Unwavering (*mi g.yo ba*), 9. Excellent Discernment (*legs pa'i blo gros*), 10. Dharma Cloud (*chos kyi sprin*).

146. *The Purification of Heruka*, 125A–125B.

147. *The Purification of Heruka*, 125B.

148. *The Purification of Heruka*, 125B.

leading to being rescued from the three lower evil rebirths. The trident is further reinterpreted as being like the sharpness of understanding of the body, speech and mind.[149] His staff is declared to be representative of the perfection of pure concentration, his bell the perfection of pure wisdom, his vajra the perfection of pure method, his lotus vase the perfection of pure prayer, and his lasso the perfection of pure strength.[150] Each of these objects are also equated with one of the ten stages of a Bodhisattva's journey to enlightenment. Heruka's consort, Dorje Pagmo (*rdo rje phag mo*, Sk. Vajravahari) is pronounced to be both the perfection of primordially pure wisdom, and the Dharma Cloud (*sa chos kyi sprin*)—which is the tenth and final stage of a Bodhisattva's journey to enlightenment. After reinterpreting other aspects of Heruka, for example his crown representing the five families of the Buddhas, Heruka is declared to be a glorious Buddha, completely purified, free of defilements (*'grib pa med pa*) and in essence the primordial Buddha Vajradhara (*rdo rje 'chang*).[151] Thus, Heruka appears to have been validated as a pure source of tantra practice, aligned with the higher ways of the Mahayana Bodhisattva path.

What is pertinent for this study is the perception that Heruka needed to be purified, that an attempt was made to do so, and that there appears to have been a successful outcome. His wrathful aspect, tantric implements, and associated impure practices required cleansing. It is also of interest that he could indeed be deemed to have been purified, largely, it seems, through the declarations made in this text. Further, the purification or sanitization process also included a reinterpretation of his tantric tools equating them with a more conventional path to enlightenment within the Mahayana tradition.[152]

---

149. Being pictured with a trident (*rtse gsum*) may be further evidence that Heruka is a projection of Shiva. The term *rtse gsum* is often used as a reference to Shiva's trident.

150. The term for staff (*kha Twa ga*) is a special type of tantric staff usually adorned with three skulls. MTD, 134. The term bell (*dril bu*) is commonly paired with the vajra (*rdo rje*). A lotus vase or container (*pdam'i snod*) is associated with purity and a lasso (*zhags pa*) with strength and power.

151. Buddha Vajradhara (*rdo rje 'chang*), the "Vajra Bearer" is considered to be the primordial Buddha and the embodiment of the five families of Buddhas. RJYS, entry under *rdo rje 'chang*. In the final lines of the text, it is claimed that Heruka mastered the sixteen moments of wisdom on the path of insight (*skad cig ma bcu drug*), the thirty-seven factors of enlightenment (*byang chub kyi phyogs kyi chos sum cu rtsa bdun*) and tamed the four devils or maras (*bdud bzhi 'dul ba*).

152. Robert Thurman, among others, has suggested that texts such as these were attempts to integrate the sutras into the tantras and make the tantras more acceptable and less controversial. This purification process then was also an attempt to de-emphasize

Whether this text was the primary reason for Heruka's adoption as the main purification deity of the higher tantras is an open question. Likely, Heruka practice was already in wide circulation, albeit surreptitiously, and this text served to validate and perhaps justify the ready acceptance of the tantras in Tibet. Gray is confident that *The Purification of Heruka* was the primary cause: "There is no doubt whatsoever that Sraddhakara was completely successful in this attempt at "purification," for not only was Heruka "purified" in the eyes of most Tibetans, but he also became the preeminent means of purification."[153] In any case, Heruka was widely accepted and became the principle deity of the three most sacred mountains in Tibet.[154] In the Nyingma tradition, which also closely adheres to Vajrasattva practice, Heruka became known as both Che Chog (*che mchog*) "Supreme Greatness" and Yangtak (*yang dag*) "Ultra Pure."[155] Heruka and his consort also became the principle deities in the widely popular highest tantra, *The Hevajra Tantra*.[156] Heruka is one of the main deities of the Gelukpa sect, being the central deity in the highest tantra practice, *The Heruka Yoga of Triple Purification*.[157] A brief analysis of this text will now follow.

---

the esoteric and controversial heretical practices and make them more acceptable into mainstream Mahayana Buddhism. See Thurman, "Tsongkha-Pa's Integration"; Arnold, "Tsongkhapa's Coordination." *The Purification of Heruka* also gives further weight to the belief that tantras are the fast path to enlightenment, by condensing each of the ten perfections and ten stages of a Bodhisattva into a single tantric text.

153. Gray, "On Supreme Bliss," 499.

154. The three sacred mountains are Mount Kailash (*gangs rin po che/gangs ti se*), Mount Lapchi (*la phyi*) and Mount Tsari (*tsa ri*). In the literature review, particularly the work of Toni Huber, the significance of pilgrimage to sacred sites as a mode of purification has been well documented. Heruka appears to be more commonly known as Demchog (*bde mchog*) "Supreme Happiness" when ascribed as the deity of these three important sacred sites. Lama Zopa Rinpoche claims that the three holy mountains of Heruka represent "one each for the holy body, holy speech, and holy mind." He further maintains that "Bathing in or drinking water from Lake Manasarovar, which is near Mount Kailash, purifies negative karma and liberates you from the lower realms." L. Z. Rinpoche, *Chat About Heruka*, 85, 87.

155. Germano, "Seven Descents," 236.

156. See Snellgrove, *Hevajra Tantra*; Farrow and Menon, *Concealed Essence*.

157. For some in the Gelukpa sect there is no separation between the practice of Heruka or Vajrasattva and thus the practice is also known as Heruka Vajrasattva, with Heruka being the wrathful form of Vajrasattva or Vajrasattva being the peaceful emanation of Heruka. But in the highest tantras, it is the wrathful form which is worshipped. The Gelukpa teacher, Lama Zopa Rinpoche, claims that many great masters of Vajrayana have achieved enlightenment in one lifetime by practicing Heruka. L. Z. Rinpoche, *Chat About Heruka*, 17. Geshe Kelsang Gyatso is even more effusive in his praise of the efficacy

STEPS TOWARD A TIBETAN UNDERSTANDING OF PURITY

The Heruka Yoga of Triple Purification

Unlike the previous text, *The Heruka Yoga of Triple Purification* (*dpal 'khor lo sdom pa'i dag pa gsum gyi rnal 'byor*) is a yoga practice and thus comes with the usual procedural elements of devotion, dedication, recitation, and visualization.[158] The larger tantra discourse regarding Heruka is the text, *Sri Chakrasamvara Tantra* (*'khor lo bde mchog*).[159] That text is also known as *Heruka Chakrasamvara* or *'khor lo dbe mchog*—"The Wheel of Supreme Happiness." The *Sri Chakrasamvara Tantra* text outlines fifty-one procedures for various rituals and yogic practices, with Heruka being the central deity. However, the central text of the highest yoga of Heruka praxis, still in use today, is *The Heruka Yoga of Triple Purification*.[160]

Essential to tantric practices is the conception that the perceived three main elements of human existence, the body, speech, and mind (*lus ngag yid gsum*), are inextricably woven together and therefore each need to be engaged in order for a yoga practice to be complete. Tadeusz Skorupski further elaborates on the highest tantras that the "Highest Yoga Tantra attaches the greatest importance to the control and purification of the mind (citta, *sems*) as the chief agent of all human activities."[161] In *The Heruka Yoga of Triple Purification*, the practitioner is invited to engage in the three-fold

---

of Heruka claiming that "In the *Condensed Root Tantra* it is said that just by seeing a sincere Heruka practitioner we purify our negativities and attain liberation." He adds that this happens "because the actual deities of Heruka abide within the body of the practitioner and therefore seeing the practitioner is not so different from seeing Heruka himself." G. K. Gyatso, *Essence of Vajrayana*, 7.

158. The text I studied is titled "*DPal 'khor Lo Sdom* [Heruka Yoga of Triple Purification]." Note that I have translated the name in the title *dpal 'khor lo sdom pa* as Heruka (though the literal meaning is "Glorious Wheel of Vows"), as this title is an epithet of Heruka, and it is clearer here to continue referencing the name Heruka.

159. Gray, *Cakrasamvara Tantra*; Gonsalez, *Chakrasamvara Root Tantra*. This text is also known as *The Heruka Tantra* or *The Heruka Cakrasamvara*. (Note the alternative spellings of Cakrasamvara and Chakrasamvara.) The text gained further appeal, and therefore Heruka's notoriety as the central deity, largely because of a famous commentary Tsong Khapa wrote about this tantra—*A Clear Illumination of All Hidden Meaning* (*sbas don kun gsal*).

160. This text is also known as the *Yoga of the Three Purifications of Shri Chakrasamvara*.

161. Skorupski, "Canonical Tantras," 101. This tripartite grouping of body, speech and mind frequently occurs in Tibetan texts and is also common in the vernacular where one can speak of doing something with all one's energies and putting one's "body, speech and mind" to the task.

purification of the body, speech, and mind through identification with the body, speech, and mind of Heruka and his consort.

After paying homage and taking refuge, the text moves into a pledge that one will become Heruka in order to lead all sentient beings to also attain Heruka's exalted state. The practitioner is then invited to do a short Vajrasattva meditation and purification, using the seed syllables of OM, AH and HUM. After the recitation of certain mantras, and the visualization of Vajrasattva, practitioners then request that Vajrasattva make them, and all other sentient beings, clean and purified (*byang zhing dag pa*) of all negativities, defiling obscurations, and broken vows.[162] After this petition, all the negativities and defiling obscurations of sentient beings are declared to have been cleansed (*sbyangs*). Offerings are made and the three doors of body, mind, and speech of the practitioner are believed to have been made completely clean.[163] A mantra then follows that invokes the power of Heruka for purification.

The text then works through the purification of the mind, body, and speech in more detail. A general overview will be given here. Firstly, the practitioner contemplates each syllable of Heruka's name (HE RU KA SRI) as a means for purifying one's mind and is subsequently to imagine that one's mind is being made pure (*yid dag pa byed pa'o*). Secondly, practitioners visualize themselves as the dark blue Heruka embracing his red consort Vajravahari.[164] After the recitation of a short mantra of Heruka's name, practitioners are to imagine that their bodies are being purified (*lus dag pa byed pa'o*). Thirdly, in order to have one's speech purified, one is to recite eight lengthy mantras and to then imagine that one's speech is

---

162. *Heruka Yoga of Triple Purification*, 167–68.
163. *Heruka Yoga of Triple Purification*, 168.
164. Central to all tantric practice are the stages of generation (*skyed pa, skyed rim*) and completion (*sgrub pa, rdzogs rim*). The first stage involves generating oneself as the deity of one's meditation. Through this visualization and identification, the deity is then believed to dissolve into the practitioner at the completion stage, where one is engulfed in clear light and pristine understanding. This sadhana follows that standard practice. The main difference in this text appears to be the emphasis on purifying the body, mind, and speech which Heruka and his consort, through this prescribed praxis, are believed to be able to affect. L. Z. Rinpoche goes further saying that in the generation stage "Shri Heruka, Vajra Varahi, the four heart yoginis and the countless dakas and dakinis from the twenty-four holy places will actually enter into your body." And "Having entered into your body, Heruka, Vajra Varahi, and all the dakas and dakinis will bless you." L. Z. Rinpoche, *Chat About Heruka*, 90, 104.

being purified (*ngag dag pa byed pa'o*).¹⁶⁵ Homage, praise and prostrations are then made to Heruka and Vajravahari. The text is rounded out with a final dedication of the practitioner resolving to become Heruka for the sake of all sentient beings, and to lead them to Heruka's glorified state. The practice concludes with a request that all the heroic yoga practitioners, and all who dwell in the twenty-four sacred places of the world, to assist in attaining the goal of becoming Heruka. Though similar to the Vajrasattva texts, this text is explicitly practiced for the purification of the mind, body and speech, and the meditational deities are wrathful and gruesome, unlike the more serene Vajrasattva. Central, of course, to any perceived efficacy are the repeated recitations of mantras.

Summary of Texts of Praxis

Being texts of orthopraxis, as opposed to simply doctrinal treatise, the confessional, preliminary, Vajrasattva, and Heruka texts share common elements. Continuing to approach Tibetan notions of purity through a religious and cosmological framework, rather than a social anthropological one, these texts reveal certain ontological and soteriological conceptions. Firstly, the ontological reality of the human condition; that there are indeed things, namely moral failings, broken vows, and defiling obscurations of sullied and ignorant perceptions of reality, which need cleansing, of being changed from an impure and imperfect state to a pure, stainless, and perfect one. Secondly, the belief that it is possible to be transformed from an unclean and impure state to a new state of being cleansed and pure, unsullied by the defects of samsara. As Yael Bentor notes, "the notion of purification implies that the transformation of the impure into a pure entity is possible."¹⁶⁶ And thirdly, this transformation can be affected through elaborate tantric practices. In short, these texts would seem to indicate that there exists in Tibetan consciousness a perceived problem of impurity, a desired solution of purification, and a mechanism by which to achieve this desired state.

Since these purification rituals need to be performed regularly, and are dependent upon the urgency, sincerity, repetition and volume of performance, purification cannot be viewed as either instant or permanent; it would appear to be gradual and accumulative. The permanency of purity is not apparent until the final state of purified enlightenment occurs. Precisely

---

165. The mantras account for more than two pages of the text.
166. Bentor, "Body in Enlightenment," 79.

when that happens is unclear, nor is it clear what happens to the physical body, other than it is believed to be engulfed in radiant light when subsumed into the purity of the meditational deity. Gavin Flood suggests that characteristic of tantric visualization practices is "The purification of the body through dissolving its constituent elements into their cause."[167] Which is to say that practitioners become one with the deities of their meditation. It remains unclear from the texts themselves what happens to the physical body, but the visualization and generation practices of the tantric methods displayed in these texts place the practitioner's own body as the site for becoming completely purified, for becoming one with the purity of the deity of one's devotion.[168]

There are many stages on the path to enlightenment, but purification, it would appear, according to these texts, is a foundational one. Whether through the confession of moral fallings, ritual and liturgical formulations, or specific esoteric tantric practices, the pursuit of purity appears to be a necessary and compelling component in the salvific pursuit of escaping from the defiled world of samsara and reaching the purified state of Buddhahood. One could perhaps state that these texts of praxis, observed by many monastic practitioners, are an essential foundation for achieving the enlightened, purified state.

Koichi Shinohara has rightly observed that, "The core of the Esoteric rituals consists in the recitation of spells."[169] Indeed, the texts examined thus far have borne this out; foundational to all tantras and texts of praxis, is the recitation of mantras or incantations. As has been seen, these texts rely on mantras as the efficacious means of purification, and without them,

---

167. Flood, "Purification of the Body," 28.

168. The Gelukpa tradition expresses the view that a purified body is an illusory body made up of the wind and the mind (*rlung sems tsam*). The transformation of the physical body into the purified illusory body is believed to occur just prior to enlightenment. Bentor, "Body in Enlightenment," 86. These abstract notions have been the subject of much discussion and these questions about the perceived nature of the enlightened body are a topic for a separate investigation, beyond the scope of this study. See also Clay, "Purity, Embodiment," 240–44. Suffice to say that in the minds of the practitioner, the pursuit of purification is a concrete reality. In asking these questions to Tibetan colleagues and friends, invariably their conception is less abstract and more concerned with not being reborn in a lower realm and hopefully being reborn in a pure realm of bliss. The nature of the physical body is less of a concern, though it is imagined to be free of pain and suffering.

169. Shinohara, *Spells, Images, and Mandalas*, xiii. Note that Shinohara equates "Esoteric" with Tantric and Vajrayana Buddhism. This is a designation East Asian scholars typically make. See Shinohara, *Spells, Images, and Mandalas*, xi.

and their perceived power, no purification would take place. Attention will now be given to a class of texts within the Kangyur known as *gzungs*—incantations or spells, the bread and butter, as it were, of any confessions, preliminaries, higher yoga praxis, esoteric rituals, liturgies, chants, or aspirational prayers.

Spells and Incantations

The Dege Kangyur lists two hundred and sixty-five texts which have been classified as *gzungs* (Sk. *dharani*)—incantations or spells.[170] Though a certain number of *gzungs* have been included in the Kangyur, the number of extant incantations is far greater. Gergely Hidas estimates there to be more than 1,300 incantations in existence within the broader Buddhist world.[171] An incantation or spell (*gzungs*) differs from a mantra (*sngags*) in that *gzungs* are typically longer than a mantra—which are often six syllables, and they combine both meaningful words and magical sounds devoid of coherent meaning. The longer, one hundred syllable form of Vajrasattva's mantra, for example, is more precisely considered to be a *gzungs*, and the shorter, condensed, six-syllable version, a mantra. There is a certain mnemonic element to a *gzungs* that helps to facilitate recitation and memorization. Van Schaik provides this definition: "A dharani (Tib. *gzungs*) is a sequence of Sanskrit syllables used to attain a variety of worldly and transcendent goals."[172] However, a complete *gzungs* can also contain meaningful Tibetan words of homage and dedication before and after the central incantation.

The terms "spell" or "incantation" seem appropriate English equivalents for the term *gzungs*, as *gzungs* are believed to contain special magical powers in and of themselves. In effect, *gzungs* are not prayers of supplication (*gsol ba*), but rather magical formulas believed to affect a particular desired outcome, such as protection from harm or success in business. The spells listed in the Kangyur are generally regarded to have been uttered by Buddha Shakyamuni in the first instance, but many variations are now

---

170. The Dege Kangyur breaks down the 265 *gzungs* into the two categories of a "Compendium of Dharanis" (*gzungs 'dus*) of 250 texts, and an "Aspiration" or "Dedication" (*bsngo smon*) section of 15 texts. The Lhasa Kangyur does not make such a delineation and instead includes all *gzungs* in the tantra section.

171. Hidas, "Dhāraṇī Sūtras," 131. It is not clear how Hidas produced this number, but in reality, it could conceivably be more than this.

172. Van Schaik, "Tibetan Avalokiteśvara Cult," 58–59.

MONASTIC TEXTS OF PRAXIS

in existence.[173] Skorupski observes that, "The presence of these formulas, spells and incantations, endowed with certain efficacious powers for the achievement of both worldly and supramundane results, is attested in all periods and forms of Buddhism."[174] Hidas notes that the use of incantations contributed to the spread of tantrism and esoteric Buddhism.[175] In Tibet, the use of magical spells became very widely practiced, and the use of mantras and magical formulas was, of course, in wide usage by shamans and Bön practitioners prior to Tibet's assimilation of Buddhism.[176]

Spells and incantations serve both mundane and supramundane purposes. Ronald Davidson suggests incantations are used primarily in "apotropaic, soteriological and devotional environments."[177] Spells and incantations are considered more effective when uttered quietly and repeatedly "with barely any perceptible movement of lips and tongue."[178] Though incantations are recited, one is actually entering into the incantation rather than just reciting it. That is, upon reciting it, one is saying sounds that represent Buddhist teachings and therefore one is entering into the doctrines of the dharma, even if one may not understand them.[179] Incantations also represent a condensed or abbreviated form of Buddhist scriptures, which is particularly useful for those who are unable to chant copious pages of scriptures at length. This encapsulation of the scriptures also adds to a spell's perceived power.[180]

The majority of the incantations appear to be used for protection from harm, either from the spirit world or the physical world. There are special spells for protections from floods, hail, storms, drought, calamities, and for

---

173. Hidas, "Dhāraṇī Sū tras," 129.

174. Skorupski, "Canonical Tantras," 98.

175. Hidas, "Dhāraṇī Sūtras," 130.

176. See Bellezza, *Spirit-Mediums, Sacred Mountains*. Bellezza notes "[for] ritual performances to be effective, the correct enunciation of the spells is imperative" (97).

177. Davidson, "Studies in Dharani Literature I," 106. Davidson notes that the category of dharani can be rather "polysemic and context-sensitive," meaning that dharani or *gzungs* can appear in many different genres. Davidson, "Studies in Dharani Literature I," 98. He also makes the pertinent observation that a dharani (*gzungs*) is not a dharani "until it is incomprehensible to the readers of the Sanskrit text," reaffirming that the sounds themselves are all important as there is typically no coherent meaning to the utterances. Davidson, "Studies in Dharani Literature I," 107.

178. Castro-Sánchez, "Indian Buddhist Dhāraṇī, 62.

179. Davidson, "Studies in Dharani Literature I," 130; Halkias, *Luminous Bliss*, 65.

180. Davidson, "Studies in Dharani Literature I," 133.

positive outcomes such as fertility and abundant harvests. Many incantations are also for supramundane soteriological concerns such as purification from negative karma. Some spells are designed for deliberately causing harm to others.[181] As well as being recited, incantations are placed in stupas and sacred statutes where they are believed to sacralize the stupas and statues and augment their special powers. As Yael Bentor notes, "In Tibet an elaborate practice of depositing many different types of relics and *dharanis* has long existed."[182]

Incantations for Purification

Incantations have traditionally been classified by their length, their content, and the deity to which they are associated.[183] In this study, the two hundred and sixty-five incantations in the Dege Kangyur have been filtered through the lens of lexical content germane to the subject of purity and purification. This selection of incantations has been further narrowed down to a small sample of the types of incantations that contain purity references. The focus in this section, then, will be on incantations that promise purification from negativities and defiling obscurations, purification from previously accumulated bad karma, purification from an evil rebirth into the three lower realms, and incantations which promise a purified rebirth into a higher realm or even into a pure realm. These incantations follow a somewhat standard formula, beginning with a homage or salutation to a deity, followed by the incantation (which is a phonetic representative of the Sanskrit in Tibetan and has no meaning in itself), a declaration of what the incantation is alleged to have achieved or is capable of achieving, perhaps a final supplication or dedication, and a final statement that the incantation is complete.[184] Of most relevance to this study is the perceived benefits these

181. Hidas, "Dhāraṇī Sūtras," 130.

182. Bentor, "On the Indian," 248.

183. Halkias, *Luminous Bliss*, 66; Halkias, "Tibetan Buddhism Registered," 66–68.

184. Note that I have not made any comments about the actual content of the phonetized incantations themselves, other than the observation here that the tantric seed syllables of AH, HUM and OM, for example, can often be punctuated throughout. As mentioned, the sounds themselves, their various combinations, and the repeated recitation is what is paramount. The standard format is homage-incantation-declaration-dedication. This is an oversimplification but will suffice for the purposes of this study. Davidson has provided a thorough examination of the dharani genre and rightly notes that the category of dharani literature is "sufficiently complex to resist easy categorization." Davidson, "Studies in Dhāraṇī Literature II," 11.

incantations are believed to effect. These benefits are made explicit in the texts and will be the focus of the commentary that follows.

The Incantation of Praise to the Glorious Eternal One

The text *The Incantation of Praise to the Glorious Eternal One* (*'phags pa yon tan bsngags pa dpag tu med pa zhes bya ba'i gzungs*),[185] begins by paying homage to the Triple Refuge of the Buddha, the dharma and the sangha, and proceeds directly to the incantation. The perceived benefits are listed after the incantation, and they are as follows:

1. If the incantation is recited once, all of one's accumulated karmic obscurations of one hundred thousand eons will be purified.
2. If the incantation is recited three times a day, every day, all of one's negativities will be cleansed, and one will obtain the root of virtue of the one thousand Buddhas.
3. If recited twenty-one times, one will be cleansed from the roots of the four downfalls.[186]
4. If recited one hundred thousand times, one will see Glorious Chamba.[187]
5. If recited two hundred thousand times, one will see Glorious Chenrezi.[188]
6. If recited three hundred thousand times, one will see the Buddha of Infinite Light.[189]

The text concludes by stating that since there are innumerable benefits, this list is just a brief summary of them.

---

185. Note that a numbered list does not appear in the text itself. I have added the numbers for ease of reading.

186. The four downfalls (*ltung ba bzhi*) are: 1. impure conduct (*mi tshangs par spyod pa*), 2. stealing (*ma byin par len pa*), 3. taking a life (*srog gcod pa*), 4. telling lies (*rdzun du smra ba*). There is also a longer list of ten downfalls (*ltung ba bcu*) in which these four are included. TDCM, 1087.

187. Glorious Chamba (*'phags pa byams pa*, Sk. Maitreya) is the future Buddha.

188. Glorious Chenrezi (*'phags pa spyan ras gzigs*, Sk. Avalokiteshvara) the Buddha of Compassion.

189. Buddha of Infinite Light (*'od dpag med* Sk. Amitābha) who dwells in the Pure Land of Sukhāvatī (*bde ba can*).

STEPS TOWARD A TIBETAN UNDERSTANDING OF PURITY

The Incantation of The Essence of Buddha Shakyamuni

The incantation *The Essence of Buddha Shakyamuni* (*shAkya thub pa'i snying po'i gzungs*), after paying a brief homage to Buddha Shakyamuni, provides a short incantation which one is invited to recite. After the incantation, the benefits of it are stated. The main benefit is that if recited just once, whatever sins one has committed during 10,180,000 eons will be cleansed and purified.[190] The text concludes by stating that the spell is the essence of the Glorious Buddha Shakyamuni. A related spell, *The Incantation of the Essence of Chenrezi* (*'phags pa spyan ras gzigs kyi snying po*) states that if this incantation is read, regardless of one's understanding, one will be remembered for 100,000 generations and even in death will be born into the pure land of Sukhāvatī.[191] Another related spell, *The Incantation of Buddha Amitābha* (*bcom ldan 'das snang ba mtha' yas kyi gzungs sngags*) promises, if recited three times, to purify all accumulated defiling karmic obstacles of 100,000 eons. If recited twenty-one times, the root of the four downfalls will be completely cleansed. Curiously, this incantation does not promise a rebirth into the pure land of Sukhāvatī (*bde ba can*), which is the abode of Amitābha. However, other incantations, such as *The Essence of Chenrezi*, and others that will be referenced later in this section, do make such a promise.[192] Spells such as these provide insight not only into the perceived power of the devotional object of the spell, but also what is believed will occur to the subjects who recite them.

---

190. Note that the hyperbolic number 10,180,000 eons, could also be translated as "countless" or "immeasurable" as that is the connotative meaning.

191. There does appear to be a clear reference to Sukhāvatī, the Pure Blissful Realm of Amitābha (*bde ba can gyi 'jig rten*), in this spell, though this could also be understood as a blissful place within a samsaric rebirth. Likely the readers and hearers of the spell associate this realm with the Pure Land as the term *dbe ba can* is highly attested to in the spoken vernacular. It is also of interest that the *Essence of Chenrezi* (Sk. Avalokiteshvara) the Buddha of Compassion, who the Dalai Lamas of the Gelukpa lineage are said to be an emanation of, is here clearly linked to the Pure Land of Sukhāvatī. Given the popularity of the cult of Avalokiteshvara in Tibet, this could be another reason the concept of a Pure Land gained such resonance with laity sensibilities.

192. Amitābha is translated into Tibetan with *snang ba mtha' yas*—"Infinite Awareness" and *'od dpag med*—"Infinite Light." The former epithet is used in this incantation.

The Incantation for Completely Purifying Offerings

The text *The Incantation for Completely Purifying Offerings* (*yon yongs su sbyong ba'i gzungs*), does not contain a Sanskrit title which suggests an original Tibetan composition. Implied in the recitation of this spell is the regular practice of making offerings, which typically are daily water offerings (*yon chab*), food (*zas*), incense (*spos*), barley or rice wine (*chang*), or small amounts of money (*dngul*). After providing the title of the spell, the text proceeds directly into the incantation. The promise is made that if this spell is recited once, all offerings, even those as large as Mount Meru, will be purified. The practitioner is thus encouraged to recite the incantation five or six times.[193] A related text, *The Cleansing of Offerings* (*yon yongs su sbyong ba zhes bya ba*), which has a longer incantation, claims, even through just one recitation, to cleanse all one's sins as well as cleanse as many offerings as one can make.

The Incantation for Circumambulation of the Three Jewels

Implied in the recitation of this incantation is the practitioner circumambulating either a monastery, temple, or sacred site. (Doing a *skor ra*, a circuit around a religious site, either by walking or prostrating, while reciting a mantra or incantation, is a very common Tibetan practice.) *The Incantation for Circumambulation of the Three Jewels* (*dkon mchog gi rten la bskor ba'i gzungs*), begins with an opening homage and prostrations to Buddha Shakyamuni. After the incantation, it is stated that reciting it once is in fact equivalent to prostrating before, and circumambulating around, the eternal and omnipresent Triple Refuge.[194] Furthermore, all one's accumulated sin from endless time will be purified, one will quickly attain Buddhahood and one will be set free from all enemies, spiritual obstacles, sickness and demons. The incantation follows the standard format by concluding with a repetition of the title of the incantation and declaring it to be finished.

---

193. The Tibetan term in the text, *ri rab*, more literally means "excellent mountain," being an epithet for Mount Meru (Sk. Sumeru), the huge mountain in the center of the world of Buddhist cosmology.

194. The term for "eternal" is more literally "past, present, and future" and the term for "omnipresent" is more literally "the ten directions"—that is, the eight cardinal points plus the vast space of all that is above (*steng*) and below (*'og*).

STEPS TOWARD A TIBETAN UNDERSTANDING OF PURITY

The Incantation that Purifies All Karmic Obscurations

The text *The Incantation that Purifies All Karmic Obscurations* (*'phags pa las kyi sgrib pa thams cad rnam par sbyong ba zhes bya ba'i gzungs*), is a longer incantation, but begins with a very brief homage. It is promised that if this incantation is always recited, then all the continuous thread of one's karma will be completely purified. If the incantation is recited three times, the five inexpiable sins will be cleansed. If recited once, bad omens, bad dreams and bad luck will cease to exist and one will never have untimely or premature deaths.[195] The text also states that if the incantation is compassionately spoken into the ear of sentient beings such as herbivores, birds, people, and any non-humans at the point of their death, they will not be reborn into the lower realms.[196] If someone does die, and if, at the time they pass away, their name is spoken aloud with kindness and compassion, one hundred, one thousand or one million times, even if that sentient being has already passed into hell, at that moment, they will be saved from hell.[197] The text provides other perceived benefits of this incantation related to one's rebirth in the higher realms and then reiterates the benefits previously mentioned.

The Incantation that Purifies All Hindrances

After a long homage, and a lengthy incantation of over five lines, the benefits of even hearing the *Incantation that Purifies All Hindrances* are stated.[198] These benefits include all demons, all one's opponents, and all enemies being completely destroyed. If the incantation is recited, then all the obstacles to previous unripened karma will be completely purified and all one's

---

195. The text contains "premature deaths" or "untimely deaths" *(dus ma yin par 'chi ba rnams)* explicitly marked in the plural, which of course suggests ongoing rebirths and deaths within samsara. The text does not promise liberation from samsara, but to be cleansed from a rebirth into the lower realms and rebirth in one of the three higher realms.

196. The term "non-humans" *(mi ma yin)* is used in the sense to incorporate all beings that are not visible. Of course, it is not possible to speak into the ear of a being one cannot see or know when they may be at the point of death, but the emphasis here is to compassionately imagine reciting this incantation for the sake of any and all sentient beings, seen or unseen.

197. The sense here is again of being inclusive of all sentient beings, whether their name is known or not.

198. The name of the text in Tibetan is *'phags pa bar du gcod pa thams cad rnam par sbyong ba zhes bya ba'i gzungs.*

purposes will come to fruition. The text also includes a wish that all sorcery and magic powers that have caused opposition, and all evil spirits and corrupting influences be destroyed, and that all good and perfect things will come to pass. The text concludes with two short mantras.

The Incantation that Purifies All Evil Rebirths

The text *The Incantation that Purifies All Evil Rebirths* (*ngan song thams cad yongs su sbyong ba'i gzung*), claims that should precious sons and daughters comprehend all the words of the incantation, they will be remembered for one hundred and forty thousand continuous generations.[199] Furthermore, they will have all their defiling karmic obstacles cleansed, will quickly attain true understanding, and none of their merit will be exhausted until they reach the essence of enlightenment. Though not stated explicitly, it is clearly implied that through the recitation of this incantation, one will be cleansed from all evil rebirths of the three lower realms. A similar incantation, *The Incantation of Yeshe Dalala that Purifies All Rebirths* (*'phags pa ye shes ta la la zhes bya ba'i gzungs 'gro ba thams cad yongs su sbyong*), promises to cleanse all possible rebirths from the six realms.[200] The sense of being cleansed (*sbyong ba*) in this text is that of being liberated from the endless cycle of rebirth into the six realms and this is made explicit in the text.[201]

Another related incantation, *The Incantation of the Crown of the Head of the Victorious Buddha that Purifies All Lower Rebirths*, promises to also completely purify all those in the lower realms.[202] The same text goes further and states that through the recitation of the spell, sentient beings will be reborn in a pure land, even those who have already passed away.[203] The

---

199. The expression "precious sons and daughters" (*rigs kyi bu'am rigs kyi bu mo*) is a term of endearment a lama may use of his disciples. The expression more literally means "son or daughter of the family."

200. Yeshe Dalala (*ye shes ta la la*) is the name of a previous Buddha.

201. The text in part reads *yongs su thar bar 'gyur*—"to be completely liberated." Section 131b.

202. The name of the text in Tibetan is *'phags pa ngan 'gro thams cad yongs su sbyong ba gtsug tor rnam par rgyal ba zhes bya ba'i gzungs*.

203. *shi 'phos nas kyang 'jig rten gyi khams bde ba can du skye bar 'gyur ro/* This line is repeated in two places, in section 217B and 218A. Note that this reference to a pure land (*'jig rten gyi khams bde ba can*) may not necessarily be referencing the Pure Land (*bde ba can*, Sk. Sukhāvatī) of Amitābha (*'od dpag med*), as the reference here could also be to a pure or blissful realm located within the worldly system of samsara. However, it is most

incantation also states that if, on the 15th day of the month, during the full moon, one ritually bathes and repeats the incantation one thousand and eight times, even if one's life is exhausted, at the point of death, one will, at that moment, have one's life extended, be set free from illness, be cleansed from defiling obscurations, and be liberated from rebirth in any of the evil lower realms.[204] The text also states the benefits of speaking the incantation into the ear of a deceased sentient being.

An incantation which clearly references rebirth in the Pure Land of Sukhāvatī is *The Essence of Sukhāvatī* (*dbe ldan gyi snying po*). The text begins with a homage to Buddha, the dharma, the sangha, Glorious Chenrezi and Great and Victorious Bodhisattvas. A wish to obtain the knowledge and understanding of those Great Ones is then given. After the incantation itself, the text states that if the incantation is read aloud with whatever understanding and awareness one has, one will be remembered for eight thousand generations, and even in death will be reborn in Sukhāvatī, Pure Land of Bliss.[205]

Such incantations as these gave rise to many of them being recited for the deceased in the hope of a better reincarnation. While the Tibetan terms for "being cleansed" (*sbyong ba*) and becoming "completely clean and purified" (*rnam par dag pa*) are used throughout these kinds of incantations, the conceptual framework is that of being cleansed so as to avoid the evil realms, and of being reborn in one of the higher realms, with the eventual goal of being completely cleansed and set free from samsara. These types of incantations are considered to be particularly important when someone has just died and is in the intermediatory state (*bar do*) between rebirths into one's next life.

---

likely that in the minds of the hearers of this incantation that Sukhāvatī comes to mind. (Pure Land aspirational prayers (*bde smon*) to be reborn in Sukhāvatī will be examined in more detail in chapter three).

204. Note that a full moon (*zla ba nya*) is considered to be auspicious for merit making, and the term *khrus* refers to ritual cleansing through the use of water which was mentioned in the purity terms section in chapter one. The ritual of *khrus* will be examined in more detail in chapter four.

205. Another popular incantation for rebirth in Sukhāvatī is *The Incantation of Accomplishing the Infinite Gateways* (*'phags pa sgo mtha' yas pa sgrub pa'i gzungs*), a condensed version of the large sutra *The Teaching on the Purification of the Infinite Gateways* (*'phags pa sgo mtha' yas rnam par sbyong ba bstan pa'i le'ur byas pa*). This sutra contains over 120 direct references to purification, with the term (*rnam par dag pa*) occurring 124 times.

The Incantation of the Essence of the Kangyur

The text *The Incantation of the Essence of the Kangyur* (*bka' 'gyur ro cog gi snying po bsdus pa'i gzungs bzhugs so*), is ascribed to Guru Chokyi Wangchuk (*gu ru chos kyi dbang phyug*, 1221–1270) and is considered a "revealed treasure," that is, an incantation which had been buried centuries earlier and later discovered.[206] Unique to this text is that it is a compilation of incantations, which the author believed contained the essence of the Kangyur—all the words of Buddha. The text begins with an incantation, which, when recited, is claimed to be the equivalent to reciting the 100,000-verse sutra, *The Perfection of Wisdom* (*shes rab kyi pha rol tu phyin pa 'bum*, Sk. Prajnaparamita). Other mantras follow which likewise claim to be the equivalent to smaller versions of *The Perfection of Wisdom* sutras.[207] A short incantation follows which is titled *The Heart Essence of All Buddhas* (*de bzhin bshegs pa thams cad kyi snying po zhes bya ba'i gzungs*).[208] It is claimed that reciting this incantation once will remove all defiling obscurations, without exception, of one hundred million eons. The text then moves to more incantations involving other *Perfection of Wisdom* sutras before citing the text of *The Incantation for Completely Purifying Offerings*, mentioned early in this section. It is claimed that reciting this incantation will purify the five inexpiable sins. The text then works through each of the five sins individually, providing a separate incantation for each one which are believed to individually cleanse these sins. The text concludes by stating that if one reads and writes this incantation, and the names of Buddha, and confesses one's sins, one will be purified, without exception, from all defiling obscurations.

Summary of Incantations

This selective sample of incantations make rather bold claims of both a mundane and supramundane nature. The incantations promise benefits in

---

206. Guru Chokyi Wangchuk is also known as Guru Chowang and was renowned as a great treasure revealer. See D. Rinpoche, *Nyingma School*, 760–70.

207. The text mentions *The Perfection of Wisdom* sutra of 25,000 verses, and of 8,000 verses. This sutra, which has varying lengths (there are 23 sutras in the *Perfection of Wisdom* series), is an important one in the Mahayana system and foundational to developing the mind of a Bodhisattva. See Conce, *Perfection of Wisdom*.

208. The condensed form of this incantation demonstrates how a *gzungs* is believed to encapsulate a large body of teaching.

the mundane world of samsara by, for example, clearing away bad luck, bad dreams, demons and eliminating obstacles such as corrupting influences or one's enemies, and cleansing the necessary offerings for merit accumulation. Evil spirits, demons, and spiritual obstacles are perceived to be unclean and impure and need to be destroyed or overcome for the practitioner to be cleansed and obtain a desired outcome. These incantations also make supramundane salvific claims of cleansing and deliverance from the lower rebirths and give hope of a higher rebirth, even for those already deceased. Other spells promise rebirth in a pure realm, even the Pure Land of Bliss, again predicated upon a certain sense of the practitioner having themselves first been cleansed of moral defilements or previous negative karma. It would appear that the recitation, writing down, and hearing of these incantations is essential in this purification and liberation process. Davidson has observed that incantations function as "the vehicle for the sonic power of mantras, whether these are for worldly purposes, as in the case of protection or other goals, or for soteriological purposes."[209] The textual, lexical, and semantic data of the incantations examined here, would appear to bear this out. One could make the observation of the incantations examined here that the soteriological goals are a cleansed or purified state, leading to being rescued from a heinous rebirth in the lower realms into a higher realm and the possibility of being reborn in a pure one, even into Sukhāvatī, the Pure Land of Bliss.

The General Sutra Discourses

This study intended to begin with an examination of purity within the general body of sutra discourse texts (*mdo ste*). However, it soon became apparent, that while notions of purity can be found there,[210] the textual

---

209. Davidson, "Studies in Dharani Literature I," 117–18.

210. The following sutras contain high lexical weightings of content associated with purity. However, the conception of purity within these texts is quite abstract, linking purity and emptiness to the primordially pure mind. This teaching appears to be uniform across the sutras. For example, the *Sutra of the Teaching of the Purification of the Limitless Gateways* (*'phags pa sgo mtha' yas pa rnam par sbyong ba bstan pa'i le'u zhes bya ba theg pa chen po'i mdo*) contains 124 references to purification (*rnam par dag pa*), the *Sutra of the Explanation of Intentions* (*'phags pa dgongs pa nges par 'grel pa zhes bya ba theg pa chen po'i mdo*) contains 72 references to purification (*rnam par dag pa*), and the *Sutra of the White Lotus of the Holy Dharma* (*dam pa'i chos pad ma dkar po zhes bya ba theg pa chen po'i mdo*) contains 18 references to purification (*rnam par dag pa*). There is also a high frequency of purification references within the *Perfection of Wisdom* (*phar phyin*) literature.

weight of purity concerns was to be found within the texts of praxis, the tantras, and the incantations. In a sense, this is not surprising given that Tibetan Buddhism is so heavily geared towards Vajrayana Buddhism and the "fast-track-to-enlightenment" practices of tantra. In commenting upon the tantras, Bentor has noted that they "offer methods with a magic-like power to transform the contaminated body into a pure essence, as alchemy is said to transform iron into gold."[211] When faced with the much longer "many-lifetimes" path to enlightenment through the gradual processes outlined in the sutras, it is the "magic-like" appeal of the tantras and texts of praxis which have gained the most currency in Tibetan Buddhism, and where notions of purity are most evident. While the primary focus of this chapter is the monastic texts of praxis, as has been examined, a few brief and very general comments and observations regarding notions of purity in the sutra discourses will be made.

Justice cannot be done here to notions of purity in the sutras, and indeed would warrant a separate study, but as a broad generalization the concept of purity and purification within the sutras is more abstract and directly linked to the fundamental Buddhist doctrine of emptiness (*stong ba nyid*).[212] This is not to say the teaching on emptiness does not appear in the tantras, rather that it is more prominent in the sutras as a foundational, core doctrine.[213] The doctrine of emptiness states that all phenomena, being devoid of inherent existence are one and the same in emptiness. This is a teaching that is pervasive throughout the discourses, especially the *Perfection of Wisdom* sutras.[214] Emptiness, in the Buddhist schema, is predicated upon the doctrine of "dependent arising" (*rten 'bral*) which, in short, claims that all things are dependent on something else for their existence and therefore do not exist inherently in themselves. On this basis, all phenomena, then, are considered to be devoid of an actual entity in and of

---

211. Bentor, "Body in Enlightenment," 79.

212. The Dege Kangyur contains 399 sutras and the Lhasa Kangyur 32 volumes so any observations here can only be considered of a general nature. A thorough examination of the Buddhist teaching on emptiness would require a separate study. There are at least twenty conceptualizations of emptiness (*stong pa nyid nyi shu*). See ITED, entry under *stong pa nyid nyi shu*. See also Hopkins' seminal work, *Meditation on Emptiness*.

213. Rolf, in her study of purity in Tsong Khapa's writings on tantra, noted the connection between emptiness and purity: "the notion of purity in a tantric context: purity as both emptiness, at the timeless level of ultimate reality, and as a total lack of accumulated defilements, at the level of deceptive reality and as a final attainment to be realized." Rolf, "Sacred Illusion," 259.

214. See for example, Conce, *Perfection of Wisdom*, 25, 51–52, 142–43, 149, 237.

themselves. Nothing is what it appears to be, and therefore our perception of reality is an illusion (*'khrul snang*), devoid of the qualities we ascribe to that which we think we perceive in our deluded state. In relation to purity, in a metaphysical sense, the mind which understands the fundamental nature of reality (*chos nyid*), that is, that it is empty (*stong pa*) of intrinsic characteristics, is said to be pure (*rnam par dag pa*). And the purification of the mind is central in the quest for enlightenment.

The Sutra of the Purification of Karmic Obscurations

The text *The Sutra of the Purification of Karmic Obscurations* (*'phags pa las kyi sgrib pa rnam par dag pa zhes bya ba theg pa chen po'i mdo*), is one example which illustrates well the difference between notions of purity contained in the general discourse sutras and the text of praxis.[215] *The Purification of Karmic Obscurations* is framed around the moral failings of a monk who breaks his vows of celibacy and sleeps with a prostitute. Upon admitting his transgression, the monk is not asked to confess, to show regret or remorse, to perform prostrations, to practice the four antidotes, or to recite lengthy liturgies, mantras, or incantations and is not instructed to visualize any deities or pay homage to them. In this sutra, the Buddha, in dealing with the monk's infraction, places no emphasis on his moral failings nor prescribes any processes for purification. Rather, the Buddha instructs the monk to contemplate the ultimate view of emptiness, the lack of any intrinsic nature of all phenomena, as the solution to be purified from defiling karmic obscurations.

In a long discourse, the Buddha expands on the theme of emptiness, telling the monk such things as: "all phenomena lack existence, their very essence is like a mirage,"[216] "all phenomena are devoid of reality, they are not real entities,"[217] and "all phenomena are like hallucinations and appear mistakenly, they are like illusions."[218] The Buddha concludes his speech by stating that "as all phenomena are at all times unafflicted, they are perfectly

---

215. The full name of the text is *The Glorious Mahayana Sutra of the Purification of Karmic Obscurations*.

216. *chos thams cad ni med pa ste/smig rgyu lta bu'i nga bo nyid yin no/ The Purification of Karmic Obscurations*, section 442B, line 1.

217. *The Purification of Karmic Obscurations*, section 442B, line 2.

218. *The Purification of Karmic Obscurations*, section 442B, line 7.

pure by nature."²¹⁹ Upon hearing this lengthy explanation from the Buddha, the monk experiences joy and relief at having learned of the nature of phenomena and is delighted that he now has no karmic obscurations, that he has been purified of his moral transgression based on this view of ultimate reality having no inherent nature.

Further on in the discourse, when the monk asks how a Bodhisattva can be purified from karmic obscurations, part of the Buddha's lengthy reply is, "Those who see all phenomena as objects of delusion will attain purification from karmic obscurations."²²⁰ In this text, it would seem the teaching of emptiness has precedence over moral conduct, and there is no apparent need for the monk's improper conduct to be cleansed and cleared away. It is mental assent to the doctrine of emptiness that is propounded as the way to be purified from the defilements of karma. This focus on mental assent, and the training of the mind, is in keeping with the teachings of the sutras, and indeed pervades all levels of Buddhist teaching.²²¹ Though it is a generalization, it is also fair to state that this notion of purity and purification as being subsumed into the teaching on emptiness, is taught across the sutras (and other genres) and marks a significant contrast to the praxis of the tantras. In the teachings of the sutras, ultimately it is the mind alone that has the capacity to purify. As the Buddha himself has said elsewhere, "living beings are defiled through the contamination of the mind . . . and they are purified through the purification of the mind."²²² And it is the mind that needs to be trained to view all phenomena as inherently empty.²²³ Here, in

---

219. *The Purification of Karmic Obscurations*, section 444A, line 3.

220. *The Purification of Karmic Obscurations*, section 450A, line 4. The Buddha later states that those who attain purification are those who "do not distinguish between the phenomena of immoral conduct and the phenomena of moral conduct." Section 451B, line 3. Note that there is a long list of qualifications of the Bodhisattvas who attain purification and I have only highlighted a few examples.

221. For example, the large body of texts in the Mind Training or Mental Purification genre (*blo sbyong*) stress the focus on training the mind to overcome deluded perceptions of reality and to be dedicated to appropriate moral conduct, particularly in regard to the treatment of others. Two of the primary texts in this genre are: *Eight Stanzas on Mental Purification* (*blo sbyong tshigs brgyad ma*) by Langri Thanpa (*glang ri thang pa*, 1054–1123), and *Seven-Point Mind Training* (*blo sbyong don bdun ma*) by Chekawa Yeshe Dorje (*mchad kha ba ye she rdo rje*, 1101–1175). An analysis of this genre was beyond the scope of this study. See Jinpa et al., *Mind Training*; and Sweet, "Mental Purification (Blo Sbyong)." See also The Dalai Lama, *Complete Foundation*.

222. As quoted in Skorupski, "Consciousness and Luminosity," 43.

223. Hopkins observes that "The mind has the capacity to purify afflictions." Hopkins, *Meditation on Emptiness*, 88. Sferra also notes that "purification [is possible] and

this sutra, there is no calling upon a higher moral source, or the invocation of mantras, as there is in the texts of praxis and the tantras, to effect purification. Purification becomes a mental exercise.

There is a certain unanimity across the sutra discourses which espouse that the mind can be trained to return to its innately pure state through meditation and contemplations of emptiness.[224] The sutras provide some understanding of notions of purity. However, since Tibetan Buddhism is essentially Vajrayana Buddhism, examining the texts associated with purification within the texts of praxis and the tantras not only proves more illuminating in regards to gaining a more comprehensive understanding of Tibetan notions of purity, but is also where the weight of textual data lies.

Chapter Two Summary

This chapter has provided an examination of notions of purity and purification contained within a selection of texts from the texts of praxis included in the genres of confessional, preliminary, Vajrasattva and Heruka tantra, and incantation texts. A cursory mention was made of purity within the sutras, and the connection between purity and emptiness was observed. The contrasting notions of purity, and the means to attain purification, as revealed in the sutras and the texts of praxis was also highlighted. The confessional, preliminary, tantra and incantation texts, have shown that Tibetans believe ontologically that there exists a state of defilement caused by both moral infractions and through conducting the quotidian affairs of mundane samsaric existence—and from both of these one needs to be cleansed. These texts indicate that Tibetans further believe that purification is possible and highly desirable.

Purified Realms

In the text of praxis, a higher moral source, a deified Buddha, is the one who is believed can help to effect purification, provided the correct processes are followed, the right mantras are recited, and the process is repeated regularly. Earthly gods, by comparison, can bring about no such effect and are not

---

depends on the purification of the mind." Sferra, "Concept of Purification," 87.

224. This focus on training the mind within the Mahayana sutras is known as the "mind only" school (*sems tsam*). A "middle way" school (*dbu ma*) also developed which placed less emphasis on the mind and incorporated other practices.

the object of one's devotion and visualization. Rather, the gods themselves need to be purified from the defiling acts of humans. From a soteriological perspective, only those beings believed to have escaped from samsara can offer salvific hope to those still trapped there. Further, the desire of escaping from a rebirth from the lower realms and the possibility of a higher rebirth, or even rebirth in a pure realm, is predicated upon a certain perception of being made clean (*sbyangs pa*) and becoming pure (*rnam par dag pa*)—key Tibetan terms used prolifically throughout the texts studied. The use of mantras and incantations was observed as being crucial in this process.

The Purified State

The various Vajrasattva tantra texts studied in this chapter emphasize the necessity of being absorbed into the purity of Vajrasattva and his consort and being one with the deity, and of the efficacy of his mantra. The highest tantric texts emphasize esoteric yoga practices, complete devotion to one's lama, and self-identification with the meditational deity as necessary for purification to occur. In addition, the Heruka tantra practice emphasizes the purification of the mind, speech, and body as the necessary progression for being subsumed into the purity of the wrathful Heruka. This threefold purification is seen as a necessary step towards attaining Buddhahood. As the fourteenth Dalai Lama has stated, "Who is Buddha? Buddha is a being who attained complete purification of mind, speech, and body."[225] Geshe Jampa Gyatso has also noted the centrality of this threefold purification within Tibetan Buddhism: "The practices of purifying negativities and accumulating merit are the heart of the many methods taught in the Buddhist sutra and tantra teachings for attaining enlightenment. To gain any mental, or spiritual, development whatsoever, it is absolutely necessary to purify the negativities of body, speech, and mind that we have accumulated throughout our beginningless lives."[226] One could assert, based on these texts, that the goal of Tibetan Buddhism can quite comfortably be framed within a purity paradigm. That is, one of the express goals of Tibetan Buddhism, and essential for reaching nirvana, is to become *rnam par dag pa*—completely pure. In fact, an argument could be made that this textual evidence suggests that the primary goal of Tibetan Buddhism is to achieve a purified state.[227]

---

225. The Dalai Lama, *Kindness, Clarity, and Insight*, 40.
226. G. J. Gyatso, *Purification in Tibetan Buddhism*, Kindle location 90–92.
227. Cabezón suggests that "In the Mahayana Buddhist, and especially in the Tantric

Purification as a Process

The analysis of the texts in this section can also lead one to conclude that purification is a process. That is, through the observance of specific rules of conduct and the purification of broken vows and impure conduct, recitation of liturgies, mantras and incantations, and the practice of elaborate yogic techniques one moves towards a purified state. Purification is an accumulative process that requires sustained effort. Lopez suggests that "The process of the path, therefore, is a gradual process of purification, removing defilements through a variety of practices until the utter transformation from afflicted sentient being to perfect buddha has been effected."[228] The current Dalai Lama confirms not only the possibility of being purified, but that it is a process over time which leads to the ultimate soteriological goal of Buddhahood. He states, "our normal mental states are permeated with the pollution of the various afflictions and that these afflictions must be removed gradually, layer after layer. It is through such a gradual process that our mind becomes increasingly purified, a process that eventually culminates in the attainment of Buddhahood."[229] The Dalai Lama also makes this claim about Buddha Shakyamuni, clearly placing purification as an essential component for enlightenment: "Initially, Shākyamuni Buddha was Siddhārtha, an ordinary being troubled by delusions and engaging in harmful thoughts and wrong actions—someone like ourselves. However, with the help of certain teachings and teachers, he gradually purified himself and, in the end, became enlightened."[230] Though this transformation is gradual, it has also been observed that the appeal of the Vajrayana esoteric tantric yoga practices is the hope of expediting the purification process with the ultimate goal of perhaps attaining enlightenment within one lifetime.

In summary, the data presented in these texts of praxis have demonstrated the cosmological and soteriological realities which underpin Tibetan notions of purity and purification. The analysis of these texts suggests

---

case, the path to liberation is viewed as a path of purification in which the body, speech, and mind of the individual are transformed into the perfect body, speech, and mind of an enlightened being." Cabezón, "Liberation," 196. Masao Abe states that "We therefore take the relation between the impure and the pure, between delusion and enlightenment, as a process of moving from the impure to the pure, from delusion to enlightenment." Abe, "Idea of Purity," 186.

228. Lopez, *Buddhism in Practice*, 23.
229. The Dalai Lama, *Introduction to Buddhism*, Kindle location 1051–52.
230. The Dalai Lama, *Kindness, Clarity, and Insight*, Kindle location 440–42.

that purity is a state worth pursuing and a pure realm worth aiming for, predicated upon the practitioner becoming purified of the defiling stains of samsaric worldly existence and moral infractions. Purity is both an aspirational state, and a desired realm to be reborn into, and the means to achieve this is the process of purification of the practitioner. In soteriological terms, purity is seen as an ultimate state of liberation from the stain of samsara. The salvific means to achieve this, at least in considerable part, is the need for purification through repeated processes of elaborate means.

This study will now move to an examination of selected texts associated with purity and purification which have a certain currency among the laity. This will be the subject matter of chapter three.

3

Texts of Lay Aspiration and Folk Traditions

Introduction

THE PRIMARY FOCUS OF this chapter will be texts which appear to have influenced lay notions of purity and purification. As mentioned in the introduction to the previous chapter, the demarcation between what may be considered strictly a "monastic" text and what may be considered a "lay" text is by no means a fixed one. Rather, it is a porous division where there remains an ongoing interplay between the two. Lawrence Epstein and Peng Wenbin, scholars among others, have observed that, "Tibetan folk and more formal religious traditions have interpenetrated each other to the extent that it is difficult to disentangle them."[1] Suffice to say that the previous chapter primarily dealt with esoteric texts of tantra, which are typically not the domain of the uninitiated laity. Here the study will be focused on exploring texts which are generally regarded as those which identify more closely with the laity. Though there is a certain subjectivity in the phrasing "generally regarded," as will be seen, the texts that follow may well allow for such a classification. To be sure, a number of the texts that will be examined have been composed by monks and Tibetan masters and are also

---

1. L. Epstein and Wenbin, "Ritual, Ethnicity, Generational Identity," 121. They further observe that "Monks, for example, often perform readings of religious texts for laymen, which in the eyes of the latter, accomplish the same this-worldly ends as do, say, folk rituals of purification. They also confer some degree of otherworldly merit on them. Similarly, Buddhist or Bon rituals and texts are often employed in folk rituals."

significant texts within the monastic communities themselves. However, these texts have both appealed to lay sensibilities and, being devoid of the restrictive tantric elements, have been more accessible to them, thus gaining a widespread appeal.

More specifically, this chapter will explore texts within the corpus of Pure Land literature. The examination of Pure Land texts will focus on the autochthonous genre of texts known as *bde smon*—Aspiration Prayers. Hence, the first part of the title of this chapter "texts of lay aspiration" refers to this genre of aspirational prayers.[2] The study and analysis of this genre will form a large section of this chapter. Continuing with the theme of aspirational folk texts, a closer examination of the most prolific Tibetan mantra, *om mani padme hum*, in particular what it reveals about notions of purity, will be undertaken. This will necessitate consideration of the cult of Avalokiteshvara, who is the exalted patron of this six-syllable mantra. The remainder of the chapter will deal with "texts of folk traditions" which will look at purity and purification within the genres of proverbs, and texts of moral instructions. These grassroot texts, as it were, will allow for closer insights to a lay understanding of purity.

Tibetan Pure Lands

It is not the intention of this study to trace the origins of Pure Land beliefs in Tibet, nor their development within the four major schools of Tibetan Buddhism. Rather, the purpose is to examine key texts which have influenced lay sensibilities regarding purity and purification. Though never an official school of Tibetan Buddhism, Pure Land Buddhism (also referred to as "Pure Lands") has had a profound influence among Tibetan people groups. Indeed, the literature review has shown the cult of Amitābha to be "an integral part of the Mahayana Buddhist tradition of Tibet."[3] Naturally, within this Tibetan Buddhist Mahayana tradition of Pure Lands are also included many Vajrayana tantric elements of devotion to Buddha Amitābha.[4] Halkias and Kapstein have demonstrated how extensive and widely accepted Pure Land teachings are among both monks and

---

2. This is not to suggest that these texts are not aspirational texts for the monastics, which many of them clearly are. Rather, the focus here is upon the influence of these texts among the laity.

3. Payne and Tanaka, *Approaching*, 5.

4. Halkias, *Luminous Bliss*, 103, 139–62; Skorupski, "Tibetan Prayer for Rebirth," 209.

the laity.⁵ There appears to be no sectarian division among the schools of Tibetan Buddhism in regards to Pure Land teachings, with all schools embracing them. This may have been an additional factor as to why Pure Lands gained such widespread acceptance among the laity. As Kapstein has noted, "there is no evidence that sectarian identity was ever peculiarly tied to the Pure Land of Amitābha. His was an ever-inclusive cult, involving Tibetan Buddhists overall."⁶

In essence, Pure Land Buddhism suggests that there exists a pure realm, a blissful land in which rebirth into, within one lifetime, is available to all, both lay and monastic, should the requisite faith and devotion to the merciful Buddha Amitābha, and his abode of Sukhāvatī, be sufficiently manifest by the sincere practitioner. The allure of Pure Lands as accessible to all members of society predicated by faith alone is central to its wide appeal. As Skorupski has observed, "it seems apparent that no one has been excluded from being reborn in the Sukhāvatī. On the contrary even the worst sinners are assured of being saved."⁷ Unlike the elaborate purification praxis of the tantras, Pure Land teachings, at the fundamental level, purport that rebirth in Sukhāvatī is possible for anyone through faith, devotion and aspirational prayer. Yet like tantra, which espouses the possibility of enlightenment within one lifetime, rebirth in Sukhāvatī is also possible within a single human existence.⁸ In its simplest form, Pure Land Buddhism provides hope for Tibetans who, it is fair to claim, are preoccupied with death and fear of the afterlife. Lowell Cook makes the observation that, "Pure Land Buddhism's central function is to address the fundamental human concern with death. Indeed, rebirth in Sukhāvatī must necessarily be premised on passing away in this life. Death is a central theme in Tibetan Buddhism, where we are reminded time and time again of the certainty of death."⁹ Kapstein has also pointed out the strong connection between the tantric 'pho ba

---

5. Halkias, *Luminous Bliss*; Kapstein, "Pure Land Buddhism."

6. Kapstein, "Pure Land Buddhism," 41.

7. Skorupski, "Tibetan Prayer for Rebirth," 213. Lowell Cook also observes that "The fact that Sukhāvatī is accessible to potentially anyone meant that all members of a given society—whether in India's caste society, Tibet's feudal system, or otherwise—had an equal opportunity at rebirth there and eventual awakening." Cook, "Ju Mi Pham," 23.

8. Corless has suggested that the focus on purity and the "fast-tracking" of purification in tantra is one of the main similarities between Pure Land and Vajrayana teachings. Corless, "Pure Land."

9. Cook, "Ju Mi Pham," 21.

ritual of the transfer of consciousness at the point of death to the pure land of Sukhāvatī—a ritual that is still widely practiced in Tibet today.[10]

Perhaps it is no wonder, given the hardships of life in Tibet and the fear of death, that the hope of a blissful land, open to all, free from the impurities and pollution of samsara, gained widespread appeal. As Kapstein has rightly observed, "it seems clear that the ideal of Sukhāvatī succeeded in Tibet precisely because it captured the real aspirations of the peasants and nomads, who knew all too well toil and hardship from cradle to the grave."[11] Skorupski draws a similar conclusion: "Thus the combination of the Sukhāvatī as a happy buddha-field and the possibility of attaining it by anyone who invokes the name of Amitābha, removes all anxieties about afterlife, and consequently dispels all worries about the dead, provided they heard the name of Amitābha before they died."[12]

Many Pure Lands—Which Is Which?

Geshe Kelsang Gyatso provides a straight forward definition of a pure land as, "A pure environment in which there are no true sufferings."[13] Indeed, there are numerous pure lands within Tibetan Buddhist cosmology that could come under that definition. A brief overview of the nomenclature and associated pure lands may prove helpful.

The most generic term for a pure land is *dag pa'i zhing khams* (also *dag pa'i khams*) which more literally means a "pure land," "pure realm," or "pure field."[14] Though the term "pure land" is a generic term, it is also often used in the literature as a metonym for Sukhāvatī, and in the spoken vernacular it is common for Tibetans to pray to be reborn in *dag pa'i zhing khams*, by which they are typically referencing Sukhāvatī. The Great Tibetan-Chinese Dictionary defines a pure realm as "one that has not been stained

---

10. Kapstein, "Pilgrimage of Rebirth Reborn"; Kapstein, *Tibetans*, 213–14. See also Gouin, *Tibetan Rituals of Death*, 16, 23–25, 44–45, 103–4. She notes that much of the funeral rite is dedicated to "purifying the deceased's karma" with the goal of "sending the deceased's consciousness to a pure land." Gouin, *Tibetan Rituals of Death*, 104.

11. Kapstein, "Pure Land Buddhism," 41.

12. Skorupski, "Tibetan Prayer for Rebirth," 220.

13. G. K. Gyatso, *Essence of Vajrayana*, 494.

14. *zhing* refers to a field, as in a field sown with a crop, and *khams* refers to a realm or place typically invisible to the human eye.

by impurities."[15] The generic term for a Buddhafield, the place where an enlightened Buddha resides, is known as a *zhing khams*. These realms are purified lands of bliss for those who have achieved the pure, enlightened, and fully awakened mind of Buddhahood.[16] The five highest and purest Buddha fields (*rigs lnga'i zhing khams*)[17] are:

1. "Nothing Below" (*'og min*, Sk. Akanishtha), the highest realm inhabited by Buddha Vairocana (*rnam par snang mdzad*), a realm considered to be in the center of the universe.

2. "Revealed Joy" (*mngon sum dga' ba*, Sk. Abirati) presided over by Buddha Aksobhya (*mi bskyod pa, mi 'khrugs pa*), is a pure realm believed to be situated in the east.

3. "Endowed with Glory" (*dpal dang ldan pa*, Sk. Shrimat) is the abode of Ratnasambhava (*rin chen 'byung gnas*), believed to be situated in the south.

4. "Endowed with Bliss" (*bde ba can*, Sk. Sukhāvatī, also referred to as "Lotus Mound" *pad ma btsheg*) is the abode of Amitābha (*'od dpag med*), a realm situated in the west.

5. "Excellent Accomplishment" (*las rab grub pa*, Sk. Karmaprasiddhi), is a realm inhabited by Amoghasiddhi (*don yod grub pa* "Completely Acomplished One"), situated in the north.

Beyond these five realms, there are other realms that are not the final stage of Buddhahood but are, to varying degrees, realms that are progressively closer to ultimate Buddhahood. In other words, there are other realms which are not the ultimate nirvana of enlightenment, but rather are a final stage before enlightenment. Though Sukhāvatī, for example, is considered to be outside the wheel of samsara, and is listed as one of the five Buddha fields, it is, in fact, not the final destination of complete liberation; rather it is the final stage before ultimate Buddhahood is attained.[18] The

---

15. TDCM, under *dag pa'i khams*, 1237.

16. TDCM, under *zhing khams*, 2388.

17. RJYS, under *rigs lnga'i zhing khams*. These Buddhafields are also known as *sangs rgyas kyi zhing*. There are five other pure realms *gnas gtsang ma'i sa lnga, gtsang ris lha gnas* which are not specific Buddha fields as such. See ITED under *gnas gtsang ma'i sa lnga*.

18. The *bde smon* texts themselves confirm this and Skorupski has noted that "beings born in Sukhāvatī are destined to be reborn once more constitutes, of course, an integral part of the Pure Land teachings." Skorupski, "Tibetan Prayer for Rebirth," 214.

TEXTS OF LAY ASPIRATION AND FOLK TRADITIONS

location of these realms is not always clearly defined, but generally they are hidden lands beyond the worldly sphere of samsara.[19] Though Sukhāvatī is the realm typically associated with Pure Land Buddhism, the mythical realm of Shambala (*bde 'byung, sham blha la*) is likely more well known among Western audiences.[20] This may be due in part to the popularity of the Kalachakra Tantra, in which Shambala features, being a tantra the current Dalai Lama has performed numerous times in the West.[21] The land of Shambala, also considered a pure land (and from which the term "Shangri-La" is believed to have been derived),[22] is a realm deeply embedded in Tibetan consciousness.[23] Other pure lands are the "Joyous Heaven" of Tuṣita (*dga' ldan*), where Maitreya (*byams pa*), the future Buddha is believed to currently reside.[24] Padmasambhava's pure realm, known as the "Copper Colored Mountain" (*zangs mdog dpal ri*), and the "Celestial Pure Heaven" (*dag pa mkha' spyod*, Sk. Khechara) where Heruka and his consort Vajrayogini (*rdo rje rnal 'byor ma*) reside, are other pure lands.[25] The pre-Buddhist religion of Bön has a famous pure land known as Olmo Lungring (*'ol mo lung ring*). This realm is also known as Tazig Olmo Lungring, being the alleged birth place of Shenrab (*gshen rab*), founder of the Bön religion, and a mythical pure realm of bliss.[26] Like all of these realms, Olmo Lung Ring is considered to be a "completely pure and spiritual land" which is "beyond the impure nature of this existing world."[27]

In scholarly literature, "Pure Land Buddhism" typically refers to the cult of Amitābha (also known as Amidism) and his pure abode of

---

19. Davidson, "Hidden Realms."

20. Shambala is translated from Sanskrit into Tibetan as "Source of Happiness" (*bde 'byung*) and is also transliterated as *sham+p+lhla* and *sham blha la*.

21. See The Dalai Lama, *Kalachakra Tantra*.

22. James Hilton's *Lost Horizon* helped popularize the term "Shangri-La."

23. See Davidson, "Hidden Realms," 166–68

24. *dga' ldan* is the name of a famous Gelukpa monastery in Tibet. James Apple suggests that "The pure land of Tuṣita is also thought to be within part of this world system (*lokadhātu*; *'jigs rten kyi khams*) and therefore easier to reach than the western paradise of Sukhāvatī (*bde ba can*)." Apple, "Maitreya's Tuṣita Heaven," 198.

25. Khechara is also referred to in English as "Dakini Land" on account of Vajrayogini being a dakini (*mkha' 'gro ma*) or sky goddess. G. K. Gyatso, *Guide to Dakini Land*, 527, and G. K. Gyatso, *New Guide to Dakini*, xi.

26. Tazig (*ta zig*) is an ancient term for Persia.

27. G. N. D. Rinpoche, *Opening the Door*, 5; Martin, "'Ol-Mo-Lung-Ring."

Sukhāvatī.²⁸ Buddha Amitābha has been translated from Sanskrit into Tibetan as "Endless Light" (*'od dpag med*) and he has also been given the epithet "Infinite Awareness" (*snang ba mtha' med*), often being referenced this way in *bde smon* texts. Amitābha is also often equated with the Buddha Amitāyus, translated in Tibetan as "Infinite Light" (*tshe dpag med*), an epithet he is accorded in many of the aspirational prayers. Though many texts do use the two names interchangeably, Amitāyus is more technically considered to be the celestial or "complete enjoyment" form or aspect of Buddha Amitābha.²⁹ Since the two Buddhas, Amitābha and Amitāyus, regularly occur in the same texts, and faith in either or both of them is efficacious for rebirth in Sukhāvatī, it is fair to assume that for most practitioners of Pure Lands, the two are interchangeable, referencing the same being.³⁰ While both of them are mentioned in the texts that will be examined in the following section, and are clearly seen as archetypal savior figures, prayer directly to Amitābha is more common throughout. Clearly, the notion of a "pure land" beyond this world of suffering has long resonated with Tibetan sensibilities. While there are believed to be many pure lands and "Buddha fields," it is worth stressing again the most prominent one, which also has the most textual support, is the pure land of Sukhāvatī. As Halkias has noted, "Among all the Mahayana pure lands that translocated from India to Tibet, none attained the religious prominence and popular acceptance of Sukhāvatī."³¹

Aspirational Prayer Texts

There are two main sutras in the Tibetan canon concerned with Pure Land teachings, which have clearly influenced the aspirational prayers of *bde smon* and are known as the "long" and "short" Sukhāvatīvyuha sutras.³² As

28. Halkias, *Luminous Bliss*, Kindle location 190.

29. There are three main aspects or "bodies" of a Buddha (*sku gsum*, Sk. trikaya)—1. the "dharma" or "reality" body (*chos kyi sku*, Sk. dharmakaya), 2. the "complete enjoyment body" (*longs spyod rdzogs pa'i sku*, Sk. sambhogakaya) and 3. the "emanation body" (*sprul pa'i sku*, Sk. nirmanakaya). See ITED, under *sku gsum*.

30. Skorupski uses the two names interchangeably in his writings, equating them as the same Buddha. Skorupski, "Tibetan Prayer for Rebirth," 213, 214, 215, 220. Jan Nattier does likewise and also notes the names are interchangeable in Chinese. Nattier, "Realm of Akṣobhya," 72. Johnathon Silk follows the same convention. Silk, "In Praise," 498, 502.

31. Halkias, "Visions," 140.

32. These sutras are considered to be the words of Buddha. The longer sutra is titled

mentioned, there exist many other types of Pure Land texts such as incantations (some of which were discussed in chapter two), treasure texts, tantric consciousness transferal texts, commentaries, and tantric sadhana texts of praxis.[33] However, that largest body of Pure Lands literature is found within the *bde smon* genre. The term *bde smon* more literally means "happy wish" and is an abbreviation of the longer expression *dbe ba can du skyes pa'i smon lam* "an aspirational prayer for rebirth in Sukhāvatī." It was this indigenous genre of prayers that developed in Tibet and has become the predominant texts of Pure Land teaching and praxis. Silk has suggested that some of the earliest examples of *bde smon* texts may date back to the eighth or ninth century.[34] In any case, Pure Land teachings have a long history among Tibetans. While the *dbe smon* prayers themselves will be the focus of this section, the *dbe smon* genre also encompass a range of literature including commentary works discussing Pure Land theology, and Vajrayana forms of devotion and practice, all linked by "a shared typology of liberation and faith in the buddha field of Buddha Amitābha."[35] One of the larger and more recent collections of *bde smon* aspirational prayers (recently republished in 2007), is the two volume work, *An Anthology of Sukhāvatī Prayers*.[36]

Scholars agree that the seventeenth-century Kadampa Kagyu master, Karma Chagme (*karma chags med*, 1613–1678), was the most prolific writer and promulgator of Pure Land literature. Though by no means the first indigenous author of Tibetan Pure Land texts, he became one of its greatest

---

'*od dpag med kyi bkod pa'i mdo*, *The Display of Amitābha* and the shorter sutra *bde ba can gyi bkod pa'i mdo*, *The Display of Amitābha of Sukhāvatī*. There is a third Pure Land sutra, the *Amitāyurdhyāna Sutra*, which is not as well attested to in the Tibetan Buddhist canon. Hisao Inagaki and Harold Stewart have undertaken an English translation of the three Pure Land sutras from Chinese. See Inagaki and Stewart, *Three Pure Land Sutras*. These sutras have clearly informed the *bde smon* texts in their descriptions of Sukhāvatī and Buddha Amitābha and his efficacious saving nature.

33. One of the most famous Pure Land tantric texts, which later on became a class of texts in its own right, was *Means for Attaining the Sukhāvatī* (*bde chen zhing sgrub*), a text believed to be composed by Migyur Dorje (1645–1668), a famous treasure revealer who was a student of Karma Chagme. See Kapstein, "Pure Land Buddhism," 32–32; and Wilson, "Pure Land Iconography."

34. Silk, "In Praise," 498. Silk suggests that these texts were influenced by Chinese Pure Land teachings and may have either been translated from Chinese or composed in a bilingual environment. The widespread appeal of Pure Land teachings in China is well attested to.

35. Halkias, *Luminous Bliss*, Kindle location 314.

36. *Bde Smon Phyogs Bsgrigs*, [*Anthology of Sukhāvatī Prayers*].

proponents. Halkias has noted that, "Karma chags-med was passionate about Pure Land practice and was the greatest systematizer of Pure Land ritual literature the Tibetan tradition has ever known. In his hagiographies it was prophesized that his teachings will lead one hundred million sentient beings to Amitābha's Pure Land."[37] The most well-known and celebrated of Karma Chagme's aspirational prayers is *A Prayer for Rebirth in Sukhāvatī*.[38] It is a prayer that is recited by many people of all walks of life, and certain lines from the prayer are well attested to in Tibetan spoken vernaculars. It would appear that Halkias is accurate to claim that, "Indisputably, his [Karma Chagme's] Aspirational Prayer for the Pure Land Sukhāvatī is the most widely recited prayer in Tibet and among Tibetan Buddhists in exile."[39] Attention will now be turned to this prayer.

A Prayer for Rebirth in Sukhāvatī

Though often referred to in abbreviated form as *Karma Chagme's Aspirational Prayer* (*chags med bde smon*), the full title is *An Aspiration Prayer of Sukhāvatī, the Perfectly Pure Realm of Great Bliss*.[40] Given the length of the prayer, it is not possible to examine every part of it. An overall commentary will be provided with examples from the text given throughout. The text is a long continuous poem, with no section breaks, composed in poetic verse form with each line consisting of nine syllables. The text appears to have been prepared for ease of recitation and memorization, typical of this genre. Before the prayer itself, Chagme begins with an encouragement to the practitioner to make this prayer a daily commitment and practice, and to share it with as many people as possible because "there is no greater

---

37. Halkias, *Luminous Bliss*, Kindle location 2831.

38. The title of the text in Tibetan is *rnam dag bde chen zhing gi smon lam rgyas bsdus bzhugs so/*

39. Halkias, *Luminous Bliss*, 115.

40. The full title in Tibetan is *mkhas grub rA ga a syas mdzad pa'i rnam dag bde chen zhing gi smon lam rgyas bsdus bzhugs so/* Karma Chagme often used a writer's name or pseudonym and here he has called himself "Accomplished Scholar Ragasya." A famous commentary on Chagme's prayer by Lagla Sonam Chodrub (*glag la bsod nams chos 'grub*, 1862–1944) is entitled *A Commentary Illuminating the Path of Liberation* (*rnam dag chen zhing gi smon lam kyi 'grel bshad thar lam snang byed*). For an outline of this commentary in English see Halkias, *Luminous Bliss*, 116–19.

TEXTS OF LAY ASPIRATION AND FOLK TRADITIONS

benefit than this prayer."[41] Chagme then sets the scene for the prayer with the well-known opening lines:

> Emaho—How wonderful!
> From here towards the westerly direction of the setting sun,
> Beyond many countless worlds,
> In a slightly elevated, glorious land,
> Lies the perfectly pure realm of great bliss—Sukhāvatī!
> Though not visible to my veiled eyes,[42]
> To the clear, purified mind, the path is radiantly clear.
> Here resides Victorious Amitābha.[43]

The prayer continues with a description of Amitābha and delicately extols his many virtues. Visually, Amitābha is depicted as sitting on a lotus flower with one thousand petals, which has strong symbolic overtones of purity, the lotus being one of the main symbols of purity. The land of Sukhāvatī is depicted, perhaps not surprisingly, as being full of lotuses. Relevant to this study is that Amitābha's retinue includes, seated to his right, the Bodhisattva Avalokiteshvara (*spyan ras gzigs*), who is holding a white lotus, and to his left Vajrapani (*phyag na rdo rje*), who is holding a vajra.[44] Given that Avalokiteshvara is the Bodhisattva of Compassion, who is emanated through the perpetual lineage of the Dalai Lamas, his presence in Sukhāvatī provides another layer of understanding as to why the cult of Amitābha has found such resonance among Tibetans. Another long section outlining the virtues of Amitābha follows the opening sections and is concluded by Chagme paying homage to the "omniscient Amitābha."[45]

Chagme then addresses the practitioner, encouraging all those who recite this prayer in faith that they will indeed be born in Sukhāvatī, and

---

41. '*di las phan yon che ba med/ An Aspirational Prayer*, plate no. 468.

42. The expression "veiled eyes" is more literally "blistered eyes" (*chu bur mig*), but the connotative sense is obscured, veiled, not able to see or perceive clearly.

43. *An Aspirational Prayer*, plate no. 468–69.

44. In the Tibetan text, Vajrapani is given the epithet "Great Sorcerer" (*mthu chen thob*), and the caption under the illustration in the *dpe cha* version, plate number 469, he is given the title "Almighty Lord of Secrets" (*mthu stobs dbang phyug gsang ba'i bdag po*). Vajrapani is most commonly known as *phyag na rdo rje*—"Vajra Bearer." In the caption under Amitābha's illustration, as depicted in plate 468 in the *dpe cha* version, Amitābha is given the epithet "Glorious Protector of Sukhāvatī" (*bde ldan zhing gi mgon po mchog*) and Avalokiteshvara, plate number 469, the title "Avalokiteshvara Embodiment of Compassion" (*snying rje'i rang gzugs spyan ras gzigs*).

45. *An Aspirational Prayer*, plate no. 472.

their guide, Amitābha, will lead them directly there after death from the intermediate state of *bar do*.[46] Chagme states that even hearing the name of Amitābha creates great merit and is efficacious for rebirth in Sukhāvatī.[47] In describing Sukhāvatī as a paradise, Chagme highlights that no one is "ever being born as a female but has a pure birth."[48] That Sukhāvatī is perceived as a pure heaven devoid of women follows the generally held belief that women cannot be enlightened, but first must be reborn as men.[49]

The prayer then continues with a lengthy list of confessions, where Chagme includes himself as one who has committed all manner of moral infractions, including the breaking of vows. Perhaps the inclusion of a long list of sins shows that Chagme is in tune with his audience, and deeply aware of their, and his own, moral failings. He concludes this long section with a wish to be completely purified, and he dedicates any merit and virtue he may have obtained to the benefit of all sentient beings.[50] Chagme continues his prayer by asking that he, and all those associated with him, be shown the path to Sukhāvatī as soon as they pass on from this life. He then lists the evils and sufferings of samsara and prays for deliverance. He again asks to be purified from all obscurations, and requests to be born in the heart of a lotus flower. A constant request throughout his prayer is that other people—family, friends, and disciples, also be led to Sukhāvatī upon their deaths.[51]

Chagme continues to praise Sukhāvatī as the unsurpassed and most glorious of all the pure realms. In aureate language, he continues to extol all the glories of Sukhāvatī, including the softness of the earth, which is soft as the palm of one's hands, and supple and spongy to walk upon. The whole land is seen as blazing with light and adorned with wish-fulfilling trees (*dpag bsams shing*), which are decorated with leaves of silk and jeweled ornaments. Beautiful sounding song birds inhabit the trees and there exist scented rivers, lakes and bathing pools, bedecked with jeweled stairways

46. *An Aspirational Prayer*, plate no. 472.
47. *An Aspirational Prayer*, plate no. 472–73.
48. *An Aspirational Prayer*, plate no. 473.
49. Skorupski notes that in the Sukhāvatīvyuha sutras "there is a pronounced stress on the absence of women in Sukhāvatī," Skorupski, "Tibetan Prayer for Rebirth," 207. Halkias has noted that other Pure Land texts proclaim that in Sukhāvatī one "will not be born as a woman," but rather "will live a pure life raised by a noble family." Halkias, *Luminous Bliss*, 127.
50. *An Aspirational Prayer*, plate no. 476, 478.
51. *An Aspirational Prayer*, plate no. 482, 483.

and terraces. There is no suffering, no poverty of any kind, and no beings from the three lower realms. Such evils, sufferings, and impurities are unheard of in Sukhāvatī.[52] Since there are no women and no human births, all beings are born out of lotus flowers.[53] Though there are no women, it is land full of goddesses. Chagme repeats the refrain of wishing to be reborn in this realm of countless wonders and virtues. The sublime virtues of Sukhāvatī are again extolled—perfect weather, neither hot nor cold, beautiful beds adorned with gems and mattresses of silk, and delightful music and melodious sounds of the dharma ringing forth. "To this wish-filling land may I be born," Chagme requests over and again.[54] He draws the prayer to a close by taking refuge in, and paying homage to, Amitābha. He makes one final supplication to Amitābha that all his wishes included in this prayer will be fulfilled and concludes by paying homage to the Triple Refuge.[55]

Karma Chagme has added a final note, which is not part of the prayer itself, encouraging the practitioner to recite this prayer as often as possible, to face a westerly direction while doing so, and to imagine in one's mind the realm of Sukhāvatī and Buddha Amitābha. He reassures his followers that should they recite this prayer with their hands pressed together in a praying position with resolute faith and devotion, they will be freed from the obstacles of this life, and without a doubt be reborn in Sukhāvatī in their next life.[56]

As has been seen, punctuated throughout this prayer is the repeated supplication to be reborn in Sukhāvatī. And it is this formula "May I be born in the land of Sukhāvatī!" which has become so popular as a prayer among the laity.[57] It would be fair to say that very few Tibetans, if any, would be unfamiliar with this one-line prayer of aspiration, even if they have not expressly prayed it themselves.[58] It is this hope of being freed

---

52. *An Aspirational Prayer*, plate no. 484–85.

53. Chagme reiterates three times in his prayer that there are no women in Sukhāvatī.

54. *yid bzhin 'grub pa'i zhing der skye bar shog/ An Aspirational Prayer*, plate no. 486.

55. *An Aspirational Prayer*, plate no. 489.

56. A short *bde smon* prayer, either composed or revealed as a treasure text by Migyur Dorje (*mi 'gyur rdo rje*, 1645–1667), is included at the end of Karma Chagme's prayer in the *dpe cha* version I studied. *An Aspirational Prayer*, plate no. 489–90.

57. This short prayer in Tibetan is *bde ba can gyi zhing la skye bar shog*.

58. Many years ago, I undertook a small study on the most common prayers lay people pray when they prostrate and circumambulate. Putting to one side the ubiquity of the *om mani padme hum* mantra, which is on the lips of every level of practitioner, the study confirmed what was already common knowledge—that the two most common

from the sufferings and impurities of this life, and being instantly reborn upon death into a pure celestial realm of bliss, that has driven the prayer life, and the composition of copious amounts of aspirational prayers of Tibetans throughout many centuries.

Though there is a certain tension as to whether it is by the faith alone of the practitioner, or by the amount of effort one exerts in earnest prayer, and the accumulated merit derived from this, or whether it is simply by the power of Amitābha's grace and benevolence, that one can arrive in Sukhāvatī, it would seem that a combination of all three is necessary.[59] There are frequent references in *bde smon* texts to the salvific claim of just hearing the name of Amitābha as being efficacious in rescuing one from samsara and arriving in Sukhāvatī.[60] While there does appear to be a certain power contained in saying or hearing the name of Amitābha, faith and devotion seem to be the primary predicating factors. After examining a particular Pure Lands text, Halkias concludes that, "In brief, faith in Amitābha and a strong aspiration to be born in his Pure Land are essential for taking birth in Sukhāvatī."[61] Other *dbe smon* prayers would appear to bear this out.

---

prayers are to be reborn as a male, and to be reborn in Sukhāvatī. Halkias is right to claim that Karma Chagme's prayer is indeed among the most recited and quoted prayers by Tibetans. Halkias, *Luminous Bliss*, 115.

59. Numerous Tibetan commentators have written on these doctrinal issues. One of the more famous treatise on the doctrinal elements of Pure Lands is Mipham Rinpoche's *Training for Sukhāvatī with Luminous Faith: Sun-like Instructions of a Sage* (*bde ba can gyi zhing sbyong ba'i dad pa gsal bar byed pa drang srong lung gi nyi ma*). This text discusses the issue of whether it is faith and aspiration, accumulated merit, or if by the power and grace of Amitābha alone which enables rebirth in Sukhāvatī. See Halkias, *Luminous Bliss*, 121–30. Halkias suggests Mipham arrives at the conclusion that "generally speaking, one cannot take birth in Sukhāvatī by offering prayers and so on if one had not previously accumulated a vast amount of merit," 126. For a more detailed examination of this commentary see Cook, "Ju Mi Pham."

60. The belief that hearing the name of Amitābha is efficacious for salvation is a consistent teaching throughout Pure Land literature in China and Japan. Jeff Wilson, among others, has noted this in some detail. See Wilson, "Pure Land Iconography." See also Ghose, "Karma and the Possibility," 268–69.

61. Halkias, *Luminous Bliss*, 123. He also notes that "Ordinary persons are born in Sukhāvatī by the power of their aspirations and faith," 125.

Additional Sukhāvatī *bde smon* Aspirational Prayers

Though Chagme's prayer is the most celebrated of the *dbe smon* literature, it is worthwhile to briefly examine other, shorter, *bde smon* prayers which have also gained widespread popularity. Among the many writings of the fifteenth Karmapa, Khakhyab Dorje (*mkha' khyab rdo rje*, 1871–1920), is a short prayer to Buddha Amitābha.[62] After paying homage to Amitābha, the embodiment of all Buddhas, and the protector of Avalokiteshvara, Khakhyab Dorje makes the direct petition for himself, and all beings, after having been freed from sin and negativities and having attained the body of a Bodhisattva, to journey in their next lives to the pure realm of Great Bliss. He further asks to be blessed with the same power as Amitābha to lead other sentient beings to Sukhāvatī.[63]

In a similar vein, highly esteemed Tibetan master Jamyang Khyentse Chokyi Lodro (*'jam dbyangs mkhyen brtse chos kyi blo gros*, 1893–1959), among his many influential writings and teachings, wrote the short *Aspiration for Rebirth in Sukhāvatī*.[64] In this prayer, he petitions Amitābha directly to have mercy on him when he is at the point of death, so that he may experience no pain and be born in the realm of Great Bliss. He further prays that any who are connected with him, even those who have only heard his name, may be purified and cleansed from sin, negativities, obscurations and suffering, and be born in the realm of Sukhāvatī.[65] Jamyang Khyentse expresses these same sentiments of purification and rebirth in Sukhāvatī, in a similar, and also well-known prayer *Aspiration for Sukhāvatī*. In this prayer, he also wishes that any who are remotely associated with him to never experience the suffering of the lower realms, but to be reborn in the sublime realm of Sukhāvatī.[66] Shamar Chokyi Wangchuk's (*zhwa dmar chos kyi dbang phyug*, 1538–1630) *bde smon* prayer, *Sharmar's Aspiration for Sukhāvatī*, also expresses a desire that he, and all who know him, be reborn in the blissful realm of Sukhāvatī.[67]

62. Dorje, K. *'od dpag med gsol bdebs bzhugs*.
63. *A Prayer to Buddha Amitābha*, lines 7–10.
64. Chokyi Lodro and Jamyang Khyentse *bde ba can du skye ba'i smon lam*.
65. *khya par bdag la 'brel ba thob pa dang/ming tsam thos pa'i sems can de rnams kyang/las nyon sdig sgrib sdug bsngal rab byang nas/bde ba can gyi zhing du skye bar shog*—this last line is again the exact formula that is repeated countless times every day by Tibetans. *Aspiration for Rebirth in Sukhāvatī*, lines 9–12.
66. *Aspiration for Sukhāvatī* (*bde chen zhing gi smon lam*), lines 29–31.
67. The title in Tibetan is *zhwa dmar pa chos kyi dbang phyug gi bde smon bzhugs*.

At the beginning of Mipham Rinpoche's (*'ju mi pham*, 1846–1912) *Sukhāvatī Aspiration*, he recommends that all who wish to be reborn in Sukhāvatī should single mindedly focus on Buddha Amitābha and recite his prayer seven times a day. His prayer follows a similar format to other *bde smon* prayers, asking that as soon as he departs from this world, he be reborn in Sukhāvatī and that his perfection, purity and karmic ripening be brought to completion.[68] Included in Mipham Rinpoche's many writings is a treatise on Pure Land doctrines where he discussed the nuances of faith, accumulated merit, devotion, and aspiration as requirements for rebirth in Sukhāvatī.[69] Migyur Dorje (*mi 'gyur rdo rje*, 1645–1667), who was a student of Karma Chagme, and an important treasure revealer of the Nyingma lineage, is said to have composed his *Condensed Sukhāvatī Aspiration* prayer at thirteen years of age.[70] His prayer follows a similar format to his teacher, Karma Chagme's prayer, and he asks that he may go directly to Sukhāvatī without going through the intermediate realm of *bar do*, and, whereupon being reborn in Sukhāvatī, he requests to see Amitābha face to face.[71] Migyur Dorje also composed a short prayer, *Beholding Amitābha in Dreams*, where he wished that even in his dreams he would journey to Sukhāvatī and there meet Amitābha.[72]

Tsong Khapa and *bde smon* Texts

An examination of the *bde smon* literature would not be complete without covering some of the many prayers of Tsong Khapa, who, though a tantric master of the Gelukpa school, was also a prominent and active promoter of Pure Land teachings. It is claimed that just before Tsong Khapa died, after completing some elaborate tantric rituals, he undertook an extensive Pure Land prayer liturgy, such was his devotion to Amitābha and rebirth

---

68. *Sukhāvatī Aspiration*, lines 10, 12.

69. The text is titled *Training for Sukhāvatī with Luminous Faith: Sun-like Instructions of a Sage* (*bde ba can gyi zhing sbyong ba'i dad pa gsal bar byed pa drang srong lung gi nyi ma*).

70. The note at the end of the prayer claims the prayer was written by Migyur Dorje when he was thirteen years old, on the seventh day of the month of Saga Dawa, in the year of the Fire Bird. See M. Dorje, *smon lam bsdus pa bzhugs*.

71. *Condensed Sukhāvatī Aspiration*, lines 8–9.

72. *Beholding Amitābha in Dreams* (*rmi lam bzung ba'i gsol 'bebs*), lines 4–5.

in Sukhāvatī.⁷³ Among his copious writings, Tsong Khapa wrote poetry of praise and devotion to Amitābha and aspiration for rebirth in Sukhāvatī. One of Tsong Khapa's many achievements was the establishment of the Great Prayer Festival (*smon lam chen mo*), at the beginning of the fifteenth century. This festival became an annual three-week prayer vigil held at the Jokhang Temple in Lhasa.⁷⁴ Prayers to Sukhāvatī were recited at this festival, including condensed versions of Tsong Khapa's own *bde smon* prayers.⁷⁵ Though Tsong Khapa was also a devotee of the pure realm of Tuṣita, the abode of Maitreya, and wrote praises to him, there are no records of any prayers of his to be reborn there.⁷⁶

Tsong Khapa wrote two well-known poems of praise to Amitābha, *Praise to Protector Amitābha—Dawn of the New Sun* and *Praise to Protector Amitābha—Gateway to the Sublime Realm*.⁷⁷ In these two poems, Tsong Khapa extols the many virtues of Amitābha, and the wonders of Sukhāvatī—where not even the word "suffering" is heard.⁷⁸ Naturally, he requests to be born in this wonderful realm upon his death and even asks to be born inside a lotus flower.⁷⁹

Tsong Khapa's most famous *bde smon* prayer, *Prayer for Birth in Sukhāvatī*, contains the typical requests for rebirth in the Land of Bliss, and also includes numerous references to purity and purification.⁸⁰ Though aspiring to be reborn in the pure realm of Sukhāvatī, after having been set

---

73. S. Tsering, "Role of Texts," 135; Thurman and Tulku, *The Life and Teachings of Tsong-Khapa* (Gangra, H.P. (India): Library of Tibetan Works & Archives, 2006), 31. Tsong Khapa's death is still remembered today in the annual ritual *dga' ldan lnga mchod* on the 25th day of the 10th month in the Tibetan calendar, where candles are lit as an offering and remembrance to him.

74. Hugh Richardson estimated that at one time around 20,000 monks attended this festival, as well as many of the laity. The prayer festival is no longer held in modern times. Richardson, *Ceremonies*, 22.

75. Halkias, *Luminous Bliss*, 106.

76. For example, Tsong Khapa's Praise to Maitreya (*byams pa'i bstod chen bzhugs so*). See Kilty, *Splendor*, 114–49.

77. In Tibetan these are *mgon po tshe dpag med la bstod pa nyi gzhon 'char ka bzhugs so/* and *mgon po 'od dpag med la bstod pa zhing mchog sgo 'byed ma bzhugs so/*

78. Kilty, *Splendor*, 80.

79. Kilty, *Splendor*, 74.

80. The text I studied *bde ba can du skye ba'i smon lam* can be found in the common book of prayers and liturgies *Zhal 'don Phyogs Bsgrigs [A Collection of Liturgies]*, 176–86. Thurman and Tulku claim the prayer was composed by Tsong Khapa in 1395. Thurman and Tulku, *Life and Teachings*, 204.

free from the "prison of samsara," and the "oceans of karmic existence," Tsong Khapa expresses his desire to travel from Sukhāvatī to the impure realms so that he can teach others the pure path of the exalted dharma, and ultimately lead them to the Pure Land of Bliss.[81] He also requests that after being miraculously reborn in Sukhāvatī, may he become a guide to all sentient beings of the impure realms, and further wishes to be established in the ways of purification and freedom from ignorance.[82] Tsong Khapa's *bde smon* texts became highly influential not only among monastics who wrote many commentaries about them, but also among the laity, who still recite lines from his prayers today. For many centuries, his *Prayer for Birth in Sukhāvatī* was recited annually at the Great Prayer Festival in Lhasa.[83] Tsong Khapa remains an exalted and much venerated saint of Tibetan Buddhism to this day.

Summary of Pure Land Texts

The key terms for purity *dag, byang, rnam par dag pa, dag chen* and *dag pa'i zhing khams* are used frequently throughout these texts, reflecting a similar lexical weighting as the texts examined in chapter two. The same notions of purity are also evident in these texts; that of being cleansed, being made clean and pure, being set free from impurities, and the existence of various pure realms. Based on the texts examined in this section (and not withstanding the Pure Land dharani texts from the previous chapter), one could draw an initial conclusion that in Tibetan consciousness there exists a certain ontological reality of pure realms and impure ones, and that sentient beings exist in either a pure or impure one. This dichotomy appears to be clearly delineated in Tibetan consciousness. Furthermore, one's current existence is by default an impure one, with samsara being perceived as inherently impure and humanity's presence in it as inherently polluting, and there exists a concrete desire to be transported to a pure realm. This desire to be transferred to a pure realm of bliss is not merely fanciful or wishful thinking but is perceived to be a real and distinct possibility given the right measure of faith, devotion and prayer. It would be fair to say that in Tibetan Buddhist cosmology there is a division of two main realms—the pure and the impure. The world of samsara we currently inhabit is a

---

81. *Zhal 'don Phyogs Bsgrigs [A Collection of Liturgies]*, 178.
82. *Zhal 'don Phyogs Bsgrigs [A Collection of Liturgies]*, 179.
83. Halkias, *Luminous Bliss*, 106.

defiled and impure one, stained by ignorance, suffering, and evil. In contrast, the pure realms, particularly Sukhāvatī, are purified, blissful realms, free from the impurities and defilements of sickness, suffering, aging, and death. While a pure land is not the final destination of enlightened Buddhahood, but rather a final stage before enlightenment, these pure lands are highly desirable and sought-after rebirths. And there exists the confident assurance that once one has arrived in Sukhāvatī, one cannot fall back into samsara. The texts have also indicated that this desire is not confined to just an individual desire for one's own rebirth in a pure land; rather, there exists a strong longing for family and friends, and especially for those in the throes of death, to be reborn in the pure realm of Sukhāvatī. Indeed, there is increased energy and effort at the point of death to help maximize the possibility of rebirth in Sukhāvatī. Halkias has astutely observed that, "Pure Land teachings dispense a universal remedy against the most fundamental human anxiety about death and the beyond, offering a blissful ontological alternative and a cosmological and ritual infrastructure to assist the departed and those who must go on living. The soteriological features of buddha fields addressed the preoccupations of the people of Tibet . . . concerning death, the afterlife, and the longevity of the family."[84] This hope for a better life in a pure realm of bliss, beyond this world of impurity and suffering, has been made manifest over the centuries by the practice and proliferation of aspirational *bde smon* prayers.

Unlike the tantric purification texts of praxis, where the goal is for the practitioner to be transformed into the purified state of one's meditational deity through elaborate and esoteric processes, in Pure Land Buddhism, the soteriological goal would appear to be direct passage to a pure realm, bypassing any possible lower rebirths, whether one is fully purified or not. At one level, this teaching could be viewed as being the "easy" path of Tibetan Buddhism, especially when the relative effort of simple faith is measured against the desired outcome of perpetual bliss. Prayer plus faith in Amitābha's benevolence leads to a new life in a pure celestial heaven.

Were one to draw a comparison to other religious faiths, Pure Land Buddhism, in a limited way, could be likened to Christianity more than any of the other major faiths. Kapstein, in describing the influence of Karma Chagme, suggests that the cult of Amitābha in Tibet "comes closest to elaborating a conception of salvation by Amitābha's unique grace."[85] Should

---

84. Halkias, *Luminous Bliss*, 38.
85. Kapstein, "Pure Land Buddhism," 23.

one wish to encapsulate Pure Lands teachings in parallel with two of the five solae of reformed Christianity, then "faith alone, grace alone," could provide one level of summation. This perceived connection to Christianity may be one reason, as Halkias, Kapstein, and others have noted, Pure Land Buddhism in Tibet did not initially attract interest from Western scholars. In contrast to the sutras and tantras, Pure Lands did not apparently appear sophisticated enough for academic sensibilities.[86]

In summary, the notion of a pure realm, and the desire to be reborn there, particularly in Sukhāvatī, rescued, saved and released from one's current impure realm by the savior Amitābha, is deeply embedded into Tibetan consciousness. The *bde smon* prayers reveal the underlying ontological, cosmological and soteriological realities which have profoundly impacted lay sensibilities over the centuries. This deep longing to be born in a pure land of bliss remains a remarkably constant thread of Tibetan existence.

The Foremost Mantra

The texts examined in chapter two illustrated the essential role of mantras and incantations, and the perceived power they contain. This section will examine the most prolific Tibetan Buddhist mantra, *om mani padme hum*, pre-eminent in Tibetic oral vernaculars and written texts. Given the enormity of such a study, the focus will again be narrowed to how the mantra may inform an understanding of purity. The ubiquity and centrality of the mantra within the Tibetan religious system, which overflows into the daily rhythm of life, cannot perhaps be over stated. Indeed, the six-syllable formula is an essential part of the fabric of Tibetan life and existence. The mantra is highly visible in Tibet, whether carved or painted on cliffs and rock faces, spelled out with painted rocks on mountainsides, pasturelands and fields, or engraved on cairns of rocks and tablets (*ma Ni rdo phung*)

---

86. Or perhaps there was a certain incredulity at how universal the longing for "heaven" is within humanity, or it reminded scholars too much of Christianity. In any case, Pure Lands has yet to make an impression on Western Tibetan Buddhist converts who appear to prefer the elaborate tantra path. For a discussion on this apparent lack of interest in Pure Lands by Western scholars, see Nattier, "Realm of Akṣobhya," 71–73; Kapstein, "Pure Land Buddhism," 19; Halkias, *Luminous Bliss*, Kindle locations 283–98; Bishop, *Dreams of Power*, 87. After a rather long-winded discussion about the validity of Pure Lands as being worthy of inclusion in the Buddhist tradition, James Steadman seems to reluctantly concede that Pure Lands could be considered "at least partially within the Buddhist Tradition." Steadman, "Pure Land Buddhism," 421. It appears that only in more recent years Pure Lands in Tibetan Buddhism has attracted scholarly attention.

TEXTS OF LAY ASPIRATION AND FOLK TRADITIONS

dotted all over the Tibetan landscape at mountain passes, sacred sites, and temples. Prayer wheels also contain scrolls filled with the mantra and are spun day and night—whether intentionally by a hand-held prayer wheel (*ma Ni 'khor lo, ma Ni lag skor*), or spun by the movement of water (*ma Ni chu 'khor*), wind (*ma Ni rlung 'khor*), the rising heat of a candle, or, more recently, by electricity.[87] Furthermore, the airwaves resound with the soft echo of the mantra from early morning until late at night. As Lama Govinda has observed, the mantra is "on the lips of all pilgrims, it is the last prayer of the dying and the hope of the living. It is the eternal melody of Tibet."[88] Tibetan scholar Janet Gyatso has also noted, "The stereotype of the Tibetan who constantly chants 'manis' with rosary and prayer wheel in hand is hardly exaggerated."[89]

The Origins of the Mantra

It appears well-established in Tibetan folklore that the first words a Tibetan child learns to speak are the mantra *om mani padme hum*.[90] This could be attributed to the reality that the mantra is repeated countless times every day, especially by the elderly who often look after the young.

There is a particular story about how *om mani padme hum* was originally conceived as a means for purifying negative actions. The story is told of a devout monk who went on a quest to India searching for a teaching that would enable him to purify the negative karma he had accumulated. He found a teacher who entrusted him with a secret teaching that he claimed would purify all his negativities. Using a bamboo pipe to speak directly into the ear of the monk, to avoid others over hearing, the teacher recited to him the mantra *om mani padme hum*. The monk, confused and with pangs of doubt, thought to himself, "This is the mantra repeated throughout Tibet by old men, women, and even children."[91] He nevertheless accepted the teaching and returned to Tibet. This folk tale is suggestive of both a certain longing for, and need of, purification from sin and negative karma, and

---

87. For example, small electric prayer wheels can be seen in modern Tibetan homes or on the dashboard of a taxi driver's car.

88. Govinda, *Foundations of Tibetan Mysticism*, 257.

89. J. Gyatso, "Literary Transmission," 102.

90. Kapstein, "Remarks," 85.

91. Roerich, *Blue Annals*, 1026–27 as quoted by Van Schaik, "Tibetan Avalokiteśvara Cult," 67.

of the possibility that there exists a teaching, in this case a mantra, which could provide an efficacious solution. It so happened that the solution was already being used in Tibet, giving, one suspects, further validation to the power, and thus the promulgation of the six-syllable formula.

Though oral traditions regarding the practice and spread of the mantra appear entrenched in folklore, the first reliable textual evidence of the mantra is found in the *Karandavyuha Sutra* in the Kangyur.[92] Alexander Studholme has estimated this sutra may have been composed in the late fourth or early fifth century AD.[93] The influence of this sutra in Tibet, however, would have come much later, either during the first or second dissemination of Buddhism, when it was likely translated into Tibetan. There is strong evidence to suggest the mantra was in widespread use in the eighth century.[94] This sutra does not just mention the mantra casually in passing; rather it is the central theme of the text and, as Studholme observes, should be considered "a work whose central concern is the dissemination of the formula."[95] As well as expounding upon the various efficacies of the mantra, the supremacy of Avalokiteshvara, and presenting the six syllables as analogous to the six perfections of a Bodhisattva (a common feature of later commentarial texts on the mantra), the sutra clearly shows that the formula was inextricably linked to rebirth in the pure land of Sukhāvatī. Studholme draws the conclusion that the sutra demonstrates the mantra had become "located within a Mahayana doctrinal system in which rebirth in Sukhāvatī, the pure land of Amitābha, is the overarching religious goal," and, furthermore, that recitation of the mantra brought to one's mind Avalokiteshvara, who was "commonly associated with the goal of Sukhāvatī."[96] Other textual evidence, as will be presented here, would suggest that such a conclusion is warranted, or at least, rebirth in Sukhāvatī is a primary one of numerous perceived efficacies of the mantra. Regardless of the origins, through both textual and oral traditions, the mantra has gained a status in Tibet as "the salvific mantra *par excellence*"[97] (italics in original).

92. The *Karandavyuha Sutra* in Tibetan is titled '*phags pa za ma tog bkod pa zhe bya ba theg pa chen po'i mdo, The Basket's Display—A Noble Mahayana Sutra*.

93. Studholme, *Origins*, 14.

94. The influence of the monumental work, the *Mani Kabum* (*ma Ni bka' 'bum*), which will be discussed further, provides strong textual support for this claim. See also Francke, "Meaning," 403–4.

95. Studholme, *Origins*, 4.

96. Studholme, *Origins*, 6.

97. This is the fair assessment of Van Schaik who suggested that this status of the

The Meaning of the Mantra

The authoritative Tibetan dictionaries define the mantra as "the six syllables of the essence of Chenrezi's (Avalokiteshvara) incantation."[98] The mantra is also referred to as the "mani mantra" (*ma Ni*) and the "six-syllable mantra" (*yi ge drug ma, yig drug*).[99] Dilgo Khyentse Rinpoche, in recognizing the potency of mantras, highlights the phonic valency: "Chenrezi's six-syllable mantra, OM MANI PADME HUM, is the compassionate wisdom of all the Buddhas manifested as sound."[100] In emphasizing the importance of the sound, Dilgo Khyentse is pointing to where the perceived power of the mantra is contained. Indeed, there is a certain ease of pronunciation in Tibetan which allows for frequent repetition, and this may contribute to the mantra's perceived power.[101]

A great deal has been written about the mantra in both Tibetan and English, and Donald Lopez's chapter, *The Spell*, in *Prisoners of Shangri-La*, has documented in detail the Western fascination with the formula, and the various attempts to translate it into English.[102] That the formula is connected to Avalokiteshvara is beyond doubt, but questions have long lingered regarding the precise grammatical construction.[103] The mantra has typically been rendered into English as a vocative, "Hail, the Jewel in the Lotus," with "Jewel in the Lotus" functioning as an epithet of Avalokiteshvara.[104] How-

---

mantra likely came about from outside the textual tradition, or in other words through oral folk traditions, such was the groundswell of laity support. Van Schaik, "Tibetan Avalokiteśvara Cult," 67. As has been noted, the mantra was likely in widespread use during the eighth century and the cult of Avalokiteshvara also finds its roots in that time. By the tenth century, both the mantra and Avalokiteshvara worship were widely entrenched. Of the 198 deity paintings discovered in the Dunhuang caves dating back to the tenth century, 143 of them were of Avalokiteshvara. Van Schaik, "Tibetan Avalokiteśvara Cult," 64–65.

98. oM ma Ni pad+me hU~M spyan ras gzigs kyi snying po gzungs sngags ye ge drug ma'o/ TDCM, 3146. TGCM, 2205, and RYJS under *om mani padme hum*.

99. RJYS, ITED, under *ma Ni* and *yi ge drug ma*. TDCM, 2044, 2564, 2568.

100. P. Rinpoche and Khyentse, *Heart Treasure*, 58.

101. The first two syllables blend easily into each other through nasalization and the final syllable is also nasalized.

102. Lopez, *Prisoners of Shangri-La*, 114–35.

103. Van Schaik has suggested that "the deity Avalokiteshvara is so closely associated with the six-syllable mantra that the two are almost interchangeable." Van Schaik, "Tibetan Avalokiteśvara Cult," 66.

104. Francke, "Meaning," 402–3; F. Thomas, "Om Maṇi Padme Hūṃ," 464; Lopez, *Prisoners of Shangri-La*, 134–35.

ever, as others have pointed out, "jewel *in* the lotus" as a locative, is better rendered either in the nominative as "jewel and lotus," or as a compound "Lotus Jewel" or "jewel-lotus," while still retaining the clear reference to Avalokiteshvara.[105] Both jewels and lotuses are symbols of Avalokiteshvara, who is often pictured in the iconography holding a jewel or gem in one hand, and a white lotus in the other. The terms *mani padme* can also suggest a lotus made of jewels, and this would certainly be in keeping with the depiction of Sukhāvatī, Avalokiteshvara's abode, as being replete with lotuses and bedecked with jewels and gems, and indeed also "replete with lotuses made of jewels."[106] Losang and Zangpo provide such a meaning: "MANI PADME means: jewel lotus or lotus of jewels."[107]

The meaning of the mantra is traditionally taught in its totality as one unit, and also broken down individually into each of the six syllabic component parts. Unpacking the mantra into its component parts, OM and HUM are seed syllables, used to bracket most mantras, and, as has been discussed previously, are multivalent and multi-efficacious terms. MANI is a transliteration from Sanskrit meaning "jewel," "gem," or "wish-fulfilling gem."[108] PADME means "lotus" and is in the vocative case, which suggests calling to, or arousing the attention of, Avalokiteshvara. A straight forward rendering would point to: "Oh, jewel-lotus."[109] The mantra, then, is an invocation calling attention to Avalokiteshvara, whether to seek refuge

---

105. Francke, "Meaning," 403; Studholme, *Origins*, 7.

106. The Tibetan reads *rin po che'i pad mas khengs pa* as found in the *Sukhāvatīyuha Sutra—The Display of the Pure Land of Sukhāvatī* (*'phags pa bde ba can gyi bkod pa*), Lhasa Kangyur, 309A, line 2. The *Karandavyuha Sutra, The Basket's Display—A Noble Mahayana Sutra* (*'phags pa za ma tog bkod pa zhe bya ba theg pa chen po'i mdo*) also contains such references to jeweled lotuses (*rin po che padma*, Sk. ratnapadme) with two occurrences in the version in the Dege Kangyur, section 375A, line 2, and section 375B, line 2.

107. Losang and Zangpo, "Significance," 3.

108. "mani" is an abbreviation for the six-syllable mantra, and also an abbreviated form of the hand-held prayer wheel *ma Ni 'khor lo* and *ma Ni lag skor*.

109. The standard term for "lotus" is *padma*, without the "e" diacritic vowel marker. But in the mantra, *padma* becomes *padme*. This is an unusual case of Sanskrit grammar influencing the Tibetan because the "e" diacritic does not mark the vocative case in Tibetan. It has been preserved in the mantra with clear grammatical intent. The textual evidence for this is compelling. The Tibetan grammar, *An Exposition of the Sanskrit Nominal Case* (*sgra'i rnam par dbye ba bstan pa*), found in the Tengyur, dating back to the ninth century, when listing the vocative case, gives the example of *mani padme*, clearly showing that a correct understanding of the grammar points to a rendering of "Oh, jewel-lotus." See Verhagen, "Mantra."

in him, request a blessing, call upon his protective and beneficent powers, or to accumulate merit. Patrul Rinpoche provides this summation: "The first syllable of Chenrezi's mantra, OM, symbolizes the five wisdoms: as the syllable of auspiciousness, it begins most mantras. MANI means "jewel," PADME means "lotus," and HUM is the syllable proclaiming and invoking Chenrezi's omniscience. The whole mantra can be rendered: 'You, the Lotus Jewel, grant your omniscience.'"[110]

Of course, it is of less significance what the mantra may mean in English.[111] Rather, the greater significance is what the mantra denotes to a Tibetan, and what are the perceived powers, benefits, and efficacies. This is not to say that the mantra does not contain latent meaning in itself; it clearly does, and this will be elaborated upon further. Suffice to say that while many Tibetans would be more concerned with what the mantra can achieve, its perceived power and benefits, rather than an elaboration of the meaning, many Tibetan texts have been written about the symbolic meaning, power, and benefits of the mantra, and are worthy of exploration.

The Benefits of the Mantra

Aside from the accumulation of merit, inherent in all religious activities, there are numerous perceived benefits which come from reciting the mantra, and only some can be touched upon here. Reciting the mantra is often said to be equivalent to reciting vast portions of Tibetan scriptures. Dilgo Khyentse, among others, claims that "to recite the *mani* once is the same as reciting the whole of the twelve branches of the Buddha's teachings. Reciting the six syllables of the *mani* perfects the six paramitas and firmly blocks any possibility of rebirth in the six realms of samsara."[112] The current Dalai Lama, in explaining the meaning of the mantra, and the importance of its perpetual usage, concludes, "Thus the six syllables, *om mani padme hum*, mean that in dependence on the practice of a path that is an indivisible

---

110. P. Rinpoche and Khyentse, *Heart Treasure*, 141.

111. As observed in chapter two in the section on dharanis, the potency of incantations is the combination of sounds in themselves, and hence are ineffective when translated into another language.

112. P. Rinpoche and Khyentse, *Heart Treasure*, 58. The six paramitas are the six perfections of a Bodhisattva (*phar rol tu phyin pa drug*).

union of method and wisdom, you can transform your impure body, speech and mind into the pure exalted body, speech and mind of a Buddha."[113]

Losang and Zangpo, after carefully examining the component parts of the mantra, and the range of semantic meaning, conclude that the six-syllable mantra is "very powerful in purifying your downfalls and unwholesome actions."[114] Eminent treasure revealer, Jatson Nyinpo (*'ja' tshon snying po*, 1585–1656), in paying homage to the supremacy of the mantra, indeed the "king of mantras"[115] is documented as having written: "Even merely remembering the six letters, like the rising sun shining on the snow, all the evil karma of negativities and polluting obscurations, which have been accumulated in samsara from beginningless time will be purified, and one will be born in Sukhāvatī. Even through touching the six letters one will obtain the limitless power of Buddhas and Bodhisattvas."[116] The link between the mantra and rebirth in Sukhāvatī again is worth noting.

Lama Zorpa suggests the benefits of the mantra are not just for an individual but can be spread and shared to others. He claims that if the mantra is recited one thousand times per day, and the practitioner washes or bathes in a river, then the water becomes purified, as do all the creatures living in it. He continues that if, after one thousand recitations, one touches another person, this will also purify them because the mantra "purifies the mind of karma and delusions."[117] He goes on further to say, "if you recite a thousand *Om mani padme hums* every day, then your children and grandchildren and so on up to seven generations will not be reborn in the lower realms."[118] Patrul Rinpoche (1808–1887), in his long exposé about the supremacy and importance of the mantra, writes that as "One deity, Chenrezi, embodies all Buddhas," so "One mantra, the six syllables, embodies all mantras." He implores the practitioner thus: "knowing the one which liberates all, recite the six-syllable mantra!"[119] Such is Patrul Rinpoche's conviction of the efficacy

---

113. The Dalai Lama, *Kindness, Clarity, and Insight*, 136.

114. Losang and Zangpo, "Significance," 7.

115. *gsang sngags kyi rgyal po*, *The Perpetual Rain of Benefit to All Beings*, manuscript plate no. 354. The full title of the text is: *The Perpetual Rain of Benefit to All Beings—A Brief Commentary on a Meditation and Recitation to the Great Compassionate One, the All-Pervading Benefits to All Beings* (*'phags mchog spyan ras gzigs kyi bsgom bzlas 'gro don mkha' khyab ma'i zin bris nyung bsdus 'gro don char rgyun zhes bya ba bzhugs so*).

116. *The Perpetual Rain of Benefit to All Beings*, manuscript plate no. 355.

117. L. Z. Rinpoche, *Wheel of Great Compassion*, xii.

118. L. Z. Rinpoche, *Wheel of Great Compassion*, xii.

119. P. Rinpoche and Khyentse, *Heart Treasure*, 201.

of the formula as the ultimate path to enlightenment, that in his eighty-one stanzas of text he implores the practitioner on fifty-three occasions to recite the mantra.[120]

Component Parts of the Foremost Mantra

As mentioned previously, there is more to the mantra than the totality of the sonic valency and perceived power as a whole unit. The mantra is also believed to have power and efficacy within each phoneme or syllable. There has been a long tradition of teaching the six syllables and ascribing particular benefits, power, and efficacies. Each syllabic component has a certain function which is believed to be unique to that particular syllable. The meaning and significance of the first syllable OM is often unpacked in this way: OM is comprised of the letters "a," "u," and "m", and these three represent the body, speech, and mind. These three are impure and need to be cleansed. The three letters also symbolize the pure and exalted body, speech, and mind of a Buddha—a state which the recitation of the mantra helps to effect. Put another way, a standard explanation is "the syllable *om*, which is composed of three sounds—A, U, M—symbolizes the practitioner's impure body, speech, and mind, which will be purified through practice into the exalted body, speech, and mind of a buddha."[121]

The typical way of unpacking the meaning of the mantra is through ascribing key doctrines to each of the six syllables.[122] The relevant texts typically do this by associating the six syllables with the six realms of existence, the six perfections of a Bodhisattva, the six Buddha Families, and the six obscurations to enlightenment. The text which has made these associations most comprehensively is the famed *Mani Kabum*. This text, and one other,

---

120. P. Rinpoche and Khyentse, *Heart Treasure*, 180–201, stanzas 23 to 76.

121. L. Z. Rinpoche, *Wheel of Great Compassion*, 10. See also Losang and Zangpo, "Significance," 3; The Dalai Lama: "The first, Om is composed of three letters, a, u, and m. These symbolize the practitioner's impure body, speech, and mind; they also symbolize the pure exalted body, speech, and mind of a Buddha." in The Dalai Lama, *Kindness, Clarity, and Insight*, 135.

122. Studholme observes that "One method of explicating this aspect of the formula has been to make each of its syllables stand for one of the elements of a variety of six-part doctrinal schemes." Studholme, *Origins*, 108. Losang and Zangpo outline more than ten ways the syllables relate to specific Tibetan Buddhist doctrines. See Losang and Zangpo, "Significance."

will now be examined in more detail as to the various ascriptions given to each of the six-syllables of the mantra.

Mani Kabum

The first textual evidence for the ascription of meaning to the six component parts of the mantra is found in the *Mani Kabum* (*ma Ni dka' 'bum*, "The 100,000 Mani Precepts"), a vast assortment of texts concerning the teachings of Avalokiteshvara. Though the exalted seventh-century Tibetan king, Songtsen Gampo, is the alleged author of this monumental work, the text itself was discovered by treasure revealers over a lengthy period of time during the twelfth century, some five centuries after it was believed to have been written.[123] The *Mani Kabum* reinforced Avalokiteshvara as the patron deity of Tibet, of whom King Songtsen Gampo was believed to be an emanation. The text naturally contains much about the six-syllable mantra, most of which is recorded in the third section of the collection, *The Cycle of Precepts*. Kapstein has rightly pointed out that one of the important functions of the *Mani Kabum* is "its significance for the development of a Tibetan worldview."[124] Both Avalokiteshvara and his mantra were crucial components to that development.

The version of the *Mani Kabum* from which the following Tibetan text has been taken is the two-volume work published in Lhasa in 2013. The relevant section is the chapter, *The Precepts of the Six Syllables* (*yi ge drug pa'i zhal gdams kyi skor*).[125] The chapter is dedicated to espousing the many benefits of the mantra by explaining the doctrinal associations of the syllables. Three sections of the text will be presented here. The first section asserts:

> When *om mani padme hum* is applied to the cleansing of the six abodes then;
> OM cleanses the realm of the gods,
> MA cleanses the realm of demigods,
> NI cleanses the realm of humans,
> PAD cleanses the realm of animals,[126]

---

123. Kapstein, *Tibetan Assimilation of Buddhism*, 145.

124. Kapstein, *Tibetan Assimilation of Buddhism*, 147.

125. Gampo, *Ma Ni Bka' 'bum*, 39–60. While Songtsen Gampo is listed as the author of this work, the revealer of this "treasure text" is given as *grub thob dngos grub sogs*.

126. Note that the term *byol song*, used in the text here, is not the typical word for

TEXTS OF LAY ASPIRATION AND FOLK TRADITIONS

ME cleanses the realm of hungry ghosts,
HUM cleanses the realm of hell.
The cleansing of the six realms occurs through the recitation of the six letters.[127]

As has been observed elsewhere, and highlighted again here, the significance of the cleansing of the six realms is clearly an important doctrinal teaching in the Tibetan Buddhist salvific schema. In the Tibetan text, the syllables themselves are the active instruments of the cleansing. That is, they are in the instrumental case, and are thus marked as the cause of the cleansing through the active recitation of the mantra. The second section of the text asserts:

When *om mani padme hum* is applied to overcoming the sufferings of the six migrations then;
OM cleanses the suffering of the transferal and downfall of the gods,[128]
MA cleanses the infighting between demigods,[129]
NI cleanses the suffering of the death transferal of humans,
PAD cleanses the suffering of the ignorance and stupidity of animals,
ME cleanses the suffering of hunger and thirst of the hungry ghosts,
HUM cleanses the suffering of the heat and cold of the hells.[130]
The cleansing of the six migrations occurs through the recitation of the six letters.[131]

The third section of the text asserts:

When *om mani padme hum* is applied to cleansing polluting obscurations then:
OM cleanses the polluting obscurations of the body,
MA cleanses the polluting obscurations of speech,

---

animals or beasts, with *dud 'gro* being the standard term used in "wheel of life" depictions of the six realms of samara.

127. Gampo, *Ma Ni Bka' 'bum*, 40.

128. That is, transferring or falling down to a lower realm of existence.

129. The demigods in this realm are perceived as always being in warfare and conflict with each other since they are neither humans nor gods. Thus, they are tormented by the intermediate state of being a demigod.

130. There are believed to be eight hot hells (*tsha'i dmyal ba brgyad*), and eight cold hells (*grang ba'i bmyal ba brgyad*) of varying temperature intensity.

131. Gampo, *Ma Ni Bka' 'bum*, 40.

NI cleanses the polluting obscurations of the mind,
PAD cleanses the polluting obscurations of ignorance,
ME cleanses the polluting obscurations of habitual tendencies,
HUM cleanses the polluting obscurations of knowledge.
The six polluting obscurations will be completely cleansed through the recitation of the six letters.[132]

The ability of the recited six letters themselves to cleanse polluting obscurations is repeated throughout the text.[133] The six syllables are also believed to be able to cleanse all of one's sin and pollution, as well as cleanse the sins of pride and avarice, lust and desire, and jealousy.[134] The verb "to cleanse" (*sbyong ba*) used in each case here, is a transitive, volitional verb that requires active agency. In other words, without the agency of the syllables (which are marked in the instrumental case throughout the text), no cleansing would take place. The need for cleansing from polluting obscurations is again clearly seen as an essential doctrine in the Tibetan salvific schema.

Khakhyab Dorje's Commentary

The second text to be examined is a commentary by the fifteenth Karmapa, Khakhyab Dorje (*mkha' khyab rdo rje*, 1871–1920).[135] This text is an elaborate explanation of the famous meditation text on Avalokiteshvara by the celebrated folk hero, Thangton Gyalpo (*thang stong rgyal po*, c. 1361–1485).[136] It is worth expanding here upon the person of Thangton Gyalpo and noting his influence upon the laity. Though Thangton Gyalpo's name means "King of the Empty Plain," he was not a king but rather a master practitioner of Tibetan Buddhism, and was also a prodigious builder

---

132. Gampo, *Ma Ni Bka' 'bum*, 41.

133. Gampo, *Ma Ni Bka' 'bum*, 51–53.

134. Gampo, *Ma Ni Bka' 'bum*, 60, 51.

135. The title of Khakhyab Dorje's commentary is: *The Perpetual Rain of Benefit to All Beings—A Brief Commentary of a Meditation and Recitation to the Great Compassionate One, the All-Pervading Benefits to All Beings* (*'phags mchog spyan ras gzigs kyi bsgom bzlas 'gro don mkha' khyab ma'i zin bris nyung bsdus 'gro don char rgyun zhes bya ba bzhugs so*). This text is a commentary to accompany Thangton Gyalpo's meditation of Avalokiteshvara, *All Pervading Benefit of Beings* (*'gro don mkha' khyab ma*).

136. The title of Thangton Gyalpo's meditation is: *A Meditation and Recitation to the Great Compassionate One, the All-Pervading Benefits to All Beings* (*thugs rje chen po'i bsgom bzlas 'gro don mkha' khyab ma bzhugs so*).

TEXTS OF LAY ASPIRATION AND FOLK TRADITIONS

of metal bridges, monasteries, and temples throughout Tibet.[137] He is also credited with establishing Tibetan opera (*lha mo*), a tradition which continues today. Thangton Gyalpo became famous for his bridge building and was affectionately known as "Iron Bridge Man" (*lcags zam pa*). His contributions to the daily lives of Tibetans won him their affections and he remains the archetypal folk hero.[138] Though the exact dates of his life are uncertain, it is widely held that he lived for more than 120 years.[139]

Pertinent to the study at hand is Thangton Gyalpo's deep devotion to Avalokiteshvara and the promulgation of his six-syllable mantra. It is claimed that as soon as Thangton Gyalpo was born, he uttered the six-syllable mantra.[140] Though considered a great Tibetan Buddhist adept, he did not remain in the cloistered world of the monastery but rather he taught ordinary people, such as traders and farmers. One of the main doctrines he taught was the importance of reciting *om mani padme hum*. It is claimed he taught that all Tibetans should recite the mantra at least five hundred times per day. He further instituted the continuous recitation of the mantra on Chagpo Mountain (*lcags po ri*, "Iron Mountain") in Lhasa during religious festival holidays.[141] His meditation on Avalokiteshvara became a famous text, widely known among Tibetans in all stations of life. His meditation focuses on the supremacy of the six-syllable mantra and its efficacy for rebirth in Sukhāvatī. Centuries later, a text that also became famous was Khakhyab Dorje's commentary on Thangton Gyalpo's meditation. This commentary will now be briefly examined.

Khakhyab Dorje's commentary is known for its lucid and expansive exposition on the significance of the *mani* mantra. For the sake of brevity, a summary of his analysis of each of the six syllables will be given. The following translations are excerpts from his commentary where he describes each of the six syllables and their respective attributes. True to a standard interpretation, each syllable is associated with a particular color. (Colorful

---

137. It is alleged that he constructed over fifty iron bridges, remarkable for that time. For a detailed account of the bridges Thangton Gyalpo built, see Gerner, *Chakzampa Thangtong Gyalpo*, 49–116.

138. Thangton Gyalpo's legacy still lives on today and folk stories about his life can be found in current school textbooks. See for example, *Skad yig lo rim bdun pa [Language Book Seven]*, 181–86.

139. J. Gyatso, "Genre, Authorship, and Transmission," 95; Gerner, *Chakzampa Thangtong Gyalpo*, 1, 14.

140. J. Gyatso, "Literary Transmission," 107.

141. J. Gyatso, "Literary Transmission," 107.

representations of the mantra can be seen wherever the mantra is visually represented.) Selected sections of the text, the order of which has been preserved, read as follows:

> The white colored OM represents the nature of the perfection of meditative absorption and cleanses the affliction of anger, along with cleansing the particular resultant effects of the suffering of the gods—death and the suffering of falling down to the lower realms of existence. This syllable guides the six migrators to the southern pure realm and enables them to attain the body of Buddha Ratnasambhava.[142]
>
> The green colored MA represents the nature of the perfection of forbearance and cleanses the affliction of jealousy, along with purifying the particular resultant effects of the suffering of the internal conflict between demigods. This syllable guides the six migrators to the northern pure realm and enables them to attain the body of Buddha Amoghasiddhi.[143]
>
> The yellow colored NI represents the nature of the perfection of morality and cleanses the stain of the ignorance of the dualistic grasping at self, along with purifying the particular resultant effects of the great four rivers of human suffering—birth, aging, sickness and death. This syllable guides the six migrators to the completely pure realm of the expanse of the dharma and enables them to attain the body of Buddha Vajradhara.[144]
>
> The azure colored PAD represents the nature of the perfection of wisdom and cleanses the affliction of ignorance, along with purifying the particular resultant effects of the suffering of wild beasts—ignorance, stupidity and exploited servitude. This syllable guides the six migrators to the central pure realm and enables them to attain the body of Buddha Vairochana.[145]
>
> The red colored ME represents the nature of the perfection of generosity and cleanses desire and avarice, along with purifying the

---

142. *The Perpetual Rain of Benefit to All Beings*, manuscript plate no. 346.

143. *The Perpetual Rain of Benefit to All Beings*, manuscript plate no. 346, 347.

144. *The Perpetual Rain of Benefit to All Beings*, manuscript plate no. 347–48.

145. *The Perpetual Rain of Benefit to All Beings*, manuscript plate no. 348. (Note that the Tibetan text may be in error here as the perfection of wisdom *shes rab kyi pha rol tu phyin pa* is mentioned twice; here and also under the syllable HUM. Typically, the perfection of wisdom is listed as the final and ultimate perfection. Likely the perfection of perseverance *brtson 'grus*, which is the only one of six perfections not listed, is intended here. This a potential copyist error.)

TEXTS OF LAY ASPIRATION AND FOLK TRADITIONS

particular resultant effects of the suffering of hunger and thirst of hungry ghosts. This syllable guides the six migrators to the pure realm of Sukhāvatī and enables them to attain the body of Buddha Amitābha.[146]

The black colored HUM represents the nature of the perfection of wisdom and cleanses the anger of dualistic grasping at self, along with purifying the particular resultant effects of the suffering of the hot and cold hells. This syllable guides the six migrators to the pure realm of Manifest Joy and enables them to attain the body of Buddha Akshobhya.[147]

Each syllable is described as having three main aspects: they represent one of the six perfections of a Bodhisattva, they cleanse a particular sin or negativity and the resulting effect of that sin, and they guide the deceased to a pure realm to attain the body of a Buddha. The verbal constructions in the text are again instrumental, indicating that the syllables are the agents of the cleansing and transferal to a pure realm. The mantra is clearly important in the purification processes necessary for rebirth in a pure realm and ultimately attaining Buddhahood.

Summary of the Foremost Mantra

Though having a wide range of usages, the *om mani padme hum* mantra is an essential component in the Tibetan schema of purification. Indeed, the mantra appears to play a crucial role in the purification process necessary for rebirth in a pure realm and the eventual attainment of Buddhahood. Doctrinally, the utterance of the mantra is believed to be efficacious in enabling the purification of bad karma, sin and negativities, polluting obscurations, and the cleansing and removal of the endemic suffering in the six realms of samsara. The frequency of repeated utterances of the mantra, or rotations of it within a prayer wheel, is believed to effect the desired outcomes. The more recitations, the greater chance of those outcomes materializing.

Furthermore, being inextricably linked to the deity cult of Avalokiteshvara, the mantra is believed to have salvific power for rebirth in Sukhāvatī. The frequent references in these texts to rebirth in the Pure Land of Bliss, as a direct result of reciting the mantra, allow for such a conclusion. Like the *bde smon* prayers of aspiration, the prayers of Patrul Rinpoche, Dilgo

---

146. *The Perpetual Rain of Benefit to All Beings*, manuscript plate no. 348, 349.
147. *The Perpetual Rain of Benefit to All Beings*, manuscript plate no. 349–50.

Khyenste, Thangton Gyalpo, Khakhyab Dorje, and the Mani Kabum, among many others, are replete with supplications to be reborn in Sukhāvatī and believed to be effected through the repeated recitation of the mantra *om mani padme hum*.¹⁴⁸ As Studholme has rightly concluded, "recitation of the six syllables has remained linked, in the collective consciousness, to the idea of rebirth in Sukhāvatī."¹⁴⁹ Though the typical Tibetan, for whom this mantra is perpetually on their lips and in their hearts and minds, may not necessarily be constantly thinking about the greater meanings and significance of the mantra, one could, however, conclude that the notion of purification, and rebirth in the Pure Land of Sukhāvatī, is very likely among them.

Proverbs

Proverbs are often attributed to providing insights into worldviews and thought patterns. Indeed, paremiology can provide a certain window into a given culture's values, pre-occupations, struggles and joys, religious sensibilities, and distilled wisdom passed down through generations. Tom Steffen has suggested that proverbs "express the values of a people in a concise way. They are hidden stories waiting to be unpacked."¹⁵⁰ Jay Moon, in his comprehensive study of African proverbs, suggests that "Proverbs can be looked *through* to see the worldview that they reveal."¹⁵¹ In advocating the use of proverbs as a tool for the development of indigenous theological communities, Moon further states that "proverbs touch both the emotions and provide instruction at the same time."¹⁵²

Tibetans have a long and rich history of proverbs, adages, aphorisms, and spoken idioms that reflect how they perceive themselves and the world around them. It is a tradition they are proud of, and, as others have observed, proverbs "have been cherished by the Tibetan people in all kinds of social settings... throughout the ages."¹⁵³ Some of their own proverbs inti-

---

148. In the final prayer in *The Precepts of the Six Syllables* (*yi ge drug pa'i zhal gdams kyi skor*) in the *Mani Kabum*, the author repeatedly requests (more than fifteen times) to be born on Mount Potala (*ri po ta lar skye bar shog*), the celestial abode of Avalokiteshvara in Sukhāvatī. Gampo, *Ma Ṇi Bka' 'bum*, 59–60.

149. Studholme, *Origins of Om Mani*, 118.

150. Steffen, *Reconnecting God's Story*, Kindle location 467.

151. Moon, *African Proverbs*, 47; italics original.

152. Moon, *African Proverbs*, 125.

153. Cüppers and Sørensen, *Collection of Tibetan Proverbs*, xxvi.

mate such an affinity: "As beer tasty to the mouth is nectar, so words pleasant to the ear are proverbs,"[154] and "Words without proverbs are difficult to comprehend, just as containers without handles are difficult to hold."[155] Of the thousands of proverbs (*gtam dpe, kha dpe*) one could analyze, only a small sample are presented here.[156] The focus has again been narrowed to proverbs which inform a Tibetan understanding of purity, and thus have been filtered accordingly. The two main data sources from which proverbs have been taken are Lhamo Pemba's *Tibetan Proverbs* and the large collection, published in Lhasa, *A Collection of Tibetan Proverbs*.[157] There are various ways one could group the following proverbs, but the system employed here has been to divide the data into two large categories. The first category is proverbs which deal directly with the subject of purity and use explicit purity terms. The second category are those which contain symbolic language, metaphors, motifs, or tropes which clearly allude to purity and purification without necessarily using explicit purity terms.

Proverbs with Explicit Purity References

The proverb which perhaps most succinctly encapsulates Tibetan religious sensibilities is the well-known proverb, "Purity results in Buddhahood, impurity results in hell."[158] The term for purity here is *dag*, well attested to in the texts studied thus far, being a state one attains after a long and detailed process of purification. The ultimate state of Buddhahood is one completely free from the stains of samsara. As the previous texts have shown, there are various means by which one can become purified, but the goal of purity,

---

154. Cüppers and Sørensen, *Collection of Tibetan Proverbs*, 83.

155. Hor Khang, *Bod kyi dtam dpe*, 153.

156. The term for proverb *gtam pde* more literally means "speech example" and the term for "saying" *kha dpe* is more literally "mouth example." Cüppers and Sørensen's, *Collection of Tibetan Proverbs and Sayings* contains more than 10,000 proverbs, adages, aphorisms, maxims, and spoken idioms. Cüppers and Sørensen, *Collection of Tibetan Proverbs*, ix.

157. Pemba, *Tibetan Proverbs*; Hor Khang, *Bod kyi dtam dpe*. Some proverbs included in this section are also drawn from my personal collection which I have documented over the years. Though I have known, studied, heard, and myself said many of these proverbs over a period of many years, I again read through each of these proverbs with a Tibetan colleague to further clarify and refine my understanding.

158. *dag pa sangs rgyas/ma dag dmyal ba/*, Pemba, *Tibetan Proverbs*, 89; Hor Khang, *Bod kyi dtam dpe*, 185.

and the process of purification, is an essential component to Tibetan Buddhism. Conversely, impurity (*ma dag*), the default state of samsara and humanity, must be dealt with in order to avoid a terrible rebirth in hell. There is a certain finality contained within this terse proverb. There is no other path than these two; the one of purity and the other of impurity. To remain impure and unpurified results in going to hell and being reborn as a hell being. There is also no demarcation between monks and the laity. This is the pathway for all. Perhaps this two-line quadrisyllabic proverb captures in a certain way the essence of Tibetan Buddhism.[159]

Another proverb directly related to notions of purity is, "Hindus clean on the outside, Tibetans clean on the inside."[160] The context here is a religious and ritualistic one and is not referring to bodily cleanliness or hygiene, nor a domestic reference of keeping one's house clean, either outside or inside. The proverb is commonly used in association with pilgrimage or visiting sacred sites, both of which are a significant part of the purification process.[161] A more specific context of this proverb is in relation to pilgrims visiting an area such as Mount Kailash, which is sacred to Hindus and Buddhists alike. Hindus wash themselves in the pure streams and lakes in this area to become ritually clean and purified. Tibetans, on the other hand, concerned, as they claim, with inner rather than external purity, do not wash in the cold streams and sacred rivers.[162] Rather, they circumambu-

---

159. The quadrisyllabic proverb, typically in two lines of four syllables, is one of the most common forms of proverbs and adages in Tibetan. A linguistic analysis of the different types of proverbs is beyond the scope of this study. The focus here is on the semantic content and the relevance to purity concerns. For more on the structure of quadrisyllabics see Naga and Rigzin, *Tibetan Quadrisyllabics*; Cüppers and Sørensen, *Collection of Tibetan Proverbs*, xiv–xv.

160. *phyi pa'i phyi gtsang/nang pa'i nang gtsang*, Huber, *Cult of Pure Crystal*, 223. There is a play on words in the Tibetan; the word for Hindu is literally "outsider" corresponding to the Tibetan preposition "outside." Conversely, the term for Tibetan is "insider" which corresponds to the preposition "inside." A more literal rendering is "The outsider cleans on the outside; the insider cleans on the inside." (The term for "outsider" is a generic term applied to all foreigners or "outsiders" but can specifically refer to Hindus. The term "insider" is also a generic reference to Tibetan Buddhists). A variant of the proverb is: *rgya phyi gtsang/bod pa nang gtsang*, Tournadre and Robin, *Le Grand Livre*, 220.

161. Huber has observed, "Pilgrimage is seen by Tibetans as a fundamental method of removing, purifying or cleansing embodied *grib* and *sdig* and is thus a ritual of relevance to a wide range of general material, social and salvational concerns, from which all levels of practitioner can benefit." Huber, *Cult of Pure Crystal*, 16.

162. There are other reasons why Tibetans do not bathe in the lakes and rivers, and

late or prostrate around these lakes and mountains, while spinning prayers wheels and intoning the foremost mantra. Though Tibetans do have cleansing water rituals (which will be discussed in chapter four), they are not fastidious about washing their bodies as part of the purification process in the manner of Hindus and Muslims, and they do not do so at sacred sites.[163] Perhaps the salient point of this proverb is that there exists an acute awareness of the need to be made clean, not just ritually but morally, in the innermost part of one's being.[164] The focus is on the heart and the mind becoming clean and pure; clean from the pollution of obscurating desires, ignorance, darkness, moral turpitude, and the endless cyclical sufferings of birth, aging, sickness, and death. The typical means to achieve this for the lay person is through pilgrimage, circumambulation, prostrations, mantras, religious festivals, burning incense, and so forth. These two proverbs would indicate that the need to be morally clean is paramount in the Tibetan religious schema.

The following proverb, which contains a double imperative, urges people to be morally pure and clean: "Words and thoughts must be truthful, just as bodies and hands must be clean."[165] The idiom of "clean hands" refers to "honest" hands that do not steal and belong to a trustworthy person. A "pure body" refers to refraining from sexual misconduct or any sins which defile the body. One's speech and one's inner thoughts (the Tibetan is "stomach," which refers to one's inner most thoughts and intentions) must always be true and honest, just as one's body and hands are to be clean and pure. The hands are seen as an extension of the body and thus both the body and the hands must be morally clean. A related proverb is the play on words: "Clean are the mouths and hands of the people of Tsang."[166] The play on words is

---

this is primarily because they do not wish to upset the nagas (*klu*) who they believe inhabit these waters and are notorious for causing humans harm if disturbed.

163. Huber, *The Cult of Pure Crystal Mountain*, 17.

164. This emphasis on the inside of a person, their inner thoughts and aspirations (*khog pa, sems*), and the notion of what is on the inside as being more important than superficial, external appearances, is also evident in the very well-known proverb: "The stripes of a tiger are on the outside, the stripes of a person are on the inside," *stag gi ri mo phyi/mi yi ri mo nang*, Hor Khang, *Bod kyi dtam dpe*, 170.

165. *kha dang khog pa drang po gyis/lus dang lag pa gtsang ma gyis/*, Hor Khang, *Bod kyi dtam dpe*, 29; Pemba, *Tibetan Proverbs*, 17.

166. *kha gtsang bas gtsang ma/lag gtsang bas gtsang pa/*, Pemba, *Tibetan Proverbs*, 19; Tournadre and Robin, *Le Grand Livre*, 203. A more literal translation of this proverb would be "A clean mouth is a Tsang women and clean hands is a Tsang man." (There are feminine/masculine case markings in the Tibetan).

that one of the major areas of Tibet is named Tsang which means "clean." This proverb, when said by a person from Tsang, is esteeming the people of that area, but can also be said tongue in cheek, particularly when said by someone who is not from Tsang. The salient point here is that the concept of "clean" contains a strong moral element—clean and pure speech, trustworthy and honest hands, and clean bodies free from defilement and sexual impurity, all of which are aspirational ideals and esteemed cultural values.[167]

This theme can further be seen in the proverb "Pure hearts and pure deeds will receive pure benefits in one lifetime."[168] This proverb is stating that if one has a pure heart and does pure and virtuous deeds, one will receive the fruit of that in one's lifetime. In other words, there are direct benefits resulting from pure conduct, such as good health, prosperity, long life, merit for one's next reincarnation, and perhaps even resulting in enlightenment in one lifetime.[169] The proverb "Preaching religion first requires one to have pure vows" continues the theme of the necessity of pure motives and pure actions.[170] Preaching to others first requires one to be pure and clean. There is no value, and no spiritual power, in proclaiming anything about the dharma if one is not first committed to purity.

Proverbs with Symbolic Purity References

George Lakoff and Mark Johnson, in their seminal work, *Metaphors We Live By*, make the case that metaphor is not merely a linguistic device employed

---

167. A related proverb is "Your mouth and heart must be honest, just as your lungs and intestines must be clean." *kha dang khog pa drang po dgos/glo ba rgyu ma gtsang ma dgos/*, Pemba, *Tibetan Proverbs*, 17. The emphasis is again on honesty and inner purity. The word for "heart" in the Tibetan is literally "stomach" (*khog pa*) but again refers to the innermost part of one's being.

168. *sems bzang rnam par dag pa'i las byas na/mi lus gcig la 'bras bzang byung ba yin/*, Hor Khang, *Bod kyi dtam dpe*, 443. Note that the expression *mi lus gcig* refers to "one lifetime" and not "one human body." Also note that the word *bzang* has been added to *'bras* in the Tibetan above, even though it did not appear in Hor Khang's version, as this is how this proverb is typically expressed. This omission would appear to be a typing error because *'bras bzang* has parallelism in the first clause to *sems bzang* and also balances the syllable count to nine per phrase, an important structural feature of proverbial expressions.

169. In Tibetan Buddhism, as has been noted, it is possible to attain enlightenment in one lifetime, particularly if one pursues the "fast track" of the tantra path. This proverb is also alluding to this possibility.

170. *chos mi la shod par/rang nyid sdom pa gtsang dgos/*, Pemba, *Tibetan Proverbs*, 65; Hor Khang, *Bod kyi dtam dpe*, 132.

for poetic purposes, rather the use of metaphor reflects human thought processes which are largely metaphorical. They suggest that the "human conceptual system is metaphorically structured and defined."[171] They also suggest that this is universal to human experience: "The most fundamental values in a culture will be coherent with the metaphorical structure of the most fundamental concepts in the culture."[172] In Tibetan culture, the color white has a strong metaphorical association with purity, and the color black with impurity and evil.[173] White colored animals are favored above others and white scarves (*kha btags*), given at significant times in people's life, are symbolic of purity (as well as prosperity and good luck).[174] White snow is also symbolic of purity and the color black is seen as a contaminate that can defile the "whiteness" of purity.

The proverb "Where white is planted, white will be reaped. Where black is planted, black will be reaped," clearly illustrates this metaphorical association of white and black to purity and impurity.[175] Though the proverb has been translated literally to reflect the binary terms of white/black in the Tibetan, "white" is not understood as just a color but rather as "pure actions" performed with a pure heart. Likewise, "black" is understood as "evil actions" performed with an impure heart. This proverb clearly enunciates the karmic law of cause and effect. The karmic results are clear: "white" pure actions result in "white" pure outcomes and "black" impure actions result in "black" impure outcomes. The proverb could more accurately be translated: "Where purity is planted, purity will result. Where impurity is planted, impurity will result."

The proverb "Pursuing purity is uphill, pursuing impurity is downhill" also reflects white/black associations.[176] Again, the term for purity is the color white and the term for impurity or evil is the color black. A more literal translation is "Pursuing white is up, pursuing black is down." The cognitive association here is that being pure, and following the right path, is an uphill pursuit, and thereby much harder work. Conversely, pursuing

---

171. Lakoff and Johnson, *Metaphors We Live By*, 6.

172. Lakoff and Johnson, *Metaphors We Live By*, 22.

173. Lhamo Pemba states that "Black and white: Symbolizes impurity and purity respectively." Pemba, *Tibetan Proverbs*, xiii.

174. For example, "A white dzo (cross between a female yak and a cow) is more highly prized than any other colour." Pemba, *Tibetan Proverbs*, 218.

175. Hor Khang, *Bod kyi dtam dpe*, 5; Pemba, *Tibetan Proverbs*, 3.

176. dkar po gyen 'ded dang /nag po thur 'ded/, Hor Khang, *Bod kyi dtam dpe*, 5.

impurity is easier and seen as going down. There is another associative meaning here, quite pronounced in Tibetan consciousness, that "up" is perceived as good or pure and "down" is perceived as bad or impure. That is, "up" is the place of the pure and good, and "down" is the place of the impure and evil. This is also apparent in the perception that one goes "up" to a pure realm and falls "down" to the impure realm of hell. Lakoff and Johnson suggest that this "orientational metaphor" of "up" as good and "down" as bad, is well attested to in many cultures.[177] The clear message of this proverb is that purity is worth pursuing, with a positive and desired outcome, but it is also harder work and requires prolonged and sustained effort, just like walking up a high mountain pass, for example. Evil or impurity is conversely seen as undesirable with undesirable outcomes, yet it is the easier, downhill path.

Though purity is an aspirational goal, and worthy of pursuing, there is a cautionary note in the following proverb that purity can easily be stained or lost: "The higher and longer something is, the easier to be broken. The whiter and cleaner something is, the easier to be stained."[178] The instruction here is that one must be careful not to damage one's purity through careless immoral actions. Purity takes considerable effort but can be quickly lost or stained, and therefore requires prolonged and sustained effort. If one is not careful, the hard-gotten gains of a pure clean life can quickly be lost to a thoughtless indiscretion. The tone here is that of a warning to be careful to preserve the purity one has attained.

The black/white dichotomy is again seen in the very well-known proverb "To put a black hat on a white person."[179] This proverb is typically used when an innocent or "pure" person is accused of doing something wrong or evil. The "black hat" is symbolic of evil and impurity. The proverb can be spoken by a third person observer who sees that someone has clearly been wronged, and it can also be used by the person who believes they have been falsely accused. The image is quite a powerful one as placing a hat on a person is typically a public act, and to place something onto someone's head is not taken lightly. The proverb has a longer version: "Putting a black hat on the head of a white person and putting black reins on a white

---

177. Lakoff and Johnson codify spatialization metaphors and tropes as "orientational metaphors." Lakoff and Johnson, *Metaphors We Live By*, 14–21.

178. *mtho zhing ring ba chag pa sla/dkar zhing gtsang ba nag nog sla/*, Hor Khang, *Bod kyi dtam dpe*, 182; Pemba, *Tibetan Proverbs*, 87. The term *nag nog* (an abbreviation of the expression *nag ge nog ge*) can mean "dirty," "filthy," "impure," and also "indistinct," "vague," and "hazy."

179. TDCM, 2630.

horse."¹⁸⁰ Both the shorter and longer version communicate injustice and inappropriateness—something or someone who is pure has been wrongly considered to be impure. Another example of white/black association is the pithy aphorism: "White mouth black heart."¹⁸¹ This saying expresses the duplicity or insincerity of someone who appears to speak pure, or kind words yet is evil and impure on the inside.

Though the aspiration to be pure and to pursue purity is a fundamental part of the Tibetan religious and conceptual framework, there are some people who are considered just too evil and incorrigible to ever become clean and pure. The saying, "Wash a crow and it does not become white," attests to this.¹⁸² Crows are black and no matter how much one may wash them, they will never become white. The connotative meaning is that some evil people, or evil situations, will always remain that way no matter how much effort may be exercised to make the person or situation otherwise. This proverb is said with a certain resigned frustration; some people or situations are habituated to evil and impurity and will forever remain so.

Another proverb referencing crows is, "The black sin and impurity of the crow, causes the golden geese to get stuck in the mud."¹⁸³ Here the impurity of the crow is so great that it causes harm to the highly treasured golden geese. The broader meaning is that some people are so bad and impure that they impact and influence the behavior of good people, or, in other words, they contaminate them. Extreme "blackness," such as that of a crow, can contaminate the pure goodness of even the best "golden geese" like people. This concept of black being associated with impurity, evil and sin, and white with purity and moral goodness appears widely attested to in other cultures. Sherman and Clore's study on "The Color of Sin" suggests black is commonly associated with impurity, sin and evil, that it contaminates purity, and that it needs to be washed clean.¹⁸⁴ As has been observed, this association is also manifestly evident in Tibetan culture.

---

180. *mi dkar mgo la zhwa nag dang/rta dkar mgo la mthur nag/*, Hor Khang, *Bod kyi dtam dpe*, 297; Pemba, *Tibetan Proverbs*, 149.

181. *kha dkar gting nag/* This proverb is taken from my personal collection but is also listed in Cüppers and Sørensen, *Collection of Tibetan Proverbs and Sayings*, 17. The word *gting* means "deep" but here refers to the inside or heart of a person, the essence of what someone is really like.

182. Gergan, *Thousand Tibetan Proverbs*, 6. There is a similar proverb "Wash charcoal and it will not become white." (*sol ba khrus te dkar po mi chags*, personal collection.)

183. Cüppers and Sørensen, *Collection of Tibetan Proverbs*, 21.

184. Sherman and Clore, "Color of Sin"; and Zhong and Liljenquist, "Washing Away

Pure, good, and virtuous people being associated with the color white is further reflected in the common saying, "Your heart is whiter than a snow mountain."[185] The motif of snow being symbolic of purity is pervasive in both the oral vernacular and written texts. A related saying is, "A white thought is like a snow mountain."[186] The following quadrisyllabic aphorism also indicates the positive connotations of the color white: "White mind golden words" which, translated more expansively, means "Pure thoughts result in words of gold."[187] A related proverb is "Pure mouths do not speak harsh words and pure actions do not give birth to evil intentions."[188] The giving of ceremonial white scarves at auspicious times in a person's life is a central component to Tibetan life. The saying, "It is not the length of the scarf which matters, but the purity of the intention" further reflects white as being associated with purity.[189] There is no benefit in giving a scarf if one does not have pure intentions and pure words (literally a "clean white mouth") towards the recipient. There is also a reference to hypocrisy here. Do not give a white scarf unless you have pure "white" intentions; otherwise, you are a hypocrite.

The very well-known proverb, "If one's heart is pure, one's path will also be pure. If one's heart is evil, one's path will also be evil," makes a connection between purity and life in the mundane world of the here and now.[190] This proverb, with a clear karmic message, is commonly said to others as a way to encourage a virtuous life because one will reap the benefits in both this life and the one to come. It is a proverb that is often said to children as an instruction. The sense of "path" (*lam*) here (a common motif in religious texts), is the path one takes in life, whether that be a life of virtue or a life of sin and evil. The term for "pure" (*bzang*) in this proverb has a broader

---

Your Sins." Though these studies were undertaken in North America, there are elements of their findings which resonate in cross-cultural settings.

185. *sems gangs ri las dkar ba*, taken from my personal collection. This saying is commonly said, often as a complement after someone has done a kind act.

186. Richardus, "Selected Tibetan Proverbs," 69; Cüppers and Sørensen, *Collection of Tibetan Proverbs*, 274.

187. Cüppers and Sørensen, *Collection of Tibetan Proverbs*, 273. A similar saying is "White heart pleasing speech" or more expansively "The pure-hearted speak pleasing words," Cüppers and Sørensen, *Collection of Tibetan Proverbs*, 268.

188. Hor Khang, *Bod kyi dtam dpe*, 37.

189. Pemba, *Tibetan Proverbs*, 17; Hor Khang, *Bod kyi dtam dpe*, 26.

190. *sems pa bzang na sa dang lam yang bzang/sems pa ngan na sa dang lam yang ngan/*, personal collection. This proverb is frequently said, especially to children.

semantic range that includes kindness, goodness and virtue, as well as being pure hearted and acting towards others with pure intentions. A related proverb, which is typically said in conjunction with the former one (they form a pair), states: "Better are the small songs of the pure than the many *mani* prayers of the evil."[191] There is again a strong didactic element in this proverb. Here the focus is on this world, but also with a view to the next life. Recitation of the foremost mantra (which is what *mani* refers to) devoid of a life of moral virtue is of no benefit. In contrast, even the small songs of the pure are of greater benefit for the accrual of merit. Both proverbs place an emphasis on pure moral conduct as mediating karmic benefits both here in samsara and in one's next life.

Summary of Proverbs

While this sample of proverbs does not provide a complete picture of the Tibetan worldview or cultural understanding, it does strongly point towards, and further confirm, that notions of purity are a significant component of Tibetan ontological, religious, and cosmological sensibilities. Some proverbs are explicitly religious and clearly place purity and purification as an essential element in Tibetan Buddhism. Other proverbs place purity and a pure heart as virtuous and aspirational goals for one's life and earthly conduct. Moral conduct is perceived as being "white"—pure and clean, and immoral conduct as being "black"—impure and unclean, which can also defile and contaminate others. These proverbs also communicate a sense of urging, encouraging, and striving towards the pursuit of purity. One could suggest that the textual data here reveals that purity is an ideal state worth pursuing, that it requires effort, that it is possible to attain, and that it produces karmic benefits both here and now and in the afterlife. Conversely, impure actions, and "black" unclean hearts and desires, ultimately lead to highly undesirable outcomes and negatively influence others. Though perceived as easier to pursue, moral uncleanness has disastrous and lasting consequences. Following the framework of Lakoff and Johnson as metaphors being indicative of underlying conceptual systems, one could suggest that these proverbs point to purity and impurity being a significant component of the "fundamental values" of Tibetan culture.

---

191. *sems ngan can gyi maNi grangs ba las/sems bzang can gyi glu chung len par dga'/*, personal collection.

Texts of Moral Instruction

There is a large body of texts that could be included in the category of "texts of moral instruction." However, there is a certain class of Tibetan texts that are considered to be more oriented towards the laity as moral advice or instructions. These texts are often in the form of oral teachings that have been given as public teachings, often at a monastery, and then later committed to writing. Indeed, many of the commentaries on the Buddhist canon were first given as oral teachings before later being written down. This tradition of giving oral instructions and teachings has played a critical role in the transmission of Tibetan Buddhism.[192] Given the fact that these texts are oral teachings, the language in them reflects the spoken vernacular and are thus more accessible to the laity than the higher register Buddhist scriptures. There are two main genre types that come under this broad category; *zhal gdams* "oral teachings" or "oral instructions" and *bslab bya* (Sk. shiksha) "instructions," "trainings," or "precepts."[193] As these two categories are interrelated, they are often listed together as *zhal gdams bslab bya* "oral teachings and instructions."[194] Though a vast genre, only two texts will be briefly examined here.

One Hundred Instructions to the People of Tingri

One of the more famous instructional texts, and one that has endured the test of time, is the *One Hundred Instructions to the People of Tingri*.[195] According to tradition, this text was composed, and also given as an oral teaching, in the eleventh century by the Indian master Padampa Sangye (*pha dam pa sang rgyas*, Sk. Paramabuddha). The meaning of Padampa Sangye is "Holy Father Buddha," and he is esteemed as a great saint by Tibetans. Though he was from southern India, he made five trips to Tibet

---

192. Cabezón and Jackson, among others, have pointed out the key role oral traditions played in the transmission of Tibetan Buddhism and Tibetan culture. Cabezón and Jackson, *Tibetan Literature*, 13–14.

193. In the term *zhal gdams*, *zhal* is honorific for mouth and *gdams* refers to teachings or instructions. These teachings then are considered noble or honorable oral teachings or instructions from the mouth of a lama. They are also known in the non-honorific form as *gdams ngag*.

194. TDCM, 2380, under *zhal gdams*.

195. The title in Tibetan is *pha dam pa sangs rgyas kyi zhal gdams ding ri brgya rtsa ma*, (also known as *ding ri brgya rtsa ma*).

and is believed to have spent most of his time in the area of Tingri, a small village settlement close to the border of Nepal, in the southern area of the Tibetan province of Tsang.[196] It is believed that on his final trip to Tibet, Padampa Sangye remained in Tingri for over twenty years and gave his *One Hundred Instructions* at the Tingri Langkhor Monastery situated there.[197] Using lower register colloquial language, his teachings are given in an affectionate way, and at the end of each instruction, he implores the "People of Tingri" (*ding ri pa*) to pay heed to them.

Padampa Sangye's instructions provide a general overview of Buddhist teachings, such as the law of karmic cause and effect, the endless cycle of suffering, the certainty of death and the afterlife, detachment from this world and worldly desires, and the need to follow the dharma and one's lama closely. He implores the people of Tingri to be virtuous, kind, generous, hard-working and to associate with virtuous people. He begins his instructions by calling on the people to devote themselves whole-heartedly to the dharma with their bodies, speech, and minds.[198] Padampa Sangye concludes his instructions by imploring the people to abandon their sins, even the smallest ones, and to do virtuous deeds, even small ones.[199] In his final instruction, Padampa Sangye urges the people to follow in his footsteps and emulate his practice.

More pertinent to the study at hand, Padampa Sangye also highlights the need for purification as an essential practice for the people of Tingri. In instruction number thirty-seven, he implores his listeners, "Through prostrations and circumambulations the sins of the body are purified. So,

196. Padampa Sangye and Khyentse, *Hundred Verses of Advice*, xv. Tingri is a village area on the high Tibetan plateau that is still in existence today and has for centuries been a frontier area for trade between Nepal and Tibet.

197. Molk and Wangdu, *Lion of Siddhas*, 15, 18. Padampa Sangye also gave many other teachings at this monastery. He was also famous for introducing the *chod* teachings to Tibet, which detail a particular type of tantric teaching and praxis of "cutting through" ignorance and delusion.

198. *One Hundred Instructions*, instruction 1, manuscript 1, plate no. 430. In the *dpe cha* version, manuscript 1, the refrain "people of Tingri" is not included after every instruction but is substituted by the symbol "x" to save space, paper, and ink. In the original version, "people of Tingri" is rendered *ding ri ba*, but in modern times the vernacular pronunciation is *ding ri pa*. I have followed the contemporary pronunciation. Also, the instructions are not numbered in the *dpe cha* version though they were added in some later versions. I consulted two versions in *dpe cha* form as one of them was missing some of the final instructions.

199. *One Hundred Instructions*, instruction no. 96, manuscript 2, plate no. 1 and instruction 97, manuscript 2, plate no. 1.

STEPS TOWARD A TIBETAN UNDERSTANDING OF PURITY

People of Tingri, abandon worldly deeds!"[200] Continuing this theme, in instruction thirty-eight, he states, "Through recitations and taking refuge, the sins of the mouth are purified. So, People of Tingri, do not engage in vulgar and baseless talk."[201] He further adds, in instruction thirty-nine, "Through devotion and longing, sins of the mind are purified. So, people of Tingri, carry your lama on the crown of your head."[202] The sense of "longing" here is associated with devotion to one's lama and longing to emulate them and follow their teachings.

The three aspects of body, speech, and mind, outlined by Padampa Sangye, follows a consistent pattern in the texts studied thus far. That is, the need for these three components to be cleansed and purified again demonstrate this teaching as being foundational in the Tibetan religious schema. Padampa Sangye also reiterates the importance of one's lama, adhering to what he says, following him in all things, and esteeming him to the point of "carrying him on the crown of your head." This image of placing one's lama on one's head indicates a place of high esteem, importance, and devotion. Padampa Sangye is confident in his own behavior and thus instructs the people to follow his example: "I have unwaveringly practiced [the dharma], you also must follow after me."[203]

The text has been composed in an easy to follow style that facilitates recitation and memorization. There is a certain affection displayed towards the laity and the people of a relatively small village area in Tibet. Though purification is not the only teaching contained in these instructions, it does form part of a general teaching on Tibetan Buddhism. The need for purification in the process of escaping from samsara and attaining Buddhahood is again reinforced. And these purification teachings remain core practices of Tibetans; prostrations and circumambulations (for cleansing one's body), recitations of mantras (for cleansing one's speech), and devotion towards one's lama (for cleansing one's mind). This text provides an example of an instructional text which has been passed on down through the generations, is a generic teaching with no sectarian biases, has had a wide reach beyond the area of Tingri, and continues to inform a Tibetan understanding of purity and purification praxis.

200. *One Hundred Instructions*, instruction 37, manuscript 1, plate no. 434.
201. *One Hundred Instructions*, instruction 38, manuscript 1, plate no. 434.
202. *One Hundred Instructions*, instruction 39, manuscript 1, plate no. 434.
203. *One Hundred Instructions*, instruction 100, manuscript 2, plate no. 1–2.

The Sixteen Precepts of Pure Conduct

Another text, which has also survived the passage of time, is the instructional text, *The Sixteen Precepts of Pure Conduct*, which are sixteen codes or precepts of "pure" or "clean" human conduct.[204] This text is attributed to the seventh-century king, Songtsen Gampo, whose copious writings are allegedly recorded in the *Mani Kabum*, a section of which was discussed earlier. Given the popularity of these sixteen pure codes of conduct, this text can be found in many places. The one presented here is from an elementary school level Tibetan language textbook, a book that all Tibetan children in Tibet study as part of their formal education.[205] What may be more remarkable about these codes of conduct, and pertinent to the topic at hand, is not so much the codes themselves, but that Songtsen Gampo chose to give them the name "pure human conducts." He explicitly used the term "clean" (*gtsang ma*) and clearly had a certain ideal in mind that civil society would behave in a "clean" or "pure" manner.

Though the first two instructions are religious in nature in calling for people to respect and be devoted to the Triple Refuge and to always practice the dharma, the remaining fourteen deal with civil conduct towards others. For example, one is expected to show respect to one's parents and return their kindness, to show respect to the learned and those of higher status, to be a loyal and faithful friend, to help one's neighbors and the poor, to be honest and reliable, to live within one's means, to repay the kindness of others, to show no favoritism, to speak politely, and to be diligent in whatever one does. Songtsen Gampo saw these virtuous behaviors as constituting a pure or clean life. In his concluding remarks about these sixteen behaviors, he states that since they have not been stained or infected with evil, these practices are therefore considered clean.[206] Furthermore, Songtsen Gampo continues, since these codes of conduct are beneficial to all people, everyone should heed these practices and "strive without error to uphold these right and pure practices."[207]

---

204. The name of the text in Tibetan is *mi chos gtsang ma bcu drug* which can also be variously translated as "The Sixteen Pure Human Laws" or "The Sixteen Codes of Pure Human Conduct."

205. *Skad yig deb dang po [Language Book One]*, 8–9. The major dictionaries also contain this list of the sixteen codes of pure conduct. See TDCM, 2067–68, DGCM, 1599–60, and RJYS under *mi chos gtsang ma bcu drug*.

206. *Skad yig deb dang po [Language Book One]*, 9.

207. *Skad yig deb dang po [Language Book One]*, 9.

Though not all Tibetans would likely know each one of these sixteen codes of conduct, it is a fair estimation to say that the majority would be familiar with the name of the text, and in general, the aspirational content of what is considered to be a virtuous life. The existence of this text, and its perseveration through perpetuity, would suggest that these "clean" behaviors, and the ideal of what constitutes "pure" civil conduct, have impinged upon and shaped Tibetan sensibilities for many centuries. Indeed, purity, purification, clean and unclean, pure and impure, would appear to be categories that have deep resonance within Tibetan consciousness.

Chapter Three Summary

This chapter has examined texts which have influenced a lay understanding of purity and purification. The various texts included the genre of the popular Pure Land *bde smon* aspirational prayers, texts associated with the foremost mantra, *om mani padme hum*, proverbs and sayings, and moral instructional texts. The Pure Land texts indicate certain ontological and cosmological realities of the existence of pure and impure beings, and pure and impure realms beyond the realm of samsara. The aspirational prayers demonstrate that Tibetans earnestly desire rebirth in a pure realm, particularly that of Sukhāvatī, with Buddha Amitābha representative of an archetypal savior. Faith and devotion were seen as the key requirements for entry into the pure and pristine Land of Bliss.

The texts associated with the foremost mantra clearly indicate that purification is an essential element of the perceived efficacy of the mantra. The mantra is believed to effect the purification of negative karma, moral infractions, and polluting obscurations. Furthermore, recitation of the mantra is important in the purification and clearing away of the suffering of samsara. Being directly linked to Avalokiteshvara, the exalted patron of the Gelukpa lineage, the mantra is a call for blessing, protection, and purification, and given that Avalokiteshvara resides in Sukhāvatī, is further seen as being efficacious for rebirth there.

The proverbs and sayings, which offer a particular window on cultural understanding, suggest that purity and purification are aspirational goals and are informative in constructing a Tibetan worldview. This worldview sees pure and impure, and clean and unclean as important demarcations which impact both life in the mundane realities of human interactions and the supramundane realities of the afterlife. It was seen that these proverbs

TEXTS OF LAY ASPIRATION AND FOLK TRADITIONS

reflect certain fundamental values of Tibetan society. The texts of moral instruction likewise show that notions of purity and purification are part of the mainstream consciousness of the laity and have been an enduring feature of oral teachings and instructions over many centuries. One could perhaps state that these texts demonstrate that purity and purification, and the concepts of clean and unclean, and pure and impure, clearly inform Tibetan soteriological, cosmological, and ontological beliefs and form a central part of Tibetan Buddhist doctrine and lay understanding and praxis.

4
Ritual Texts and Symbols

Introduction

CONTINUING THE GOAL OF seeking to gain a comprehensive understanding of Tibetan notions of purity, this chapter will explore some of the common, everyday rituals performed by Tibetans such as prostration, the spinning of prayer wheels, incense burning, and lustral water purification rites. More specifically, the annual incense burning festival, World Purification Day (*'dzam gling spyi bsang*), will be briefly discussed in the section on incense burning, and particular attention will be given to a certain water ritual (*byabs khrus*) that forms part of a daily purification praxis. A brief examination of some of the main symbols of purity will be made at the end of the chapter. This investigation will again be facilitated by examining a selection of salient Tibetan texts. Given the vast corpus of texts on this topic, and the myriad of rituals and festivals one could choose to examine, out of necessity this chapter will only briefly introduce a selection of rituals relevant to purity and purification.[1]

Though the confessional and tantric purification texts examined in chapter two are the basis for a variety of elaborate rituals, and the recitation of prayers and mantras (essential to all ritual) are in themselves a form of ritual, the term "ritual" is being used here in a broader sense to incorporate regular practices which form part of the daily existence of the life

---

1. For a general overview of the various types of Tibetan rituals see Cabezón, *Tibetan Ritual*, 1–34. Though in modern times some festivals are no longer celebrated, or not celebrated on the scale they once were, in traditional Tibet there were at least fifty days of the year on which particular rituals or festivals were observed. See Richardson, *Ceremonies*.

of a Tibetan. Van Schaik has rightly observed that "the practice of ritual is at the heart of Tibetan Buddhism."[2] Cabezón has also noted that ritual "pervades the Tibetan religious landscape."[3] Though much has been written about ritual in general, and various methods of studying them,[4] the approach followed here is to give voice to the emic understanding found in indigenous texts. No attempt will be made to provide an all-encompassing theory regarding the structure and function of Tibetan rituals. However, as a general working definition, "ritual" will be considered as the regular practice of the application of religion to one's daily life, thus representing a certain intersection between the mundane reality of human existence and the supramundane realities of the transcendent.[5] Gabezón makes a useful distinction between the tantric rituals of the monastics (sometimes referred to as "elite" rituals) and the magic and pragmatic rituals (sometimes referred to as "popular" rituals) which are made available to the laity by the appropriate ritual experts. However, he also notes, as has been observed in previous chapters, that drawing a definitive demarcation between the activities of monks and the laity is problematic.[6] The Tibetan term *cho ga*, which is typically translated into English as "ritual," offers a broad definition of "a method to bring about a certain outcome, a particular procedure or practice, or a sequence of steps."[7] Such a definition, which allows for rituals with or without the facilitation of a ritual expert, will suffice here.

---

2. Van Schaik, *Spirit of Tibetan Buddhism*, 135.

3. Cabezón, *Tibetan Ritual*, 2.

4. See, for example, Hiebert et al., *Understanding Folk Religion*, Kindle location 5132–5917, and Cabezón, *Tibetan Ritual*, 12–13.

5. Skorupski defines ritual as "applied religion." Skorupski, "Tibetan Prayer for Rebirth," 243 n46. Hiebert et al., suggest that "The most important rituals are sacred ceremonies that link life experiences to the sacred, to the transcendent." Hiebert et al., *Understanding Folk Religion*, Kindle location 5340.

6. Cabezón, *Tibetan Ritual*, 14–20. Cabezón notes that there exists a blurring of "elite" and "popular" rituals between monks and the laity, and that such a division is porous. He further suggests that while some rituals have soteriological concerns and others more pragmatic ones, such as protecting crops from hail, it is again difficult to neatly separate them. This is because Tibetan Buddhist praxis, as has been observed, often has the dual goals of impacting life in the here and now, and the higher goal of salvation from the endless cycle of samsara.

7. TDCM, 821–22.

Prostration as a Purificatory Ritual

Following the definition of ritual as a particular practice to bring about a desired outcome, the ubiquitous ritual practice of prostration will now be examined. As well as being an essential element of confessional and tantra purification rituals, where the prescribed number of prostrations is often 100,000, full body prostrations are a core element of pilgrimages, temple and monastic visits, and general acts of worship and devotion. The act of prostration is a primary way of accumulating merit and also a means for achieving purification from defilement.[8] Pilgrims often prostrate for long distances, taking months, or even years, to arrive at a particular sacred site. It is common for pilgrims to circumambulate around sacred sites with full body prostrations, often traversing high mountain passes in the process. Circumambulation by walking is considered a purifying act, and circumambulation by prostration even more so. There are numerous texts which stress how both prostration and circumambulation are believed to cleanse the sins and defilement of the body.[9]

The term for prostration, *phyag 'tshal ba*, more literally means "to beseech with one's hands" and is a generic term for paying homage or obeisance to a higher being.[10] However, the term also refers specifically to the physical act of bowing down, laying prostrate on the ground, stretching out fully one's arms, retracting them, and standing upright again before repeating the same action, all as an act of worship and devotion. Tibetans typically prostrate before an image of a deity, one's lama, a temple, stupa or

---

8. The Dalai Lama, *Complete Foundation*, Kindle location 1795, 2285.

9. Statements such as "being purified from bodily defilements through prostration and circumambulation" (*lus kyi sgrib pa sbyong phyir phyag 'tshal dang skor ba*) can be found in a variety of texts. See, for example, Huber, *Cult of Pure Crystal*, 17, and 233 footnote 18. Huber suggests that "Variations on this common formulation appear to have been introduced into Tibet during the eleventh and twelfth centuries." The practices themselves predate this period but the existence of explicit textual evidence appears to date from this time.

10. The term for hand *phyag* (in *phyag 'tshal ba*) is the honorific form indicating that the showing of respect and homage is towards one who is of greater importance, rank or status. However, the term is also etymologically linked to *phyags*, the verb meaning to clean or wipe clean. This term is also cognate with *phyags ma* the word for broom, with clear associations of sweeping something clean. Geshe Palden Drakpa has noted this link suggesting *phyag* in this context should be understood to mean cleansing oneself of physical, mental and verbal obscurations. Drakpa, *Freeing Yourself*, 68. Ekvall has also noted this semantic association with the term *phyag*, suggesting that prostration then becomes "a rite of cleansing or purification." Ekvall, *Religious Observances in Tibet*, 203.

other holy object, and around sacred sites. One of the major Tibetan dictionaries defines prostration as "a supreme act of reverence and devotion through the three pathways of body, speech, and mind."[11] Tibetans make a distinction between two types of prostration. The first type, *brkyangs phyag*, is a full prostration where one's body, forehead, knees and both palms of one's hands contact the ground. The second type, *bskums phyag*, is where only one's knees touch the ground, and one bends forward without one's body connecting with the ground.[12] As one can imagine, full prostrations are more meritorious and efficacious not only because they require more effort, but, as the Dalai Lama states, "your whole body connects to the sacred ground."[13]

Tibetan scholar Sagong Wangdu, in his book *One Hundred Tibetan Customs*, makes it clear that the purpose of prostration is to purify and remove all negativity and defiling obscurations, and to enter into the path of liberation.[14] Wangdu further states that in order to achieve the exalted state of Buddhahood, nothing can surpass the act of prostration which he considers to be "the supreme act of homage through the means of appropriating one's body, speech and mind."[15] It is of course important that during prostrations one keeps one's mind focused, pure, and full of faith and devotion.[16] Wangdu outlines how one may choose to do one hundred, one thousand or even 100,000 prostrations as a means to purify one's defilements.[17] Typically, prostrators do sets of one hundred prostrations and count them off on their rosaries as they go.

---

11. TDCM, 1735, under *phyag 'tshal ba*.

12. TDCM, 178, under *brkyangs phyag*, 182 under *bskums phyag* and Wangdu, *Bod mi'i yul srol goms gshis*, 25–26. L. Z. Rinpoche claims that in all prostration "the 'five limbs' that should always touch the ground are the two hands, two knees, and forehead." L. Z. Rinpoche, *Preliminary Practice of Prostrations*, Kindle location 1182. See also Drakpa, *Freeing Yourself*, 65–68.

13. The Dalai Lama, *My Tibet*, 132.

14. Wangdu, *Bod mi'i yul srol*, 25–26.

15. Wangdu, *Bod mi'i yul srol*, 25.

16. As well as reciting mantras while prostrating, it is also believed that focusing on the color white and imagining being absorbed in radiant light is an effective means of purifying one's misdeeds. L. Z. Rinpoche, *Preliminary Practice of Prostrations*, Kindle locations 440, 517.

17. Wangdu, *Bod mi'i yul srol*, 26.

The Benefits and Advantages of Prostration

One of the primary texts concerning prostration, the prayers of which are often quoted while performing prostrations, is the famous text *The Benefits and Advantages of Prostration* (*phyag 'tshal ba'i phan yon*) attributed to Sakya Pandita Gunga Gyaltsen, (1181–1251).[18] This text is still widely used and recited today.[19] For the sake of brevity, attention will only be given to those sections of the prayer relevant to purity and purification. The prayer begins in typical fashion by paying homage to and taking refuge in one's lama, the Buddha, the dharma and the priesthood. The supplicant then prays, "Through the offering of prostrations to the Holy Triple Refuge, may I, and all beings, be purified from negative misdeeds and defiling obscurations."[20] The prayer continues with a wish: "by placing my hands together at the crown of my head, may I be reborn in the pure realm of Sukhāvatī."[21]

After the preliminary supplications, the prayer then works through the purification of each of the three elements of body, speech, and mind, a common thread that has been observed throughout the purification texts previously examined. The first aspiration is that through the placing of one's hands together in a praying position, and touching them on one's forehead, one's misdeeds and polluting obscurations of the body may be purified. The second aspiration is that through the placing of one's hands at one's throat, one's misdeeds and polluting obscurations of speech may be purified. The third supplication requests that by placing one's hands together at the position of one's heart, one's misdeeds and polluting obscurations of the heart and mind may be purified.[22] The prayer then outlines each element of prostration and an associated wish. For example, by placing one's knees on the ground,

---

18. Sakya Pandita, *phyag 'tshal ba'i phan yon*. I also studied another related text by Sakya Pandita, *Aspiration Prayer While Prostrating* (*phyag 'tshal skabs 'don rgyu'i smon tshig*).

19. When reading over this text together with one of my close Tibetan colleagues, he recalled how he recited this text from a young age, wrote it out on a piece of paper and placed it on the wall over his bed. He enthusiastically read over this prayer with me.

20. *bdag gis mchog gsum dam par phyag 'tshal nas/bdag cag 'gro kun sdig sgrib 'dag par shog*, *The Benefits and Advantages of Prostration*, line 2/3.

21. *thal mo spyi bo'i gtsug tu sbyar ba yis/zhing mchog bde ba can du skye bar shog*, *The Benefits and Advantages of Prostration*, lines 6/7. It is of interest to note the consciousness of Pure Land Buddhism in this prayer. If this text was composed in the twelfth to thirteenth centuries, this is further evidence of the early dispersion and adoption of Pure Land teachings in Tibet.

22. *The Benefits and Advantages of Prostration*, lines 7–14.

may all beings be freed from the lower realms of samsara, and, by placing one's forehead on the ground, may the level of Complete Illumination be attained.[23] The prayer continues with the request that by touching the ground with one's body, and rising up again, may one not remain in samsara but attain the path of liberation. Furthermore, the prayer petitions: "Through the meritorious power of the offering of full body prostrations, may I obtain long life devoid of sickness and replete with perfect abundance."[24] The desire to be reborn in Sukhāvatī is again restated as is the wish to attain the perfect and complete stage of Buddhahood. The prayer concludes with a restatement of a desire for all these things to be accomplished.

The recurrent theme that the three elements of body, speech, and mind must be purified as a precursor to any attempts at liberation from samsara and reaching the final stage of Buddhahood, is again evident in this text. Indeed, as has been seen elsewhere, any liberation, escape from samsara, or attainment of a higher rebirth is predicated upon first being made clean from sin and defilement. The desire to be reborn in the pure realm of Sukhāvatī is again clearly seen as an aspiration for all prostrators. Though this prayer is an aspirational prayer, typically prayed while prostrating, the name of the prayer, *The Benefits and Advantages of Prostrations*, reflects the strong belief that prostration in itself can bring about these desired outcomes.[25] As has been observed, the number of prostrations, and the sincerity of the practitioner, is paramount to any perceived efficacy. In other words, a few casual prostrations done now and again will not bring about the desired results of purification and rebirth in a pure realm. Prostration is a solemn and sacred undertaking that pervades all aspects

---

23. *The Benefits and Advantages of Prostration*, lines 15–16, 19–20. The term "Complete Illumination" (*bcu gcig kun tu 'od*) refers to the eleventh stage of Bodhisattva perfection of becoming completely radiant, full of universal light of understanding and perfection, and free from all impurities.

24. *The Benefits and Advantages of Prostration*, lines 29–30.

25. Among the many benefits of prostration that Lama Zopa Rinpoche lists are its efficacy for purifying negative karma, freeing one from terrifying samsara, attaining moral purity, and, of course, the achievement of ultimate enlightenment. L. Z. Rinpoche, *Preliminary Practice of Prostrations*, Kindle locations 444, 445, and 479. Drakpa asserts that prostrations can cleanse one of all non-virtues and all physical, verbal and mental defilements and achieve great merit. Drakpa, *Freeing Yourself*, 57–58, 65. In asking many Tibetans over the years the benefits of prostration, the typical reply is that any accumulated merit they hope will benefit them in their next life, and invariably they add that even if it does not benefit them in their next life, it is at least beneficial physical exercise that improves their health and well-being in this life.

of Tibetan religious life. Lama Zopa Rinpoche, in stressing the imperative of regular prostration as an inextricable part of Tibetan Buddhist practice, highlights the urgent need:

> Death can come at any time, even in this hour or this minute. I could be born in the lower realms any moment ... Therefore, how can I stand to live for even one second without purifying this negative karma? There is no way to relax without doing something to purify the cause, without doing the practice of purification. It is like you have eaten poison and you want to get rid of it the quickest way possible. So therefore, we do prostrations.[26]

The Spinning of Prayer Wheels as a Purificatory Ritual

The rituals of prostrations, spinning prayer wheels, reciting the foremost mantra *om mani padme hum*, and burning incense form some of the most fundamental elements of Tibetan religious life. Though these four rituals are evident in all religious activity, including specific rituals and festivals, they are also rituals within their own right, typically performed in the daily rhythm of life. They are also rituals which require no qualified religious expert to administer and are freely open to all. The spinning of prayer wheels in many ways represents the quintessential Tibetan Buddhist religious practice.[27] Prayer wheels can be found at all temples and monasteries in various forms and sizes. The most common form found in Tibetan households is the hand-held device, the spinning of which is governed by the momentum of a ball and chain attached to a metal cylinder containing a scroll of mantras. A generic definition of the prayer wheel is "a wheel containing many coiled-up copies of the six-syllable mantra."[28] The larger prayer wheels, which Simpson described as a type of "ritualistic machine," are often designed to be blown by the wind or powered by water.[29] Typi-

---

26. L. Z. Rinpoche, *Preliminary Practice of Prostrations*, Kindle location 507.

27. Martin, "On the Origin," 13. Simpson, *Buddhist Praying-Wheel*, 3.

28. TDCM, under *ma Ni 'khor lo—ma Ni yig drug mang po'i dril ba'i 'khor lo*, 2044–45. The term *ma Ni 'khor lo* typically refers to the handheld spinning device, though there is also a specific term *lag 'khor* "hand wheel." The term *ma Ni chu 'khor* refers to a prayer wheel spun by the force of water and *ma Ni rlung 'khor* a prayer wheel spun by the force of wind. *ma Ni rdo phung* refers to heaped prayer cairns containing tablets and stones engraved with the six-syllable mantra.

29. Simpson, *Buddhist Praying-Wheel*, 20.

cally, the mantra *om mani padme hum* is printed thousands of times on the paper scroll that is coiled inside the wheel. Each rotation of the wheel is believed to be equivalent to reciting all of the thousands of mantras contained inside.

Legend has it that Nagarjuna (*klu sgrub*), the Indian master of Buddhism who lived during the second to third centuries AD, magically brought the prayer wheel into the human realm, which centuries later, made its way to Tibet.[30] Others claim the device was an adaptation of the large revolving bookcases found in Chinese Buddhist monasteries.[31] The conception of a rotating wheel can be traced to the commencement of the Buddha's first teachings which became known as *chos 'khor*—"the turning of the wheel of the dharma."[32] There is an annual festival *chos kyi 'khor skor ba'i dus chen* that commemorates Buddha's first turning of the wheel of the dharma. The spinning of prayer wheels, then, harkens back to the initial teaching ("turning") of the dharma. The importance of the wheel is that the mantra needs to be spun in order to produce the desired effect. In short, the mantra is not effective if left dormant inside the wheel and hence the reason there are prayer wheels powered by wind and water. Though the accumulation of merit is a primary motivation in the ritualistic turning of a prayer wheel, it is also believed to be efficacious in the process of purification.

A Short Treatise of Prayer Wheels

One of the primary textual sources for this understanding of prayer wheels being effective in the process of purification is *A Short Treatise of Prayer Wheels* (*'khor lo'i rnam gzhag mdor bsdus bzhugs*) by Gung Thang (1762–1823).[33] Though a brief text, it provides insights into the prayer wheel as being an agent of purification. In listing the benefits of spinning a prayer wheel, the text states that it provides the best form of protection from harm, that it stops rebirth in the six realms of samsara, and that it purifies the intermediatory state of *bar do*. Gung Thang even makes the bold claim that the spinning of a prayer wheel is more purifying than just reciting the mantra contained within it.[34] The text continues that the rotation of prayer wheels has many

---

30. L. Z. Rinpoche, *Wheel of Great Compassion*, 13–14; Martin, "On the Origin," 20.
31. Winder, "Aspects of the History," 25–26. Martin, "On the Origin," 16.
32. TDCM, under *chos 'khor*, 826, and TDCM, under *chos kyi 'khor skor ba*, 830–31.
33. Gung Thang's full name is *gung thang dkon mchog bstan pa'i sgron me*.
34. *A Short Treatise of Prayer Wheels*, plate no. 000736.

superior benefits over mantra recitation alone. Though this statement of the supremacy of the spinning of the wheel over the mantra itself may be hyperbolic, it does highlight the high esteem placed on these devices and their perceived efficacy. Indeed, the best scenario is to actively spin the wheel, which puts into motion the power of thousands of mantras, and to recite the mantra at the same time. Lama Thupten Zorpa claims that reciting the mantra and turning the wheel simultaneously "helps us to complete the accumulation of extensive merit and purify obscurations so as to achieve enlightenment as quickly as possible."[35] He also claims that Buddha Amitābha stated that, "Anyone who recites the six syllables while turning the Dharma wheel at the same time is equal in fortune to the Thousand Buddhas."[36]

A Short Treatise of Prayer Wheels makes additional claims that when the light which emanates from the spinning of a prayer wheel strikes one's body it can purify all sin and polluting obstacles, and cause the blessings of all the Buddhas to enter one's being.[37] Furthermore, the light rays from the prayer wheel, which spread in all directions, can cleanse the world and its inhabitants from all impurities.[38] The text also claims that even if a mantra is written on a piece of wood, and spun around just a few times, the power generated from these rotations will be able to stop contagious diseases, frost, hail, and the like.[39] The emphasis in the text here is both on the mantra and the action of rotating or spinning it. The need for pure motives in performing this ritual is also evident from the text: "So if one spins a mantra with pure motives, unimaginable benefits will result. Even the wind from the spinning of a prayer wheel, should it touch one's body, will purify many sins and obscurations, and establish the seeds of liberation."[40]

The prayer wheel has a long and celebrated history in Tibet, and its rotation is perceived to bring many benefits in this life and is a necessary agent in the process of liberation from the endless suffering and misery of samsara. When Tibetans spin their prayer wheels and recite the foremost mantra, protection from harm, the accumulation of merit, purification

---

35. L. Z. Rinpoche, *Wheel of Great Compassion*, ix.

36. L. Z. Rinpoche, *Wheel of Great Compassion*, viii. Lama Thupten Zopa further states that "reciting the mantra and turning the wheel . . . instantly eliminates all the immeasurable negative karmic obscurations." viii–ix.

37. *A Short Treatise of Prayer Wheels*, plate no. 000737.

38. *A Short Treatise of Prayer Wheels*, plate no. 000738.

39. *A Short Treatise of Prayer Wheels*, plate no. 000738.

40. *A Short Treatise of Prayer Wheels*, plate no. 000738.

from sin, the avoidance of an impure rebirth in samsara, and the hope of being reborn in a pure realm, may be among the various motivating factors that lead them to do so.

Purificatory Fumigation Rituals

Together with prostrations, the spinning of prayer wheels, and reciting mantras, the burning of incense is another daily activity that pervades the religious life of Tibetans. Though almost all rituals involve burning incense, offering up incense is a daily ritual in itself which also speaks to Tibetan notions of purity. The vast majority of Tibetan households have incense burners (*spos gzhong, spos sgam*) inside their houses as well as incense burners (*bsang khung*) on the roof or an outside wall. Incense burners can be found at the entrances to temples and monasteries, and along the pathways of circumambulation circuits around sacred sites. Kapstein offers a concise definition of the practice of burning incense: "*Sang*, literally 'purification,' is a ubiquitous Tibetan custom in which the fragrant smoke of juniper and other substances is offered to the gods and spirits pervading the land."[41] Tibetan scholar Chabpel Tseten Phuntsok writes that the ritual of incense burning (*bsang gtong ba*) is an essential preliminary practice for removing the impurities and uncleanness of the human realm which are offensive to local deities.[42]

The concept of the human realm being inherently unclean and impure has its roots in the Bön religion where in preparation for deities to descend from the heavens, incense was first to be burned in order to purify their passage.[43] According to legend, prior to the first Tibetan king, Nyatri Tsenpo (*gnya' khri bstan po*, ca.127 BC), descending to earth, three divine beings were dispatched in order to purify the defiled human realm through the burning of incense.[44] Samten Karmay further elaborates that purification rituals developed "based on the idea that the deities and the environment have been defiled (*phog pa, 'bags pa*) as a result of man's own impure nature

---

41. Kapstein, *Tibetan Buddhism*, 8. Note that the spelling of *sang* (without the prefix *ba*) is an attempt to capture the pronunciation (even though it is pronounced "sung") rather than the correct spelling of *bsang*.

42. In Wangdu *Bod mi'i yul srol*, 14–15. Chabpel Tseten Phuntsok, in a separate article, also states that the purification rite of incense burning is "performed in order to purify environmental pollution so as to make a place pure enough to invite deities." Phuntsok, "Deity Invocation Ritual," 9.

43. Wangdu, *Bod mi'i yul srol*, 14; Phuntsok, "Deity Invocation Ritual," 9.

44. Rigzin, *Festivals of Tibet*, 37; Wangdu, *Bod mi'i yul srol*, 8.

and activity... the deities are offended by what man does to himself and to his environment."⁴⁵ As a result of this defilement, the gods withdraw their favors and cause harm and suffering to the human realm. Therefore, the practice of purification through the fumigation of incense burning needs to be performed regularly as one may unwittingly commit a defiling act that displeases the local deities and be subject to their wrath.⁴⁶ This practice of purifying the gods by fumigation spread widely throughout Tibetan areas and became known as a fragrant offering (*bsang mchod*) ritual.⁴⁷ Wangdu notes that the primary motivation for burning incense is to purify the land from the filth and defilement of humans.⁴⁸ For the most part, this ritual is an individual act that does not require a ritual specialist, and is "practiced in one form or another by virtually all Tibetans, monks and laypersons, men and women, rich and poor."⁴⁹

Purificatory Fumigation Texts

An important purification by fumigation textual source is the compendium *The Preliminary Practices of Purification through Fumigation* (*bsang gi dag gtsang sngon 'gro*), attributed to the Bön master Nyamme Sherab Gyaltsen, (*mnyam med shes rab rgyal mtshan*, 1365–1415). In this compilation of liturgies and ritual practices, the purpose of burning incense is made clear. A short excerpt will suffice. After exhorting the practitioner to prepare an incense offering with a pleasant fragrance, the liturgy then encourages the recitation of:

> Let us purify the gods above
> Let us purify the naga below
> Let us also purify the spirits in between
> Let us purify our seats
> May our clothes be purified
> Indeed, may everything be made pure!⁵⁰

45. Karmay, "Local Deities," 383.
46. Karmay, "Local Deities," 383.
47. Phuntsok, "Deity Invocation Ritual," 26; Karmay, "Local Deities," 381.
48. Wangdu, *Bod mi'i yul srol*, 15.
49. Kapstein, *Tibetan Buddhism*, 8.
50. *The Preliminary Practices of Purification through Fumigation*, (*bsang gi dag gtsang sngon 'gro*), 2, as quoted in Karmay, "Local Deities," 382. Though I was able to source this work, I was unable to gain access to all of the contents and thus have relied on the

RITUAL TEXTS AND SYMBOLS

Practitioners today often elicit liturgies such as these, or one of two lines of them, as they burn incense. This style of liturgy forms the basis of generic daily practices of burning incense in one's home, temple, or monastery.

Though incense is offered to appease an array of deities and gods, one primary function is to satisfy the wishes of nagas, (mentioned in the liturgy above) who are underground serpents believed to be particularly sensitive to human defilement, and the cause of much harm to humans. There are dedicated texts and ritual manuals which explain in detail how to make incense offerings specifically to cleanse nagas from the pollution caused by humans. One example is the ritual instruction manual, *A Brief Guide to the Purification of Nagas* (*klu bsang gtong tshul mdor bsdus bzhugs so*) being one text in a large compendium of ritual procedures and liturgies.[51] This text outlines the procedure to be performed by a ritualist specialist such as a monk or shaman. However, the laity would be encouraged to recite the particular mantra and liturgy contained within it. The text makes bold claims that through the recitation of the long mantra, and the burning of incense, all the great eight nagas will be cleansed and all the naga protectors of the world will be purified.[52] The text also claims that all places where nagas congregate, including lakes, rivers, springs, ponds, cliffs, trees, will, along with all land spirits, without exception, be purified.[53] Karma Chagme's celebrated prayer, *A Great Fumigation Offering to Nagas* (*klu bsangs bla sel chen po bzhugs so*) follows a similar theme and further highlights the preoccupation with nagas as primary agents of harm and misery, and their need to be placated through purifying fumigation.

The question may be asked what specifically does one need to be purified from in order to maintain the proper equilibrium with the gods, spirits and nagas? One text which answers this question in some detail is the instructional text, *The Purification of Defilements and Pollution* (*mnol bsang dang/grib bsang gnyis bzhugs so*).[54] This text begins by highlighting a particular mantra that needs to be recited at least three times while performing the incense burning ritual. The practitioner or ritualist specialist is to follow

---

excellent scholarship of Samten Karmay in providing access to the source text. I have added the final line in the Tibetan which was missing from Karmay's citation. Note that the active construction in the Tibetan expression *bsang ba bya*—means to effect purification through fumigation.

51. *gto rigs phyogs bsgrigs*, 193–96.
52. *gto rigs phyogs bsgrigs*, 194–95.
53. *gto rigs phyogs bsgrigs*, 194.
54. *gto rigs phyogs bsgrigs*, 182–83.

a liturgy which specifies the type of defilements that can purified.⁵⁵ For example, the text states that the defilement caused by eating unclean food, wearing unclean clothing, breaking one's promise, fighting, being afflicted with contaminating diseases, slaughtering animals, defiled land, meeting a bride, leprosy, foul smelling smoke, and all polluted gods and humans, will be cleansed, without exception, through this offering of fumigation.⁵⁶ Another liturgy, which is also to be recited by the practitioner while burning incense, includes the defilements of the murder of close relatives, incest, contact with a corpse, widowhood, and stepping over someone. According to this text, the combination of reciting the appropriate mantra, following the liturgy, and burning incense, will result in all impurities, without exception, being purified.⁵⁷

World Purification Day

Though all festivals incorporate incense burning (typically juniper *shug pa*), there is an annual festival called World Purification Day (*'dzam gling spyi bsang*) which is solely devoted to making incense offerings. This festival falls each year on the fifteenth day of the fifth month of the Tibetan calendar. Originally, this festival was inaugurated to celebrate the successful completion of Tibet's first monastery, Samye monastery, in the eighth century.⁵⁸ History records that the tantric master Guru Rinpoche (Padmasambhava) subdued all the territorial spirits that were hindering the building of the monastery, and that he appeased the spirits and deities "through a grand offering of juniper incense."⁵⁹ The Tibetan king at that time, Trisong Detsen (*khri srong lde bstan*), also commissioned a purification

---

55. The first liturgy was composed by the fourth Panchen Lama, Losang Chokyi Gyaltsen, (*blo bzang chos kyi rgyal mtshan*, 1570–662).

56. *gto rigs phyogs bsgrigs*, 182. The pollution of "foul smelling smoke" is also known as *thab grib* a type of contamination that comes from burning or cooking anything impure on a hearth or stove. Meeting a bride before she is about to be married is considered polluting.

57. *gto rigs phyogs bsgrigs*, 183. This second liturgy was composed by Chusang Lama Rinpoche, (*chu bzang bla ma rin po che*) ca. eighteenth century. His lineage lives on today, the fifth incarnation of Chusang Rinpoche being born in 1959. Note that it is considered polluting to walk over someone when they are lying down.

58. Wangdu, *Bod mi'i yul srol*, 102.

59. Rigzin, *Festivals of Tibet*, 37. Guru Rinpoche also wrote a famous text on purification through fumigation, *Fumigating the gods through Gifts and Provisions* (*rgyags rngan lha bsang*).

rite of incense burning to purify the environment. Though the burning of incense is attested to prior to this period, the establishment of the World Purification Day festival is traced backed to this occasion.[60] This festival is still remembered today when Tibetans burn incense on mountains passes and sacred sites in multiple places, from early morning to late in the evening. On this day, clouds of incense smoke billow across all major Tibetan settlements. In more recent times, while the focus is still on purifying local territorial spirits and deities, and the environments of human habitation, there is also an element which extends this festival beyond Tibetan borders, viewing it as contributing to the purification of the world at large.

The major text which outlines the purposes and ritual practices of World Purification Day is the large compilation of ritual incense burning texts, *The Land of Snow's World Purification Non-Sectarian Collection of Incense Offering Texts* (*gangs ljongs kyi bsang yig ris med phyogs sdeb 'dzam gling spyi bsang*). Given that the content of this collection is similar to the liturgies previously examined, some general comments will be made rather than a specific analysis of a particular text. The collection is replete with formulaic liturgies which are used to purify an array of gods, spirits and demons as well as human defilements and impurities. Of relevance to the World Purification Day festival are comments from selected Tibetan masters who extol the virtues and the necessity of burning incense on this day. These religious figures encourage practitioners to burn as much juniper as possible on this auspicious occasion when it is believed to be possible for all the gods and spirits to be purified.[61] Indeed, they state that the most important offering for territorial spirits is the burning of incense.[62] According to Shuchen Tshultrim Rinchen (*zhu chen tshul khrims rin chen*, 1697–1774), "The sweet smelling purifying incense offering cleanses all the pollution of crimes and mistakes, and has the power to bring good fortune."[63] He further reiterates that on this festival day all unclean things will become clean and all impure things pure.[64]

As can be seen from these fumigation texts, the burning of incense is an integral part of the Tibetan schema of purification. Though clearly having an apotropaic function, the mantras, liturgies and fumigating smoke are

60. Wangdu, *Bod mi'i yul srol*, 102.
61. Rwa yum skyabs, *Gangs Ljongs Kyi Bsang Yig*, 4.
62. Rwa yum skyabs, *Gangs Ljongs Kyi Bsang Yig*, 6.
63. Rwa yum skyabs, *Gangs Ljongs Kyi Bsang Yig*, 8.
64. Rwa yum skyabs, *Gangs Ljongs Kyi Bsang Yig*, 8.

also believed to effect the cleansing of human ritual and moral defilement, and to purify the spirits who have been contaminated by defiling human activity. Bellezza provides a further summary: "Incense is the instrument that purifies the deities and the environment in which they and all living beings reside. It is popularly believed that purification through fumigation restores the integrity and contentment of the deities, leading to a strengthening of the concord with human beings."[65]

Water Purification Rituals

Unlike the four preceding rituals, which do not require a trained specialist, water purification rituals do require the services of a ritual expert. In further contrast to fumigation rites, which seek to purify the gods from human generated impurities, water rituals aim to purify the participant, and gain the blessing of the deity upon whom the ritual is centered. Though the incense offering liturgical texts claim to purify all defilements, in fact they are unable to purify them all hence the need for water purification rituals.[66] Whereas the term *bsang ba* denotes purification through fumigation of incense burning, the term *gstang ba* denotes purification through the sprinkling of water (*khrus*) on defiled spaces, and the application of consecrated lustral waters (*bsang chu*) upon the supplicant. Water rituals are typically performed by monks as a religious service for any laity who believe such a ritual would be of benefit. The meditational deity upon whom the ritual is centered, and through whom the water is consecrated, is critically important in these rituals.[67] Textual evidence suggests these water rituals have their origin in the Bön religion where notions of purity and impurity were strictly observed. Purity in ancient Bön had both a spiritual and physical aspect where one was to carefully guard against coming into contact with anything considered impure.[68] There are also accounts of ritual bathing being required before certain liturgies could be performed, and bathing with purified lustral waters was an essential part of Bön consecration ceremonies.[69]

---

65. Bellezza, *Spirit-Mediums, Sacred Mountains*, 183.
66. Karmay, "Local Deities," 385.
67. Karmay, "Local Deities," 397.
68. Tucci, *Religions of Tibet*, 240.
69. Tucci, *Religions of Tibet*, 241; Bellezza, *Dawn of Tibet*, 246, 258, 268, 274; Berounský, "Wind-Horse Galloping," 188–89.

Lustral Water Purification Texts

Current day water rituals in Tibet can broadly be divided into two categories; those which involve the sprinkling of water over a polluted or contaminated area (*khrus, khrus gsol*) and those which require the imbibing of lustral water and application to one's body (*byabs khrus*). The first kind is a generic form of water purification typically performed by a monk who has been called upon by the laity to perform a cleansing ritual specific to a certain household. For example, someone in a family may be having persistent nightmares, or the household has been riddled with bad luck, sickness, demonic oppression, or they want to cleanse some land from the influence of nagas in preparation for building a house or dwelling. A monk, or group of monks, is invited to perform a cleansing water ritual (*khrus*). There is also the water ritual of *yul khrus* "land cleansing" which is the purification of a village or larger area which has experienced a particular calamity. In one "land cleansing" instructional text, a list is provided of scenarios where such a ritual would be beneficial. These include village areas that have been plagued by misfortune through hailstorms, floods, poor crops, famines, epidemics—both human and with livestock, earthquakes, and "all manner of harm that comes upon the earth."[70] The same text also includes a long list of ritual and moral defilement that can be purified through a cleansing of the land.[71] In the rituals of *khrus* and *yul khrus*, consecrated water, prepared in a particular type of vase, is sprinkled on the ground where the defilement, spiritual obstacles and calamities have occurred. Mantras and liturgies are recited, and incense is burned.[72]

One of the main textual sources regarding water purification rites, which is still used today, is the large compilation of ritual procedures, *A Collection of Ritual Instructional Manuals* (*gto rigs phyogs bsgrigs*).[73] These manual texts provide detailed instructions regarding water purification

---

70. *Land Cleansing Through the Power of Buddha, Lord of the Nagas* (*bcom ldan 'das klu'i dbang phyug rgyal po'i sgo nas yul khrus bzhugs so*) in Dge 'dun 'od zer, *gto rigs phyogs bsgrigs*, 85. Hiebert et al. would classify this type of ritual as a "crisis ritual" or "crisis rite." Hiebert et al., *Understanding Folk Religion*, Kindle location 5780–818.

71. *Land Cleansing*, 84.

72. *gto rigs phyogs bsgrigs*, 85. Mantras are typically to be recited at least three times.

73. This manual is readily available in bookstores in Lhasa and Tibetan areas, and in Tibetan bookstores in Kathmandu. One bookseller, an elderly man I have known for many years, told me that it was a popular book, especially the sections on purification rituals.

rituals including the necessary implements, the meditational deities, the prayers and liturgies, and the desired outcomes. From this collection of texts, three water ritual instructional manuals, where lustral waters are partaken of by the participants (*byabs khrus*), were examined.[74] Common to all the texts is that they are based upon a particular deity, either a Buddha or Bodhisattva, that they require the water to be consecrated through prescribed preparations and mantras, the recitation of liturgies, the use of small monastic cymbals and bells and other musical instruments, and the vajra (*rdo je*), the essential tantric implement. Incense is also burned throughout the ritual. The three texts dealing with the *byabs khrus* ritual contain lengthy descriptions regarding the preparation of the necessary implements and the process of consecrating the libation waters. Given that the content of these texts is similar, general remarks will be made rather than a detailed analysis of a specific text.

For the *byabs khrus* ritual, the ceremonial vase (*bum pa*), which contains the consecrated water (*bsang chu*), should also contain strands of *kusha* grass and peacock feathers, (which stand upright in the vase)—both of which are believed to be efficacious in the cleansing of spiritual pollution and protection from defilement.[75] Once the mantras have been recited, the monk is to pour a small amount of the consecrated lustral water into the hands of the supplicants who then dab the water onto the crown of their heads. The symbolic placing of water on one's head represents the cleansing of the whole body from the crown of one's head to the heels of one's feet, and of being cleansed both externally and internally of all impurities,

---

74. *Water Purification through the Power of Vajrapani* (*phyag na rdo rje sgo nas byabs khrus bzhugs so*), 53–60, *Water Purification through the Power of Vajra Vidarani* (*bcom ldan 'das rdo rje rnam 'joms ma'i sgo nas byabs khrus bzhugs so*), 61–70, and *A Cleansing Sin and Pollution Manual by Water Purification through the Power of Yeshe Khrung Nag* (*ye shes khyung nag gi sgo nas byabs khrus bya tshul sdig grib spyod byed bzhugs so*) 75–81, in *gto rigs phyogs bsgrigs*. Note that all three deities are tantric deities.

75. *gto rigs phyogs bsgrigs*, 63. Both *kusha* grass and peacock feathers are essential elements in water purification rites. *Kusha* grass is a long brush-like grass that can grow up to two feet. It is efficacious for purity and protection from harm. It is alleged Shakyamuni Buddha may have sat on a mat comprised of *kusha* grass when he attained enlightenment. Beer, *Encyclopedia of Tibetan Symbols*, 189, 336; Beer, *Handbook*, 22. Peacock feathers are believed to be highly effective agents in removing impurity and providing protection against defilements. Drakpa, *Freeing Yourself*, 84. It is maintained that peacocks are able to eat all sorts of things including poisonous and noxious plants, yet are unaffected by them and remain clean, pure and beautiful. Peacock feathers, authentic or made of plastic, are popular items for sale in market places.

RITUAL TEXTS AND SYMBOLS

illnesses, demons, obscurations, sin, and all uncleanness.[76] Water is again to be poured into the hand of participants who place it in their mouths. Partakers may also choose to apply water to their foreheads, eyes, necks or other areas they believe need cleansing. In this way, the cleansing of the three elements—body, speech, and mind are ritually cleansed.[77] One text states that, "As metal filings immediately stick to a magnet, so too will one be cleansed from infectious diseases, epidemics, demons, and all impurities and spiritual obstacles."[78] Other potential benefits of *byabs khrus* are the hope that it will cleanse one from an untimely death, the effects of curses, accidents, misfortune, bad omens and signs, bad dreams, harm from noxious spirits, bad luck, harm from "black" evenings, the snare of demons, messengers of the Lord of Death, obstructing spirits, corrupting influences, and interfering and opposing spirits.[79] The texts are replete with mantras and liturgies which are for the most part to be recited by the ritual officiant; the participant is simply to receive the lustral waters and move along through the line of people.[80]

The *byabs khrus* ritual is popular with the laity in Tibet and there are three primary locations where it is offered as a daily purification ritual. The most popular location is in the Cham Khang Temple (*byams khang*) in Lhasa, a temple devoted to the future Buddha.[81] Hundreds of people line up each day from early in the morning to partake of these purifying lustral waters with a range of hopes and aspirations to be achieved.[82] As

76. *gto rigs phyogs bsgrigs*, 55–56.
77. *gto rigs phyogs bsgrigs*, 62, 65.
78. *gto rigs phyogs bsgrigs*, 57.

79. *gto rigs phyogs bsgrigs*, 67. In Tibetan astrological calculations, certain days, months and years are considered "black," occasions when it is believed that calamities are more likely to happen. The evening of a black day is believed to be a time of increased potential harm from evil spirits. The expression "the snare of demons" is more literally "the lasso of demons." The lasso (*zhags pa*) is a motif of inescapable harm and entrapment used frequently in religious texts.

80. At the site of a *byabs khrus* in a monastery, there is a typically a trough, which pilgrims lean over, to collect any water that may spill. A donation box for alms sits at the end of the procession.

81. The future Buddha is known as *byams pa* or *ma 'ongs pa'i byams pa* (Sk. Maitreya), an epithet which means "Future One of Loving-Kindness." The two other locations are in Lhoka and Nedong counties, with Yasang Monastery (*g.ya' bzang dgon pa*) being the primary place of officiating water purification rites in those counties.

82. Many years ago, I interviewed a number of participants after they had received the lustral waters asking them the reason for their participation. Responses varied from

these water rituals do not provide permanent purification, many pilgrims partake of them frequently.

Symbols of Purity

The study of symbols, motifs, artwork, and colorization schema has attracted growing scholarly attention as a key area for gaining cultural insights. Hiebert et al. have suggested that, "At the center of a culture is its sacred symbols. These integrate and give expression to a people's worldview—the mental picture they have of the way things in reality actually are."[83] Steffen has likewise highlighted the centrality of symbols as representative of a community's

---

the desire to be cleansed from bodily pains and illnesses, cleansed from bad dreams and the generic cleansing from all spiritual obstacles (*bar cad*). In April 2022, I witnessed a monastic cham dance at Sharpa Monastery (*shar pa dgon pa*), a Nyingma monastery in Kathmandu, which included a *byabs khrus* water rite for the laity. The ritual was performed by the designated monks using the various implements and consecrated lustral waters. Hundreds of people lined up for hours hoping to receive this special blessing and empowerment. Each person was first given a *kha btags* (white scarf), symbolic of purity, which was hung around their necks. They then received the consecrated water in their hands, put some on the crown of their heads, and some in their mouths. After this, they received an empowerment by being touched on the head with a white conch shell (also a symbol of purity) by a special lama. Those who wished to were also touched on the head with a consecrated dagger (*phur ba*). As the participants proceeded along, they received a special "empowerment" (*tshe dbang*) from the monastery's Rinpoche by being touched on the head with Tibetan scriptures. This was followed by being given special balls of edible dough and a spoonful of rice wine. In talking with the monks, they stated that these rituals are to help cleanse the pollution, negativities, sins and impurities of the laity, and to empower them to be free of sickness, spiritual obstacles, such as demon oppression, and to give them long life. Several of the monks stressed to me that it is not possible to cleanse one's sins and pollution just by receiving this water ritual alone. Rather, it is a lengthy process over the duration of one's lifetime and this ritual is just one part of the process that helps towards the overall goal of being free from sin and impurities. On multiple occasions I have also observed monks administering lustral waters to pilgrims at the central stupa in Boudha in Kathmandu. In short, practitioners stated that they see lustral waters as effective in providing good fortune, staving off harm from evil spirits, healing sicknesses and bodily aches and pains, and helping towards the cleansing of sin and impurities. All this to say that water purification rituals are still very much part of lay consciousness and monastic praxis. Though not fastidious about regular bodily washing, Tibetans do have an annual week-long bathing festival *skar ma ri Shi shar* (also *skar ma dod pa*), during the seventh month, when rivers and streams are believed to have certain healing and purifying properties. Tibetans will also wash their carpets and clothes in rivers and streams at this time.

83. Hiebert et al., *Understanding Folk Religion*, Kindle location 4494.

worldview and values, and the necessity of studying them closely.[84] And for the purposes of this section, this is what a symbol will considered to be—a visual or physical representation of a certain perceived reality.[85]

Symbols are embedded and woven into the Tibetan corpus of writings and no definitive indigenous text which systematically codifies them appears to be in existence (at least, none that I have been able to find). More recently, Tibetan scholars have written about the main symbols in Tibetan Buddhism, largely, it seems, as a response to inquisitive foreigners. Given the lack of a definitive Tibetan text, this section will draw on the works of Tibetans who are writing primarily for a Western audience, and from other related secondary sources. To be sure, there are many symbols and symbolic references in Tibetan Buddhism, and the absence of a definitive text should not diminish the importance and significance of them. This section then will be a brief survey of the primary symbols in Tibetan Buddhism which relate to purity concerns.

The Lotus

As has been seen thus far, particularly in the texts referencing the pure realm of Sukhāvatī, the lotus flower is a recurring symbol of purity. Images of the lotus can be found in Tibetan homes, temples, monasteries and wherever artwork is displayed. Steffen would consider the lotus a "master symbol," given its proliferation and significance.[86] Master symbols are clearly important markers in defining and understanding worldview. The lotus is one of the eight lucky symbols (*bkra shis brtags brgyad*), which typically appear as a set of eight, but is also a symbol in its own right, and is more widely employed than the other auspicious symbols. The main reason given as to why the lotus is a symbol of purity is that though it grows in mud, it is not stained by its surroundings but remains clean, pure, uncontaminated and beautiful. Wangdu states that, "the lotus flower represents one who dwells in samsara but is not attached to it and not contaminated with the stains of ignorance."[87] Karma Chagme, in his famous prayer, writes: "Just as the

---

84. Steffen, *Worldview-Based Storying*, 159–85.

85. The two Tibetan terms *rtags* and *mtshan* mean symbol, sign, badge, insignia, representation or symbolization. The verb *mtshon*, (cognate with the noun *mtshan*), means to represent, display, show or symbolize.

86. Steffen, *Worldview-Based Storying*, 180, 183.

87. Wangdu, *Bod mi'i yul srol*, 59–60.

lotus is not stained with mud, so it is not stained with the three realms of existence."[88] Tseten Namgyal suggests that the lotus flower "represents the pure acclaimed state of Buddha's mind, body, and speech."[89] He further states that, "The lotus flower is considered to be a symbol of purity or of pure divine origination, represented as mental and spiritual purity."[90] Tibetan scholar Loden Sherap Dagyab Rinpoche adds, "The lotus is altogether one of the best-known symbols. It is considered to be a symbol of purity, or of pure or divine origination, for, although it has its roots in the mud of ponds and lakes, it raises its flower in immaculate beauty above the surface of the water . . . the lotus stands for purity, especially mental purity."[91]

The prevalence of this symbol of purity cannot perhaps be overstated. The pure realm of Sukhāvatī is carpeted with lotuses, and Buddhas reborn there are said to be reborn seated in a lotus.[92] The name of the great Guru Rinpoche (*padma 'byung gnas*) means "originating from a lotus." Spontaneous birth from a lotus is a clear mark of great purity and Bodhisattvas are often considered to be "supreme lotuses of humanity."[93] Sitting in the lotus position is significant in tantric meditation and certain lamas or ritual experts wear a lotus shaped hat.[94] The lotus is also symbolic of a divine womb and the pudenda and is an important symbol in tantric meditation.[95] The word "lotus," as has been seen in chapter three, is central to the most common mantra. As has been well documented, because the lotus was identified as the primary symbol of purity within the Tibetan schema, it was used by the Church of the East in their attempts to contextualize Christianity in Buddhist contexts.

---

88. *Karma Chagme's Aspirational Prayer*, plate no. 484. The three realms of existence (*srid gsum*) are 1. the realm of nagas below the earth (*sa og*), 2. the realm of humans on the earth (*sa steng*) and 3. the realm of gods above the earth (*sa bla*). TDCM, 2976 under *srid pa gsum*.

89. Namgyal, "Significance," 39.

90. Namgyal, "Significance," 29.

91. Dagyab Rinpoche, *Buddhist Symbols*, 23. Beer states that the lotus "blossoms unstained from the watery mire, is a symbol of purity, renunciation and divinity." Beer, *Encyclopedia of Tibetan Symbols*, 175. See also Gomez, "Contributions," 163–64.

92. *Karma Chagme's Aspirational Prayer*, plate no. 468–69. Studholme, *Origins*, 114.

93. Studholme, *Origins*, 113–14.

94. Kapstein, *Tibetan Buddhism*, 47.

95. Beer, *Handbook*, 8.

The White Scarf

Ceremonial white scarves (*kha btags*) are used in many and varied situations, from guiding the souls of the dead in a funeral procession, to being offered to a lama, to giving to a friend on a special occasion such as graduating from school, attending a wedding, or wishing someone well on a journey. The *kha btags* is typically draped over a person's neck as a respectful salutation and they are used prolifically in Tibetan daily life. Pemba defines them thus: "A khada is usually made of white cotton or silk, used on all occasions to signify the offeror's pure intention and concern."[96] One major dictionary states that the white scarf represents "a pure mind of good aspiration."[97] Wangdu suggests that *kha btags* are offered primarily to represent the purity of one's speech and motives.[98] Though white is the most common color of a *kha btags*, they are also available in other colors such as orange and red, and often have auspicious symbols or mantras imprinted on them. These ceremonial scarves may also be draped over an image of a deity to represent the pure intention of one's offering and are also representative of a deity's "unblemished purity."[99] Sacred images are often wrapped in white scarves to prevent defilement, particularly when being transported. In the age of social media, memes and emojis of *kha btags*, and Tibetans offering them, are popular.[100] Though *kha btags* have a wide range of uses, they are in general indicative of pure or "white" intentions of the giver who wishes to convey a wish of good fortune or blessing upon the recipient.

Colors

As has been observed in the section on proverbs in chapter three, the color white is indicative of purity, and the color black of impurity, evil and negativity. Dagyab Rinpoche confirms that in Tibetan color symbolism white is equated with "peace and purity" and black or dark blue with "wrath and

---

96. Pemba, *Tibetan Proverbs*, 205.
97. ITED, under *kha btags*.
98. Wangdu, *Bod mi'i yul srol*, 1.
99. Beer, *Encyclopedia of Tibetan Symbols*, 115, 165.
100. I have ten emojis on my phone featuring *kha btags*. A popular one that gets sent to me often has a picture of a long flowing, white scarf with the caption, "Congratulating you with unstained, pure, divine white silk." (*dri med lha dar dkar pos rten 'brel zhu*).

pollution."[101] The color white is believed to symbolically represent the pacification of illnesses, demons, and obstacles to enlightenment, and thus is the predominant color of houses, temples and monasteries.[102] Bright and radiant light is associated with purity and ultimate enlightenment is often pictured as being engulfed in radiant light. The clear white light that radiates from gem stones is considered purifying and able to repel harmful forces.[103] Crystal is also symbolic of purity.[104] White lotus flowers are particularly auspicious, and Tseten Namgyal suggests they "represent mental and spiritual purity."[105]

Secondary Symbols of Purity

Within the designated eight auspicious articles or substances, *bkra shis rdzas brgyad* (which are different to the eight lucky symbols), several of them are representative of purity, though this would not be their primary association. The eight auspicious articles are often used in tantric rituals but can also be given as individual offerings to deities. The third auspicious substance, yogurt or curd (*sho*) is typically regarded as pure, being a form of pure nourishment both physically and spiritually. It is one of the three "white foods" (*dkar zas*) of milk, curd, and cheese. Yogurt is widely used as a purifying substance in many tantric rituals.[106] The fourth substance, durva grass (*rtsva dur ba*), is similar to the *kusha* grass used in water purification rituals, and likewise is considered to have symbolic purifying properties.[107] The fifth substance, *bilva* or wood-apple fruit (*shing tog bil ba*, Sk. bilva), is said to have purifying medicinal properties.[108] In terms of animals which may be symbolic of purity, Thurston has suggested that, "tigers, leopards, and snow leopards are evoked frequently in order to elicit positive images of strength, purity, and auspiciousness."[109] Deer are often

---

101. Dagyab Rinpoche, *Buddhist Symbols*, 56.

102. Wangdu, *Bod mi'i yul srol*, 65–66. There is also an annual festival of painting the walls of buildings white *dkar rtsi dus chen*.

103. Schaeffer et al., *Sources of Tibetan Tradition*, 280.

104. Khenpo Yeshe Phuntsok, *Vajrasattva Meditation*, Kindle location 454.

105. Namgyal, "Significance," 40.

106. Beer, *The Handbook of Tibetan Buddhist Symbols*, 21.

107. Beer, *Encyclopedia of Tibetan Symbols*, 189.

108. Beer, *Handbook*, 23.

109. Thurston, "Introduction to Tibetan," 63.

depicted in pure realms symbolizing peace and the absence of fear.[110] As mentioned previously, peacocks and peacock feathers are symbolic of purity and considered highly efficacious in cleansing and protecting against ritual and moral defilement.

Chapter Four Summary

The textual evidence presented in this chapter again suggests that Tibetans have a pronounced sense of their need to be purified and cleansed from impurity and ritual and moral filth. The texts have shown that the daily rituals of prostrations, spinning prayer wheels, burning incense and undertaking lustral water rites all speak of a preoccupation with a certain ontological predisposition. That is, Tibetans regard humans by default as defiled and impure, as is the samsaric world they find themselves in, and human activity defiles local deities who can in turn be purified and regularly need to be. In order to minimize the harmful effects of fickle and wrathful deities, daily rituals of purification through fumigation, and the rites of lustral waters are performed. Such rituals need to be repeated frequently as their effectiveness is for a limited duration.

These everyday rituals, that Tibetans from all levels of society engage in, appear to be vital in the quest to quell the harm of malevolent spiritual forces, and, from a soteriological perspective, are essential in accumulating merit and effecting purification in order to journey to a pure realm, free from the stains of this world. Tibetan symbols, ubiquitous in houses, monasteries, temples and sacred sites, and annual Tibetan festivals, further reinforce a worldview which places purity and purification as an aspirational goal and a necessary salvific step for obtaining a better rebirth, escape from samsara and ultimately the attainment of enlightenment. Tibetan scholar Karmay Samten provides a telling and pertinent summary statement regarding Tibetan notions of purity: "The concept of purification reveals itself as one of the primary elements that constitute the basis of Tibetan culture. Even though it has undergone much change with different interpretations for centuries, it remains basically fundamental."[111] It is on the basis of this profound sense of purity and purification that the next chapter will begin to explore the missiological implications of these findings.

---

110. Beer, *Encyclopedia of Tibetan Symbols*, 83.
111. Karmay, "Local Deities," 405.

5

Missiological Reflections and Considerations

Introduction

THIS CHAPTER WILL EXPLORE how the data presented in this study can inform an understanding of the Tibetan worldview and discuss some missiological considerations and potential applications. In order to do this in a systematic way, a review of the findings will first be given, including possible points of contention. A diagrammatic representation of the findings will be attempted, leading to a discussion of the popular tripartite paradigm of cultural analysis. Following this, issues of contextualizing the gospel in light of Tibetan Buddhist notions of purification will be discussed. This will entail a discussion of purity language in the Bible, and an exploration of contextualized gospel presentations with a purification emphasis. Potential implications of the findings of this study for those who seek to minister to Tibetans will also be presented. Some questions for further research will be raised before some final concluding remarks are made.

Review of the Findings

This dissertation has sought to answer the question of how Tibetan Buddhists conceptualize notions of purity and purification. The study has expressly followed the goal of seeking to answer this question not through a social anthropological lens by tracing the demarcations of the ritually impure, but rather through the religious lens of Tibetan Buddhism. The argument was made in chapter one that the purification schema cannot be separated from the religious realm, neatly delineated as a mere social phenomenon, and thus needed to be examined within the domain of religious discourse. The primary means for answering the question of Tibetan notions of purity has been to seek an emic voice through examining a comprehensive range of indigenous Tibetan texts, incorporating both the monastics and laity, which explicitly deal with notions of purity. The semantic domains of Tibetan terms for purity and impurity, which were outlined in detail in chapter one, have been identified in these texts and traced throughout the textual analysis.[1] The texts presented in chapter two examined key monastic texts of praxis from the genres of confessional, preliminary, and tantric texts, as well as from the large corpus of spells and incantations. Chapter three explored lay texts of aspiration and folk traditions by examining aspirational prayers and liturgies for rebirth in the pure land of Sukhāvatī, as well as the foremost Tibetan mantra, proverbs, and texts of moral instruction. Chapter four surveyed texts of ritual praxis, festivals, and symbols. The overwhelming finding has been that the high lexical weighting of purity terms, in a wide range of contexts, and the pervasiveness of ritualized purification practice, gives rise to the conclusion that purity and purification is of central concern to Tibetans; it has a considerable bearing on how they view themselves, the world around them, how they respond to those perceptions and how they conduct their daily lives.

Three Key Findings

The textual data presented in the preceding chapters suggest there are three key elements which inform a Tibetan understanding of purity in the religious schema and hence provide insights into the Tibetan worldview. These are:

1. Ontologically, Tibetans perceive sentient beings as either pure or impure with the default position of humanity as being impure, and the world of samsara being defiled by ignorance, sin, and suffering. While this does not discount the doctrine of primordial purity,[2] the

---

1. Specific purity/pollution (p/p) Tibetan terms with high lexical weighting are: *dag pa, mi dag pa, sbyong ba, byang ba, gstang ba, mi gstang ba, grib, sgrib, sgrib sbyong, sdig sbyong, sdig grib sbyong ba, bsang, bsang gtong ba, bde ba can, sangs rgyas, bde ba can gyi zhing khams, dag pa'i zhing khams*.

2. It is important to note, as was highlighted in chapter two, that while Tibetans do readily admit to humanity being impure, the teaching of primordial purity, which suggests all humans are in fact inherently pure and that, through elaborate tantric means

Tibetan worldview does acknowledge there is a problem with humans and the world they inhabit. Humans are trapped in a world of stains, defilements, negativities, ritual and moral impurities, non-virtuous thoughts, and evil behaviors. These need to be cleansed and cleared away in order to gain a better rebirth, hopefully in a Sukhāvatī-like pure realm, and ultimately to obtain enlightenment. People and places can be defiled, and both require purification through various rituals. Tibetans believe in the pursuit of individual purification through a variety of elaborate and pervasive means. There is a continuum in the pursuit of purity leading to an ultimate state of total purification.

2. Soteriologically, Tibetans believe it is possible to attain a permanent state of purification from ritual defilements and moral infractions. Being purified is necessary for liberation and salvation from the impure realm of samsara. The three components of human existence—the body, speech and mind (*lus ngag yid gsum*) need to be fully purified before one can escape samsara. In the Pure Land traditions, a savior Buddha is believed to effect salvation and lead one into a pure realm. In the tantric tradition, purification is possible through elaborate rituals, with particular reliance upon one's guru, meditational deities, and powerful mantras. Everyday rituals such as incense burning, prostrations, mantra recitation, lustration waters and so forth, also contribute to the process of purification. In actuality, it could be argued that the specific soteriological goal of Buddhism is purity—that is, complete purification from the stains of samsara leading to Buddhahood. Not only is this an explicit aspiration, but the process of purification is also a primary salvific pursuit for both monks and the laity. Indeed, any spiritual quest—protection from harmful spirits, the accumulation of merit, attaining spiritual blessing and empowerment—is predicated upon the practitioner pursuing purification through a variety of means available to them.

---

can be restored to a pure, pristine state, is a pervasive teaching across all the schools of Buddhism. On the one hand, sentient beings who inhabit samsara are by default impure, by virtue of the fact that they were reborn there, samsara being the abode of those not yet fully purified. On the other hand, the philosophical position of many schools of Tibetan Buddhism is that humans, though impure, also possess a latent, primordial purity that can be restored through exhaustive human effort. It is on this basis that Tibetan Buddhism rejects the doctrine of universal human depravity. One could perhaps argue that the teaching of primordial purity may have some conceptual link to the purity and innocence of Adam and Eve prior to the Fall.

3. Cosmologically, Tibetans believe in pure and impure realms, and a spirit world that comprises a vast array of local spirits and deities who can be defiled by human activity. These beings in turn need to be purified and placated in order to avoid being harmed by them. The pure realm of Sukhāvatī is a highly desirable rebirth, the longing for which is deeply engrained in Tibetan consciousness. Whether one can attain rebirth in a pure realm is contingent upon one's virtuous behavior, merit accumulation and the pursuit of purification.

These three key elements are foundational to gaining an understanding of Tibetan notions of purity and are thus foundational to their worldview. As the Tibetan proverb succinctly states: "Purity is Buddhahood, impurity is hell."[3]

Possible Contentions to the Findings

Though these findings would appear to accurately reflect the data, it is possible that some contentions could be raised. One possible contention is that the texts examined are predominantly ancient texts and therefore are not of relevance today. Such a contention would not be cognizant of the preservation, veneration, and continued usage that the texts examined still enjoy today. It is difficult to argue against the influence of these texts, which is clearly quite profound, and which, as the data shows, is the voice of Tibetans themselves. Indeed, these voices are from Tibetans in all stations in life, from high monks and lamas, including the Dalai Lama, the monastic community at large, local shamans, the laity, and Tibetan scholars and historians. Many of the texts studied appear in current day textbooks and are readily available for sale in bookstores or as downloads from multiple online sources. The proverbs and symbols are still current, and the daily rituals remain ubiquitous. What was striking throughout this study was the prevalence of texts on this subject (many were excluded to keep within the dissertation limits), and the pervasiveness of purity concerns within them. This study was not confined to one particular esoteric set of texts but spread across a broad spectrum.

In a similar vein, a further possible contention might be that the findings are somewhat skewed as the texts examined were only dealing with purity and purification, and not other concerns, even though this was the

---

3. *dag pa la sangs rgyas/ma dag pa la dmyal ba/*

express goal of the study. One reply is to state that this study was specifically focused on purity and was not attempting to cover all aspects of Tibetan religion and culture, nor make definitive claims about them. What continued to be a revelation throughout this study, however, was the prevalence of texts on this subject and the rich lexicon of purity terms and expressions. Again, this study was not confined to a certain set of exclusive texts but spread across a wide literary range. The goal was for Tibetans to speak through their texts, and they would appear to have spoken clearly and comprehensively.

Another contention might be that these findings do not adequately represent notions of purity among younger Tibetans, caught in a world of cultural change, and increasing influence from outside sources. This contention may have some weight, as one cannot claim with any level of certainty about the current state of Tibetan youth culture or their perceptions of purity and impurity. The first reply is that this study has not sought to explore an answer to this question, being a research topic for another occasion. Even if it were possible to gauge the vagaries, fluctuations, and fluidity of Tibetan youth culture, a textual and semantic analysis of Tibetan notions of purity is a more objective and robust approach. A second reply is that many of the texts presented here, as previously mentioned, appear in school textbooks that the majority of educated Tibetans would have studied at some point. Young people also see and experience the daily activities of their parents and neighbors, and are not shielded from purification rituals.[4]

Another possible contention is that notions of purity and purification are somewhat abstract and that many people groups, as has been well noted by others, prefer concrete concepts over abstract ones.[5] Again, such a contention is ignorant of the underlying realities; Tibetan notions of purity are concrete and practical, and the lexical items for such notions reflect the concrete realities of washing, cleaning, and purifying. These realities are well understood by the laity, many of whom are non-literate, and who regularly observe an array of purification practices. Things get dirty and need to be cleaned. Likewise, humans are dirty and need to be cleaned in order to make any spiritual progress, in order to make merit, in order to obtain any spiritual power, in order in to escape the impure realm of samsara and be reborn in a pure realm, and ultimately to attain Buddhahood. The Tibetan

---

4. As a general observation, one can say that younger Tibetans are less concerned with religious practice but often there is a shift when they become older and closer to death, they typically begin in earnest their pursuit of merit making for their next reincarnation.

5. For example, Dyrness, "Can We Do Theology," 56; Wu, "Contextualizing the One Gospel," 36, 40.

practices identified in this study, even the esoteric tantra ones, are practical, physical activities that contribute to the overall goal of being made clean. The gods have been made dirty by human activity and require the smoke of incense to make them clean and keep them from causing harm. Indeed, all rituals outlined in this study are physical, concrete responses to the perceived problem of uncleanness and impurity.

More than Purification

While the central focus of this study has been purity, it has also recognized there are other factors that comprise a Tibetan worldview.[6] Other themes have emerged from the data, which have been highlighted along the way, and it would be remiss not to restate them. Two of these themes are the need for merit, and the pursuit of spiritual power. These two concerns have been prominent in the data, and it is difficult to neatly delineate them from the pursuit of purity. They are intertwined and inter-related. The need for spiritual power to influence the unseen spiritual realm is clearly evident through the use of spells, incantations, and mantras. Indeed, all the rituals and practices presented here are dependent upon mantras for their efficacy. No spiritual pursuit is attempted without them. The perceived power of one's lama and local shamans has also been identified. Likewise, the pursuit of merit accumulation has also been seen; specifically, the merit derived from circumambulations, prostrations, the spinning of prayer wheels, water rituals, incense burning, and the recitation of mantras. Mention should also be made of the underlying need for faith, aspiration, and unswerving devotion for these three—purification, power, and merit—to be achieved. In order to represent these findings in a visual form, a diagrammatic representation has been attempted.

---

6. There is another key element in Tibetan Buddhism, and Buddhism at large, which has not been highlighted here, (since it was outside the realm of this study, and it did not appear in the texts) and that is the pursuit of wisdom. This is a generic pursuit within Buddhism, and in a sense is assumed. One of the two key elements in pursuing the Mahayana path of a Boddhisattva is the accumulation of wisdom—*ye shes kyi tshogs*, the other being the accumulation of merit—*bsod nams kyi tshogs*.

STEPS TOWARD A TIBETAN UNDERSTANDING OF PURITY

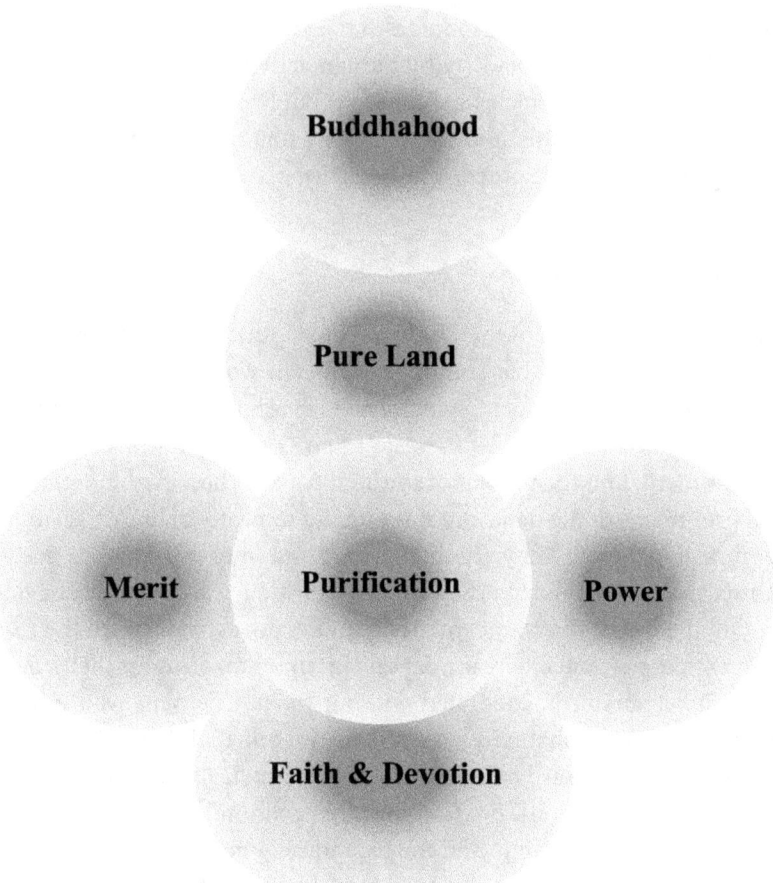

Figure 1.1 Diagrammatic Representation of the Findings

Overlapping circles provide one way to visually represent the findings. Circles are an appropriate shape to illustrate the interconnectedness of these elements as opposed to a linear "boxed" approach that may be suggestive of bound or closed sets rather than fluid and inter-related ones. Circles are also a reflection of Tibetan Buddhist culture, indicative of a worldview that is more circular than linear, with circles being the dominant cultural shape reflected, for example, in prayer wheels, circumambulation circuits, the wheel of dharma, the wheel of life, and reincarnation. The dyadic pairing of purity/pollution has not been employed as this is suggestive of opposing states, whereas the underlying reality is a more nuanced continuum. That is, there is a progression in the pursuit of purity, merit and power. This continuum is represented by the outer parts of the circle being lighter and the center of each circle as darker. These graduated colors represent both the continuum of progression towards the goals of merit, purity, and power, and also the degree to which this key element may be prominent in an individual's religious endeavors.

Generalizations are by nature problematic. For some Tibetans, merit accumulation may be more central as a driving force in their lives, particularly when they are older and want to accumulate as much as possible before they die. For others, the pursuit of power may be of greater importance, particularly in times of sickness and calamity. For the earnest pilgrim and the ritually impure, pursuing purification may be central. Naturally, these motivations may vary according to one's stage in life, or the particular circumstances one finds oneself in. For most, it is likely that a combination of motivations exists, even at an unconscious level; they may just be following the traditions handed down to them, simply trying whatever they believe will help in that moment to minimize their suffering or assist in their next reincarnation.

The texts have also shown that in any religious endeavor, faith and devotion are essential and, in a sense, are a given. That is, without faith and devotion, no spiritual progress can be made. As has been repeatedly noted, devotion requires countless repetitions of ritualized praxis. Hence, "faith and devotion" are pictured underpinning the three main themes which the data has identified. In reality, merit or power could also be at the center of this diagram, depending on one's individual focus, but given that purification is crucial for a better outcome in one's next life it assumes a position of central importance. It is also the primary predicating factor for rebirth in a pure realm and is vital for enlightenment. This is the reason only the top two circles, representing a pure land of rebirth and Buddhahood, the ultimate soteriological goals, are overlapping with purity. This is not to suggest that progression to a pure realm is always necessary before attaining Buddhahood; one can be directly enlightened. In summary, the data has shown that faith and devotion are foundational, that a wide variety of ritualized religious practices contribute, in varying degrees, to the three goals of merit, purity, and power, all leading to the hope of being reborn in a pure realm and eventual Buddhahood.[7] If one were to itemize each of the three

---

7. I was able to discuss this diagram in detail with a Tibetan colleague who holds

elements of the middle layer of the diagram, with the primary ritualized praxis that could be associated with them, they could be put in columns such as has been done below.

Merit	Purification	Power
prostrations	confessional praxis	tantra
circumambulations	preliminary praxis	mantras
mantra recitation	tantra	highest yoga
prayer wheels	mantras	lama veneration
festivals	highest yoga	deity meditation
incense burning	water rituals	preliminary praxis
lustral waters	incense burning	symbols
	prostrations	shaman utilization
	prayer wheels	spells & incantations
	aspirational prayers	
	festivals	
	symbols	

Table 1.1 Three Key Elements with Associated Praxis

As can be seen from the table, many praxes are overlapping with multiple desired outcomes. While such a table may be informative, it represents linear and compartmentalized thinking; each element is overlapping and cannot be so neatly delineated. The following circular word diagram is likely more representative of the reality; that these elements, and the ritualized praxis, are mixed, intertwined, overlapping and fluid. The key element and associated praxis shown below are not intended to be seen as static but in motion, reflecting the mix of motivations and emphases one may have according to a variety of factors—for example, one's current circumstances, the stage of one's life, or one's desired overall goal.

---

a master's degree in Tibetan Buddhist Philosophy from a prestigious university. He thought the diagram was an accurate representation of Tibetan Buddhism, recognizing there are other elements, such as the pursuit of wisdom, that also comprise Tibetan Buddhist thought and praxis. He affirmed the main focus of Tibetan Buddhism as being the pursuit of being cleansed and cleared of defiling obstructions (*sgrib bsangs ba, sgrib sbyong ba*), and to be cleansed of the three poisons of ignorance, hatred, and desire (*dug gsum sbyong ba*), and of moral failings (*sdig pa sbyong ba*). He was in complete agreement that the only way to be reborn in a pure realm, or attain Buddhahood, is by first being purified and cleansed of all ignorance, obscured perceptions of reality, and moral defilements.

MISSIOLOGICAL REFLECTIONS AND CONSIDERATIONS

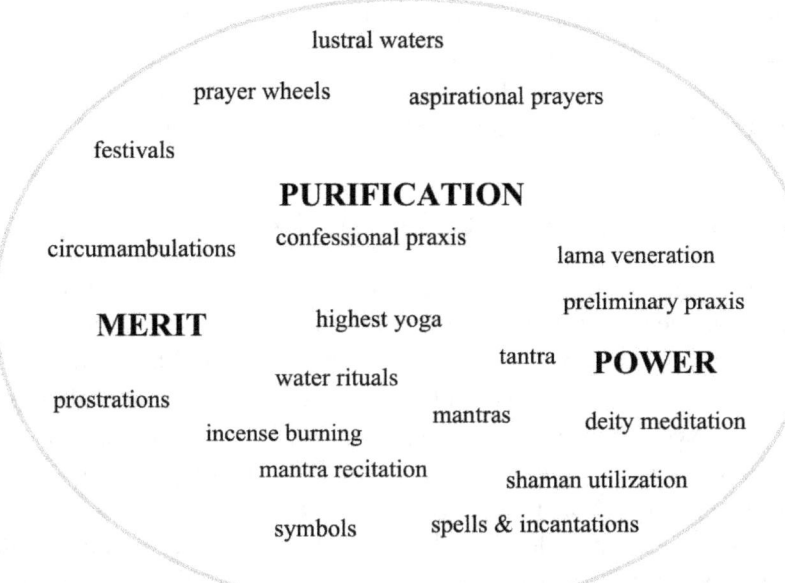

Figure 1.2 Word Diagram of Three Key Elements with Associated Praxis

What is also of note from the findings is the absence of shame and honor terms within the religious dialogue. To be sure, honor/shame (h/s) dynamics are prominent within Tibetan culture, but h/s terms do not appear to be part of the soteriological discourse.[8] In other words, while h/s is a dynamic cultural force, it is not the language used within the religious domain. There may be a conclusion here, at least for Tibetan Buddhists, that because a people group exhibits h/s dynamics this does not automatically mean it is the language of religion, or the best pathway for making a bridge to the gospel. It may well be, as the case here, that using the h/s

---

8. H/S and face dynamics are a prominent part of Tibetan culture evidenced by the high frequency of usage of "face" terms within the vernacular, and the complex honorific system. (Central Tibetan has honorific forms of pronouns, nouns and verbs). There is, naturally, some connection between defilement and shame. In many social contamination or ritual defilement scenarios, there is an element of associated shame and loss of face. However, this state is typically temporary and restorative once the defilement has passed or been removed through the appropriate ritual. The removal of defilement does not lead to honor. There is no movement from shame to honor, rather shame to restoration, the normal equilibrium of life.

schema is not only outside the framework of religious dialogue, but it is underwhelming and simply does not resonate. Jesus taking away one's shame or embarrassment may not be nearly as compelling or relevant as Jesus making one clean.[9] This conclusion leads to a further observation regarding the concept of cultural frameworks and their application.

Cultural Frameworks and Cultural Analysis

Though the granulated and complex components of human communities can be classified into larger generic groupings, as has been made popular by the *3D Gospel* binary pairings of fear/power (f/p), honor/shame (h/s), and guilt/innocence (g/i), which can provide a certain level of understanding, a more nuanced and perspicacious approach might be to first dig deep into the complexities of a culture, study closely what is being said and done, and then carefully construct some possible conclusions. The approach of overlaying an existing cultural grid onto a complex human community, and viewing everything through that grid, may in fact result in only a limited understanding, or worse, a skewed or wrong understanding. In the case of the *3D Gospel*, little attention is paid to purity and pollution concerns. To be sure, purity/pollution (p/p) is mentioned, but only very briefly as a subset of the honor and shame framework.[10] Steffen has rightly contested this, suggesting it is an oversight, and that at a minimum, given the pervasiveness of p/p concerns across a wide range of cultures, the *3D Gospel* should at least be the 4D Gospel, and perhaps even more beyond that.[11] The findings of this research would support such a claim; it may have been remiss to exclude p/p in the initial codifying of only three cultural frameworks.

As mentioned in the introduction of this dissertation, the premise on which the *3D Gospel* approach is based appears to be faulty, or, at least, incomplete, in that it rests on the responses to human sin and moral infractions being limited only to guilt, shame, and fear.[12] Surely feeling polluted or

---

9. Cozens and Ochs make a similar observation about the limitations of honor-centered gospel presentations. Cozens and Ochs, "Putting the Shameful Body," 238–39.

10. Georges, *3D Gospel*, 39–40.

11. Steffen, "Clothesline Theology," 45, 47; Steffen, *Worldview-Based Storying*, Kindle locations 3717–33, 5590–614, 6848, 6896.

12. Others who have more recently questioned the *3D Gospel* include: Merz, "Culture Problem"; Cozens, "Shame Cultures"; Beech, "Shame/Honor"; Cozens and Ochs, "Putting the Shameful Body"; Whiteman, "Shame/Honor." Had this study begun with the 3D Culture Test, and the results shown Tibetan Buddhists to be an h/s orientated society,

dirty is also one of them, among potentially other human responses to sin. To be fair, in their book, *Ministering in Shame-Honor Cultures*, Georges and Baker do address p/p concerns, but again only within a h/s framework.[13] And there is no mention of p/p within Buddhist contexts.[14] As helpful as the tripartite framework may be to initiate inter-cultural dialogue and awareness, one also must address the limitations of such an approach. It may well fail to discover a broader range of themes, concerns, values, and cultural traits while limiting discovery to only that which fits into predetermined boxes.[15] The overlaying of an etic framework onto complex cultural systems seems to be approaching cultural analysis from the "outside in" rather than from the "inside out." Or put another way, it may be better to first start from the "ground up." Starting from the ground up potentially brings richer findings.[16] Advocates of contextualization are in agreement that one needs to understand the language of religious dialogue of the receptor culture in order present the gospel as clearly as one can.[17] As Johannes Merz has

---

this preconceived idea could have been assumed to be the primary mode of religious dialogue. This study has shown this not to be the case and highlights the potentially misinformed conclusions one can derive from the 3D approach. However, I appreciate that Georges also recognizes that cultures are complex and cannot always be so neatly codified. Georges, *The 3D Gospel*, 15–16.

13. Georges and Baker, *Ministering in Honor-Shame*, Kindle locations 811, 895, 916, 2886–924.

14. Mischke et al. in their chapter on purity do briefly mention, in one short paragraph, p/p being a feature of Buddhism. Mischke et al. *Global Gospel*, Kindle location 5086.

15. In commenting on the *3D Culture Test* of Georges' honor/shame website, Cozens goes so far as to say, "Dividing cultures at the nation-state level into one of three categories is at best clumsy reductionism and at worst cultural stereotyping." Cozens, "Shame Cultures, Fear Cultures," 333.

16. For example, there is the possibility of discovering other underlying narratives such as how the themes of "light and darkness" might pervade the religious dialogue or how a preoccupation with the end of the world might be prominent. Naturally, there may be other dominant social themes such as the essential role hospitality plays in forging meaningful relationships, or the strong values of loyalty, and the high value placed on honesty and justice within a deeply corrupt system, and patron-client dynamics, are other examples that might be missed by only seeing the host culture through a limited threefold matrix. The 3D approach also stereotypes g/i as being the default position of legally based Western cultures and suggests that it is not prominent elsewhere. This can lead to the conclusion that non-Western cultures are not concerned about justice, whereas in reality, oppressed minority groups may indeed have a profound sense of justice and a strong desire to see justice and fairness come to pass.

17. For example, Wu states that "Contextualizers use whatever cultural language best

rightly suggested, one first needs to "identify the words, and notions behind them, that people use to express their own values."[18] Only then, when one has some understanding of the religious system, based on their words and concepts, can one begin to unpack other cultural traits and patterns. Rather than suggesting that the 3D Gospel be rewritten as the 4D Gospel, it might be better to emphasize a "ground up" approach, one which seeks the emic perspective without, as much as possible, relying on preconceived stereotypical frameworks, and binary terminology which may not always have such neatly defined counterparts in the receptor culture.

Tibetan Notions of Purification and Contextualization

If one of the missiological goals of this study has been to seek an understanding of Tibetan notions of purity in order to pursue the contextualization of the Christian message, then the question as to what extent can Tibetan notions of purity and purification be used as bridges to the gospel needs to be explored. Or put another way, to what degree can the gospel speak into a Tibetan worldview that is heavily influenced by notions of purity and purification? Can the gospel be framed in a way that may appeal to Tibetan sensibilities yet remain faithful to the Biblical message? In order to answer these questions, it is important to first address the differences between a Tibetan Buddhist understanding of purity and a Biblical one.

Two Contrasting Systems

On the surface, there may appear to be certain ontological and soteriological parallels between Christianity and Tibetan Buddhism, and likewise their purity schemas may appear to have certain commonalities. To elaborate, the concept of clean and unclean is a central theme in the Old Testament, pervasive in all aspects of Jewish life and also prominent within the New Testament. The demarcation between the sacred and the profane, the holy and the unholy, the clean and unclean, both ritually and morally, is the central thrust of the purity code outlined in book of Leviticus and other parts of the Old Testament. Though many clean/unclean demarcations are made in Leviticus, and numerous scenarios of ritual contamination

---

conveys the ideas needing to be expressed." Wu, "Contextualizing the One Gospel," 37.

18. Merz, "Culture Problem," 138.

MISSIOLOGICAL REFLECTIONS AND CONSIDERATIONS

are outlined, God provides a summary task for Aaron and his sons in that they were to "distinguish between the holy and the common, and between the unclean and the clean" (Lev 10:10).[19] God himself took great pains to clearly articulate these specific demarcations as he set apart for himself a people who would be holy and consecrated to him, and who needed to follow the requisite offerings and sacrifices for interaction with a holy God (Exod 19:10; Lev 5–7; 11:44; 15:31; 19:2; 20:7).[20] While the purity code demarcated the clean from the unclean, the purpose was not just to delineate such a hierarchy but rather to make it possible for people to rectify their particular states of impurity whether ritual or moral.

Various purificatory ritual practices included the burning of incense as a daily fragrant offering (Exod 30:7; 2 Chr 13:11), and the burning of incense in Numbers chapter sixteen, in an attempt to avert God's wrath, gives the appearance of being apotropaic in intent (Num 16:47–48). Water libations, and the use of the "water of purification" (Num 8:7) for purifying the Levites were regularly practiced.[21] Bodily washing and the washing of clothes, were also regularly practiced as purification rites for the ritually defiled,[22] and particularly for corpse defilement (Num 19:11–22; 31:19, 24). Purifying unclean objects by fire was also practiced (Num 31:23). Failure to perform purification rites, or observe the purity code, led to being cut off from the community.[23] In Nehemiah chapter twelve, after the priests had been purified, the people, the gates, and the wall were also purified (Neh 12:20). In Nehemiah chapter thirteen, Nehemiah had the temple storerooms purified after he considered them defiled (Neh 13:9). There are many other examples of the unclean being made clean and, of course, Jesus' reshaping of the purity code in the New Testament also highlights the purity focus within the whole of the Biblical text. However, though these examples may suggest a certain resemblance to Tibetan ritual praxis, and an apparent shared commonality in the need to be made clean and pure, the two systems are at variance. There are at least four primary areas of disparity, which are outlined below.

19. Unless otherwise noted, Biblical references are taken from the *Holy Bible: English Standard Version* (2001).

20. The purity code also included the consecration of the Tabernacle, the items within it, and the consecration of the priests.

21. Exod 29:4; 40:12; Num 8:1–15; 19:7–8; 19:17–21.

22. Exod 19:10; Lev 11:25, 40; 13:6; 14:8–9; 15:5; 16:4; 26–28; Num 31:23–24.

23. Lev 7:20–21; 15:31; 22:3; Num 5:2–3; 19:13.

Creator God

The first crucial difference is that Christianity is built upon the existence of a Creator God, who created the world, the universe, and all that is in it, whereas Tibetan Buddhism (and Buddhism at large) does not acknowledge this.[24] Tibetan Buddhism is human centered, while Christianity is God centered. Tibetan Buddhism starts with humanity and, in the best-case scenario, after multiple lifetimes, ends with a deified human. Christianity starts with God and ends with those who belong to him dwelling with him forever. Tibetan Buddhism exalts the creature over the Creator (Rom 1:23, 25). Tibetan purification is for advancement towards enlightenment, to become a deified, divine, morally pure and pristine Buddha. There is no concept of being purified and made clean in order to have a right relationship with a holy and supreme Creator God. Furthermore, though Tibetan Buddhism does espouse a doctrine of primordial purity, which may suggest a conceptual link to the purity and innocence of Adam and Eve prior to the Fall, there is no concept of humanity originally having a pure and unstained relationship with God.

The Nature of Sin

Though Tibetan Buddhism does acknowledge moral failings and the sins of doing wrong against other people, it does not see sin as offending a holy God, as rebelling against God our maker, failing to meet his standards, transgressing his decrees, not living as how he intended, and not honoring him.[25] Tibetan Buddhism does not see sin as something which infects the core of human existence, and it rejects the doctrine of universal human depravity. Rather, sin is seen as negative karma which needs to be mitigated against by obtaining good karmic merit through elaborate human endeavor. Moral infractions are not seen as violating God's established order, but as non-virtuous behavior. Therefore, any measure of purity is not measured against the eternal, transcendent holy God, but against other humans and those who are believed to have reached ultimate purity in attaining Buddhahood—something in itself that is unknown and unmeasurable.

---

24. In one of his teachings, Geshe Palden Drakpa states that Buddhism "never adheres to the standpoint which asserts existence of 'the creator of all' and 'the protector of all' who has control over all spheres of existence and their inhabitants." Drakpa, *Freeing Yourself*, 1.

25. Gomez, "Contributions," 168–69.

The Way of Salvation

Tibetan Buddhists pursue the goal of a purified, divine self primarily through their own efforts; no one else can or should save them. To be sure, Bodhisattvas and savior-like Buddhas such as Amitābha, can assist in this process, but it still requires utmost devotion and frequent invocations. Furthermore, a Savior Buddha is not cleansing one from the consequences of sin as infractions against a holy and supreme God, rather he is helping one to escape from, to be cleansed from, the weight of defiling negative karma so as to leave the world of samsara. Tibetan Buddhism, and Buddhism at large, is a self-salvific, *autosoteria* religion. In the Christian schema, the universality of human sin, which has created a chasm of broken relationship between a pure God and impure humanity, means that no one is able to effect his or her own salvation or save anyone else; all humans are ineligible of saving themselves or saving others. Sin is endemic; humans sin because humans are sinners. There is nothing one can do to expunge this defilement, no amount of human effort can make humans clean.[26] Purification from sin requires outside agency because the problem is too deep, existing in the core of one's being. In the Christian faith, one is made right with God, cleansed before Him, not based on anything one has done, or any accumulated merit (indeed, all of one's good deeds are the equivalent of filthy rags, Isa 64:6), but on the righteousness of Christ, and what he has accomplished through his death and resurrection (Rom 3:22, 28; 5:18–19). The believer's righteousness in Christ is a declarative position, having been declared right with God, reckoned and credited as being righteous (Gen 15:6; Rom 4:3, 5–6, 22; Gal 3:6). This has a certainty and assurance because it is not based on the amount of purity, merit or power any individual can muster, but on what someone else, namely God, in the person of Jesus, has done. Only Jesus can make people truly clean, cleansed from sin, negativity, moral depravity, ritual pollution, obscurations, and all forms of impurity (1 John 1:9).

The object of one's faith in Tibetan Buddhism is centered on esteemed monks and lamas, Buddhas of previous eons, mantras and liturgies, and elaborate ritualized praxis. In contrast, the object of one's faith in Christianity is Christ alone; nothing further is required to be restored to a right relationship with God. Furthermore, the Christian does not become equal with God in moral perfection or become a deified being. As Tarrant has

---

26. Müller states that "Mankind is unclean. It is not just that man is totally depraved, mankind is totally defiled." Müller, *Honor and Shame*, 60.

noted, even after a lifetime of being sanctified, believers "do not become identical with the essence of Christ."[27]

Heaven and Earth

Tibetan Buddhism has a very dim view of the samsaric realm humans inhabit. Samsara is full of misery and suffering; it is a world devoid of joy and one's very existence in itself is evidence of one's moral impurity. That is, only impure and unenlightened beings inhabit samsara. As such, there is no notion of human flourishing or of seeking to improve the plight of others. Human effort is centered on personal purification so that one can escape the endless circle of birth, sickness, aging, and death. Naturally, there is no notion of God's will being done on earth just as his will is done in heaven. In contrast, Christianity, though also longing for another world, a holy, pure, eternal world of living in God's presence, affirms human flourishing and the joy of belonging to God right here and now, and of doing his heavenly will here on earth, full of suffering and misery though it may be. The "eternal life" believers have is something they experience now and forever (John 10:10; 17:3).

Links to the Gospel

In light of these differences, does this render the two systems as irreconcilable and that an understanding of Tibetan notions of purity has no value for contextualizing the good news to Tibetans? Or is it possible that the purification schema of Tibetans is in some way a distant echo of God setting eternity in people's hearts (Eccl 3:18)? The Tibetan longing to be purified may be a reflection of God's indelible footprint on humanity, that he has not left himself without a testimony (Acts 14.17). The existence of a profound sense of the need to be purified, (albeit from a different conceptual framework) may in fact suggest the gospel can indeed speak into this felt need. The way forward, then, is perhaps to not only recognize the differences and shortcomings of the purity system of Tibetan Buddhism, but to see it as a reference point, as a bridge or a link to frame the gospel in a way that may make sense to a Tibetan. The Apostle Paul strove to preach the gospel clearly, in a winsome and compelling way, in whatever setting he found

---

27. Tennent, *Theology in the Context*, Kindle location 4589.

himself (1 Cor 9:20–23). He even asked the Colossian believers to pray that he would proclaim the message clearly "as I should" (Col 4:4). The goal of contextualization, then, is to follow Paul's example, and to communicate clearly within the framework and thought patterns of the receptor culture so that the gospel "both comes to authentic expression in the local context and at the same time prophetically transforms the context."[28]

The Gospel of Purification

The suggested approach, then, is to frame the gospel within the Biblical context of purity and purification in a way that may appeal to Tibetan sensibilities. The Bible is replete with purity language, metaphors and motifs, p/p narratives and interactions.[29] If such a focus were highlighted in presenting the gospel to Tibetans, this may help them have a greater understanding and appreciation of the Christian message. The following is a brief look at some of the purity language in key Biblical passages.

Sin and Impurity

In the Old Testament, both ritual and moral impurity needed to be cleansed through sacrifice and ritual praxis.[30] This can be seen in Leviticus chapter sixteen, in the directives for the high priest:

> Thus he shall make atonement for the Holy Place, because of the uncleanness of the people of Israel and because of their transgressions, all their sins. And so he shall do for the tent of meeting, which dwells with them in the midst of their uncleanness. (Lev 16:16)

---

28. Flemming, *Contextualization*, 19.

29. The expression "The Gospel of Purification" has been preferred over "The Purity Gospel" because of potential connotations of chastity or sexual purity, but it also better reflects a contextualized approach in that "purification" is a central notion of Tibetan Buddhism and also a clear aspect of the gospel.

30. This is not to suggest that there was no difference between ritual and moral defilements. Ritual defilements were typically unavoidable, being a natural part of life whereas moral defilements were avoidable. Ritual defilement was contagious whereas moral defilement was typically noncommunicable. For more on these differences see Thiessen, *Jesus and the Forces*, Kindle location 404–63; Van Maaren, "Does Mark's Jesus Abrogate," 31–35.

Both ritual uncleanness and moral transgressions made people unfit to be in God's presence or to be in right relationship with him, and therefore required perpetual cleansing. Leviticus 16:30 continues, "For on this day shall atonement be made for you to cleanse you. You shall be clean before the LORD from all your sins." In order to approach God, the Israelites needed to be cleansed of both their ritual and moral impurity. Both "clean hands" and a "clean heart" were required for worship (Ps 24:3-4).

Sin, in both the Old and New Testament, is often described in purity terms as being defiled, unclean or impure, and forgiveness as being cleansed or washed clean (Isa 1:16; 4:4; Jer 2:22; 4:14; Ezek 36:25).[31] In Psalm 51, King David cries out, "Wash me thoroughly from all my iniquity, and cleanse me from my sin!" (Ps 51:2). Sinful behavior also defiled the land (Num 35:33-34; Ezek 22:4; 36:17; Jer 2:7; 3:1). In Isaiah 1:16, God cries out to the people to, "Wash yourselves; make yourselves clean; remove the evil of your deeds from before my eyes; cease to do evil," and further on God himself is the one who will "remove all your impurities" (Isa 1:25). Isaiah, transported into the holy presence of God, declares himself as "a man of unclean lips," dwelling among "a people of unclean lips" (Isa 6:5). In the book of Jeremiah, God again cries out, "Woe to you, O Jerusalem! How long will it be before you are made clean" (Jer 13:27). In Malachi 3:3, God is pictured as the Purifier of his people. And in Ezekiel 36:25, God promises to restore his people of Israel saying, "I will sprinkle clean water on you, and you shall be clean from all your uncleannesses, and from all your idols I will cleanse you."

In the New Testament, ritual defilement, though still deeply embedded in Jewish consciousness and practice,[32] is less of a focus in itself, with the defiling power of sin being seen as immoral actions which flow from morally defiled hearts. Jesus made it clear it was the things that came out from the heart of a person that defiled them rather than ritual contamination (Matt 15:11; Mark 7:15).[33] Jesus also exposed the hypocrisy of the

---

31. See also DiFransico, "Washing Away Sin."

32. See, for example, Wassen, "Jewishness of Jesus"; Thiessen, *Jesus and the Forces*; Kazen, *Jesus and Purity Halakhah*; Holmén, "Jesus and the Purity"; Dunn, "Jesus and Purity."

33. This would seem to be the central point of Mark chapter seven. Jesus is concerned with the heart, with the moral defilement of the internal rather than the ritual defilement of the external. He is not dismissive of ritual purity as such (as can be seen in Mark 1:44), but rather he appears to be prioritizing moral purity. Roger Booth, among others, arrives at a similar conclusion. Booth, *Jesus and the Laws*, 218-21.

Pharisees for appearing pure and clean on the outside, but on the inside being full of "everything unclean" (Matt 23:27). The writers of the epistles also used p/p language in describing sin as impurity. Paul describes humanity as "slaves to impurity" (Rom 6:19), and the works of the flesh as "impurity" (Gal 5:19, Eph 4:19; 5:3, 5; Col 3:5). Paul also urges believers to "purify ourselves from everything that contaminates body and spirit" (2 Cor 7:1). Peter and James speak of the defilements and pollutions of the world (2 Pet 2:20; James 1:27; 3:6) and being cleansed from sin (2 Pet 1:9). James exhorts believers to "Cleanse your hands, you sinners, and purify your hearts, you double-minded" (James 4:9).

The Atonement

The purpose here is not to examine the various atonement theories,[34] or pit them against one another, but to continue to explore the purity language in the Bible regarding the atonement, with the purpose of discovering potential gospel links for Tibetan Buddhists. As has been mentioned, the atoning sacrifices in the Old Testament were cleansing both uncleanness and moral transgressions in order to have a right standing before God, and to be restored back into his community of set apart people.[35] In the New

---

34. See, for example, Ott, "Power of Biblical Metaphors"; Blocher, "Biblical Metaphors"; Baker and Green, *Recovering the Scandal*; Mischke et al., *Global Gospel*; Wu, "Contextualizing the One Gospel." By "atonement," I am following a standard definition of being covered over, of having sins covered through Christ's sacrifice, or wiped cleaned and removed so that sinners can be at one with God, hence the term "at-one-ment." The Hebrew verb for "make atonement" *kaphar* also includes the meaning element of cleansing or wiping clean. *Hebrew Lexicon* https://biblehub.com/hebrew/3722.htm.

35. Not wanting to weigh in on the atonement debate, as many others have already done, but just to make the point that it would appear that one main aspect of the atonement is the cleansing, the clearing away of sin (Exod 30:8–10; Lev 4–5; Lev 16:16, 30). Jacob Milgrom has argued that the "sin offering," outlined in Lev 4–5, should be considered a "purification offering," with the wiping of the blood on the altar for cleansing, allowing for such an understanding. Milgrom, *Anchor Bible: Leviticus 1–16*, 226–92. Robert Alter also suggests that purification from offenses is implied in the sin offering. Alter, *Five Books of Moses*, 382–83. In commenting on the purification of the Levite priests in Num 8:5–8, Alter makes a novel suggestion that rather than a doctrine of original sin, the purification practices might be more indicative of "original impurity," (504). But this is a discussion for another occasion. Suffice to say that it does not appear to be heresy to speak of the atonement in terms of cleansing one from sin, rather than exclusively focusing on shed blood as due payment for sin. (And there is a certain paradox in that blood was both a contaminating substance, requiring ritual purification, and also one of the primary agents of purification).

Testament, it is through the death, and perfect sacrifice of Christ, and the power of his resurrection, that people are cleansed from the defilement of sin and restored into relationship with God and his people. The book of Hebrews employs purity language when describing what Christ has accomplished. Hebrew 1:3b states that Christ, "After making purification for sins, he sat down at the right hand of the Majesty on high." The Greek term for purification *katharismos* is suggestive here of being cleansed through a "ritual purgation or washing."[36] Jesus is described as the superlative high priest because "he is holy and blameless, unstained by sin" (Heb 7:26). Unlike other animal sacrifices, which did not effect a permanent cleansing, the blood of Jesus is able to "purify our conscience from dead works" (Heb 9:14), and to effect a lasting and permanent cleansing from the stain of sin (Heb 10:1–22). The writer of Hebrews makes this confident assurance explicit when he writes: "let us draw near with a true heart in full assurance of faith, with our hearts sprinkled clean from an evil conscience and our bodies washed with pure water" (Heb 10:22).

In Titus, Paul explains Jesus' sacrifice in terms of giving his life "to redeem us from all lawlessness and to purify for himself a people for his own possession" (Titus 2:14), and in saving us Jesus "washed away our sin, giving us new birth and new life through the Holy Spirit" (Titus 3:5, NLT).[37] Jesus offered himself as a sacrifice so that the church, the community of believers, could be made "holy and clean, washed by the cleansing of God's word" (Eph 5:26, NLT). Paul further makes this explicit in 1 Corinthians, reminding the believers that "you were cleansed; you were made holy; you were made right with God by calling on the name of the Lord Jesus Christ and by the Spirit of our God" (1 Cor 6:11, NLT). The Apostle John uses purity language in clearly stating that, "If we confess our sins, he is faithful and just to forgive us our sins and to cleanse us from all unrighteousness" (1 John 1:9). In Acts 3:19, Peter implores his audience to repent of their sin and turn to God "so that your sins may be wiped away" (NLT). In Acts 15:9, God "cleansed" the hearts of the Gentiles through faith, and in Acts 22:16, Paul is instructed to "Rise and be baptized and wash away your sins, calling on his name." Furthermore, one of the pictures of heaven is of pure, white radiance with the inhabitants dressed in pure, white garments (Rev 3:4–5; 4:4; 6:11; 7:9, 14; 21:27).

---

36. *Thayer's Greek Lexicon*, Strongs NT 2512, https://biblehub.com/greek/2512.htm.
37. *Holy Bible: New Living Translation* (NLT).

Viewed through the lens of purity language, the atonement speaks of being made clean, cleansed, made new, set free from defilements, restored back to relationship with God our maker, and his community, and gives believers the assurance of dwelling forever in a purified, pure realm in heaven with the primordial pure and holy God, and his purified people.

Jesus and the Gospel of Purification

Jesus' ready willingness to touch the unclean and make them clean and whole again, shows his love and concern for the ritually impure and the outcasts of society. It also reflected his desire to cleanse all who were defiled by sin and in need of inner cleansing.[38] The Gospel of Mark is replete with purity references and would appear to be one of the main emphases of the book.[39] Jesus is first introduced in the book of Mark in the context of water baptism, a potent symbol of purification and of being washed clean of moral impurities. Though perfect, and in no need of purification, Jesus inaugurated his ministry with the washing of water baptism.[40] Jesus then begins his miracles in Mark with the casting out of an unclean spirit from a man who was inside the sacred space of a synagogue, on the sacred and set apart day of the Sabbath. The unclean man declares the purity of Jesus by crying out, "I know who you are—you are the Holy One of God" (Mark 1:24). Mark appears to be intentionally using *pneumati akatharto* (unclean spirit), rather than the generic term for demon *daimonia*, to highlight his theme of purity.

---

38. For example, in Luke 17:11–19 Jesus heals ten lepers and in Mark 14:3–9 Jesus visits the house of Simon the Leper. In Mark 2:15–17 Jesus associates with unclean and impure outcasts such as sinners and tax collectors. Clearly Jesus was prepared to mix with those considered to be unclean.

39. Jerome Neyrey states that "The basic presentation of Jesus in Mark's Gospel is done in terms of purity." Neyrey, "Idea of Purity," 124. Thiessen suggests that Mark's Gospel demonstrates that "Jesus is involved in a broadscale purification mission." Thiessen, *Jesus and the Forces*, Kindle location 4804. Elizabeth Shively makes a case that Mark's focus was on the purification of the body and that he "presents not only a theology of the cross, but also a theology of resurrection as the purification of God's people." Shively, "Purification of the Body," 89.

40. deSilva notes that "John's baptism resembles a purificatory washing to remove the pollution of sin, to restore a condition of cleanness so that one can encounter God." deSilva, *Honor*, 304. For more on baptism as a purificatory rite see Thiessen, *Jesus and the Forces*, Kindle location 625–46; Blidstein, "'All is Pure'" 213–28, and Blidstein, *Purity, Community, and Ritual*, 15, 107–34.

It may be of no coincidence that the three main sources of ritual impurity in the Old Testament—skin disease, genital discharges and corpse contact, are three of the main encounters Jesus has with the ritually impure in the New Testament. These three are clearly in focus in the book of Mark.[41] In Mark 1:40–45, Jesus reaches out and touches a leper, but rather than himself being defiled, Jesus imparts a cleansing purity which treats the source of the leper's impurity and thus makes him clean. The cause of the man's impurity has now gone, and Jesus is concerned not just for his cleansing, but also that he be restored back into the community. In Jesus we see a certain kind of reversal of the contagion principle of ritual impurity.[42] Where ritual impurity is contagious through human contact, Jesus is able to transfer purity, cleansing, and wholeness to the ritually unclean. But Jesus' mission is more than just healing and cleansing the ritually impure. In Mark 2:1–12, in the healing of the paralytic, the challenge is put forward whether Jesus can cleanse moral impurities and not just physical ones. Jesus clearly shows that he is able to effect ultimate cleansing through the forgiving of sin. He both has the power and the authority to cleanse ritual and moral impurity. And this is why Jesus ultimately came—to cleanse people from the moral impurity of their sin.

Mark chapter five has a high weighting of p/p interactions. The chapter begins with the cleansing of an unclean Gentile, possessed by unclean spirits, who lived in unclean tombs, in a land of unclean pig farmers.[43] Jesus both cleanses the man and the land from defilement. When in a large crowd of people, Jesus' garment is touched by an unclean woman who had been subjected to twelve years of bleeding (Mark 5:25–34), and again, a healing purity flows from him. He is not contaminated but cleanses the woman and deals

41. In Numbers 5:2, God says, "Command the people of Israel that they put out of the camp everyone who is leprous or has a discharge and everyone who is unclean through contact with the dead." In the Markan account, Jesus first encounters an unclean leper (Mark 1:40–45), then a woman suffering from an unclean discharge (Mark 5:25–34), and then a ceremonially unclean dead body (Mark 5:35–43). Mark appears to be intentional here, and it would seem that his preservation of the order in which the ritually defiled appear in Numbers is not coincidental. (These ritual defilements are also detailed in Lev 12–15 and Num 19).

42. Wassen notes that "In traditional Judaism, impurity was transmitted between people, but purity was obtained through divine agency, that is through God or the Holy Spirit." Wassen, "Jewishness of Jesus," 24. Thiessen suggests the Markan portrayal of Jesus is of one who embodies "a contagious power of holiness that overwhelms the forces of impurity." Thiessen, *Jesus and the Forces*, Kindle location 217.

43. From a Jewish perspective, one could hardly think of a worse combination of defiling factors.

with the source of her defilement by stopping the bleeding.⁴⁴ Jesus is again concerned for both the woman's physical cleansing and her restoration to the community by publicly declaring her as having been healed and thus made clean. At the end of Mark chapter five, Jesus is taking the hand of a defiled corpse and bringing a young girl back to life (Mark 5:41). Corpse defilement, though the strongest form of impurity,⁴⁵ does not affect Jesus, and rather than being defiled, he imparts his purity and cleanses the source of the impurity, death itself. The young girl is healed and cleansed and is thus removed from any defilement. In the Gospel of Mark, Jesus deals with the source of all defilement and impurity whether it is ritual, moral, or demonic unclean spirits.

It is perhaps in death that Jesus most identifies with humanity and absorbs not just all the consequences of divine justice, but also all of humanity's defilement and decay. It is by his taking on all of the defilement of sin and death, and being rejected by the community of the Godhead, that believers can know the purification and forgiveness his resurrected victory over death brings.⁴⁶ As Paul writes to the Colossians, "Yet now he has reconciled you to himself through the death of Christ in his physical body. As a result, he has brought you into his own presence, and you are holy and blameless as you stand before him without a single fault" (Col 1:22, NLT). Just as purification offerings were burned outside of the camp, so too Jesus was sacrificed in the place of uncleanness outside of the city (Isa 53:8, Heb 13:12). As deSilva suggests, "Jesus' journey outside the margins of the camp is a ritual act of sacred power, his death becoming a purification offering."⁴⁷ Likewise, just as Jesus dealt with the real source of ritual uncleanness in his cleansing healings, in his death and resurrection he defeated the true source of all defilement—sin and death itself, so that believers could be made clean and new, restored to fellowship with God and his people. This was all accomplished through Christ "who abolished death and brought life and immortality" (2 Tim 1:10).⁴⁸ It is only through Jesus that humanity can

---

44. Not only had the woman been unclean for all those years, likely this rendered her infertile as constant bleeding does not allow for pregnancy, putting to one side the fact that no man would have relations with an unclean woman. Jesus, in restoring her wholeness, also potentially gave her the opportunity to bring new life into the world. Wassen, "Jesus and the Hemorrhaging Woman," 644.

45. Num 5; 19. See also Thiessen, *Jesus and the Forces*, Kindle location 2599–619 and Shively, "Purification of the Body," 70.

46. Deut 21:22–23; Heb 13:11–13; Gal 3:13; Rom 8:3.

47. deSilva, *Honor*, 308.

48. Furthermore, "through death he might destroy the power of death," Heb 2:14, and also Col 1:22; Acts 2:24; 1 Cor 15:54.

be made clean and pure and restored into a right relationship with a pure and holy God. And all of this may well be good news for a Tibetan.

Implications and Applications

One of the potential implications of this study, particularly for any who are ministering to Tibetan Buddhists, is firstly an awareness of the purification schema and how this impacts the worldview of Tibetans. The existence of such a schema may not be immediately obvious, particularly for Western Christians who do not have such categories within their cultures.[49] An understanding of p/p concerns may also require probing further into a culture and looking beyond just h/s or f/p dynamics. Seeking such an understanding may start with first applying a "ground up" approach to cultural analysis rather than simply overlaying an etic framework. Another potential implication is an awareness of the dark spiritual nature of Tibetan Buddhism, particularly the tantric practices. With such an emphasis on spells, incantations, mantras, and demonic tantric practices, one needs to be sensitive to the spiritual realities that are present in the Tibetan Buddhist schema, and to be prepared for spiritual warfare. There is a sense that in ministering to Tibetan Buddhists, one is entering a new level of potential demonic interactions. One should be prepared for spiritual obstacles and to appropriate the armor of God.

Applying the Gospel of Purification

Articulating the Gospel

In seeking to share the gospel with Tibetans, there may be a case not to start with initial gospel presentations which have a legal or juridical emphasis. Rather than starting with sin as law-breaking, it may be expedient to first speak of sin in terms of defilement, pollution, and impurity. This is not to diminish the seriousness of sin, or dilute it to some syncretic form, but to first frame it in terms that lead to greater understanding.[50] In sharing the

---

49. Even though Hiebert et al. have suggested that "Concepts of moral order based on mechanistic notions of purity and pollution are almost universal," p/p concerns appear to have been less of a focus among missionaries and missiologists, at least in Buddhist contexts. Hiebert et al. *Understanding Folk Religion*, Kindle location 3816.

50. Others who have suggested it is appropriate for sin to be spoken of as pollution

gospel in a Japanese context, Paul Sadler found that, "Rather than starting with a concept like sin, which in Japanese includes strong connotations of crime, it is often far more natural to begin with the inherent beliefs of the Japanese regarding purity and from there introduce the demand for purity of a holy God, and the purification that Jesus provided through his death on the cross."[51] The so called "legal" gospel of penal or forensic substitution may be better preserved for an expanded understanding of the gospel rather than the initial presentation. This is not to say that Tibetans cannot understand the idea of substitution, indeed, someone dying for someone else is considered honorable.[52] However, the concept of a "guilty conscience" appears unremarkable in Tibetan consciousness, and certainly there is no concept of being guilty and condemned before a holy God.[53] But of feeling dirty and unclean, there is strong resonance. Furthermore, the notion of Jesus taking away one's sin is conceptually difficult because Tibetans have such a strong belief that everyone should take the karmic consequences of their own sin; no one else can or should. There is a well-known proverb which states that one must take the consequences of one's own accumulated sins.[54] However, to speak of being made clean from the stain of sin may well strike a chord of understanding.

---

and defilement include Hiebert, "Clean and Dirty"; Dyrness, "Can We Do Theology," 57; Hibbert and Evelyn, "Contextualising Sin"; Ott, "Power of Biblical Metaphors," 367; Dye and Zachariah, "Five Key Questions," 191. Robert Priest makes the case that in initial evangelism concepts of sin which resonate with the consciousness of the indigenous culture, rather than that of the missionary, must be emphasized. Priest, "Missionary Elenctics," 309–11. See also Dye, "Toward a Cross-Cultural Definition."

51. Sadler, "Japanese Gospel Message," 28. (p/p concerns in Japanese culture appear well attested to. See, for example, Namihira, "Pollution"). Others, in Islamic contexts, have made similar observations to Sadler. See Hibbert, "Defilement and Cleansing"; Dale, "Ritual Purity and Defilement"; B. Thomas, "Gospel for Shame Cultures."

52. There are Tibetan folk stories which portray a substitutionary death for the sake of others as heroic and honorable. For example, the children's stories of the elephant (*glang chen gyis rang lus dor ba*) and the monkey (*spre'u'i rgyal pos spre'u tshogs bskyangs pa*) who give their lives for the survival of the community are well-known. (These stories are derived from the Jataka tales (*skyes rabs*), stories of the former lives of Buddha). Suffice to say that the concept of a substitutionary death should not be completely dismissed.

53. There is no express term for "guilty conscience" in Tibetan. The closest equivalent is regret or remorse.

54. *rang gis sdig pa bsags rang gis mkhyer*. There is a similar saying in the broader Buddhist dharma which states: "One can only taint oneself, one can only purify oneself." Gomez, "Contributions," 171.

As well as looking for links to the Gospel of Purification throughout the larger Biblical narrative,[55] one can also draw on the many p/p encounters of Jesus in presenting the gospel to a Tibetan. As has been shown, the Gospel of Mark may well be a fruitful place to begin, tracing those encounters which have a purification focus.[56] In the first instance, just being aware that someone from a p/p-based culture may read the encounters of Jesus in Mark, and the other Gospels, quite differently, could be beneficial. There may be a need to explain that Jesus did not get contaminated when he associated with the ritually defiled. A study of the Markan accounts could also highlight both Jesus' willingness to cleanse the impure and his power and authority to do so. Naturally, the primary emphasis would be given to his ability to forgive defiling sin. It may also be worth emphasizing not just the individual cleansing and purification, but the restoration back into relationship with God and entrance into his community, a kingdom of God's people. Salvation has both an individual and a communal aspect, just as there is in being cleansed and restored back into community. For collectivist people groups such as Tibetans, this can be an important aspect. It may also be possible to frame the overarching narrative of the Bible, for example, the elements of Creation, Fall, Redemption and Restoration within a purity framework.[57]

Perhaps it goes without saying that central to any gospel presentations is the establishment of genuine friendships. Relationships in any endeavor

---

55. With a new awareness of p/p concerns, one may be able to look for links or threads to the Gospel of Purification, even in unlikely places. For example, (though of little concern to a Western Christian) corpse defilement and related purification rituals outlined in Numbers 19, may have a certain connection with a Tibetan. There, any form of contact with a corpse was considered ritually impure and required purification. For seven days any who had contact with the deceased would be ritually impure and cut off from the community. Those who never became clean were permanently cut off. Perhaps there is a gospel thread here. Jesus became defiled and contaminated through death and was cut off from community with God so that by his death and shed blood we could be made clean and be restored back into fellowship with God and his community. Jesus was likewise restored back into fellowship with God through his resurrection. Unlike the purification rituals for corpse defilement which needed to be repeated, the purification that comes through Jesus is permanent where God no longer considers us to be impure, but rather as clean and whole.

56. For an example see Morrison, "Sharing the Gospel," 128.

57. For generic examples, see Steffen, "Clothesline Theology," 261–62, 271–72. Steffen, *Worldview-Based Storying*, Kindle locations 6848, 6892. Ott, "Power of Biblical Metaphors," 366–68. Mischke et al., *Global Gospel*, Kindle locations 5145–70. For a specific example see Morrison, "Sharing the Gospel," 127.

are obviously key, and hospitality in Tibetan culture can be formational in building relationships.[58] Having an awareness of p/p concerns can also help to foster deeper relationships through a clearer understanding of the rituals one may encounter each day.

Translation

A particular implication for Bible translators may be to explore terms for sin which provide a more rounded, nuanced, and balanced understanding by including the meaning elements of impurity and defilement. In Tibetan, the term used for sin *sdig pa* can include moral failings but more typically means "negativities." Another term for sin, (used extensively in the Tibetan New Testament), is *sdig nyes*—which focuses on both the moral aspect of sin and of being a crime or civil offense. While both are useful terms, the natural collocation of *sdig grib* (also *sdig sgrib*)—sin and defilement, which has a high lexical weighting in the texts studied, could also be used where appropriate. This term, depending on the context, may more readily resonate with Tibetans.

There may also be a case to preserve the potential redundancy of "unclean spirits," in order to accurately capture Mark's p/p emphasis. That is, demonic beings who can inhabit humans are typically perceived as being unclean and to explicitly modify them as such can potentially seem redundant or unnatural. However, to ellipse "unclean" from the collocation "unclean spirit" may diminish the weight of Mark's p/p concerns.[59] An awareness of p/p language in both the Biblical text and the receptor language can create greater sensitivity towards tailoring a Gospel of Purification relevant for Tibetans, particularly in developing extra-biblical materials and scripture engagement resources. Providing an overview of the purity system of the Old Testament, and tracing how that relates to Jesus' purifying sacrifice, may also prove enlightening.

58. Covell, "Buddhism and the Gospel," 136. For more on hospitality see Smither, *Mission as Hospitality*.

59. The Tibetan term for a spirit or demon that can possess humans is *gdon 'dre*. This being is typically considered impure and thus modifying it with "unclean" (*mi gtsang ba*) can seem unnecessary. However, in order to preserve the full measure of Mark's p/p presentation, retaining "unclean" as the modifier of demons is well warranted. Some freer English translations do not preserve "unclean spirit" in Mark, and other New Testament passages, but rather render *pneumati akatharto* simply as "evil spirit." This may serve to dilute Mark's (and other New Testament authors') purity focus.

Ecclesial Praxis

Hiebert et al. state that, "Rituals play a central role in creating and renewing religious beliefs in most societies, and it is important for missionaries to be aware of the need to embody the gospel in living ritual forms."[60] This need may be accentuated in the case of highly ritualized Tibetan societies. On that basis, it may prove worthwhile to encourage and foster more emphasis on the sacraments of baptism and the Lord's Supper, and a holy reverence for them. In both cases, the focus could be placed on being made clean and whole, cleansed from sin and defilement, and being made clean by what Christ has done (Col 1:22). Fostering the development of communion prayers which focus on being washed and cleansed by the blood of Jesus may also be appropriate.[61] Baptism, in which the believer joins in the death, burial, and resurrection of Christ (Rom 6:3–5, Col 2:12), also initiates the believer into a community of cleansed and restored followers of Jesus who belong to God's holy and set apart people. Perhaps a heightened emphasis on baptism as an outward sign of inner purification, and of entering into a new community may also prove beneficial in ecclesial praxis.

A group of Tibetan believers, in a certain location, recently composed a song about the Lord's Supper, a song they felt they needed specifically for communion, as this is a significant ceremony for them. The first stanza of the song states that Jesus came to make unclean people clean and give them new life. When discussing the song with the main translator, he said this was what he believed was the main purpose of Jesus' death, and that remembering this through the Lord's Supper was especially important. Given that observation, it may be opportune to foster the remembrance of the Lord's Supper in a Tibetan context more regularly, not just because Christianity is by comparison to Tibetan Buddhism devoid of ritual, but because it can be such a rich and meaningful purificatory sacrament of remembrance.

For other church praxis, it may be fruitful to explore the usage of purity symbols; whether existing ones could be adapted or new ones created.

---

60. Hiebert et al., *Understanding Folk Religion*, Kindle location 5835. Steffen reiterates the need for rituals: "wherever ritual occurs, to remain relevant, Christianity must provide ritual substitutes that fall within the boundaries of Scripture." Steffen, *Worldview-Based Storying*, Kindle location 4565.

61. For example, there may be a place for encouraging prayers such as the *Prayer of Humble Access*, in the *Book of Common Prayer*, which focuses on the being made clean by Christ's body and washed through his cleansing blood. Smither, *Mission as Hospitality*, 68–69.

Discipleship training could also be encouraged with a purity focus. Though Jesus' blood cleanses believers from all sin and defilement, and one does not need to strive to be made clean in God's sight, believers still do need to endeavor to live holy and pure lives. Indeed, they are expected to live holy lives set apart for God and his glory (Eph 1:4; Titus 2:14). Often the bar for discipleship can be set quite low (what do Christians actually do?), but a purity emphasis, in which believers are to be holy and pure in their daily lives, is a lifelong challenge and commitment.[62] Discipleship could also contain a communal aspect as believers grow together as God's holy people set apart for him.[63] Naturally, there may be other potential implications and applications that others will find.

Areas of Further Research

While this dissertation may have begun to raise awareness of Tibetan notions of purity, other potential research questions remain. It may firstly be of interest to explore the purity and purification schema in other Buddhist contexts, at both the monastic and folk level. Another potential research question might be to explore further the interconnection between power and purity within folk Buddhism. A more philosophical topic could be to explore notions of purity and emptiness, and the pursuit of the mind of a Bodhisattva (Sk. bodhicitta). Whether there is a connection between wisdom and purity might also be a question of interest.

The question of notions of purity among younger generations of Tibetans may be a topic for further research, with another study focused on the consciousness of purity among modern Tibetans of the diaspora, particularly those now living in the West. Further research into the use of appropriate purity symbols and rituals in ecclesial praxis for believers from Tibetan Buddhist or Buddhist backgrounds may also be illuminating. A study of the practice of fasting (*smyung gnas*), widely undertaken in monastic communities, its connection to the pursuit of purity, and the implications for Christian believers, would also be a study of potential interest. A research topic that would be particularly pertinent is to explore

---

62. Given the highly ritualized nature of Tibetan religious praxis, it is not surprising that Tibetan believers often struggle with what Christians are to do. Tibetan believers have naturally asked the question, "What do Christians actually do other than just meet together and pray?"

63. 2 Cor 7:1; 1 Pet 1:14–15, 22; 2:9; 1 Thess 4:7; 1 John 3:3.

how Tibetan Buddhist background believers became Christians, what factors led them to follow Christ, what aspects of the gospel resonated with them, and how their faith is lived out in Christian praxis.

Concluding Remarks

This study has set out to explore Tibetan notions of purity with a view to not only gaining further insights into the Tibetan worldview, but also to explore possible missiological implications of such an understanding. One specific focus of the missiological application explored how such an understanding may be efficacious in sharing the good news of Jesus with Tibetans. Of course, it is only through the power of the Holy Spirit that Tibetans will be drawn to Christ, and God is ultimately in control of the salvation of Tibetans.[64] However, believers are tasked with proclaiming the gospel clearly, and attempts should be made to both articulate and demonstrate it in a way that enhances optimal understanding so that "the Lord's message will spread rapidly and be honored wherever it goes" (2 Thess 3:1).

The missiological conclusions of this dissertation have pointed to making a case for the Gospel of Purification as a potential avenue of meaningful transmission of the Christian message, and as a foundation for fostering indigenous ecclesial formation among Tibetans. For initial presentations of the gospel, such an approach may connect with both the heart and mind of Tibetan Buddhists, and perhaps Buddhists at large. This is not to diminish any other aspects of the multi-faceted nature of the gospel, nor to sanction an approach of selecting certain aspects one may prefer while ignoring others. The legal, judicial, forensic, substitutionary, reconciling, redemptive, honoring, powerful, victorious, and the cleansing aspects of the gospel all testify to the wonderful riches of Christ crucified and the mysteries of the cross. It is rather a matter of prioritizing that which may make more sense to one's audience in initial presentations of the good news.[65] In the fullness of time, all of these aspects can be taught as part of the wonderful unfolding of the rich tapestry of the gospel, and its unchanging power to transform

---

64. Matt 9:38; Luke 10:2; John 6:44, 65; 16:8–11; Rom 8:14.

65. As Dye and Zachariah observe, "Because there are multiple ways to explain the same truths, a Christian witness is free to choose the metaphor that will most clearly communicate accurate biblical truth. Eventually, all metaphors and facets should be introduced and explained, but not all are equally good places to begin. We start with bridges, not barriers." Dye and Zachariah, "Five Key Questions," 190.

lives and complex communities of every tongue, tribe, and nation, even closed communities who have long proved resistant. As an initial bridge to the good news, the Gospel of Purification may have a certain appeal to Tibetan Buddhist sensibilities as they discover the eternal and universal truth that the blood of Jesus Christ cleanses them from all their impurities.

In Zechariah chapter three, Joshua the high priest, a clear pre-figure of Christ, is pictured standing before the angel of the Lord dressed in filthy garments representing the filth and defilement of sin. His filthy clothes are removed, and pure and clean vestments are placed upon him, symbolically depicting the cleansing of sin (Zech 3:4–5). This is a pre-enactment of what the Branch, the Messiah, will achieve in just "a single day" (Zech 3:9), where "a fountain will be opened . . . to cleanse them from sin and impurity" (Zech 13:1). Jesus took on all the filth and defilement of our sin, was cast out into the place of uncleanness, shed his blood and tasted death, so that we could, from that day on, be made clean, whole, and new through his perfect sacrifice.

The first recorded sign in the Gospel of John traces Jesus turning the water that was stored in large purification pots into wine. The water in those pots would, at least in part, make one ritually clean. Jesus turns that water into wine. Wine is a symbol of joy, something that everyone present would have well understood.[66] But perhaps there is another layer of nuanced and protracted meaning of celebrating the purification of being cleansed and forgiven through Jesus' blood, symbolically represented by the wine at the Lord's Supper; a wine that Jesus will not drink again until believers are fully purified with him and dressed in white, pure robes of linen together with people from every tribe and language, and celebrate the complete purification from all impurity at the marriage feast, having been made clean by the blood of the Lamb.[67]

The hope might be, then, that with a new awareness of purity considerations, deeply grounded in the Biblical narrative, the Gospel of Purification may bring added understanding to the all-encompassing and compelling nature of the good news, a faithful presentation of which may yet resonate in the hearts of many Tibetans.

---

66. For wine as a symbol of joy see Num 18:12; Deut 7:13; 11:14; 33:28; Ps 104:14–15; Isa 25:6–8; Jer 31:12–14; Amos 9:13–14.

67. Rev 7:9, 14; 19:7–9.

Bibliography

Abe, Masao. "The Idea of Purity in Mahāyāna Buddhism." *Numen* 13 (1966) 183–89.
Adarsha: https://adarsha.dharma-treasure.org/
Aguilar, Mario I. "The Jesuits in Tibet at the Time of the VI and VII Dalai Lamas." *The Tibet Journal* 35.3 (2010) 61–77.
Almogi, Orna. "Analysing Tibetan Titles: Towards a Genre-Based Classification of Tibetan Literature." *Cahiers d'Extrême-Asie* (2005) 27–58.
Almogi, Orna., ed. *Contributions to Tibetan Buddhist Literature*. Beiträge zur Zentralasienforschung 14. Halle (Saale): International Institute for Tibetan and Bud-dhist Studies, 2008.
Alter, Robert. *The Five Books of Moses: A Translation with Commentary*. New York: Norton, 2019.
Apple, James B. "Maitreya's Tuṣita Heaven as a Pure Land in Gelukpa Forms of Tibetan Buddhism." In *Pure Lands in Asian Texts and Contexts*, 188–222. Honolulu: University of Hawaii Press, 2019.
Arazi, Eliran. "Corpse Impurity in Second Temple Judaism: A Revised Approach in Light of the Order of Meaning of Honor and Shame." *Journal of Ancient Judaism* 10 (2019) 354–94.
Arnold, Edward A. "Tsongkhapa's Coordination of Sūtra and Tantra: Ascetic Performance, Narrative, and Philosophy in the Creation of the Tibetan Buddhist Self." PhD diss., Columbia University, 2021.
Āryadeva. *Āryadeva's Four Hundred Stanzas on the Middle Way: With Commentary by Gyel-Tsap*. Translated by Sonam Rinchen. Ithaca, NY: Snow Lion, 2008.
Bahr, Petra. "Purity." In *The Brill Dictionary of Religion*. Edited by Kocku von Stuckrad. Vol. 1–4. Leiden: Brill, 2006.
Baker, Mark D., and Joel B. Green. *Recovering the Scandal of the Cross: Atonement in New Testament and Contemporary Contexts*. Downers Grove, IL: InterVarsity Press, 2011.
Barnett, Robert. "Notes on Contemporary Ransom Rituals in Lhasa." In *Revisiting Rituals in a Changing Tibetan World*, edited by Katia Buffetrille, 273–374. Brill's Tibetan Studies Library 31. Leiden: Brill, 2012.
Barstow, Geoffrey. *Food of Sinful Demons: Meat, Vegetarianism, and the Limits of Buddhism in Tibet*. New York: Columbia University Press, 2018.

BIBLIOGRAPHY

"bCom Ldan 'das Snang Ba Mtha' Yas Kyi Gzungs Sngags [The Incantation of Buddha Amitābha]." n.d. TWE, https://tibetan.works/etext/reader.php?collection=kangyur&index=491.

Bde Smon Phyogs Bsgrigs. [An Anthology of Sukhāvatī Prayers] 2 Vols. Chengdu: Si khron mi rigs dpe skrun khang [Sichuan Publishing House], 2007.

bDud 'joms 'jigs bral ye shes rdo rje. "sDom Pa Gsum Gyi Gso Sbyong Gi Cho Ga Mdor Bsdus Snying Por Dril Ba [The Essence of the Practice for Restoring and Purifying the Three Vows]." In *gSung 'bum 'jigs Bral Ye Shes Rdo Rje*, edited by Dorje Jigdral Yeshe. Kalimpong: Dupjung lama, n.d. BDRC, https://library.bdrc.io/show/bdr:MW20869_42DD6B

Bean, Susan S. "Toward a Semiotics of 'Purity' and 'Pollution' in India." *American Ethnologist* 8 (1981) 575–95.

Beech, Geoff. "Shame/Honor, Guilt/Innocence, Fear/Power in Relationship Contexts." *International Bulletin of Mission Research* 42 (2018) 338–46.

Beer, Robert. *The Encyclopedia of Tibetan Symbols and Motifs.* Boston: Shambhala, 1999.

———. *The Handbook of Tibetan Buddhist Symbols.* Boston: Shambhala, 2003.

Bell, Charles Alfred. *The People of Tibet.* Delhi: Motilal Banarsidass, 1992.

Bellezza, John Vincent. *The Dawn of Tibet: The Ancient Civilization on the Roof of the World.* London: Rowman & Littlefield, 2014.

———. *Spirit-Mediums, Sacred Mountains, and Related Bon Textual Traditions in Upper Tibet: Calling Down the Gods.* Brill's Tibetan Studies Library 8. Leiden: Brill, 2005.

Bendlin, Andreas. "Purity and Pollution." In *A Companion to Greek Religion*, edited by Daniel Ogden, 178–89. Blackwell Companions to the Ancient World: Literature and Culture. Oxford: Wiley-Blackwell, 2007.

Bentor, Yael. "The Body in Enlightenment: Purification According to dGe Lugs' Works on the Guhyasamaja Tantra." In *Archaeologies of the Written: Indian, Tibetan, and Buddhist Studies in Honour of Cristina Scherrer-Schaub*, edited by Vincent Tournier, Vincent Eltschinger, and Marta Sernesi. Naples: Università degli Studi di Napoli L'Orientale, 2020.

———. "On the Indian Origins of the Tibetan Practice of Depositing Relics and Dhâraṇîs in Stûpas and Images." *Journal of the American Oriental Society* (1995) 248–61.

Beresford, Brian C., trans. *The Confession of Downfalls: The Confession Sutra, with Commentary by Arya Nagarjuna, The Practice of Vajrasattva with Sadhana: Supplemented by Verbally Transmitted Commentaries from Geshe Ngawang Dhargyey, Geshe Rabten, Geshe Khyentse, Thubten Zopa Rinpoche.* Dharamsala: Library of Tibetan Works and Archives, 1993.

Berounský, Daniel. "Burning the Incestuous Fox: A Tibetan Fumigation Ritual (Wa Bsang)." *Études Mongoles et Sibériennes, Centrasiatiques et Tibétaines* 50 (2019) 1–33.

———. "Tibetan Purificatory Sel Rituals: Fragments of the Tradition from the Borderlands of the Tibetan Plateau." *Studia Orientalia Slovaca* 19 (2020) 1–66.

———. "Wind-Horse Galloping: On a Tibetan Symbol Connected with Nature." *Pandanus' 04, Signeta* (2004) 185–203.

Beyer, Stephan V. *Magic and Ritual in Tibet: The Cult of Tara.* New Dehli: Motilal Banarsidass, 2001.

Bishop, Peter. *Dreams of Power: Tibetan Buddhism and the Western Imagination.* Fairleigh Dickinson University Press, 1993.

BIBLIOGRAPHY

"bKa' 'gyur Ro Cog Gi Snying Po Bsdus Pa'i Gzungs [The Incantation of the Essence of the Kangyur]." In *[Dpal-Ldan Karma Bka'-Brgyud Kyi Rjes Su 'braṅ Ba'i Dge 'dun Rnams Kyi Thun Moṅ Tshogs Su Źal 'don Du Bya Ba'i Chos Spyod Kyi Rim Pa Legs Lam Rab Gsal Las Gces Btus Ñuṅ Gsal Du Bkod Pa] /Compiled By Śes-Rab-Rgyal-Ntshan [Sic]*. [Delhi]: [Sherab Gyaltsen], n.d. BDRC, https://library.bdrc.io/show/bdr:MW00EGS1016759_24CE20.

Bkra'-shis tshe-ring, and Ciren Zhaxi. *English-Tibetan-Chinese dictionary = Dbyin-bod-rgya-gsum śan-sbyar-gyi tshig-mdzod =Ying Zang duizhao cidian*. Beijing: Minzu Chubanshe, 1997.

Blidstein, Moshe. "'All Is Pure for the Pure': Redefining Purity and Defilement in Early Greek Christianity, from Paul to Origen." PhD diss., Oxford University, 2014.

———. *Purity, Community, and Ritual in Early Christian Literature*. Oxford: Oxford University Press, 2017.

Blocher, Henri. "Biblical Metaphors and the Doctrine of the Atonement." *Journal of the Evangelical Theological Society* 47 (2004) 629–45.

Booth, Roger P. *Jesus and the Laws of Purity: Tradition History and Legal History in Mark 7*. Journal for the Study of the New Testament Supplements 13. Sheffield: JSOT Press, 1986.

Bray, John. "French Catholic Missions and the Politics of China and Tibet 1846–1865." *Tibetan Studies: Proceedings of the 7th Seminar of the International Association for Tibetan Studies* 1 (1995) 85–95.

———. "Heinrich August Jaeschke: Pioneer Tibetan Scholar." *Tibet Journal* 8 (1983) 50–55.

———. "Sacred Words and Earthly Powers: Christian Missionary Engagement with Tibet." *The Transactions of the Asiatic Society of Japan* 3 (2011) 93–118.

Buddhaghosa, Bhadantacariya. *The Path of Purification: Visuddhimagga*. Sri Lanka: Buddhist Publication Society, 2010.

The Buddhist Canons Research Database: http://databases.aibs.columbia.edu/.

Buddhist Digital Resource Center: https://www.tbrc.org/.

Buffetrille, Katia. "The Blue Lake of A Mdo and Its Island: Legends and Pilgimage Guide." *The Tibet Journal* 19.4 (1994) 2–22.

———, ed. *Revisiting Rituals in a Changing Tibetan World*. Brill's Tibetan Studies Library 31. Leiden: Brill, 2012.

Bull, Geoffrey Taylor. *Tibetan Tales*. London: Hodder & Stoughton, 1966.

"Byang-Chub Sems-Dpa'i-Ltung—Ba Bshags Pa [The Bodhisattva's Confession of Downfalls]," n.d. Lotsawa House, https://www.lotsawahouse.org/bo/words-of-the-buddha/.

Cabezón, José Ignacio. "Liberation: An Indo-Tibetan Perspective." *Buddhist-Christian Studies* 12 (1992) 191–98.

———, ed. *Tibetan Ritual*. New York: Oxford University Press, 2010.

Cabezón, José Ignacio, and Roger R. Jackson, eds. *Tibetan Literature: Studies in Genre*. Ithaca, NY: Snow Lion, 1996.

Carus, Paul. "Nestorius and Nestorians." *Open Court* 3.3 (1909) 171–73.

Castro-Sánchez, Pedro Manuel. "The Indian Buddhist Dhāraṇī: An Introduction to Its History, Meanings and Functions." PhD diss., University of Sunderland, 2011.

Chagme, Karma. *Chags Med Bde Smon [Chagme's Pure Land Prayers]*. 1 vols. Bal yul mchod rten bya rung kha shor: Nyag rong lha rje rgyal sras 'jam dbyangs bstan 'dzin, 1932.

———. "Klu Bsangs Bla Sel Chen Po Bzhugs so [A Great Fumigation Offering to Nagas]," n.d. Lotsawa House, https://www.lotsawahouse.org/bo/tibetan-masters/karma-chakme/lasel-chenmo-naga-offering.

———. *Rnam Dag Bde Chen Zhing Gi Smon Lam Rgyas Bsdus Bzhugs so [An Aspiration Prayer of Sukhavati, the Perfectly Pure Realm of Great Bliss]*, n.d. BDRC, https://library.bdrc.io/show/bdr:MW00EGS1016759_96184E

———. "Sa Bdag Bshags 'bum Bsdus Pa [Confession to the Lords of the Earth]." In *gSung 'bum Karma Chags Med (Gnas Mdo Dpe Rnying Nyams Gso Khang)*. [Nang Chen Rdzong]: Gnas Mdo Gsang Sngags Chos 'phel Gling Gi Dpe Rnying Nyams Gso Khang /, n.d. BDRC, https://library.bdrc.io/show/bdr:MW1KG8321_6C4684

Chagme, Karma, and Gyatrul Rinpoche. *Naked Awareness: Practical Instructions on the Union of Mahāmudrā and Atiyoga*. Translated by Alan B. Wallace. Ithaca, NY: Snow Lion, 2000.

———*A Spacious Path to Freedom: Practical Instructions on the Union of Mahāmudrā and Atiyoga*. Translated by Alan B. Wallace. Ithaca, NY: Snow Lion, 1998.

Chamberlain, Brad. "Linguistic Watersheds: A Model for Understanding Variation among the Tibetic Languages." *Journal of the Southeast Asian Linguistics Society* 8 (2015) 71–96.

Chokyi Lodro, Jamyang Khyentse. *Bde Ba Can Du Skye Ba'i Smon Lam [Aspiration for Rebirth in Sukhavati]*, n.d. Lotsawa House, https://www.lotsawahouse.org/bo/tibetan-masters/jamyang-khyentse-chokyi-lodro/sukhavati-aspiration.

———. *Bde Chen Zhing Gi Smon Lam [Aspiration for Sukhavati]*, n.d. Lotsawa House, https://www.lotsawahouse.org/bo/tibetan-masters/shamar-chokyi-wangchuk/sukhavati-aspiration.

Chos-dbyiṅs-stobs-ldan-rdo-rje. *The Complete Nyingma Tradition from Sutra to Tantra: Foundations of the Buddhist Path*. Translated by Ngawang Xangpo. Boston: Snow Lion, 2014.

Clay, Gemma. "Purity, Embodiment and the Immaterial Body: An Exploration of Buddhism at a Tibetan Monastery in Karnataka, South India." PhD diss., Brunel University, 2016.

Clemente, Adriano. "The sGra-Bla, Gods of the Ancestors of Gshen-Rab Mi-Bo According to the sGra Bla Go Bsang from the Gzi Brjid." Edited by Per Kvaerne. *Tibetan Studies: Proceedings of the 6th Seminar of the International Association for Tibetan Studies* 1 (1992) 127–36.

Conce, Edward. *The Perfection of Wisdom in Eight Thousand Lines and Its Verse Summary: Being the Aṣṭasāhasrikā-Prajñāpāramita and Prajñāpāramitā-Ratnaguṇasaṃcayagāthā*. Bolinas: Four Seasons Foundation, 1973.

Cook, Lowell. "Ju Mi Pham on Pure Land Doctrine and Practice." MA thesis, Centre for Buddhist Studies, Kathmandu University, 2016.

Corless, Roger J. "Pure Land and Pure Perspective: A Tantric Hermeneutic of Sukhāvatī." *The Pure Land* 6 (1989) 205–17.

Covell, Ralph R. "Buddhism and the Gospel Among the Peoples of China History." *International Journal of Frontier Missions* 10 (1993) 131–40.

Cozens, Simon. "Shame Cultures, Fear Cultures, and Guilt Cultures: Reviewing the Evidence." *International Bulletin of Mission Research* 42 (2018) 326–36.

———. "What Do We Mean by the Term 'Shame Culture'?" *Australian Journal of Mission Studies* 12 (2017).

Cozens, Simon, and Christoph Ochs. "Putting the Shameful Body to Death: Some Critiques and a Way Forward in the Soteriology of Shame." *Transformation* 36 (2019) 233–45.
Croft, William. "The Role of Domains in the Interpretation of Metaphors and Metonymies." In *Metaphor and Metonymy in Comparison and Contrast*, 161–206. Berlin: de Gruyter Mouton, 2003.
Cüppers, Christoph, and Per K. Sørensen. *Collection of Tibetan Proverbs and Sayings: Gems of Tibetan Wisdom and Wit*. Tibetan and Indo-Tibetan Studies 7. Stuttgart: Steiner, 1998.
Dag yig di'i sgrig tshan chung, ed. *Dag Yig Gsar Bsgrigs [New Spelling Dictionary]*. Xining: mtsho sngon mi rigs dpe skrun khang [Qinghai Printing Press], 1994.
Dale, Moyra. "Ritual Purity and Defilement: What Place Does It Have?" *Webzine* 2.1 (2018) 1–16.
Dalton, Jacob P. "A Crisis of Doxography: How Tibetans Organized Tantra during the 8th–12th Centuries." *Journal of the International Association of Buddhist Studies* (2005) 115–81.
———. "The Questions and Answers of Vajrasattva." In *Yoga in Practice*, edited by David Gordon White, 185–203. Princeton Readings in Religions. Princeton: Princeton University Press, 2011.
———. *The Taming of the Demons: Violence and Liberation in Tibetan Buddhism*. New Haven: Yale University Press, 2011.
"Dam Pa'i Chos Pad Ma Dkar Po Zhes Bya Ba Theg Pa Chen Po'i Mdo [The Sutra of the White Lotus of the Holy Dharma]." n.d. TWE, https://tibetan.works/etext/reader.php?collection=kangyur&index=116.
Daniels, Christine. "Defilement and Purification: Tibetan Buddhist Pilgrims at Bodhnath, Nepal." PhD diss., Oxford University, 1994.
Das, Sarat Chandra. *Tibetan-English Dictionary*. 1902. Reprint, Delhi: Book Faith India, 2000.
Davidson, Ronald M. "Hidden Realms and Pure Abodes: Central Asian Buddhism as Frontier Religion in the Literature of India, Nepal, and Tibet." *Pacific World: Journal of the Institute of Buddhist Studies* (2002) 153–81.
———. "Studies in Dharani Literature I: Revisiting the Meaning of the Term Dharani." *Journal of Indian Philosophy* 37 (2009) 97–147.
———. "Studies in Dhāraṇī Literature II: Pragmatics of Dhāraṇīs." *Bulletin of the School of Oriental and African Studies* 77 (2014) 5–61.
Davidson, Ronald M, and Christian Wedemeyer, eds. *Tibetan Buddhist Literature and Praxis: Studies in Its Formative Period, 900–1400 Proceedings of the Xth Seminar of the International Association for Tibetan Studies*. Leiden: Brill, 2006.
Day, Sophie. "Embodying Spirits: Village Oracles and Possession Ritual in Ladakh, North India." PhD diss., London University, 1989.
Decleer, Hubert. "Reviewed Work: Tibetan Literature: Studies in Genre Essays in Honor of Geshe Lhundup Sopa." Edited by J.I. Cabezón and R.R. Jackson. *The Tibet Journal* 23 (1998) 67–106.
Dege Kangyur, n.d. Translating the Words of Buddha, https://read.84000.co/section/O1JC11494.html.
Dennis, Geoffrey W. "Purity and Transformation: The Mimetic Performance of Scriptural Texts in the Ritual of Taharah." *Journal of Ritual Studies* 26 (2012) 51–64.
Denwood, Philip. *Tibetan*. Amsterdam: Benjamins, 1999.

BIBLIOGRAPHY

deSilva, David A. *Honor, Patronage, Kinship & Purity: Unlocking New Testament Culture.* Downers Grove, IL: InterVarsity, 2000.

"Dbe Ldan Gyi Snying Po [The Essence of Sukhavati]," n.d. TWE, https://tibetan.works/etext/reader.php?collection=kangyur&index=484.

Dge 'dun 'od zer, ed. *gto rigs phyogs bsgrigs [A Collection of Ritual Instructional Manuals].* mtsho snong mi rigs dpe skrun khan [Qinghai Printing Press], n.d.

Diemberger, Hildegard. "Blood, Sperm, Soul and the Mountain. Gender Relations, Kinship and Cosmovision among the Khumbo (NE Nepal)." In *Gendered Anthropology*, edited by Teresa del Valle, 88–127. London: Routledge, 1993.

———. "Lovanga (Lo 'bangs Pa?) Lama and Lhaven (Lha Bon): Historical Background, Syncretism and Social Relevance of Religious Traditions among the Khumbo (East Nepal)." In *Proceedings of the 5th Seminar of the International Association of Tibetan Studies Narita 1989*, edited by Ihara Shoren and Yamaguchi Zuiho, 421–33. Narita-shi: Naritasan Shinshoji, 1992.

DiFransico, Lesley R. "Washing Away Sin: An Old Testament Metaphor and Its Influence." PhD diss., Catholic University of America, 2014.

Dilgo Khyentse Tashi Peljor. "rDor Sems Rgyun Khyer Mdor Bsdus Bzhugs [A Concise Daily Practice of Vajrasattva]." In *The Collected Writings of Skyabs-Rje Dil-Mgo Mkhyen-Brtse Rin-Po-Che*, 113–14. Delhi: Shechen Publications, 1991. BDRC, https://library.bdrc.io/show/bdr:MW21809_0465AA.

"Dkon Mchog Gi Rten La Bskor Ba'i Gzungs [The Incantation for Circumambulation of the Three Jewels]." n.d. https://tibetan.works/etext/reader.php?collection=kangyur&index=718.

Doctor, Andreas. *Tibetan Treasure Literature: Revelation, Tradition, and Accomplishment in Visionary Buddhism.* Ithaca, NY: Snow Lion, 2006.

Dodin, Thierry, and Heinz Rather, eds. *Imagining Tibet Perceptions, Projections, and Fantasies.* Boston: Wisdom Publications, 2002.

Dorje, Khakhyab. *'od Dpag Med Gsol Bdebs Bzhugs [A Prayer to Buddha Amitābha]*, n.d. Lotsawa House, https://www.lotsawahouse.org/bo/tibetan-masters/fifteenth-karmapa/amitabha-prayer.

———. *'Phags Mchog Spyan Ras Gzigs Kyi Bsgom Bzlas 'Gro Don Mkha' Khyab Ma'i Zin Bris Nyung Bsdus 'gro Don Char Rgyun Zhes Bya Ba Bzhugs so [The Perpetual Rain of Benefit to All Beings—A Brief Commentary on a Meditation and Recitation to the Great Compassionate One, the All-Pervading Benefits to All Beings]*, n.d. BDRC, https://library.bdrc.io/show/bdr:MW20749_EFC7FD.

Dorje, Migyur. "Rmi Lam Bzung Ba'i Gsol 'bebs [Beholding Amitā Bha in Dreams]," n.d. Lotsawa House, https://www.lotsawahouse.org/bo/tibetan-masters/terton-mingyur-dorje/dream-prayer.

———. *Smon Lam Bsdus Pa Bzhugs [Condensed Sukhavati Aspiration].* n.d. Lotsawa House. https://www.lotsawahouse.org/bo/tibetan-masters/terton-mingyur-dorje/brief-sukhavati-aspiration.

Douglas, Mary. *Purity and Danger: An Analysis of Concepts of Pollution and Taboo.* 1966. Reprint, New York: Routledge, 2001.

Dowman, Keith. *Everything Is Light: The Circle of Total Illumination.* USA: Dzogchen Now!, 2017.

———. *The Flight of the Garuda: The Dzogchen Tradition of Tibetan Buddhism.* Boston: Wisdom, 1994.

BIBLIOGRAPHY

"dPal 'khor Lo Sdom Pa'i Dag Pa Gsum Gyi Rnal 'byor [The Heruka Yoga of Triple Purification]." In *Dge-Lugs-Pa'i Chos Spyod Phyogs Bsgrigs [A Collection of Gelukpa Religious Practices]*, 166–74. Zixing: mTsho sngon mi rigs dpe skrun khang, 1995. BDRC, https://library.bdrc.io/show/bdr:MW19999_8EDE2E.

Dragpa, Panchen Sonam. *Overview of Buddhist Tantra: General Presentation of the Classes of Tantra, Captivating the Minds of the Fortunate Ones (Rgyud Sde Spyi'i Rnam Par Bzhag Pa Skal Bzang Gi Yid 'phrog Ces Bya Ba Bzhugs So)*. Translated by Martin J. Boord and Losang Norbu Tsonawa. Dharamsala: Dharamsala: Library of Tibetan Works and Archives, 1996.

Drakpa, Geshe Palden. *Freeing Yourself from the Cycle*. Translated by Tenzin Gyaltsen. Dharamsala: Library of Tibetan Works & Archives, 2013.

Dreyfus, Georges B. J. *The Sound of Two Hands Clapping: The Education of a Tibetan Buddhist Monk*. Berkeley: University of California Press, 2003.

Dstan 'dzin dge legs, ed. *Bod Kyi Dmangs Srol Gces Btus [A Collection of Beloved Tibetan Folk Traditions]*. Beijing: mi rigs dpe skrun khan [Nationalities Press], 1999.

Duff, Lotsawa Tony, and Peter Schaffranek. *The Illuminator Tibetan-English Dictionary*, 4.20. Padma Karpo Translation Committee, 2003.

Dung dkar blo bzang 'phrin las. *Dung Dkar Tshig Mdzod Chen Mo [Dung Dkar's Great Dictionary]*. Beijing: krung go'i bod rig pa dpe skrun khang [China's Tibetology Press], 2002.

Dunn, James D.G. "Jesus and Purity: An Ongoing Debate." *New Testament Studies* 48 (2002) 449–67.

Duschinsky, Robbie. "Recognizing Secular Defilement: Douglas, Durkheim and Housework." *History and Anthropology* 25 (2014) 553–70.

Dye, Wayne. "Toward a Cross-Cultural Definition of Sin." *Missiology* 4 (1976) 27–41.

Dye, Wayne, and Danielle Zachariah. "Five Key Questions: What Hearers Always Want to Know as They Consider the Gospel." *International Journal of Frontier Missiology* 35.4 (2018) 185–93.

Dyrness, William. "Can We Do Theology from Below? A Theological Framework for Indigenous Theologies." *International Journal of Frontier Missiology* 35.2 (2018) 53–60.

Eimer, Helmut, and David Germano, eds. *The Many Canons of Tibetan Buddhism: PIATS 2000: Tibetan Studies: Proceedings of the Ninth Seminar of the International Association for Tibetan Studies, Leiden 2000*. Brill's Tibetan Studies Library 2/10. Leiden: Brill, 2002.

Ekvall, Robert B. *Religious Observances in Tibet: Patterns and Function*. Chicago: University of Chicago Press, 1964.

———. "The Tibetan Self-Image." In *The History of Tibet*, edited by Alex McKay, 3:629–34. London: Rutledge Curzon, 2003.

Elliston, Edgar J. *Introduction to Missiological Research Design*. Pasadena, CA: William Carey Library, 2011.

Epstein, David G. "Sherpa Purity: Down to Earth?" *American Anthropologist* 76 (1974) 341–42.

Epstein, Lawrence. "Causation in Tibetan Religion: Duality and Its Transformations." PhD diss., University of Washington, 1977.

Epstein, Lawrence, and Peng Wenbin. "Ritual, Ethnicity, and Generational Identity." In *Buddhism in Contemporary Tibet: Religious Revival and Cultural Identity*, edited by Melvyn C. Goldstein and Matthew T. Kapstein, 120–38. Berkeley: University of California Press, 1998.

BIBLIOGRAPHY

Farrow, George W., and I. Menon. *The Concealed Essence of the Hevajra Tantra: With the Commentary Yogaratnamala*. Delhi: Motilal Banarsidass, 2001.

Feder, Yitzhaq. "Defilement, Disgust, and Disease: The Experiential Basis of Hittite and Akkadian Terms for Impurity." *Journal of American Oriental Society* 136 (2016) 99–116.

———. "The Semantics of Purity in the Ancient Near East: Lexical Meaning as a Projection of Embodied Experience." *Journal of Ancient Near Eastern Religions* 14 (2014) 87–113.

Fjeld, Heidi. *Commoners and Nobles: Hereditary Divisions in Tibet*. Nordic Institute of Asian Studies Monograph Series 96. Copenhagen: NIAS, 2005.

———. "Pollution and Social Networks in Contemporary Rural Tibet." In *Seminar of the IATS, 2003. Vol. 11: Tibetan Modernities: Notes from the Field on Cultural and Social Change*, edited by Robert Barnett and Ronald Schwartz, 113–37. Brill's Tibetan Studies Library 11.Leiden: Brill, 2008.

Flemming, Dean E. *Contextualization in the New Testament: Patterns for Theology and Mission*. Downers Grove, IL: InterVarsity, 2005.

Flood, Gavin. "The Purification of the Body in Tantric Ritual Representation." *Indo-Iranian Journal* 45 (2002) 25–43.

Francke, A. H. "The Meaning of the 'Om-Mani-Padme-Hum' Formula." *The Journal of the Royal Asiatic Society of Great Britain and Ireland* 47 (1915) 397–404.

Frevel, Christian, and Christophe Nihan, eds. *Purity and the Forming of Religious Traditions in the Ancient Mediterranean World and Ancient Judaism*. Dynamics in the History of Religion 3. Leiden: Brill, 2013.

Gampo, Songtsen. *Ma Ṇi Bka' 'bum [Mani Kabum, Vol. 2, Second Edition]*. Par gzhi 2. Vol. 2. 2 vols. Gangs Can Khyad nor Dpe Tshogs. Lhasa: Bod ljongs mi dmangs dpe skrun khang [Lhasa: Tibet People's Press], 2013.

———. "Mi Chos Gtsang Ma Bcu Drug [The Sixteen Codes of Pure Conduct] (c. Seventh Century AD)." In *Skad yig deb dang po [Language Book One]*, 8–9. Lhasa: bod ljong mi dmangs dpe skrun khang [Tibet People's Press], 1989.

Gayley, Holly. "Revisiting the 'Secret Consort'(*gsang yum*) in Tibetan Buddhism." *Religions* 9.6 (2018) 179–200.

Gega, Lama. *Principles of Tibetan Art: Illustrations and Explanations of Buddhist Iconography and Iconometry According to the Karma Gardri School*. Antwerpen: Kunchab Publications, Tibetan Institute, 1990.

Georges, Jayson. *The 3D Gospel: Ministry in Guilt, Shame, and Fear Cultures*. Amazon Digital Services, Inc., 2014.

Georges, Jayson, and Mark D. Baker. *Ministering in Honor-Shame Cultures: Biblical Foundations and Practical Essentials*. Downers Grove, IL: InterVarsity, 2016.

Gergan, Josef. *A Thousand Tibetan Proverbs and Wise Sayings*. Kathmandu: Global Printers, 1991.

Germano, David. "The Seven Descents and the Early History of Rnying Ma Transmissions." In *The Many Canons of Tibetan Buddhism. PIATS 2000: Tibetan Studies: Proceedings of the Ninth Seminar of the International Association for Tibetan Studies, Leiden 2000*, edited by Helmut Eimer and David Germano, 225–63. Brill's Tibetan Studies Library 2/10. Leiden: Brill, 2002.

Gerner, Manfred. *Chakzampa Thangtong Gyalpo: Architect, Philosopher and Iron Chain Bridge Builder*. Bhutan: Centre for Bhutan Studies, 2007.

BIBLIOGRAPHY

Ghose, Lynken. "Karma and the Possibility of Purification: An Ethical and Psychological Analysis of the Doctrine of Karma in Buddhism." *Journal of Religious Ethics* 35 (2007) 259–90.

Gispert-Sauch, G. "Desideri and Tibet." *The Tibet Journal* 15.2 (1990) 29–39.

Goldstein, Melvyn C. "Review of Sherpas through Their Rituals by Sherry Ortner." *Journal of the American Oriental Society*, April 1, 1980.

———. "The Revival of Monastic Life in Drepung Monastery." In *Buddhism in Contemporary Tibet: Religious Revival and Cultural Identity*, 15–52. Berkeley: University of California Press, 1998.

Goldstein, Melvyn C., and Matthew T. Kapstein, eds. *Buddhism in Contemporary Tibet: Religious Revival and Cultural Identity*. Berkeley: University of California Press, 1998.

Goldstein, Melvyn C., T. N. Shelling, and J. T. Surkhang. *The New Tibetan-English Dictionary of Modern Tibetan*. Berkeley: University of California Press, 2001.

Gomez, Luis O. "Contributions to the Methodological Clarification of Interfaith Dialogue Among Buddhists and Christians." In *The Cross and the Lotus: Christianity and Buddhism in Dialogue*, edited by G.W. Houston, 127–208. Delhi: Motilal Banarsidass, 1985.

Gonsalez, David, trans. *The Chakrasamvara Root Tantra: The Speech of Glorious Heruka*. Somerville, MA: Wisdom, 2020.

Goodman, Steven D., and Ronald M. Davidson, eds. *Tibetan Buddhism: Reason and Revelation*. Albany: State University of New York Press, 1992.

Gouin, Margaret. *Tibetan Rituals of Death: Buddhist Funerary Practices*. Routledge Critical Studies in Buddhism. New York: Routledge, 2010.

Govinda, Lama Anagarika. *Foundations of Tibetan Mysticism According to the Esoteric Teachings of the Great Mantra Om Mani Padme Hum*. London: Rider, 1969.

———. "A Tibetan Buddhist Looks at Christianity." In *The Cross and the Lotus: Christianity and Buddhism in Dialogue*, edited by G.W. Houston, 121–25. Delhi: Motilal Banarsidass, 1985.

Gray, David B. *The Cakrasamvara Tantra (The Discourse of Sri Heruka): A Study and Annotated Translation*. Somerville, MA: Wisdom, 2019.

———. "Compassionate Violence? On the Ethical Implications of Tantric Buddhist Ritual." *Journal of Buddhist Ethics* 14 (2007) 239–71.

———. "On Supreme Bliss: A Study of the History and Interpretation of the 'Cakrasamvara Tantra.'" PhD diss., Columbia University, 2001.

———. "The Purification of Heruka: On the Transmission of a Controversial Buddhist Tradition to Tibet." In *Tantric Traditions in Transmission and Translation*, edited by David B. Gray and Ryan Richard Overby, 230–56. New York: Oxford University Press, 2016.

———. "Skull Imagery and Skull Magic." *Pacific World: Journal of the Institute of Buddhist Studies*, 2006, 21–39.

Gray, David B., and Ryan Richard Overbey, eds. *Tantric Traditions in Transmission and Translation*. New York: Oxford University Press, 2016.

Gung Thang. "'khor Lo'i Rnam Gzhag Mdor Bsdus Bzhugs [A Short Treatise of Prayer Wheels]," n.d. BDRC, https://library.bdrc.io/show/bdr:MW22112_3B944E.

"gSo Sbyong Gi Gzhi [The Basis for Restoration and Purification]." In *The Sde-Dge Mtshal-Par Bka'-'gyur: A Facsimile Edition of The 18th Century Redaction of Si-Tu Chos-Kyi-'byuṅ-Gnas /Prepared Under The Direction Of H.H The 16th Rgyal-Dbaṅ Karma-Pa*. Delhi: Delhi karmapae chodhey gyalwae sungrab partun khang, n.d. BDRC. https://library.bdrc.io/show/bdr:MW22084_0001-2.

Gyalchok, Shonu, and Konchok Gyaltsen. *Mind Training: The Great Collection*. Vol. 1. Translated by Thupten Jinpa. Boston: Simon & Schuster, 2014.

Gyatso, Geshe Jampa. *Purification in Tibetan Buddhism: The Practice of the Thirty-Five Confession Buddhas*. Edited by Joan Nicell. Somerville, MA: Wisdom, Kindle Edition, 2016.

Gyatso, Geshe Kelsang. *The Bodhisattva Vow: The Essential Practices of Mahayana Buddhism*. London: Tharpa Publications, 1991.

———. *Essence of Vajrayana: The Highest Yoga Tantra Practice of Heruka Body Mandala*. Delhi: Motilal Banarsidass, 1997.

———. *Guide to Dakini Land: The Highest Yoga Tantra Practice of Buddha Vajrayogini*. London: Tharpa Publications, 1991.

———. *The New Guide to Dakini Land—the Highest Yoga Tantra Practice of Buddha Vajrayogini*. London: Tharpa Publications, 2012.

Gyatso, Janet. "Genre, Authorship, and Transmission in Visionary Buddhism: The Literary Traditions of Thang-stongrGyal-Po." In *Tibetan Buddhism: Reason and Revelation*, edited by Steven D. Goodman and Ronald M. Davidson, 95–106. SUNY Series in Buddhist Studies. Albany: State University of New York Press, 1992.

———. "A Literary Transmission of the Traditions of Thang-Stong rGyal-Po: A Study of Visionary Buddhism in Tibet." PhD diss., University of California, Berkeley, 1981.

Halkias, Georgios T. *Luminous Bliss: A Religious History of Pure Land Literature in Tibet*. Pure Land Buddhist Studies. Honolulu: University of Hawaii Press, 2012.

———. "Tibetan Buddhism Registered: A Catalogue from the Imperial Court of 'Phang Thang." *Eastern Buddhist* 36.1–2 (2004) 46–105.

———. "Visions of the Pure Land from the Mind Treasury of Namchö Migyur Dorje." In *Pure Lands in Asian Texts and Contexts*, 139–54. Pure Land Buddhist Studies. Honolulu: University of Hawaii Press, 2019.

Halkias, Georgios T., and Richard K. Payne, eds. *Pure Lands in Asian Texts and Contexts: An Anthology*. Pure Land Buddhist Studies. Honolulu: University of Hawaii Press, 2019.

Harrer, Heinrich. *Seven Years in Tibet*. London: Paladin, 1953.

Hattaway, Paul. *Peoples of the Buddhist World: A Christian Prayer Diary*. Pasadena, CA: William Carey Library, 2013.

———. *Tibet: The Roof of the World*. London: SPCK, 2020.

Hebrew Lexicon: https://biblehub.com/hebrew/

Hendry, Joy. *An Introduction to Social Anthropology: Sharing Our Worlds*. London: Palgrave, 2016.

Herrmann-Pfandt, Adelheid. "The Lhan Kar Ma as a Source for the History of Tantric Buddhism." In *The Many Canons of Tibetan Buddhism. PIATS 2000: Tibetan Studies: Proceedings of the Ninth Seminar of the International Association for Tibetan Studies, Leiden 2000*, edited by Helmut Eimer and David Germano, 129–49. Brill's Tibetan Studies Library 2/10. Leiden: Brill, 2002.

Hibbert, Richard Y. "Defilement and Cleansing: A Possible Approach to Christian Encounter with Muslims." *Missiology* 36 (2008) 343–55.

Hibbert, Richard Y., and Evelyn Hibbert. "Contextualising Sin for Cross-Cultural Evangelism." *Missiology* 42 (2014) 309–21.

Hidas, Gergely. "Dhāraṇī Sūtras." In *Brill's Encyclopedia of Buddhism*. Vol. 1, *Literature and Languages*, edited by J. Silk, O. von Hinüber, and V. Eltschinger, 129–37. Leiden: Brill, 2015.

Hiebert, Paul G. "Clean and Dirty: Cross-Cultural Misunderstandings in India." *Evangelical Missions Quarterly* 44 (2008) 90–92.
Hiebert, Paul G., R. Daniel Shaw, and Tite Tienou. *Understanding Folk Religion: A Christian Response to Popular Beliefs and Practices*. Grand Rapids: Baker, 1999.
Hilton, James. *Lost Horizon*. London: Simon & Schuster, 1933.
Holmén, Tom. "Jesus and the Purity Paradigm." In *Handbook for the Study of the Historical Jesus*, edited by Tom Holmén and Stanley E. Porter, 2709–44. 4 vols. Leiden: Brill, 2011.
Holy Bible: English Standard Version. Wheaton, IL: Crossway Bibles, 2001.
Holy Bible: New Living Translation. Carol Stream, IL: Tyndale, 2008.
Hopkins, Jeffrey. *Meditation on Emptiness*. Boston: Wisdom, 1997.
Hopkirk, Peter. *Trespassers on the Roof of the World: The Race for Lhasa*. Oxford: Oxford University Press, 1982.
Hor Khang, Bsod Nams, ed. *Bod kyi dtam dpe phyogs bsgrigs [A Collection of Tibetan Proverbs]*. Lhasa: bod ljongs mi dmangs dpe skrun khang [Tibet People's Press], 2004.
Houston, G.W. "Jesus and His Missionaries in Tibet." *The Tibet Journal* 16.4 (1991) 8–27.
Huber, Toni. *The Cult of Pure Crystal Mountain: Popular Pilgrimage and Visionary Landscape in Southeast Tibet*. New York: Oxford University Press, 1999.
———. "Putting the Gnas Back into Gnas-Skor: Rethinking Tibetan Buddhist Pilgrimage Practice." *The Tibet Journal* 19.2 (1994) 23–60.
Huber, Toni, and Tsepak Rigzin. "A Tibetan Guide for Pilgrimage to Ti-Se (Mount Kailas) and mTsho Ma-Pham (Lake Manasarovar)." In *Sacred Spaces and Powerful Places in Tibetan Culture: A Collection of Essays*, edited by Toni Huber, 125–53. Dharamsala: Library of Tibetan Works and Archives, 1999.
Inagaki, Hisao, and Harold Stewart. *The Three Pure Land Sutras*. Berkeley: Numata Center for Buddhist Translation and Research, 2003.
'jam dbyangs mkhyen brtse chos kyi blo gros. "rDor Sems Bsgom Bzlas Mdor Bsdus [A Concise Vajrasattva Visualization and Mantra Recitation]," n.d. Lotsawa House, https://www.lotsawahouse.org/bo/tibetan-masters/jamyang-khyentse-chokyi-lodro/vajrasattva-visualization-recitation.
Jäschke, Heinrich August. *A Tibetan-English Dictionary*. 1881. Reprint, Delhi: Motilal Banarsidass Publishers, 1995.
Jaspert, Nikolas. "An Introduction to Discourses of Purity in Transcultural Perspective." In *Discourses of Purity in Transcultural Perspective (300–1600)*, edited by Matthias Bley, Nikolas Jaspert, and Stefan Köck, 1–20. Dynamics in the History of Religion 7. Leiden: Brill, 2015.
Jenkins, Philip. *The Lost History of Christianity: The Thousand-Year Golden Age of the Church in the Middle East, Africa, and Asia-and How It Died*. New York: HarperOne, 2008.
Kapstein, Matthew T. "A Pilgrimage of Rebirth Reborn: The 1992 Celebration of the Drigung Powa Chenmo." In *Buddhism in Contemporary Tibet: Religious Revival and Cultural Identity*, edited by Melvin Goldstein and Matthew T. Kapstein, 95–119. Los Angeles: University of California Press, 1998.
———. "Pure Land Buddhism in Tibet?" In *Approaching the Land of Bliss Religious Praxis in the Cult of Amitābha*, edited by Richard K. Payne and Kenneth K. Tanaka, 16–51. Studies in East Asian Buddhism 17. Honolulu: University of Hawaii Press, 2004.

———. "Remarks on the Mani'bka-'bum and the Cult of Avalokitesvara in Tibet." In *Tibetan Buddhism: Reason and Revelation*, edited by Steven D. Goodman and Ronald M. Davidson, 79–92. SUNY Series in Buddhist Studies. Albany: State University of New York Press, 1992.

———. "The Purificatory Gem and Its Cleansing: A Late Tibetan Polemical Discussion of Apocryphal Texts." *History of Religions* 28 (1989) 217–44.

———. "The Royal Way of Supreme Compassion." In *Religions of Tibet in Practice*, edited by Donald S. Lopez, 69–76. Princeton Readings in Religions. Princeton: Princeton University Press, 1997.

———. *The Tibetan Assimilation of Buddhism: Conversion, Contestation, and Memory*. New York: Oxford University Press, 2000.

———. *Tibetan Buddhism: A Very Short Introduction*. New York: Oxford University Press, 2013.

———. *The Tibetans*. Peoples of Asia. Malden, MA: Wiley, 2013.

Karmapa Texts: https://www.translating-karmapas.org/.

Karmay, Samten Gyaltsen. *The Great Perfection (rDzogs Chen): A Philosophical and Meditative Teaching of Tibetan Buddhism*. Brill's Tibetan Studies Library 11. Leiden: Brill, 2007.

———. "The Local Deities and the Juniper Tree: A Ritual for Purification (Bsang)." In *The Arrow and the Spindle: Studies in History, Myths, Rituals and Beliefs in Tibet*, 380–412. Kathmandu, Nepal: Mandala Book Point, 1998.

Karmay, Samten Gyaltsen, and Yasuhiko Nagano. *New Horizons in Bon Studies*. Vol. 2. National Museum of Ethnology, 2000.

———. *A Survey of Bonpo Monasteries and Temples in Tibet and the Himalaya*. Osaka: National Museum of Ethnology, 2003.

Kazen, Thomas. "Dirt and Disgust: Body and Morality in Biblical Purity Laws." In *Perspectives on Purity and Purification in the Bible*, edited by Baruch J. Schwartz, David P. Wright, Jeffery Stackert, and Naphtali S. Meshel, 43–64. Library of Biblical Studies. New York: T. & T. Clark, 2008.

———. *Jesus and Purity Halakhah: Was Jesus Indifferent to Impurity?* Rev. ed. Vol. 2. Winona Lake IN: Eisenbrauns, 2010.

———. "Purity/Impurity." In *Vocabulary for the Study of Religion*, edited by Robert Alan Segal and Kocku von Stuckrad. 3 vols. Leiden: Brill, 2015.

Keenan, John P. "Original Purity and the Focus of Early Yogācāra." *Journal of the International Association of Buddhist Studies* 5 (1982) 7–18.

Khyentse, Dilgo. *Primordial Purity: Oral Instructions on the Three Words That Strike the Vital Point*. Boulder, CO: Shambhala, 2016.

Khyentse, Dzongsar Jamyang. *Not for Happiness: A Guide to the so-Called Preliminary Practices*. Boston: Shambhala, 2012.

Kilty, Gavin, trans. *The Splendor of an Autumn Moon: The Devotional Verse of Tsongkhapa*. Somerville, MA: Wisdom, 2001.

Kipling, Rudyard. *Kim*. United Kingdom: Wordsworth Editions, 1994.

Köck, Stefan, Nikolas Jaspert, and Matthias Bley, eds. *Discourses of Purity in Transcultural Perspective (300–1600)*. Dynamics in the History of Religion 7. Boston: Brill, 2015.

Kohn, Richard J. "An Offering of Torma." In *Religions of Tibet in Practice*, 255–65. Princeton Readings in Religions. Princeton: Princeton University Press, 1997.

Kongtrul, Jamgon. *The Torch of Certainty*. Translated by Judith Hanson. Boston: Shambhala, 1977.

BIBLIOGRAPHY

Kun-bzaṅ-'gro-'dul. "rDo Rje Sems Dpa' Gsang Ba Dri Med Las Bshags Pa'i Snying Po Sbyong Ba'i Rgyal Po Bstan [From the Stainless Secret Vajrasattva—King of Purification, The Heart Essence of Confession]." In *gSung 'bum Kun Bzang 'gro 'dul Bde Chen Rdo Rje*. Mer Chen: Mer Chen Dgon Pa [Merchen Monastery], n.d. BDRC, https://library.bdrc.io/show/bdr:MW1GS61404_A38F5D.

Lakoff, George, and Mark Johnson. *Metaphors We Live By*. Chicago: University of Chicago Press, 2003.

Lama, The Dalai. *The Complete Foundation: The Systematic Approach to Training the Mind*. Edited by Christine Cox. Translated by Jinpa Thupten. Boulder, CO: Shambhala, 2018.

———. *The Essence of the Heart Sutra: The Dalai Lama's Heart of Wisdom Teachings*. Translated by Thupten Jinpa. Somerville, MA: Wisdom, 2005.

———. *An Introduction to Buddhism*. Translated by Geshe Thupten, Jinpa. Boulder, CO: Shambhala, 2018.

———. *The Kalachakra Tantra: Rite of Initiation: For the Stage of Generation*. Edited and translated by Jeffrey Hopkins. London: Wisdom, 1985.

———. *Kindness, Clarity, and Insight: The Fundamentals of Buddhist Thought and Practice*. Translated by Jeffrey Hopkins. Boulder, CO: Shambhala, 2020.

———. *My Tibet*. Berkeley: University of California Press, 1995.

———. *The World of Tibetan Buddhism: An Overview of Its Philosophy and Practice*. Translated by Geshe Thupten Jinpa. New York: Wisdom, 2005.

Lama, The Dalai, and Thubten Chodron. *Saṃsāra, Nirvāṇa, and Buddha Nature*. Somerville, MA: Wisdom, 2018.

Landaw, Jonathan, and Andy Weber. *Images of Enlightenment: Tibetan Art in Practice*. Ithaca, NY: Snow Lion, 2006.

Lemos, Tracy M. "Where There Is Dirt, Is There System? Revisiting Biblical Purity Constructions." *Journal for the Study of the Old Testament* 37 (2013) 265–94.

Lhasa Kangyur. *Tibetan Works*. n.d. https://tibetan.works/etext/?sub=two.

Lha Sa'i Dmangs Khrod Sgrung Gtam/ Stod Cha [Lhasa Folk Stories—Volume One]. Lhasa: Tibet People's Press, 2009.

Lhalungpa, Lobsang Phuntshok, trans. *The Life of Milarepa*. London: Penguin, 1979.

Lhundup, Tashhi. "Religious Symbolism in Ladakh with Special Reference to Three Important Buddhist Symbols." *The Tibet Journal* 43.1 (2018) 49–63.

Lim, David S., Steve Spaulding, and Paul H. De Neui, eds. *Sharing Jesus Effectively in the Buddhist World*. Pasadena, CA: William Carey Library, 2005.

Linrothe, Rob. "Mirror Image: Deity and Donor as Vajrasattva." *History of Religions* 54 (2014) 5–33.

Lobpön Dé Jé Gocha. "He Ru Ka'i Rnam Par Dag Pa." In *Tangyur Golden*, translated by Rinchen Zangpo and Lobpön Dé Jé Gocha. Tibet: [Snar Thang], n.d. BDRC, https://library.bdrc.io/show/bdr:MW23702_0000T200.

Lopez, Donald S., Jr. *Elaborations on Emptiness: Uses of the Heart Sūtra*. Princeton: Princeton University Press, 2016.

———. *The Heart Sutra Explained: Indian and Tibetan Commentaries*. SUNY Series in Buddhist Studies. Albany: State University of New York Press, 1988.

———. *Prisoners of Shangri-La: Tibetan Buddhism and the West*. Chicago: University of Chicago Press, 1998.

———. "A Rite for Restoring the Bodhisattva and Tantric Vows." In *Buddhism in Practice*, edited by Donald S. Lopez, Jr. 387–96. Princeton Readings in Religions. Princeton: Princeton University Press, 2015.

———, ed. *Religions of Tibet in Practice*. Princeton Readings in Religions. Princeton: Princeton University Press, 1997.

Lopez, Donald S., and Thupten Jinpa. *Dispelling the Darkness: A Jesuit's Quest for the Soul of Tibet*. Cambridge: Harvard University Press, 2017.

Losang, Kyabje Yonzin Trijang Dorje Chang, and Yeshe Tenzin Gyatso Pal Zangpo. "The Significance of the Six Syllable Mantra OM MA NI PAD ME HUM." *The Tibet Journal* 7 (1982) 3–10.

Lotsawa House. https://www.lotsawahouse.org/.

Maberly, Allan. *God Spoke Tibetan: The Epic Story of the Men Who Gave the Bible to Tibet, the Forbidden Land*. Orange, CA: Evangel Bible Translators, 1977.

Macdonald, Alexander. "Review of High Religion: A Cultural and Political History of Sherpa Buddhism by Sherry Ortner." *Journal of the International Association of Buddhist Studies* 14 (1991) 341–44.

Malina, Bruce J. *The New Testament World Insights from Cultural Anthropology*. 3rd ed. Louisville: Westminster John Knox, 2001.

Martin, Dan. "'Ol-Mo-Lung-Ring, the Original Holy Place." *The Tibet Journal* 20.1 (1995) 48–82.

———. "On the Origin and Significance of the Prayer Wheel According to Two Nineteenth-Century Tibetan Literary Sources." *Journal of the Tibet Society* 7 (1987) 13–29.

Matisoff, James A., Stephen P. Baron, and John B. Lowe. *Languages and Dialects of Tibeto-Burman*. Berkley: Sino-Tibetan Etymological Dictionary and Thesaurus Project, Center for South East Asia Studies, 1996.

Melnick, Alison, and Christopher Bell. "Maṇi Kambum." In *Tibetan Renaissance Seminar*, 2019.

Merrriam-Webster: https://www.merriam-webster.com.

Merz, Johannes. "The Culture Problem: How the Honor/Shame Issue Got the Wrong End of the Anthropological Stick." *Missiology* 48.2 (2020) 127–41.

Milgrom, Jacob. *Leviticus 1–16: A New Translation with Introduction and Commentary*. Anchor Bible 3. New York: Doubleday, 1991.

Miller, Beatrice Diamond. "Is There Tibetan Culture(s) without Buddhism?" In *Proceedings of the International Seminar on the Anthropology of Tibet and the Himalaya : September 21-28 1990 at the Ethnographic Museum of the University of Zurich*, edited by Charles Ramble et al., 222–28. Zurich: Völkerkundemuseum der Universität Zürich, 1993.

Miller, Roy Andrew. *Studies in the Grammatical Tradition in Tibet*. Amsterdam: Benjamins, 1976.

Mills, Martin A. *Identity, Ritual and State in Tibetan Buddhism: The Foundations of Authority in Gelukpa Monasticism*. RoutledgeCurzon Studies in Tantric Traditions. London: Routledge, 2003.

———. "Living in Time's Shadow: Pollution, Purification and Fractured Temporalities in Buddhist Ladakh." In *The Qualities of Time: Anthropological Approaches*, edited by Wendy James and Martin A. Mills, 349–66. Oxford: Berg, 2005.

Mischke, Werner, Samuel Chiang, and Steven C. Hawthorne. *The Global Gospel: Achieving Missional Impact in Our Multicultural World*. Scottsdale, AZ: Mission One, 2015.

Molk, David, and Tsering Wangdu. *Lion of Siddhas: The Life and Teachings of Padampa Sangye*. Ithaca, NY: Snow Lion, 2008.

Moon, W. Jay. *African Proverbs Reveal Christianity in Culture: A Narrative Portrayal of Builsa Proverbs Contextualizing Christianity in Ghana*. Vol. 5. Eugene, OR: Wipf & Stock Publishers, 2009.

Morrison, James E. "Christianity's Journey to the Roof of the World." In *Emerging Faith Lessons from Mission History in Asia*, edited by Paul H. de Neui, 16:175–86. Littleton, CO: William Carey, 2020.

———. "Sharing the Gospel with Tibetan Buddhists through the Cultural Paradigm of Pollution and Purity." In *Majority World Theologies Theologizing from Africa, Asia, Latin America, and the Ends of the Earth*, edited by Allen Yeh and Tite Tienou, 116–30. EMS 26. Littleton, CO: William Carey, 2018.

Müller, Roland. *Honor and Shame: Unlocking the Door*. Philadelphia: Xlibris Corp., 2000.

Mullin, Glenn H., trans. *The Dalai Lamas on Tantra*. Ithaca, NY: Snow Lion, 2006.

Naga, Sangye Tandar, and Tsepak Rigzin. *Tibetan Quadrisyllabics, Phrases and Idioms*. Dharamsala: Library of Tibetan Works and Archives, 1994.

Nagarjuna, Arya. "An Explanation of the Confessions of the Bodhisattva's Downfalls (Byang Chub Ltung Ba Bshags Pa'i 'grel Pa)." In *The Confession of Downfalls: The Confession Sutra, with Commentary by Arya Nagarjuna, The Practice of Vajrasattva with Sadhana: Supplemented by Verbally Transmitted Commentaries from Geshe Ngawang Dhargyey, Geshe Rabten, Geshe Khyentse, Thubten Zopa Rinpoche*, translated by Brian C. Beresford, 3–43. Dharamsala: Library of Tibetan Works and Archives, 1993.

Namdak, Tenzin. *Bonpo Dzogchen Teachings*. Kathmandu: Vajra, 2006.

Namgyal, Tseten. "Significance of 'Eight Traditional Tibetan Buddhist Auspicious Symbols/Emblems' (Bkra Shis Rtags Brgyad) in Day to Day Rite and Rituals." *The Tibet Journal* 41.2 (2016) 29–51.

Namihira, Emiko. "Pollution in the Folk Belief System." *Current Anthropology* 28 S4 (1987) S65–74.

Namkhai Norbu, Chogyal, and John Shane. *The Crystal and the Way of Light: Sutra, Tantra, and Dzogchen: The Teachings of Chogyal Namkhai Norbu*. New York: Routledge & Kegan Paul, 2000.

Nattier, Jan. "The Realm of Akṣobhya: A Missing Piece in the History of Pure Land Buddhism." *Journal of the International Association of Buddhist Studies* 23 (2000) 71–102.

Neusner, Jacob. *A History of the Mishnaic Law of Purities*. Studies in Judaism in Late Antiquity 21. Leiden: Brill, 1979.

———. "Idea of Purity in Ancient Judaism." *Journal of the American Academy of Religion* 43 (1975) 15–26.

New Testament—A Radiant Light to the Ends of the Earth, Modern Tibetan. Central Asia Publishing, 2018.

Neyrey, Jerome H. "Clean/Unclean, Pure/Polluted, and Holy/Profane: The Idea and System of Purity." In *The Social Sciences and New Testament Interpretation*, edited by Richard L. Rohrbaugh, 80–104. Peabody, MA: Hendrickson, 1996.

———. "The Idea of Purity in Mark's Gospel." *Semeia* 35 (1986) 91–128.

"Ngan Song Thams Cad Yongs Su Sbyong Ba'i Gzung [The Incantation That Purifies All Evil Rebirths]," n.d. BDRC, https://library.bdrc.io/show/bdr:MW22084_0782.

Nida, Eugene A. *Customs and Cultures: Anthropology for Christian Missions*. South Pasadena, CA: William Carey Library, 1975.

BIBLIOGRAPHY

Ortner, Sherry B. *High Religion: A Cultural and Political History of Sherpa Buddhism.* Princeton Studies in Culture/Power/History. Princeton: Princeton University Press, 1989.

———. "Sherpa Purity." *American Anthropologist* 75 (1973) 49–63.

———. *Sherpas Through Their Rituals.* Cambridge Studies in Cultural Systems 2. Cambridge: Cambridge University Press, 1978.

Ott, Craig. "The Power of Biblical Metaphors for the Contextualized Communication of the Gospel." *Missiology* 42 (2014) 357–74.

Padampa Sangye, and Dilgo Khyentse. *The Hundred Verses of Advice of Padampa Sangye.* New Delhi: Shechen, 2004.

Payne, Richard K., and Kenneth K. Tanaka, eds. *Approaching the Land of Bliss: Religious Praxis in the Cult of Amitābha.* Studies in East Asian Buddhism 17. Honolulu: University of Hawaii Press, 2004.

Pemba, Lhamo. *Tibetan Proverbs Bod-kyi-gtam-dpe.* Dharamsala: Library of Tibetan Works and Archives, 1996.

Pha Dampa Sangs rgyas. *Ding Ri Brgya Rtsa Ma [One Hundred Spiritual Instructions to the Tingri People].* Edited by David Kittay. Translated by Lozang Jamspal. Ladakh: Ladakh Ratnashridipika, 2011.

———. "Pha Dam Pa Sangs Rgyas Kyi Zhal Gdams Ding Ri Brgya Rtsa Ma [One Hundred Instructions to the People of Tingri]," n.d. BDRC, https://library.bdrc.io/show/bdr:MW20749_1A5D31.

"'phags Pa Bar Du Gcod Pa Thams Cad Rnam Par Sbyong Ba Zhes Bya Ba'i Gzungs [The Incantation That Purifies All Hindrances]," n.d. TWE, https://tibetan.works/etext/reader.php?collection=kangyur&index=564.

"'phags Pa Bde Ba Can Gyi Bkod Pa [Sukhavatiyuha Sutra—The Display of the Pure Land of Sukhavati]," n.d. TWE, https://tibetan.works/etext/reader.php?collection=kangyur&index=118.

"'phags Pa Dgongs Pa Nges Par 'Grel Pa Zhes Bya Ba Theg Pa Chen Po'i Mdo [The Sutra of the Explanation of Intentions]," n.d. TWE, https://tibetan.works/etext/reader.php?collection=kangyur&index=109.

"'phags Pa Las Kyi Sgrib Pa Rnam Par Dag Pa Zhes Bya Ba Theg Pa Chen Po'i Mdo [The Sutra of the Purification of Karmic Obscurations]," n.d. TWE, https://tibetan.works/etext/reader.php?collection=kangyur&index=219.

"'phags Pa Las Kyi Sgrib Pa Thams Cad Rnam Par Sbyong Ba Zhes Bya Ba'i Gzungs [The Incantation That Purifies All Karmic Obscurations]," n.d. TWE, https://tibetan.works/etext/reader.php?collection=kangyur&index=690.

"'phags Pa Ngan 'Gro Thams Cad Yongs Su Sbyong Ba Gtsug Tor Rnam Par Rgyal Ba Zhes Bya Ba'i Gzungs [The Incantation of the Crown of the Head of the Victorious Buddha That Purifies All Lower Rebirths]," n.d. TWE, https://tibetan.works/etext/reader.php?collection=kangyur&index=537.

'phags pa lha, and mdo sngags bstan pa'i nyi ma. *Bzhi Brgya Pa'i Rnam Bshad Lku Dbang Dgongs Rgyan [Text & Commentary on Aryadeva's Four Hundred Stanzas on the Middle Way].* Manipal, India: Ngagyur Nyingma Institute, 2017.

"'phags Pa Phung Po Gsum Pa Zhes Bya Ba Theg Pa Chen Po'i Mdo [The Exalted Mahayana Sutra of the Three Heaps]." In *gSung 'bum Blo Gros Grags Pa [The Collected Works of Lodro Drakpa].* ['dzam Thang, 'bar Thang], n.d. BDRC, https://library.bdrc.io/show/bdr:MW19762_F982D9.

BIBLIOGRAPHY

"'phags Pa Sgo Mtha' Yas Rnam Par Sbyong Ba Bstan Pa'i Le'ur Byas Pa [The Teaching on the Purification of the Infinite Gateways]," n.d. TWE, https://tibetan.works/etext/reader.php?collection=tengyur&index=2695.

"'phags Pa Sgo Mtha' Yas Pa Rnam Par Sbyong Ba Bstan Pa'i Le'u Zhes Bya Ba Theg Pa Chen Po'i Mdo [The Sutra of the Teaching of the Purification of the Limitless Gateways]," n.d. TWE, https://tibetan.works/etext/reader.php?collection=kangyur&index=46.

"'phags Pa Shes Rab Kyi Pha Rol Tu Phyin Pa Khri Pa Zhes Bya Ba Theg Pa Chen Po'i Mdo [The Sutra of the Perfection of Wisdom in Ten Thousand Lines]," n.d. TWE, https://tibetan.works/etext/reader.php?collection=kangyur&index=13.01.

'phags Pa Shes Rab Kyi Pha Rol Tu Phyin Pa Khri Pa Zhes Bya Ba Theg Pa Chen Po'i Mdo *[The Transcendent Perfection of Wisdom in Ten Thousand Lines]*. Vol. Degé Kangyur, 31 (shes phyin, ga), folios 1b–91a and vol 32 (shes phyin, nga), folios 92.b–397.a. Padmakara Translation Group, n.d. Translating the Words of Buddha, http://read.84000.co/translation/toh11.html.

"'phags Pa Spyan Ras Gzigs Kyi Snying Po [The Incantation of the Essence of Chenrezi]," n.d. TWE, https://tibetan.works/etext/reader.php?collection=kangyur&index=657.

"'phags Pa Ye Shes Ta La La Zhes Bya Ba'i Gzungs 'Gro Ba Thams Cad Yongs Su Sbyong [The Incantation of Yeshe Dalala That Purifies All Rebirths]," n.d. TWE, https://tibetan.works/etext/reader.php?collection=kangyur&index=725.

"'phags Pa Yon Tan Bsngags Pa Dpag Tu Med Pa Zhes Bya Ba'i Gzungs [The Incantation of Praise to the Glorious Eternal One]," n.d. TWE, https://tibetan.works/etext/reader.php?collection=kangyur&index=575.

"'phags Pa Za Ma Tog Bkod Pa Zhe Bya Ba Theg Pa Chen Po'i Mdo [Karandavyuha Sutra, The Basket's Display—A Noble Mahayana Sutra]," n.d. TWE, https://tibetan.works/etext/reader.php?collection=kangyur&index=119.

Phuntsho, Karma. *The History of Bhutan*. Haryana: Random House India, 2013.

Phuntsok, Chabpel Tseten. "The Deity Invocation Ritual and the Purification Rite of Incense Burning in Tibet." Translated by Thubten K. Rikey. *The Tibet Journal* 16.3 (1991) 3–27.

Phuntsok, Khenpo Yeshe. *Vajrasattva Meditation: An Illustrated Guide*. Somerville, MA: Wisdom, 2015.

Pomplun, Trent. *Jesuit on the Roof of the World: Ippolito Desideri's Mission to Tibet*. New York: Oxford University Press, 2010.

Powers, John. *Introduction to Tibetan Buddhism*. Ithaca, NY: Snow Lion, 2007.

Preston, James. "Purification." In *The Encyclopedia of Religion*, edited by Mircea Eliade, Vol. 12. New York: MacMillan, 1987.

Priest, Robert J. "Defilement, Moral Purity, and Transgressive Power: The Symbolism of Filth in Aguaruna Jivaro Culture." PhD diss., University of California, Berkeley, 1993.

———. "Missionary Elenctics: Conscience and Culture." *Missiology* 22, no. 3 (1994) 291–315.

Rabten, Geshe. *The Preliminary Practices of Tibetan Buddhism*. Burton, WA: Tusum Ling Publications, 1974.

Radcliffe-Brown, Alfred Reginald. *Structure and Function in Primitive Society: Essays and Addresses by AR Radcliffe-Brown*. Great Britain: University of Aberdeen, 1952.

Ramble, Charles. *The Navel of the Demoness: Tibetan Buddhism and Civil Religion in Highland Nepal*. New York: Oxford University Press, 2008.

Rampa, T. Lobsang. *The Third Eye*. New York: Doubleday, 1957.

BIBLIOGRAPHY

Rangjung Yeshe. *Rangjung Yeshe Tibetan-English Dharma Dictionary 3.0*. Rangjung Yeshe Publications, 2005.

"rDor Sems Kyi Bsgom Bzlas Mdor Bsdus [A Concise Meditational Practice of Vajrasattva]." In *gSung 'bum Dharma Bha Dra*, 745–52. [Dngul Chu Bla Brang] Ngulchu Estate, n.d. BDRC, https://library.bdrc.io/show/bdr:MW6493_678B21.

Rheingans, Jim, ed. *Tibetan Literary Genres, Texts, and Text Types: From Genre Classification to Transformation*. Leiden: Brill, 2015.

Richardson, Hugh Edward. *Ceremonies of the Lhasa Year*. Edited by Michael Aris. London: Serindia, 1993.

———. *High Peaks, Pure Earth: Collected Writings on Tibetan History and Culture = Rimtho sa-gtsang zhes-bya-ba Bod kyi lo-rgyus dang rig-gnas skor gsung thor-bu phyogs-gcig tu bsgrigs-pa*. Edited by Michael Aris. London: Serindia, 1998.

———. *Tibet and Its History*. Boulder, CO: Shambhala, 1984.

Richardus, Peter. "Selected Tibetan Proverbs." *The Tibet Journal* 14.3 (1989) 55–71.

Rigzin, Tsepak. *Festivals of Tibet*. Rev. ed. 2006. Dharamsala: Library of Tibetan Works and Archives, 1993.

Rinpoche, Dagyab Loden Sherap. *Buddhist Symbols in Tibetan Culture*. Boston: Wisdom, 1995.

Rinpoche, Dilgo Khyentse. *The Excellent Path to Enlightenment: Oral Teachings on the Root Text of Jamyang Khyentse Wangpo*. Translated by Padmakara Translation Group. Ithaca, NY: Shambhala, 1996.

Rinpoche, Dudjom. *The Nyingma School of Tibetan Buddhism: Its Fundamentals and History*. Translated by Gyurme Dorje and Matthew Kapstein. Somerville, MA: Wisdom, 1991.

Rinpoche, Geshe Nyima Dakpa. *Opening the Door to Bön*. Ithaca, NY: Snow Lion, 2005.

Rinpoche, Gyatrul, and Trinley Norbu Rinpoche. *Commentaries on the Practice of Vajrasattva*. Ashland, OR: Mirror of Wisdom, 1978.

Rinpoche, Lama Zopa. *A Chat About Heruka*. Boston: Lama Yeshe Wisdom Archive, 2000.

———. *Daily Purification: A Short Vajrasattva Practice*. Boston: Lama Yeshe Wisdom Archive, 2001.

———. *The Preliminary Practice of Prostrations to the Thirty-Five Confession Buddhas*. Portland, OR: Foundation for the Preservation of the Mahayana Tradition, 2016.

———. *The Wheel of Great Compassion: The Practice of the Prayer Wheel in Tibetan Buddhism*. Edited by Lorne Ladner. Boston: Wisdom, 2005.

Rinpoche, Lati, and Jeffrey Hopkins. *Death, Intermediate State and Rebirth in Tibetan Buddhism*. Ithaca, NY: Snow Lion, 1985.

Rinpoche, Mipham. *Bde Chen Zhing Gi Smon Lam Bzhugs so [Sukhavati Aspiration]*, n.d. Lotsawa House, https://www.lotsawahouse.org/bo/tibetan-masters/mipham/sukhavati-aspiration.

———. "dPal Ldan Bla Ma Rdo Rje Sems Dpa' La Brten Nas Nyams Grib Sbyong Thabs Bzhugs [Purifying the Pollution of Broken Vows by Adherence to Glorious Vajrasattva]." In *gSung 'bum Mi Pham Rgya Mtsho*, 458. Khreng Tu'u: [Gangs Can Rig Gzhung Dpe Rnying Myur Skyobs Lhan Tshogs], 2007. BDRC, https://library.bdrc.io/show/bdr:MW2DB16631_9ACF77.

Rinpoche, Patrul. *Kunzan Lama'i Shelung [The Words of My Perfect Teacher]*. Translated by Padmakara Translation Group. Boston: Shambhala, 1998.

Rinpoche, Patrul, and Dilgo Khyentse. *The Heart Treasure of the Enlightened Ones: The Practice of View, Meditation, and Action*. Boston: Shambhala, 1992.

———. "Thog Mtha' Bar Gsum Du Dge Ba'i Gtam Lta Sgom Spyod Gsum Nyams Len Dam Pa'i Snying nor Zhes Bya Ba Bzhugs so [A Complete Virtuous Discourse on the Doctrine, Meditation and Practice of the Sacred Heart Treasure]." In *The Heart Treasure of the Enlightened Ones*, 180–201. Boston: Shambhala, 1992.

Rinpoche, Sogyal. *The Tibetan Book of Living and Dying*. London: Random House, 2008.

Roche, Gerald. "Introduction: The Transformation of Tibet's Language Ecology in the Twenty-First Century." *International Journal of the Sociology of Language* 2017, no. 245 (2017) 1–35.

Roche, Gerald, and Hiroyuki Suzuki. "Tibet's Minority Languages: Diversity and Endangerment." *Modern Asian Studies* 52.4 (2018) 1227–78.

Roerich, George N. *The Blue Annals*. Vol. 2. Delhi: Motilal Banarsidass, 1949.

Roesler, Ulrike. "Classifying Literature or Organizing Knowledge? Some Considerations on Genre Classifications in Tibetan Literature." In *Tibetan Literary Genres, Texts, and Text Types*, 31–53. Leiden: Brill, 2015.

———. "The Kadampa: A Formative Movement of Tibetan Buddhism." In *Oxford Research Encyclopedia of Religion*, 2019.

Rolf, Eva Natanya. "Sacred Illusion: On Purity and Creation in Je Tsongkhapa's Philosophy of Tantra." PhD diss., University of Virginia, 2017.

Rozario, Santi, and Geoffrey Samuel. "Tibetan and Indian Ideas of Birth Pollution: Similarities and Contrasts." In *Daughters of Hariti: Childbirth and Female Healers in South and Southeast Asia*, edited by Santi Rozario and Geoffrey Samuel, 182–208. New York: Routledge, 2002.

Rwa yum skyabs, ed. *Gangs Ljongs Kyi Bsang Yig Ris Med Phyogs Sdeb 'dzam Gling Spyi Bsang [The Land of Snow's World Purification Non-Sectarian Collection of Incense Offering Texts]*. Par gzhi dang po. 1 vols. Bod Kyi Srol Rgyun Ngag Thog Rig Gnas Deb Phreng. Lhasa: bod ljongs mi dmangs dpe skrun khang [Tibet People's Press], 2015.

Sakya Pandita. *Legs Par Bshad Pa Ring Po Che'i Gter [A Treasury of Excellent Sayings]*. Edited by Lozang Jamspal. Leh, Ladakh, India: Ladakh Ratnashridipika, 2003.

———. *Ordinary Wisdom: Sakya Pandita's Treasury of Good Advice*. Translated by John T. Davenport. Boston: Wisdom, 2000.

———. "Phyag 'Tshal Ba'i Phan Yon [The Benefits and Advantages of Prostration]," n.d. https://www.gyalyongsachen.com/?p=6376.

———. "Phyag 'tshal Skabs 'Don Rgyu'i Smon Tshig [Aspiration Prayer While Prostrating]," n.d. Lotsawa House, https://www.lotsawahouse.org/bo/tibetan-masters/sakya-pandita/aspiration-while-prostrating.

———. *Sa Skya Legs Bshad Rtsa 'grel [Text and Commentary of Wise Sayings]*. Lhasa: bod ljongs mi dmangs dpe skrun khang [Tibet People's Press], 1979.

Sadler, Paul. "A Japanese Gospel Message." *Evangelical Missions Quarterly* 50, no. 1 (January 2014) 26–33.

Samuel, Geoffrey. *Civilized Shamans: Buddhism in Tibetan Societies*. Kathmandu, Nepal: Mandala Book Point, 2006.

———. *Introducing Tibetan Buddhism*. World Religions. New York: Routledge, 2012.

———. *Tibetan Buddhism—the eBook*. State College, PA: Journal of Buddhist Ethics Online, 2013.

Schaeffer, Kurtis R. *The Culture of the Book in Tibet*. New York: Columbia University Press, 2009.

Schaeffer, Kurtis R., Matthew T. Kapstein, and Gray Tuttle. *Sources of Tibetan Tradition*. New York: Columbia University Press, 2013.

BIBLIOGRAPHY

Schell, Orville. *Virtual Tibet: Searching for Shangri-La from the Himalayas to Hollywood.* New York: Owl, 2001.

Schicklgruber, Christian. "Grib: On the Significance of the Term in a Socio-Religious Context." In *Tibetan Studies. Proceedings of the 5th Seminar of the International Association for Tibetan Studies. Naritasan Shinshoji, Tokyo*, Buddhist Philosophy and Literature Vol. 1:723–34. Naritasan Shinshoji, 1992.

Schrempf, Mona. "Taming the Earth, Controlling the Cosmos: Transformation of Space in Tibetan Buddhist and Bon-Po Ritual Dance." In *Sacred Spaces and Powerful Places in Tibetan Culture*, edited by Toni Huber, 198–224. Dharamsala: The Library of Tibetan Works and Archives, 1999.

Sferra, Francesco. "The Concept of Purification in Some Texts of Late Indian Buddhism." *Journal of Indian Philosophy*, 1999, 83–103.

Shabkar Tsodruk Rangdrol. "Nyams Len Bsdus Don Gyi Glu [Concise Song of Praise]," n.d. Lotsawa House, https://www.lotsawahouse.org/bo/tibetan-masters/shabkar/short-song-of-practice.

———. "sNgon 'gro Nyung 'dus [Concise Preliminary]." In *Zhabs Dkar Tshogs Drug Rang Grol Gyi Bka' 'bum: The Collected Works Zhabs Dkar Tshogs Drug Rang Grol (1781 1851)*, 75–76. New Delhi: Shechen Publications, 2003. BDRC, https://library.bdrc.io/show/bdr:MW23893_5D1CC3.

"shAkya Thub Pa'i Snying Po'i Gzungs [The Incantation of the Essence of Buddha Shakyamuni]," n.d. TWE, https://tibetan.works/etext/reader.php?collection=kangyur&index=481.

Shantideva, Acharya. *A Guide to the Bodhisattva's Way of Life.* Translated by Stephen Batchelor. Dharamshala: Library of Tibetan Works and Archives, 1979.

Sherman, Gary D., and Gerald L. Clore. "The Color of Sin: White and Black Are Perceptual Symbols of Moral Purity and Pollution." *PSCI Psychological Science* 20, no. 8 (2009) 1019–25.

Shinohara, Koichi. *Spells, Images, and Mandalas: Tracing the Evolution of Esoteric Buddhist Rituals.* New York: Columbia University Press, 2014.

Shively, Elizabeth E. "Purification of the Body and the Reign of God in the Gospel of Mark." *The Journal of Theological Studies* 71, no. 1 (2020) 62–89.

Shneiderman, Sara. "Barbarians at the Border and Civilising Projects: Analysing Ethnic and National Identities in the Tibetan Context." *Tibetan Borderlands*, 2006, 9–34.

Si khron dpe skgrun tshogs pa, ed. *Zhal 'don Phyogs Bsgrigs [A Collection of Liturgies].* Chengdu: si khron dpe skrun khang [Sichuan Printing Press], 2006.

Silk, Jonathan A. "In Praise of His Mighty Name: A Tibetan Poem of Amitābha from Dunhuang." In *Pure Lands in Asian Texts and Contexts*, 496–539. Honolulu: University of Hawaii Press, 2019.

Simpson, William. *The Buddhist Praying-Wheel.* London: Macmillan, 1896.

Skad yig deb dang po [Language Book One]. Lhasa: bod ljong mi dmangs dpe skrun khang [Tibet People's Press], 1989.

Skad yig lo rim bdun pa smad cha [Language Book Seven]. Vol. 2. Lhasa: bod ljong mi dmangs dpe skrun khang [Tibet People's Press], 2005.

Skyid, Sa mtsho, and Gerald Roche. "Purity and Fortune in Phug Sde Village Rituals." *Asian Highlands Perspectives* 10 (2011) 231–84.

Skorupski, Tadeusz. "The Canonical Tantras of the New Schools." In *Tibetan Literature: Studies in Genre*, edited by José Ignacio Cabezón and Roger R Jackson, 95–110. Ithaca, NY: Snow Lion, 1996.

———. "Consciousness and Luminosity in Indian and Tibetan Buddhism." *Buddhist Philosophy and Meditation Practice*, 2012, 43–64.

———. "A Tibetan Prayer for Rebirth in the Sukhāvatī." *The Pure Land: Journal of Pure Land Buddhism* 12 (1995) 205–52.

Skorupski, Tadeusz, trans. *The Sarvadurgatipariśodhana Tantra: Elimination of All Evil Destinies: Sanskrit and Tibetan Texts*. Delhi: Motilal Banarsidass, 1983.

Skreslet, Stanley H. *Comprehending Mission: The Questions, Methods, Themes, Problems, and Prospects of Missiology*. Maryknoll, NY: Orbis, 2012.

Smith, Alex G. *Buddhism through Christian Eyes*. Littleton, CO: Overseas Missionary Fellowship, 2001.

Smith, Eugene. *Among Tibetan Texts: History and Literature of the Himalayan Plateau*. Boston: Wisdom, 2001.

Smither, Edward L. *Christian Mission: A Concise, Global History*. Bellingham, WA: Lexham Press, 2019.

———. *Mission as Hospitality: Imitating the Hospitable God in Mission*. Eugene, OR: Wipf & Stock, 2021.

Snellgrove, David L. "Categories of Buddhist Tantras." In *Orientalia Iosephi Tucci Memoriae Dicata*, edited by G. Gnoli and L. Lanciotti, 1353–84. Serie Orientale Roma 56. Rome: Istituto Italiano per il Medio ed Estremo Oriente, 1988.

———. *The Hevajra Tantra: A Critical Study*. London: Oxford University Press, 1959.

Snellgrove, David L., and Hugh Edward Richardson. *A Cultural History of Tibet*. Bangkok: Orchid Press, 2003.

Sraddhakaravarma and Rinchen Zangpo. "He Ru Ka'i Rnam Par Dag Pa [The Purification of Heruka]," n.d. TWE, https://tibetan.works/etext/reader.php?collection=tengyur&index=1481.

Steadman, James D. "Pure Land Buddhism and the Buddhist Historical Tradition." *Religious Studies* 23, no. 3 (1987) 407–21.

Steffen, Tom. "A Clothesline Theology for the World: How a Value-Driven Grand Narrative of Scripture Can Frame the Gospel." *Great Commission Research Journal* 9 (2018) 235–72.

———. *Reconnecting God's Story to Ministry: Cross-Cultural Storytelling at Home and Abroad*. Downers Grove, IL: InterVarsity Press, 2005.

———. *Worldview-Based Storying: The Integration of Symbol, Story, and Ritual in the Orality Movement*. Dallas: Center for Oral Scriptures, 2018.

Studholme, Alexander. *The Origins of Om Mani Padme Hum–A Study of the Karandavyuha Sutra*. Albany: State University of New York Press, 2002.

Sum bha don grub tshe ring. *Bod Kyi Yul Skad Rnam Bshad [A General Introduction to Tibetan Dialects]*. Beijing: Krung go'i bod rigs dpe skrun khang, 2011.

Sweet, Michael J. "Mental Purification (Blo Sbyong): A Native Tibetan Genre of Religious Literature." In *Tibetan Literature: Studies in Genre*, edited by Roger Reid Jackson and José Ignacio Cabezón, 244–60. Ithaca, NY: Snow Lion, 1996.

Tambiah, Stanley J. "A Performative Approach to Ritual." *Proceedings of the British Academy*, 1979, 113–69.

Tan, Gillian G. "Differentiating Smoke: Smoke as Duwa and Smoke from Bsang on the Tibetan Plateau." *Anthropological Forum* 28.2 (2018) 126–36.

———. "Smoky Relations: Beyond Dichotomies of Substance on the Tibetan Plateau." In *In Exploring Materiality and Connectivity in Anthropology and Beyond*, edited by Philipp Schorch, Martin Saxer, and Marlen Elders, 145–61. UCL Press, 2020.

Tennent, Timothy C. *Theology in the Context of World Christianity: How the Global Church Is Influencing the Way We Think about and Discuss Theology*. Grand Rapids: Zondervan, 2009.
Terrone, Antonio. "Bya Rog Prog Zhu, The Raven Crest: The Life and Teachings of bDe Chen'od Gsal Rdo Rje, Treasure Revealer in Contemporary Tibet." PhD diss., Leden University, 2010.
———. "Householders and Monks: A Study of Treasure Revealers and Their Role in Religious Revival in Contemporary Eastern Tibet." In *Buddhism Beyond the Monastery: Tantric Practices and Their Performers in Tibet and the Himalayas*, edited by Sarah Jacoby and Antonio Terrone, 73–109. Brill's Tibetan Studies Library 12. Leiden: Brill, 2010.
Thayer's Greek Lexicon. https://biblehub.com/greek/
Thiessen, Matthew. *Jesus and the Forces of Death: The Gospels' Portrayal of Ritual Impurity within First-Century Judaism*. Grand Rapids: Baker Academic, 2020.
Thomas, Bruce. "The Gospel for Shame Cultures." *Evangelical Missions Quarterly* 30.3 (1994) 284–90.
Thomas, F. W. "Om Maṇi Padme Hūṃ." *Journal of the Royal Asiatic Society* 38, no. 2 (1906) 464.
Thompson, Phyllis. *Sadhu Sundar Singh: A Biography of the Remarkable Indian Disciple of Jesus Christ*. Carlisle, UK: OM Publishing, 1992.
Thondup, Tulku. *Hidden Teachings of Tibet: An Explanation of the Terma Tradition of the Nyingma School of Buddhism*. Boston: Wisdom, 1986.
Thupten, Jinpa, ed. *The Tibetan Book of Everyday Wisdom: A Thousand Years of Sage Advice*. Translated by Beth Newman. Somerville: Library of Tibetan Classics, 2018.
Thurman, Robert A. F., and Sherpa Tulku. *The Life and Teachings of Tsong-Khapa*. Dharamsala: Library of Tibetan Works & Archives, 2006.
Thurman, Robert A. F. *Essential Tibetan Buddhism*. Edison, NJ: Castle, 1996.
———. "Tsongkha-Pa's Integration of Sutra and Tantra." In *Soundings in Tibetan Civilization*, edited by Barbara Nimri Aziz and Matthew Kapstein, 372–83. New Dehli: Manohar, 1985.
Thurston, Timothy. "An Introduction to Tibetan Sa Bstod Speeches in A Mdo." *Asian Ethnology* 71.1 (2012) 49.
Tibetan Works: https://tibetan.works/etext/.
Tournadre, Nicolas. "The Classical Tibetan Cases and Their Transcategoriality: From Sacred Grammar to Modern Linguistics." *Himalayan Linguistics* 9.2 (2010) 87–125.
———. "The Tibetic Languages and Their Classification." In *Trans-Himalayan Linguistics*, edited by Thomas Owen-Smith and Nathan W. Hill, 105–30. Trends in Linguistics: Studies and Monographs 266. Berlin: de Gruyter, 2014.
Tournadre, Nicolas, and Françoise Robin, eds. *Le Grand Livre Des Proverbes Tibétains*. Paris: Châtelet, 2006.
Tournier, Vincent, Vincent Eltschinger, and Marta Sernesi, eds. *Archaeologies of the Written: Indian, Tibetan, and Buddhist Studies in Honour of Cristina Scherrer-Schaub*. Napoli: Università degli Studi di Napoli L'Orientale, 2020.
Translating the Words of Buddha: https://84000.co/.
Trungpa, Chogyam, and Francesca Fremantle. *The Tibetan Book of the Dead: The Great Liberation Through Hearing in the Bardo*. Boston: Shambhala, 2000.
Tsangnyon, Heruka. *The Life of Milarepa*. Translated by Andrew Quintman. Harmondsworth: Penguin, 2010.

BIBLIOGRAPHY

Tsepag, Ngawang. "Traditional Cataloguing & Classification of Tibetan Literature." *The Tibet Journal*, 2005, 49–60.

Tsering, Marku. "Islands in the Sky." In *Sharing Jesus Effectively in the Buddhist World*, 243–61. Pasadena, CA: William Carey Library, 2005.

———. *Sharing Christ in the Tibetan Buddhist World*. Chiang Mai, Thailand: Central Asia Fellowship, 2006.

Tsering, Sonam. "The Role of Texts in the Formation of the Geluk School in Tibet During the Mid-Fourteenth and Fifteenth Centuries." PhD diss., Columbia University, 2020.

Tshe ring rdo rje, rdo sbis, ed. *Deng Rabs Bod Skad Tshig Mdzod [Modern Tibetan Dictionary]*. Chengdu: bod ljongs mi dmangs dpe skrun khang [Tibet People's Press], 2016.

Tsomo, Karma Lekshe. "Review of Buddhism in Contemporary Tibet: Religious Revival and Cultural Identity by Melvyn C. Goldstein and Matthew T. Kapstein." *China Review International*, Honolulu: University of Hawaii Press, March 22, 2002.

Tsong Khapa Blo bzang grags pa. *The Great Treatise on the Stages of the Path to Enlightenment Volume One*. Edited by Joshua W.C. Cutler and Guy Newland. Translated by Lamrin Chenmo Translation Committee. Ithaca, NY: Snow Lion, 2000.

Tsong Khapa Blo bzang grags pa and Bstan 'dzin rgya mtsho. *The Great Exposition of Secret Mantra Volume One Tantra in Tibet*. Translated by Jeffrey Hopkins. Boulder, CO: Snow Lion, 2016.

———. *The Great Exposition of Secret Mantra Volume Three Yoga Tantra*. Translated by Jeffrey Hopkins. Boulder, CO: Snow Lion, 2017.

———. *The Great Exposition of Secret Mantra Volume Two Deity Yoga*. Translated by Jeffrey Hopkins. Boulder, CO: Snow Lion, 2017.

Tucci, Giuseppe. *The Religions of Tibet*. London: Routledge & Kegan Paul, 1980.

Tuttle, Gray, and Kurtis R. Schaeffer. *The Tibetan History Reader*. New York: Columbia University Press, 2013.

U Lhan, ed. *Rna Ba'i Bdud Rtsi/ Bod Kyi Dmangs Khrod Ngag Rgyun Gces Bsdus/ [A Collection of Beloved Folk Stories and Oral Traditions]*. Beijing: krung go'i bod rig pa dpe skrun khang [China's Tibetology Press], 2007.

Uray, Geza. "Tibet's Connections with Nestorianism and Manicheism in the 8th–10th Centuries." *Contributions on Tibetan Language, History and Culture*, edited by Ernst Steinkeliner and Helmut Tauscher, 399–429. Proceedings of the Csoma de Kőrös Symposium 1. Vienna: Arbeitskreis fur Tibetische und Buddhistische Studien, Universitat Wien, 1983.

Van der Geest, Sjaak. "Anthropologists and Missionaries: Brothers under the Skin." *Man* 25 (1990) 588–601.

———. "Pollution and Purity." In *The Wiley Blackwell Encyclopedia of Health, Illness, Behavior, and Society*, edited by William C. Cockerham. Chichester, UK: Wiley-Blackwell, 2014.

Van Maaren, John. "Does Mark's Jesus Abrogate Torah? Jesus' Purity Logion and Its Illustration in Mark 7: 15–23." *Journal for the Jesus Movement in Its Jewish Setting* 4 (2017) 21–41.

Van Schaik, Sam. *The Spirit of Tibetan Buddhism*. New Haven: Yale University Press, 2016.

———. "The Tibetan Avalokiteśvara Cult in the Tenth Century: Evidence from the Dunhuang Manuscripts." In *Tibetan Buddhist Literature and Praxis: Studies in Its Formative Period, 900–1400 Proceedings of the Xth Seminar of the International Association for Tibetan Studies*, edited by Ronald M. Davidson and Christian Wedemeyer, 55–72. Leiden: Brill, 2006.

BIBLIOGRAPHY

———. *Tibet: A History*. New Haven: Yale University Press, 2011.

Van Spengen, Wim. "Ways of Knowing Tibetan Peoples and Landscapes." *HIMALAYA, the Journal of the Association for Nepal and Himalayan Studies* 24.1 (2004) 95–111.

Verhagen, Pieter C. "The Mantra 'Oṃ Maṇi-Padme Hūṃ' in an Early Tibetan Grammatical Treatise." *Journal of the International Association of Buddhist Studies*, 1990, 133–38.

Waddell, L. A. *The Buddhism of Tibet, or, Lamaism*. 1895. Reprint, New Delhi: Aryan Books International, 1996.

Walter, Michael L. *Buddhism and Empire: The Political and Religious Culture of Early Tibet*. Brill's Tibetan Studies Library. Leiden: Brill, 2009.

Wangchuk, Dorji. "A Relativity Theory of the Purity and Validity of Perception in Indo-Tibetan Buddhism." In *Yogic Perception, Meditation, and Altered States of Consciousness*, edited by Eli Franco and Dagmar Eigner, 215–37. Vienna: Austrian Academy of Sciences, 2009.

Wangdu, Sagong. *Bod mi'i yul srol goms gshis [One Hundred Tibetan Customs]*. Beijing: mi rigs dpe skrun khan [Nationalities Press], 2003.

Wangchuk, Shamar Chokyi. "Zhwa Dmar Pa Chos Kyi Dbang Phyug Gi Bde Smon Bzhugs [Sharmar's Aspiration for Sukhavati]," n.d. Lotsawa House, https://www.lotsawahouse.org/bo/tibetan-masters/shamar-chokyi-wangchuk/sukhavati-aspiration.

Wassen, Cecilia. "Jesus and the Hemorrhaging Woman in Mark 5: 24–34: Insights from Purity Laws from the Dead Sea Scrolls." In *Scripture in Transition: Essays on Septuagint, Hebrew Bible, and Dead Sea Scrolls in Honour of Raija Sollamo*, edited by Anssi Voitila and Jutta Jokiranta, 647–66. Journal for the Study of Judaism Supplements 126. Leiden: Brill, 2008.

———. "The Jewishness of Jesus and Ritual Purity." *Scripta Instituti Donneriani Aboensis* 27 (2016) 11–36.

White, David Gordon, ed. *Tantra in Practice*. Princeton Readings in Religions. Princeton: Princeton University Press, 2000.

Whiteman, Darrell L. "Shame/Honor, Guilt/Innocence, Fear/Power: A Missiological Response to Simon Cozens and Geoff Beech." *International Bulletin of Mission Research* 42 (2018) 348–56.

Wilson, Jeff. "Pure Land Iconography and Ritual Intent: A Comparative Study of the Visualization Texts Kuan Wu-Liang-Shou-Fo Ching and Amitabha Sadhana." *Pure Land* 22 (2006) 167–86.

Winder, Marianne. "Aspects of the History of the Prayer Wheel." *Bulletin of Tibetology* 28.1 (1992) 25–33.

Wolf, Thom. "The Mahayana Moment: Tipping Point Buddhism." In *Buddhism and the 21st Century*. New Delhi, India: Ministry of Culture, Government of India and Nava Nalanda Mahavihara University, 2009, 1–35.

Wu, Jackson. "Contextualizing the One Gospel in Any Culture: A Model from the Biblical Text for a Global Context." *Global Missiology* 3 (2013) 1–40.

Wylie, Turrell. "A Standard System of Tibetan Transcription." *Harvard Journal of Asiatic Studies* 22 (1959) 261–67.

"Yang Dag Par Sbyor Ba Zhes Bya Ba'i Rgyud Chen Po [The Foundation of All Tantras, the Great Compendium]," n.d. TWE, https://tibetan.works/etext/reader.php?collection=kangyur&index=396.

Yeshe, Lama Thubten. *Becoming Vajrasattva: The Tantric Path of Purification*. Somerville, MA: Wisdom, 2004.

"Yon Yongs Su Sbyong Ba Zhes Bya Ba [The Cleansing of Offerings]," n.d. TWE, https://tibetan.works/etext/reader.php?collection=kangyur&index=719.

"Yon Yongs Su Sbyong Ba'i Gzungs [The Incantation for Completely Purifying Offerings]," n.d. TWE, https://tibetan.works/etext/reader.php?collection=kangyur&index=720.

Yoo, Yohan. "A Theory of Purity from the Perspective of Comparative Religion." PhD diss., Syracuse University, 2005.

Zhang, Yisun, and Bian Zhu. *Bod Rgya Tshig Mdzod Chen Mo [The Great Tibetan-Chinese Dictionary]*. Beijing: Nationalities Press, 1984.

Zhong, Chen-Bo, and Katie Liljenquist. "Washing Away Your Sins: Threatened Morality and Physical Cleansing." *Science* 313 no. 5792 (2006) 1451–52.

www.ingramcontent.com/pod-product-compliance
Lightning Source LLC
Chambersburg PA
CBHW061433300426
44114CB00014B/1667